CAPTAIN'S DIARY
2 0 0 8

CAPTAIN'S DIARY
2 0 0 8
RICKY PONTING

HarperSports
An imprint of HarperCollinsPublishers

Harper*Sports*
An imprint of HarperCollins*Publishers* Australia

First published in Australia in 2008
by HarperCollins*Publishers* Australia Pty Limited
ABN 36 009 913 517
www.harpercollins.com.au

HarperCollins*Publishers*
25 Ryde Road, Pymble, Sydney, NSW 2073, Australia
31 View Road, Glenfield, Auckland 10, New Zealand
1–A, Hamilton House, Connaught Place, New Delhi – 110 001, India
77–85 Fulham Palace Road, London, W6 8JB, United Kingdom
2 Bloor Street East, 20th floor, Toronto, Ontario M4W 1A8, Canada
10 East 53rd Street, New York NY 10022, USA

National Library of Australia Cataloguing-in-Publication data:

Ponting, Ricky.
Captain's diary 2008 : a season of tests, turmoil and
twentytwenty / Ricky Ponting, Geoff Armstrong.
ISBN: 978 0 7322 8491 6 (pbk.)
Ponting, Ricky – Diaries.
Cricket captains – Australia – Biography.
Cricket players – Australia – Biography.
Cricket – Tournaments – Australia.
Cricket – Australia.
Other Authors/Contributors:
Armstrong, Geoff.
796.358092

Cover image by Jonathan Wood/Getty Images
Cover and internal designs by Matt Stanton
Typeset in 11/17 Sabon by Kirby Jones
Printed and bound in Australia by Griffin Press
70gsm Classic used by HarperCollins*Publishers* is a natural, recyclable product made from wood
grown in sustainable forests. The manufacturing processes conform to the environmental
regulations in the country of origin, Finland.

5 4 3 2 1   08 09 10 11

It's amazing how, no matter how much you might like to think you've seen it all in international cricket, something new and totally unexpected happens every year. However, there are some constants, and for me the most important is the total support I always receive from my wife Rianna. Now, we have the beautiful Emmy to keep us company. Whatever stresses might consume my cricket life, my family life is always fantastic and for that I am extremely grateful.

GEOFF ARMSTRONG

Ricky Ponting's co-author on *Captain's Diary 2008*, Geoff Armstrong, has worked — as writer, editor or publisher — on more than 80 books on sport, more than 30 of them on cricket. Between 1993 and 2005, he collaborated with Steve Waugh on each of Steve's 12 best-selling books, including all of his diaries and the former Australian captain's autobiography *Out of My Comfort Zone*. Geoff is the author of *A Century of Summers*, the centenary history of the Sheffield Shield (featuring an epilogue by Sir Donald Bradman), *ESPN's Legends of Cricket*, which profiles 25 of the game's greatest players, *The 100 Greatest Cricketers*, and the co-author, with Mark Gately, of *The People's Game*, a history of Australia in one-day international cricket. He has worked as co-author on books by David Boon, Ian Healy, Mike Whitney, Bob Simpson and Michael Bevan, and with Ian Russell produced *Top 10s of Australian Test Cricket*, a study of Australian cricket statistics.

Geoff is also the co-author, with Peter Thompson, of *Phar Lap*, the definitive biography of the legendary racehorse, and *Melbourne Cup 1930*, the story of the most remarkable of Phar Lap's many big-race victories. In 2007–08, he worked with Ian Heads and David Middleton on the centenary history of Australian rugby league and the history of the Sydney Roosters rugby league club, and on books with Justin Langer and Wayne Bennett.

CONTENTS

PHOTOGRAPHS

The photographs that 'open' each chapter of this book are as follows:

Page 1: Ricky Ponting after Australia won the second Test v India, Sydney, January 6, 2008 (Cameron Spencer/Getty Images).

Page 35: Zimbabwe celebrate defeating Australia at the ICC World Twenty 20, Cape Town, September 12, 2007 (Tom Shaw/Getty Images).

Page 57: The Australians at the end of the one-day series v India, Mumbai, October 17, 2007 (Hamish Blair/Getty Images).

Page 89: The Australians with the Warne–Muralitharan Trophy, Hobart, November 20, 2007 (Quinn Rooney/Getty Images).

Page 115: Sir Richard Hadlee (far left), Ian Chappell (far right) with the Australians at the conclusion of the Chappell–Hadlee Trophy series, Hobart, December 20, 2007 (Cameron Spencer/Getty Images).

Page 133: The Australian fieldsmen mob Ricky Ponting (centre, in helmet) and Michael Clarke at the end of the second Test v India, Sydney, January 6, 2008 (Mark Nolan/Getty Images).

Page 187: Ricky Ponting leaves the Gabba after being dismissed in the second Commonwealth Bank Series final, Brisbane, March 4, 2008 (Ezra Shaw/Getty Images).

Page 215: Adam Gilchrist, Ricky Ponting and Matthew Hayden with the Border–Gavaskar Trophy, Adelaide, January 28, 2008 (Simon Cross/Getty Images).

Page 231: MS Dhoni and Ricky Ponting, Australia v India Twenty20 International, Mumbai, October 20, 2007 (Hamish Blair/Getty Images).

Page 247: Brett Lee, Mike Hussey and Ricky Ponting with the Frank Worrell Trophy, Bridgetown, June 16, 2008 (Chris McGrath/Getty Images).

Page 297: Ricky Ponting and Shane Watson after Watson reached his century in the third ODI v West Indies, Grenada, June 29, 2008 (Doug Benc/Getty Images).

The credits for the photographs that appear in the colour sections are listed on page 374

CO-AUTHOR'S NOTE

As he has done in past years, Ricky Ponting kept notes on all the major events that occurred during the 2007–08 season. Afterwards, the two of us went through that material, and also studied numerous newspaper and internet reports, to record in a diary format — not a day-by-day account; rather, a few days at a time — his take on what will be remembered as one of the most tumultuous 12 months ever experienced by the Australian cricket team. In addition, following his review of the Commonwealth Bank Series, Ricky provides his take on the extraordinary career of Adam Gilchrist, and then looks back on his time playing with the Kolkata Knight Riders in the first edition of the Indian Premier League.

Given the level of controversy relating to the Australia v India Test series that took place between December 26, 2007, and January 28, 2008, Ricky has also taken the opportunity to describe, from his perspective, the events that shaped that tumultuous time in cricket. This analysis, which introduces *Captain's Diary 2008*, is followed by a response from Cricket Australia's Chief Executive Officer James Sutherland, which has been written specifically for this book.

Ricky and I appreciate James contributing to the book in this way, and we are also grateful for the help provided by others at Cricket Australia, most notably Peter Young and Philip Pope. We must also acknowledge the strong support we received from Ricky's manager James Henderson and the entire team at DSEG, and from everyone at HarperCollins, especially Mel Cain, Patrick Mangan, Matt Stanton and the legendary Graeme Jones. Thanks, too, to Alexia Pettenon, Stella Tarakson and Steve Keipert for the help they provided in getting the words in the right order.

In the book, many of the Australian players are referred to by their nicknames. Some of these are self-explanatory (Gilly, Symmo, Mitch, Hadds, Jaquesy, Huss, Kato, Hoggy, et al), but a few probably need clarifying: 'Haydos' is Matthew Hayden; 'Pup' is Michael Clarke; 'Sarf' is Stuart Clark; 'Bing' is Brett Lee; 'Vin' is coach Tim Nielsen. The statistics, scores and averages that appear through the pages and at the end of the book were derived from a variety of sources, including three excellent websites — *Cricinfo.com, Howstat.com: the cricket statisticians and cricketarchive.com.*

With the exception of the photograph of Ricky, Rianna and Emmy Ponting (which was kindly provided by Newspix), all the photographs that appear in *Captain's Diary 2008* come from Getty Images. We appreciate the help provided by the good people at Getty, especially Philippa Hutson and their outstanding photographers who follow the Australian cricket team around the world.

Geoff Armstrong
August 2008

INTRODUCTION
A MATTER OF TRUST

*'My overall emotion and feeling at the end of the
game was as good a feeling as I've ever had on a
cricket field.'*

— Ricky Ponting, after the second Test v India,
January 6, 2008

'HE'S DONE IT AGAIN!'

I wouldn't say those words sent a chill up my spine, or anything that sinister, but they certainly stopped me in my tracks.

'He's done it again!' shouted Michael Clarke in my direction during the third day's play of the Australia-India New Year's Test in Sydney. 'He just called Symmo a "monkey" again!'

The 'he' was Harbhajan Singh, India's No. 1 spinner, a man known throughout the cricket world for his instantly recognisable turban, an excellent bowling résumé in international cricket that dates back to 1998, and also for the fact that he is feisty sort of character. He and I had enjoyed some battles over the previous 10 years, going back to Australia's tour of India in '98. No bowler had dismissed me more often in Test cricket, but that record was far from my mind when this incident occurred. The word that jumped out at me, however, when Pup (as Michael Clarke is known) called out to me was *again*. Harbhajan had form.

Back on the previous October 17, in Mumbai, immediately after we'd finished the final one-day international of a seven-match series, our player of the series, Andrew Symonds, a man of part Afro-Caribbean descent, informed us that when we had been fielding Harbhajan had called him a 'monkey'. If he had, it was a racist jibe, one that echoed some of the rubbish that had been coming from a section of the big crowds in the grandstands. We debated among ourselves whether we should do anything about it. Eventually, Symmo stood up and said, 'I'll fix it.' He walked out of our dressing room, knocked on the Indian team's door, asked to see Harbhajan, confronted him and said flatly, 'Don't do it again.' When Symmo returned to our room, he told us that after he explained how much the insult had affected him. While Harbhajan had not admitted that he said it, he did acknowledge that it was unacceptable, had apologised for any offence, and assured Symmo there'd be no repeat. The two men shook hands. On that basis, we decided that the right thing to do was exactly what our critics told us we should have done in Sydney: we gave him another chance. We just let it go.

THE INCIDENT IN SYDNEY started with Symmo, at mid-off, and Harbhajan, at the non-striker's end during an important stand with Sachin Tendulkar, exchanging a few words between deliveries. We had scored 463 in our first innings, of which Symmo had scored 162 not out, but now, just after tea on day three, Harbhajan and Tendulkar had brought the visitors just about level with our total, when 20 overs earlier it had seemed we'd be enjoying a significant first-innings lead. Then Harbhajan got on strike, and he slashed a Brett Lee riser for four over the slip cordon and then squeezed a yorker out behind square for a single. As he ran through for the one, he tapped Binger on the behind (we weren't quite sure why), and that got Symmo's back up even more. At the end of the over, as had occurred in

Mumbai, Harbhajan marched towards Symmo, who was walking from mid-off to mid-off, so they were face to face, and then he said something. I didn't see that confrontation, as I was more concerned with talking to our left-arm quick, Mitchell Johnson, who was about to bowl the next over. That was when I heard Pup's shout …

He's done it again! He just called Symmo a 'monkey' again!

The clarity I felt at this moment was a result, I believe, of the fact that from my perspective it was such a straight repeat of what had occurred in Mumbai, combined with the precise instructions concerning on-field racial abuse that I'd been given as captain by International Cricket Council (ICC) match referees before Test and one-day series over the previous two years. *I've got to act on it.* I talked to Symmo, to get his version as to what had happened. Then I went over and told umpire Mark Benson what we believed had just gone on, and I asked him to do something about it. Benson walked over to Harbhajan and Tendulkar, put his hand over his mouth so he couldn't be lip-read, and, I presume, asked Harbhajan if he had said what we were accusing him of saying. Harbhajan said he hadn't. Benson went back to his position, while I made a point, as I walked past the two batsmen on my way to the slip cordon, to say to the Indian spinner, 'I hope you haven't said that again.'

To which Tendulkar promptly replied, 'Leave it alone. I'll fix this, I'll sort this out.'

But it was too late for that. I'd already spoken to the umpire. It was out of my hands. I had done what I had been told to do. The match officials were going to have to work it out.

During the next over, I spoke to two of the Australian team's most senior players, Matthew Hayden and Adam Gilchrist. Haydos told me he'd heard Harbhajan's alleged insult; Gilly explained he'd been too far away to hear anything. Both men would be called before the subsequent inquiry, where they repeated what they told me straight after the clash occurred.

At the end of Mitch's over, I went off the field and told Steve Bernard, our team manager, what had happened. And then I got on with the game. The umpires were compelled to report the incident, and we were told at the end of the day's play that Mike Procter, the ICC match referee, the great South African all-rounder of the 1960s and 1970s, would hold an inquiry into the incident at the completion of the Test.

'WHY DO WE NEED TO KEEP IT QUIET?'

On the night after we made our on-field report about Harbhajan, I had a phone conversation with a senior member of the Indian touring party, who asked me straight to drop the complaint. 'Why do we need to keep it quiet?' I asked.

His reply had nothing to do with Harbhajan's guilt or innocence; this fellow was more concerned with how events were going to transpire and tried to convince me that it might not be worth the stress of going ahead with what might well be a prolonged legal process. I was determined to see that justice would be done, but I knew from the moment I put my mobile back in my pocket that the investigation might not be as straightforward as the authorities hearing the evidence, making the right decision and then we all move on. It would not look good for Indian cricket for one of their senior players to be convicted of racial abuse, and from the time their officials realised we were not going to give ground — which was probably the moment this brief conversation ended — they set out to make sure that did not happen.

James Sutherland, CEO of Cricket Australia, came into our dressing room at stumps on that third day. He sat down next to me, and asked, 'What happened?' After I explained, he said, 'What do you want to do? Where do you want this to go?' I said that if Harbhajan was found guilty, then I wanted him to be accountable for his actions. I also wanted Symmo to know his captain, his team-mates and the game supported him. I'd heard a lot about how racism in sport was unacceptable and I agreed with that sentiment totally. It was not something I'd thought about when I was a kid from Mowbray in northern Tasmania, hoping to one day play cricket for my country, but from the day racial abuse by spectators became a big issue in cricket, I'd given it plenty of thought and had come down very firmly in the 'zero tolerance' camp. I'd also seen the genuine hurt in my mate's eyes as he explained to us how much a slur of this kind upset him. If events on the field had played out as we believed they had, then — under the ICC's code of conduct — a 'Level 3.3' (racial abuse) verdict against Harbhajan would demonstrate clearly that cricket was fair dinkum about eradicating this blight from our game.

ONE OF THE GREAT frustrations of this affair was that the quality of our victory in this Sydney Test, and the excitement it generated, was largely lost in the angst that engulfed cricket in the days immediately after the game. By any measure, it was a remarkable win: three wickets needed, a maximum two overs remaining, and then Michael Clarke — a bloke who before this day had never taken a Test wicket in Australia — snared three wickets in five balls. The feeling was remarkable. That it extended our winning streak in Test cricket to 16 games; that the victory came after a roller-coaster five days, in which we'd shared and suffered so many emotions, on and off the field; that during that final day we'd anguished over when to declare, not wanting to be too reckless or too cautious, thought we were going to win, resigned ourselves to a draw, then come from nowhere to get up on the line … all these things added to our exhilaration. The fans love seeing games go down to the last half hour of the fifth day and the players love being involved. It's a good feeling when you win one.

So much happened during the final few minutes, yet much of it was forgotten in the game's turbulent aftermath. No one recalled how the Indian tailenders mucked around in what proved to be the final over, as they sought to ensure that they'd face no more deliveries than they had to.

After Harbhajan was brilliantly caught by Mike Hussey off the first ball of the over, it took him a proverbial eternity to walk off the ground. It's quite funny watching the replay — how he started to depart at normal speed and then, part way off, he stopped, turned around, watched a replay on the big screen, walked a bit further, stopped again, before slowly and sadly departing the ground.

Finally, RP Singh replaced him, and after he was lbw first ball he also left at a snail's pace. Out came No. 11 Ishant Sharma, 19 years old and nervous as can be, and after he'd walked a few metres he suddenly realised he'd come out with two right-handed batting gloves. Their 12th man, Irfan Pathan, had to provide him with a replacement mitt. At the same time, in stark contrast, we'd been making sure that we were in position as quickly as possible, waiting for the new batsman to get himself ready. Part of this was about not wasting any time; most of it was about making it a statement that this was *our* turf. I remember thinking how the atmosphere created by the SCG crowd added to this sense of *all* of us against them. Later, some people tried to suggest that the fans at the ground weren't excited by our win, but that was rubbish. There was a lot of passion about, which took a long, long time to dissipate.

A major debating point in the press box and the commentary booths throughout the final day was the timing of my declaration. From the start of day four, I had made it clear to the guys that I wanted us to get in a position where we were the only team that could win the Test, and that played a part in my decision to set them 333 to win in just 72 overs. I was aware of the fact that throughout the game runs had been scored at four runs an over, and remembered the Sydney Test in 2005–06, my 100th Test, when we scored 288 in 60.3 overs to beat South Africa. I guess the best way to judge the quality of a declaration is the result, and we won the game, but I do concede I cut it fine. What frustrated us a little was the fact that during the day some commentators spent so much time harping on my 'mistake' that word got back to us in the dressing room that we were being denigrated for our alleged conservatism. It was nice to be able to prove these knockers wrong.

We won, we celebrated on the field, shook hands with our opponents, did some on-field interviews, and then within minutes of getting into the dressing room, I was on my way to the post-Test media conference. After that, I was in a conference discussing how Mike Procter's inquiry was going to work. When I finally left the SCG about 3am I'd hardly spent any time with the boys in the dressing room at all. People have asked me what was the mood in the Australian camp after the game, but I have to be honest and say I don't really know.

I WENT IN FIRST at the media conference, before Indian captain Anil Kumble, and I've often wondered how things might have played out if this batting order had been reversed. The fallout from the racism inquiry might still have happened, but

Kumble's highly charged remarks about how we play the game might not have gone so unchallenged. Early on, I didn't sense any negativity from the Australian journalists — if you'd have told me then that two days later page one of the *Sydney Morning Herald* would be calling for my head I would have laughed at you — and while a few of the Indian writers did seem a bit agitated, I just put that down to the fact that they were disappointed with the result. First, I was asked about how I rated the victory ...

> *My overall emotion and feeling at the end of the game then was as good a feeling as I've ever had on a cricket field, winning a Test like that in the last eight or 10 minutes on the fifth day.*
>
> *I said after the Adelaide Test against England last year that was the best and this isn't far behind ...*

Then I was asked a two-pronged question about the relationship between the two teams and the umpiring, which everyone conceded had not been good ...

> *There was absolutely no doubt about this match being played in the right spirit. There's been one little issue that's come out of the game that we'll all hear about later, but otherwise the spirit between both teams in both Tests has been excellent. I don't think the players lost confidence in them (the umpires). I can't comment on the umpiring.*
>
> *All I can say about the umpires is that they're out there, like me, trying their best; to do the best job they can ...*

The Indian reporters were more aggressive, and I was okay with that until one of them told me I shouldn't have claimed to have caught MS Dhoni close in on the offside during Dhoni's fighting seventh-wicket partnership with his captain ...

I think you've got something wrong there. There is no way I grounded that ball. If you are actually questioning my integrity in the game then you shouldn't be standing there ...

I made the point that in India's first innings I had had not claimed a catch off Rahul Dravid, when he edged a catch to me at second slip and I grabbed the ball with my fingers on the grass. Truth be told, I probably did catch it, but I wasn't certain and as I've often made the point that the best person to judge these things is the fieldsman involved, I knew immediately it would be wrong to go through with an appeal. It was different in India's second innings, when Sourav Ganguly edged a ground-level chance to Michael Clarke. Soon as it happened, I rushed up to Pup and asked, 'Did you catch it?' When he said he did, for me that meant Ganguly was gone and I had no problems when the umpire gave him out ...

Doesn't that explain the way I play the game? I am saying I am 100 per cent sure I would have caught that catch off Dhoni today. As it turned out it was given not out anyway. Am I right or wrong? Am I right or wrong?
Michael Clarke today told me straight away he was 100 per cent sure he caught the ball so that's why I made my way to the umpires and let them know. That's the way this series will be played right the way through ...

As things turned out, that last sentence wasn't right, because in the turmoil of the following week the Indians decided to back out of our pre-series agreement to take the fieldsmen's word on ground-level catches. From the moment that reporter chose to question my integrity, I was angry. I'd gone into that media conference in a fairly buoyant mood; I walked out filthy that I'd basically been called a cheat.

The umpiring in the game hadn't been good, and there is no doubt that the rub of the green in this game did go our way. Ironically, in the third Test, in Perth, things worked the other way but there were no complaints from the Indian media about that. On day one in Sydney, there had been a number of mistakes, a couple of them involving me and then a couple more with Andrew Symonds. Afterwards, Symmo was upfront about his situation — he's not a 'walker' and is happy to accept the good with the bad. But not everyone agreed with his philosophy, even though it has been followed by most international cricketers since at least the 1970s, when tough cricketers such as Ian Chappell and Tony Greig made it fashionable.

In my case, I got lucky with a nick down the legside when I was 17 and then was on the wrong end of a shocking lbw decision when I was 55. When I got back to the dressing room I threw my bat across a table, which was caught by the media and which many saw as a reaction to being ripped off (and inappropriate given the earlier error that went my way). But it was much more just a response to the general quality of umpiring. When I calmed down I realised I was wrong to react in that manner, and not just because it looked petulant.

Toning down my reaction to that first-day dismissal was not the only thing I wish we'd done differently in this Test. Michael Clarke was caught first-ball at slip in our second innings but stood his ground, waiting for the umpire's decision, which given the controversies that had already occurred with the umpiring was the wrong thing to do. His dallying looked provocative and silly, and the fact that he was stunned and dejected at failing with the bat for the second time in the game was no excuse. In the later Tests, whenever Pup was dismissed, he was out of there as soon as the umpire gave his decision. A bit bizarrely, though, the next time I met with the Cricket Australia board after the Sydney Test, I used these two reactions — mine in our first innings and Pup's in the second — as examples of things we had to improve, and the great Allan Border, the former long-time Australian captain who is on the board, quickly cut me off, saying that this sort of thing has been happening in high-pressure cricket Tests for 100 years. That is true, too, but as I learned from this game, this summer, on some occasions the niceties of the sport are such that you have to tread more carefully than you might in more 'peaceful' times.

After I left the room under the Bradman Stand in which the media conference was held, Anil Kumble slid into the hot seat and — as I learned later — quickly he made the accusations that would generate headlines and muddy the waters over the next couple of days ...

'I think only one team was playing within the spirit of the game,' he began. 'We like to play hard on the field and we expect that from Australia as well. I have played my cricket very sincerely and very honestly, and that's the approach my team takes on the field. I expect that from the Australians as well ...'

From what I understand, his comments were met with rousing cheers by the Indian press corps. No one, Indian or Australian, challenged his view. They had their story. I'm not sure how extensive Anil's knowledge of cricket history is, but — as was picked up immediately by the reporters — his comments echoed those made by Australian captain Bill Woodfull during the acrimonious Bodyline series of 1932–33. 'There are two teams out there,' Woodfull said to the English managers Pelham Warner and Richard Palairet during the third Test of that series, 'One is trying to play cricket and the other is not.' Over the course of the next few hours, Mike Procter heard all the evidence concerning Harbhajan's conversation with Andrew Symonds and then suspended him for three Tests. The next day, the Indian cricket authorities reacted to that decision by threatening to quit the tour. However, because Kumble's unchallenged 'Australia do not play within the spirit of the game' criticism got so much airtime, many concluded that it was our behaviour, not the ICC match referee's verdict, that had pushed the tour to the brink. That wasn't right, but it didn't matter. For the next three days, we were fair game.

I WONDERED THEN, AND still wonder now, exactly what we did in that game that the Indian team does not do. What did we do that any other international team does not do? We didn't walk, we left the decision-making to the umpires, but there are plenty of blokes in the Indian team who don't walk either. We appealed for 'edges' that went our way but which the video later showed shouldn't have been given out (Rahul Dravid copped a particularly poor decision on the final day) but I can assure you that we honestly thought they were out and I can also assure you that the Indian team would have appealed just as loudly in the same situation. If the Test had ended differently, I doubt we would have gone through much of the commotion. The Indian camp was bitterly disappointed not to get out of the Test with a draw, because the loss meant that their chance to regain the Border–Gavaskar Trophy was gone. That, I'm sure, played a part in the scale of their reaction.

MEN IN THE MIDDLE

In Sydney, as we waited for Mike Procter's inquiry to begin, I briefly found myself talking to Mark Benson, one of the umpires who had been heavily criticised during the game. Mark was a central figure in the drama, the ump I went to when I realised I had to report what I believed had just transpired.

He told me that he had been on the road for four months, non stop, all around the cricketing world. I know what it is like to be an international player away from home for two or three months — by the end of it, you're worn down and your decision-making is not as sharp as it needs to be. My guess is that it would be harder for an umpire than it is for a player, as they are required to stand in one of two positions — square leg or non-striker's end — making precise decisions throughout every moment of a five-day Test, a high-powered 50-over game or a frenetic Twenty20 encounter. Great decisions are accepted as routine, line-ball decisions are over-scrutinised, mistakes are endlessly repeated for the benefit of viewers, usually in slow-motion. The pressure might even be enjoyable at first, but not for long. We players rarely make it easy for them, but a lot is expected of us, too.

One thing I have noticed about the recent history of Australian seasons is that, with the back to back Test matches in Melbourne and then Sydney over the Christmas-New Year period, more players get reported in Sydney and there are more bad umpiring decisions in Sydney, too. By the New Year's Test, everyone is on edge, everyone is a bit run down. Nerves get frayed, mistakes are made.

This doesn't mean we should accept poor officiating. Rather, we have to accept that mistakes occur and try to find ways to get the best out of the men recognised as the finest umpires we have.

Most of the men on the ICC's international umpires panel are good at what they do and good blokes, too, and what I and others need to be is constructive in our criticism, so we can improve this aspect of the game. Throwing bats after you've copped a dud call doesn't achieve this. In my view, there are a few things that could be done immediately to improve the overall standard — let's increase the size of the ICC panel, perhaps go back to using umpires in their own countries if they are the best men for the job, and also look hard at the use of the video to make the umpires' job easier. More of this later ...

By the time Anil made his media-conference comments, I was back in the home dressing-room, in the room at the front, looking out over the SCG, while in the bigger area out the back the rest of the team continued to celebrate our win. Music was playing, a lot of family members were there, and I could hear plenty of laughs. After that blue with the Indian reporter, and because I'd been locked out of my own party, my beer didn't taste as sweet as it should have.

Outside, the members' bar was packed, as it usually is after the final day of a New Year's Test. A few fans were hanging around the front of the dressing room, hoping for an autograph, and there were still a few security guards on the playing area, and some members of the SCG groundstaff. I had been joined by Symmo, Pup, Haydos and Gilly, who like me would be giving evidence. Steve Bernard and James Sutherland were also there, with a member of Cricket Australia's legal team, and it was explained to us exactly how the hearing would be conducted.

I must stress here that we were not out to get Harbhajan suspended. We'd cop whatever the match referee decided, so long as we got a fair hearing. I knew Symmo was still angry and upset about what had gone on and, frankly, I was sick of the people who were arguing that we should have just ignored what had occurred, as if a racial slur is just another sledge, part of the game.

Over and over in my head I recalled the fact that the matter of racism on and off the field was the first subject on the agenda at just about every match referee's meeting I had attended in the previous 24 months. If someone behaves in a racist manner, we were told, you are compelled to report it. I thought, too, of the anti-racism messages that had been displayed on scoreboards across the country over the past couple of years, since we had some disturbances with the crowds during the South Africans' tour in 2005–06. Surely, they applied to the players as unequivocally as they applied to the fans?

Gilly, Pup and Haydos were free to go once they'd given their evidence. So they were home before midnight. I was obliged to sit through the entire hearing: first our version of events, then India's. I came out of the hearing confident that Harbhajan would be found guilty, not least because I knew that Mike Procter was an experienced match referee who appreciated how unusual it was for an Australian team to be protesting about something that had been said on the field. This was not just run-of-the-mill chitchat between players. Later, Procter would be vilified in some quarters for his verdict, a reaction that I thought was outrageous; cricket can ill-afford to lose such a respected and perceptive figure. Almost immediately after he released his decision that Harbhajan would be outed for three Tests, the Indians appealed, which allowed the off-spinner to keep playing until a new hearing was conducted, before a High Court judge from New Zealand, Justice John Hansen, in Adelaide straight after the conclusion of the fourth Test.

IN THE FOUR OR five days after the Sydney Test, we came to think that the media was against us, when the truth was that it was probably fifty50 — plenty of critics, but many people backing our position, too. Inevitably, some ex-players — mostly the usual suspects — were into us, and I found their hypocrisy extremely disappointing. They were demanding standards from us that they had never kept themselves when they were Test stars. The classic came when Tony Greig suggested that the batsmen of today should be walking to make it easier for the umpires. This was coming from a bloke who in his day made a virtue out of not walking, who was praised by his team-mates for not doing so because it showed that the England team was getting 'tougher'. I always presumed that ex-players are employed by media outlets because their experience gives them a rare insight into the pressures elite cricketers are under and the way we think, but it seems to me that many of them forget all about their past lives the minute they're handed a press pass.

In one way, I found Greig's suggestion that we shouldn't be waiting for the umpire's decision revealing. Here he was bagging the Australian team and in doing so trying to add weight to Anil Kumble's argument that we don't play within the spirit of the game. But when he was asked for examples of such unsportsmanlike behaviour the best he could do was say we should be walking, something he never did when he played Test cricket. I couldn't help thinking, *Is that the best you can do?*

Two days after the Test, I had an early start at a charity golf day at the magnificent New South Wales layout at La Perouse. I was out of the house by 6am, and there was no chance to look at a newspaper before we teed off. After a few holes, I gave Rianna a quick call — she was still asleep when I left before the sun came up — and the first thing she said was, 'What's going on?'

'What do you mean, what's going on?'

'It's all over the front page of the paper,' she explained. 'You're going to lose your job!'

Peter Roebuck, one of the *Sydney Morning Herald*'s cricket writers and a high-profile ABC commentator, had written a lengthy piece that demanded I be sacked. The message in the page-one headline was loud and emphatic: Ponting Must Go.

We had copped some stick in the previous day's papers, though most of the reports were fairly constrained — the story of a thrilling last day followed by trenchant criticism of the umpires, reaction to Anil Kumble's comments about the spirit in which the game was played. The late editions carried reports of Harbhajan's three-Test suspension. Inevitably, the stories in the

Indian media, which we could access via the internet, were much angrier. Roebuck's article bought into that mood.

It began, 'Ricky Ponting must be sacked as captain of the Australian cricket team.' He was scathing in his criticism, which of course he is entitled to be, but to me he was so far over the top it was ridiculous. It was as if we'd started World War III. He suggested that the entire cricket community was 'disgusted' and 'distressed' by our performance, but that was hardly the feedback I was getting.

It was actually quite extraordinary how, when I walked down the street or stopped for a coffee in the day or two after that story appeared, people would come up and ask, 'What's going on? What's Roebuck on about?'

Gradually, the war evolved to where it seemed that the newspapers were involved in some sort of game, with the players pawns in the middle. One paper would be highly critical; its chief competitor would back us to the hilt, and I became less and less forgiving of the entire process. Anil Kumble had suggested we were not playing in the spirit of the game, Peter Roebuck had suggested I needed to be sacked as captain and that Matt Hayden, Adam Gilchrist and I must be dropped from the team. We were such ogres, the Indian team was about to go home. Meanwhile, Cricket Australia advised us to keep quiet, which we did. Their strategy, it seemed, was to sit back and let the kerfuffle burn itself out, to let everyone have their say and then we'd all move on. In fact, this became the hardest thing for the team to deal with during the affair — that we were having bullets fired at us while we had no way to defend ourselves. Eventually, I did interviews with the TV and print media, but by then much of the damage had been done.

The day after the Test, James Sutherland came out and said, 'We're supportive of the Australian team and the way they play and this tough and uncompromising way is the way Australian teams have always played.' Unfortunately, that statement was lost among the more strident comments and paragraphs that were generating headlines and encouraging angry talkback calls. I was on the phone to James every day during the week after the Sydney Test, asking him to aggressively defend us, to refute Kumble's post-Test comments, and specifically to back us over the racism charge, but anything he or anyone else from Cricket Australia said was lost amid the greater uproar. At the same time, I read that James and Cricket Australia chairman Creagh O'Connor were 'locked in meetings with senior Indian officials … in a bid to save the tour'.

Four days after the Test ended, James told the papers that 'the Australian cricket team plays the game tough and uncompromisingly — it's the way Australian cricket teams have played the game since 1877'.

'Under all sorts of different captains Australians have expected their teams to play the game hard but fair and they have been admired for that,' he continued. 'Both principles are in stride with the laws of the game of cricket. It's very important people understand where the lines are drawn there. Test cricket is what is being played here. It is not tiddlywinks. It's a tough game and out there from time to time emotions will bubble over and perhaps some of the words that are said will not be acceptable in genteel company, but they are said and that is what happens.'

I appreciated him saying that. I was also grateful that later in the same interview he reiterated that my job was not under threat.

I ENJOYED MAKING FRESH contact with my Aussie team-mates in Perth, for the third Test, six days after the Sydney Test finished. I'd been heartened by all the phone calls and text messages from the boys in the days when my position and our sportsmanship were questioned, and it was good for the Aussie team family to get back together. However, one of the first things we were required to do was attend what the papers called a 'round-table discussion' that was organised by Cricket Australia and attended by all the players, plus our coach Tim Nielsen, James Sutherland, Steve Bernard and Cricket Australia operations manager Michael Brown. The session was moderated by Ray McLean, a 'leadership consultant' employed by Cricket Australia, who had once been an officer in the Royal Australian Air Force.

It was good to clear the air, and I knew there would never be a perfect time or place for us to get together with Cricket Australia to talk about the Sydney Test and its aftermath, but the problem I had was that even the act of calling this meeting suggested strongly to me that our bosses had accepted the gist of Anil Kumble's remarks: that we did not play within the spirit of the game. Yet again, as I had with others who had thrown this accusation at me, when I asked them to nominate examples of where we were going wrong, they could not do so. It was all general stuff about the public's perception of us, and about us not giving the media opportunities to take potshots at us. At least they didn't tell us we had to start walking. Maybe I was getting paranoid, but I couldn't help thinking, *if there isn't a problem, why are we having this meeting?*

It was all very well to say, 'Don't give the papers any ammunition to fire shots at you.' But the trouble is, we can go for six months without putting a foot out of place — no mean achievement in modern professional sport — but first time we make a mistake, we're damned by the Roebucks of this world as 'Ugly Australians'. Of course, this has been happening since Ian Chappell was Australia's Test captain, and it frustrated me that I had to explain this to people who I thought were on our side. All I could promise to my masters and the masses was that we would keep playing and preparing to the best of our ability, and adhere as best we could to the 'Spirit of Australian Cricket' code we established for ourselves in 2003. I was confident that if we did this, then our supporters would be happy to back us unconditionally. The cynics, I knew, would never be so forgiving.

We went into the Perth Test distracted, no doubt about it, which — against a good team who were bent on vengeance — proved fatal. Yet I will always reckon that if I could have got through just one more over in our second innings, then we might still have won. Tall, lean, ultra-impressive Ishant Sharma, playing just his fourth Test and still eight-and-a-half months short of his 20th birthday, had bowled an awesome spell to me: seven overs where he was fast, aggressive and relentless, where I never felt as if I was truly 'in'. But even with his heroics, we were 2–117 seeking 413, I was 45 not out, Mike Hussey was 26 not out and I sensed Sharma was about to be taken off. However, after consulting with a couple of his senior colleagues, Kumble gave his teenage quick one more over. First ball, I pushed forward at a delivery that fizzed through and edged a straightforward catch to Dravid at first slip. From then on, whenever we seemed we might be a chance to reach our imposing target, we faltered. It was typical of the whole game; we weren't that far away, but we weren't quite right. India won by 72 runs, the first time a team from the subcontinent had not lost a Test match at the WACA.

Though that personal battle with Ishant Sharma ended badly, it still remains a positive memory for me, because it reminded me of what it is that makes Test cricket such a fantastic experience. All the off-field angst and argy-bargy of the previous 12 days was forgotten, and this contest between bat and ball took precedence.

The match was on the line, and I knew I was facing an impressive and challenging opponent, and that I needed all my skill and sharpness if I was to survive. Sharma was bringing everything back into me, a right-handed batsman, at some speed, a style of bowling I don't see all that often. His pace and accuracy were such that if he bowled a straight one, it had the same effect as a leg cutter. That was the ball that eventually got me. All the while, in the back of my mind, I knew that as the ball got older, he'd be quite capable of getting some reverse swing, with the ball moving away from the bat, sometimes appreciably, so I had to be on the lookout for that. It wasn't a quick Perth wicket, so I couldn't trust the bounce enough to try to pull him. At times, I felt I was pinned down his end, one delivery hit me on the gloves, there was a confident lbw shout, but then I drove past mid-on for four. I knew I had the ability to win this duel, I worked very hard to see him off, but on this occasion he was too good for me. That afternoon, over the next few days, so many people — including Tim Nielsen and a number of players in our dressing room, — commented on how it was such an unbelievable spell of bowling. It was great sport and I was lucky to be part of it.

I guess it's frustrating that when people recall this series, they won't think so much about great cricketing moments such as that spell, but about all the controversy and the off-field shenanigans. I'll be the same, thinking about the hearings and the meetings and the media as much as I savour the fact that we won 16 Tests in a row. I don't want to feel again the way I felt in the days after the Sydney Test: let down, drained, a target. I want to be as excited as I was going into that fourth day in Perth, when we were 2–65 at the start of the day, in pursuit of what would have been an Australian record successful fourth-innings run-chase. Before play began that day, I was super keen to get out there, same way I was when I was a kid in Tassie playing on Saturday mornings. I lost that pure joy of cricket for a little while, but by the end of the Perth Test, even though we lost, I felt it was coming back.

However, before the series was through there was one more episode when my attitude towards the off-field machinations of international cricket was really tested. It occurred in Adelaide, during the final Test, after I'd scored a hundred on the fourth day. During that innings, my back seized up a little, and I should have spent the night working on getting that ailment right — after all, we had a game to win the next day — but instead I was required at yet another meeting to discuss what had become something of an impasse in the Harbhajan affair. The Indians were standing firm in their opposition to the racism charge. So here Symmo and I were in a room at our team hotel, slumped on comfy chairs, talking with a number of senior figures from Cricket Australia. The debate went on for hours, often going around in circles but always coming back to the same question: *do you really want to go ahead with the charge of racial abuse?*

No one could be sure what would happen if the original verdict was upheld — the threat that the rest of the tour would be called off still lingered in the air. I understood that the previously friendly relationship between Indian and Australian cricket had to be preserved — we all wanted that — and a potential split in world cricket was too big an outcome to risk. The Indians were adamant their man had been unfairly treated, and Cricket Australia, while not necessarily swayed towards that view, was prepared to give some ground. Their understanding, based on talks with the Indians, was that Harbhajan would plead guilty to a 'lesser' charge, which would limit the angst that would come out of the final hearing, and would also ensure that he was punished, though not as severely as he had been at the end of Mike Procter's original hearing.

I understood the logic of all this, but part of it still grated with me. 'I need to know,' I said with the clock well past midnight. 'If Symmo and I do decide to go ahead with a "level three" charge, will we have the support of Cricket Australia?'

Chairman Creagh O'Connor explained that it wasn't up to him to give that commitment on behalf of Cricket Australia; he'd have to speak to his board. That was where the meeting finally ended, deep in the night, without a final resolution. The next day, during the lunch break on day five — India 2–142 in their second innings, a lead of 105 — we had another, much briefer get-together in a room at the back of the Adelaide Oval members stand, and Creagh told me that Cricket Australia's preference was to stick to their compromise, but if we wanted to go ahead they'd back us. So it was that the following morning we found ourselves in the No. 1 court of the Federal Court in Adelaide, before Justice John Hansen, still pursuing the racism charge.

We all knew, going into the hearing, that it was not a fait accompli that Justice Hansen would uphold Harbhajan's appeal. But after all the goings-on of the previous three weeks it just felt that way. Justice Hansen was an independent adjudicator who had been charged by the ICC to consider all the evidence, and it was very possible he would come to the same conclusion as Mike Procter. He accepted that Symmo, Haydos and Pup were sure they had heard the word 'monkey' and noted that they had immediately confronted Harbhajan on the field to voice their displeasure. However, unlike Procter, who concluded that Sachin Tendulkar had been too far away from Symmo and Harbhajan to hear what had been said, Justice Hansen recognised Tendulkar as a key witness. In his decision, the judge wrote:

A viewing of the video shows that people were moving around but certainly Mr Tendulkar appears to have been

closest to Mr Singh in the course of the heated exchange
we are concerned with. Contrary to reports that Mr
Tendulkar heard nothing, he told me he heard a heated
exchange and wished to calm Mr Singh down. His
evidence was that there was swearing between the two. It
was initiated by Mr Symonds. That he did not hear the
word 'monkey' or 'big monkey' but he did say he heard
Mr Singh use a term in his native tongue 'teri maki'
which appears to be pronounced with an 'n'. He said this
is a term that sounds like 'monkey' and could be
misinterpreted for it.

I was somewhat confused, as I could not recall hearing this 'native tongue' explanation during Mike Procter's original investigation. Eventually, Justice Hansen explained that, after considering all the evidence, he could not be certain that Harbhajan had abused Symmo in the manner we originally suggested.

'I need to "be sure" in relation to the allegations,' he wrote, 'and if I am left with an honest and reasonable uncertainty then I must make a finding favouring Mr Singh.' In the course of submissions, counsel for Cricket Australia, Brian Ward, informed Justice Hansen that Symmo 'took the language to be offensive and seriously insulting, but did not consider it fell under the requirements of (Level) 3.3.' Harbhajan conceded that he had used 'offensive words including the "teri maki" in his native tongue', but denied he had used the word 'monkey'. He pleaded guilty to a Level 2.8 charge — offensive abuse not amounting to racism — and copped the minimum fine: 50 per cent of his match fee. I felt empty, totally worn out, in dire need of a break from it all. Astonishingly, we learned the day after the hearing that in coming up with that penalty, Justice Hansen had not been provided with full details of Harbhajan's previous

MATESHIP MATTERS

This introduction was written in July, the best part of six months after the India series ended. I needed time to dwell on what for all of us was a mentally demanding saga, and as I pondered exactly what to write one thought nagged at me: *Am I better for the experience?*

In some ways, I think I am. I guess it's inevitable that, when you go through a tough experience like this one, you're going to learn something about yourself, and also about the people around you and the environment you work in. Loyalty has always been important to me, but never more so than on this occasion, and I will never forget the way the Aussie players, especially the senior guys, stuck together. Mateship really matters.

I also learned that while I mightn't like 'cricket politics', I have to accept they exist and that because of them the tasks performed by the game's administrators are rarely easy. In my view, what happened during the India series demonstrated clearly how there are times when we need the full backing of our bosses; but I acknowledge, too, that Cricket Australia needs the players' support. We have to be able to provide it.

The last time anyone suggested I should be sacked as Australian captain was in 2005, straight after we lost the Ashes. One thing I learned from that tour of England was that if a problem ever comes up it is important, as part of my role as captain, that I set out to fix it as soon as possible. It is a mistake to sit back and hope a problem will fix itself or go away, or to assume that someone else will set things straight.

For me, that lesson was reinforced through this saga. If something concerning the team isn't right, as captain I've got to try to fix it. This summer, things weren't fixed as quickly and efficiently as they could have been, and it impinged on our performance. I have to take some of the responsibility for that. It wasn't until after we finally had a frank exchange with Cricket Australia that our performances got back on track and I came away from our West Indies tour feeling positive about the way the team played, my relationship with my employer, and about my attitude towards the game I've always loved.

I don't think I ever took any of these three things for granted. But after all we went through during the India series, the fact I feel so optimistic about them means much more to me now than it ever has in the past.

misdemeanours, which meant that the spinner was not punished as severely as he might have been.

That was a bizarre way for the saga to end. The earlier guilty verdict to the Level 3.3 charge and the three-Test suspension that went with it were quashed.

AT THE END OF the Australian season, after we'd played in the first Indian Premier League (IPL) competition and before we went to the West Indies, we had *another* meeting, this time with the senior players and senior management from Cricket Australia.

Over time, I hope this gathering will be remembered as an important one in the history of the relationship between Australia's elite players and administrators. Throughout the saga I have described in this introduction, I never quite felt we got the level of support from Cricket Australia that we needed and deserved. I know James Sutherland does not agree with me, which is why I have given him the chance to put Cricket Australia's side of the story in this book. For me, this meeting before the Windies tour was a chance for us players to get any bitterness we felt off our chests, to start again, if you like; and for Cricket Australia it was an opportunity, having now had a chance to review all the controversy, to reassess the way they deal with their contracted players. From the day the Board of Control for Australian Cricket, the forerunner for Cricket Australia, was formed more than 100 years ago, there has been a level of animosity between it and the game's best cricketers, but in recent times — often because of the efforts of officials such as James Sutherland and Creagh O'Connor — many points of difference were eliminated. From my perspective, we lost a deal of that in 2007–08 and we have to get it back. I came away from this latest meeting believing we can do so.

The world of cricket politics is an increasingly precarious one. We know that the game's administrators have to tread carefully, and it's not for the blokes on the field to be making their job any harder than it already is. With hindsight, we players probably made a mistake in assuming that Cricket Australia knew we were making a stand for the right reasons, and we should have gone out of our way to assure them that we weren't just out to cause trouble.

For the future, as far as Cricket Australia and its national team are concerned, the key — as it is with any relationship — is honesty. At that meeting before the Windies tour, we participated in a series of workshops in which we split up into small groups made up of players and officials, and when those groups reported back to the larger meeting the question of trust was No. 1 on everyone's list. I think the guys from Cricket Australia were surprised by the depth of feeling we players had on this matter of trust, but simply because we disclosed it in such a forum, at the end of such an angry, acrimonious summer, I think we're already a way down the path towards making things much better in the future. No one, least of all me, wants to go back to the mood that pervaded Australian cricket for a time in January 2008.

Throughout the Harbhajan saga, a number of people — administrators, journalists and opponents — doubted our motives. They perceived our actions as being just another sledge, elaborate for sure but like any other sledge one designed to put the opposition off, maybe even drive away one of our chief antagonists. But it was much more serious than that, and we made the mistake of assuming that those closest to us would automatically back us and realise that our cause was noble. When we didn't get that support, we were angry and felt totally let down. I guess there was a certain naivety on my part in all of this; next time, I'll want to be just as sure about my convictions as I was this time, but I'll also want to be certain that the game is as committed to justice as I am before I put my reputation, and the reputation of my team-mates, on the line.

There is a part of me that says in future I should steer clear of 'cricket politics', that I'd be better off simply focusing on scoring runs, captaining the team on the field as best I can, trying to win as many games as possible. But I don't want to run away from my responsibilities. I couldn't then, and I won't in the future. Trust me.

CRICKET AUSTRALIA'S PERSPECTIVE

WE MUST CONSIDER THE BIG PICTURE

By James Sutherland, CEO, Cricket Australia

The 2007–08 summer included some of the toughest challenges many of us in Australian cricket have experienced.

The joy and pride of 16 Test wins after a remarkable New Year contest against a fine side of Indian cricketers at the historic SCG turned sour in a twinkling of an eye.

The drama of a racism allegation was overlaid with an outcry about fair play and the spirit of cricket.

On one hand, a diplomatic crisis with India, the cricket world's superpower. On the other, a roar of media and a tidal wave of emails to Cricket Australia demanding that we do everything from sack our captain to calling for our players to return to the alleged days of on-field decorum of some golden age long since past.

The days through Sydney, Perth and then on to Adelaide for Adam Gilchrist's emotional last Test were among the most difficult CA has experienced in my time.

Rick did media after Sydney and discussed that players might have done some things differently. I fronted a packed mass of TV cameras and media microphones on returning to Melbourne after Sydney and reminded everyone that we were playing Test cricket, not tiddlywinks, and treated suggestions about sacking our captain with the contempt they deserved.

But the summer got tougher in following days, particularly after Adelaide, as we realised that our players felt let down by Cricket Australia.

For the Australian players, with their singular focus that says Australian cricket is about winning cricket matches, there was, for a time, a drop in their trust of Cricket Australia.

Administrators and players have a slightly different focus, and this can lead to misunderstandings. For players, the singular focus is, quite rightly, on winning international cricket matches. From where they sit, everything in Australian cricket should be structured to achieve this end. For administrators, this singular focus on being world number one is important — because it achieves a greater end.

On-field success is important not just for itself, but because it is good for the Australian game and helps cricket survive from this generation to the next and then on to the next again.

Cricket Australia and its players went into Adelaide discussing CA's view that we needed to look at the big picture. We were facing an international diplomatic crisis and were in a situation where we would struggle to uphold an ICC code of conduct level-three racism charge in a formal hearing presided over by a High Court judge. The burden of evidence in that setting was always going to be tougher than in a post-match hearing by an ICC match referee.

CA argued the big picture, that the good of the game might be better served by arguing for a charge we knew would stand. The players went into Adelaide arguing that it was simple. A wrong had been done and it needed to be addressed by telling the truth and having it dealt with.

Despite the different emphasis, and some difficult discussion on the way through, we were always bound by a common view that the players would go to court and tell the truth.

And they did. They went in and argued the facts. The outcome — including the judge's decision, after hearing evidence, that a level-three racism charge would not fly and our need to then argue a level-two offensive language charge, and the later bungled ICC failure to advise the judge of Harbhajan Singh's prior history — is now a matter of record.

The summer's lessons vary.

When we sat down with Ricky and our players at the end of the season and talked, no-holds-barred, about trust and what is needed for it to prosper, we agreed that we need to communicate better. We each need to be comfortable talking straight and doing so face to face.

A second lesson to me is that racism is a complex and charged issue. For all its understanding of the challenges of cultural diversity, the ICC approach in this case was too simplistic.

CA continues to argue that forcing a captain to make a formal racism complaint and to go straight into an adversarial hearing overseen by match referees who are cricket experts but not qualified in this area is short sighted, is not going to change racist attitudes if they exist, and is going to set up nation-versus-nation diplomatic conflict. To me, the Australian Football League's confidential mediation process is more appropriate. It offers a more realistic approach to helping athletes genuinely understand each other and what is acceptable or unacceptable.

And a third lesson is that measuring the public mood is not always as simple as the talk-back commentators and columnists will have you believe.

Such was our concern about our standing after Sydney that we undertook formal market research. We found, at summer's end, that the public genuinely rates the Australian team, its individual players, and the way they play very highly. Our cricketers stood out as sportspeople who are admired and highly respected, ahead of those from almost all other sports.

The 2007-08 summer was tough, mistakes were made on all sides. But I am convinced we have emerged with Australian players and administrators understanding each other better than before, with an even clearer view of how we will work together to uphold cricket as Australia's favourite sport.

PART ONE

ICC WORLD TWENTY20

*'When you don't respect this [Twenty20] game,
it gets up and bites you.'*

— Ricky Ponting,
September 12, 2007

TUESDAY, SEPTEMBER 11

Back in the days when I was a teenage cricket fan, in the late 1980s, it always seemed that the Australian cricket season had a definite starting point. It wasn't the first Test; more likely, it was the start of the Sheffield Shield or some domestic one-dayers. When I look back at the cricket records, however, I see that the Aussie team of those days did usually have a 'spring tour' of some kind: to India in 1986; the World Cup in 1987; Pakistan in 1988; the Nehru Cup in India in 1989.

So maybe cricket life was just as hectic back then, just for the fans it didn't seem that way. Last season, we started in Kuala Lumpur, and then experienced the Champions Trophy in India before we could focus on the Ashes Tests in Australia. This year, it was something new again — what they're rather grandly calling the 'World Twenty20' which was quickly interpreted as meaning the 'Twenty20 World Championship' or even the 'Twenty20 World Cup', to be staged in South Africa. Then it's a one-day series in India; back home for Tests against Bangladesh; a three-game Chappell–Hadlee series against New Zealand; Tests against

India; the Commonwealth Bank one-dayers with India and Sri Lanka; a tour of Pakistan; a tour of the West Indies. It's all very exciting, sure, but a bit crazy, too. When I study the program, and think about all the hotel rooms, and the airports, and the press conferences, I start to feel exhausted even before a ball is bowled. If it was just about playing cricket, and representing my country, and sharing the experience with my mates, it would be wonderful. In many ways, it still is. The fear is that something might go wrong. I just look at that itinerary, and I wonder, *where is the time to regroup, to reassess, to get it right?*

As if to emphasise that time will often be short over the next few months, my departure for South Africa was delayed because my wife Rianna fell ill. Suddenly, my preparation for the big Twenty20 tournament had been thrown out, and there was a point when I thought I might have to miss the entire competition. The boys left without me on September 3, a Monday, about the time Rianna's health began to pick up, and by the following Thursday I was able to announce that I would be playing. Then a new problem came up — finding an available flight — and I wasn't able to land in Johannesburg until yesterday.

As captain, a situation where a family member falls sick is tricky, rather than difficult. Staying behind was a no-brainer, because the health and happiness of the people closest to me means more than anything else. Yet, it is impossible not to worry at least a little bit about the fact that others are doing your job. I was lucky that Cricket Australia was so understanding, and that vice-captain Adam Gilchrist and coach Tim Nielsen were so well-equipped to take on the leadership role.

Also on my flight to Jo'burg was Shane Watson, whose departure had been delayed while he was treated for hamstring soreness. We were two of a 15-man squad that looked this way: Ricky Ponting (captain), Adam Gilchrist (vice-captain), Nathan

Bracken, Stuart Clark, Michael Clarke, Brad Haddin, Matthew Hayden, Ben Hilfenhaus, Brad Hodge, Brad Hogg, Michael Hussey, Mitchell Johnson, Brett Lee, Andrew Symonds, Shane Watson. Hilfenhaus, my young Tassie team-mate whom I reckon has a fantastic future ahead of him, had come into the side after Shaun Tait withdrew because of an elbow problem.

Because of our late arrivals, my original thought was that neither of us would be included in the Aussie line-up for our opening match of the tournament, against Zimbabwe in Cape Town tomorrow. We missed practice matches against New Zealand and South Africa (the first an Australian victory; the second, a loss) and given our late arrival — just two days before the match — it was going to be a big ask for us to play. It is not as if we haven't got others in the squad who can do the job. In my case, I hadn't picked up a bat too often since the World Cup final last April 28, so part of my thinking was that I was really in need of a net or two (another section of my brain, the competitive bit, said, 'Go for it!'). Right now, though, after a decent sleep, I don't feel too bad, so I reckon I might as well play. The 6pm start for the game works in my favour, and maybe the only thing that will stop me is if our physio, Alex Kountouris, believes it is too big a risk to play so soon after such a long flight. Watto, however, will definitely be given more time to get his hammy 100 per cent right.

Maybe it was our experience after we landed at the airport yesterday evening that blasted any lethargy out of my system. The flight we got on should have given us a few hours in Jo'burg before the annual ICC awards night began, which I was obliged to attend, but of course it was late, which meant that after we escaped customs we were hustled into a van and then given a four-car police escort straight to the function. It was quite a ride at times, with the convoy reaching speeds of up to 160ks per hour, as all other traffic was stopped to let us through. There was

ICC AWARD WINNERS 2007

Player of the Year: Ricky Ponting (Australia)
Other nominees: Shivnarine Chanderpaul (West Indies), Kevin Pietersen (England), Mohammad Yousuf (Pakistan)
Test Player of the Year: Mohammad Yousuf (Pakistan)
Other nominees: Muttiah Muralitharan (Sri Lanka), Kevin Pietersen (England), Ricky Ponting (Australia)
ODI Player of the Year: Matthew Hayden (Australia)
Other nominees: Ricky Ponting (Australia), Jacques Kallis (South Africa), Glenn McGrath (Australia)
One-day Player of the Year for non-Test nations: Thomas Odoyo (Kenya)
Other nominees: Ashish Bagai (Canada), Ryan ten Doeschate (Netherlands), Steve Tikolo (Kenya)
Women's Player of the Year: Jhulan Goswami (India)
Other nominees: Lisa Sthalekar (Australia), Claire Taylor (England)
Emerging Player of the Year: Shaun Tait (Australia)
Other nominees: Ravi Bopara (England), Shakib Al Hasan (Bangladesh), Ross Taylor (New Zealand)
Captain of the Year: Ricky Ponting (Australia)
Other nominee: Mahela Jayawardene (Sri Lanka)
Spirit of Cricket Award: Sri Lanka
Other nominees: Australia, Ireland, New Zealand
Umpire of the Year: Simon Taufel (Australia)
Other nominees: Mark Benson (England), Steve Bucknor (West Indies), Daryl Harper (Australia)
World Test Team of the Year (in batting order): Matthew Hayden (Australia), Michael Vaughan (England), Ricky Ponting (Australia, captain), Mohammad Yousuf (Pakistan), Kevin Pietersen (England), Michael Hussey (Australia), Kumar Sangakkara (Sri Lanka), Stuart Clark (Australia), Makhaya Ntini (South Africa), Mohammad Asif (Pakistan), Muttiah Muralitharan (Sri Lanka); 12th man: Zaheer Khan (India)
World ODI Team of the Year (in batting order): Matthew Hayden (Australia), Sachin Tendulkar (India), Ricky Ponting (Australia, captain), Kevin Pietersen (England), Shivnarine Chanderpaul (West Indies), Jacques Kallis (South Africa), Mark Boucher (South Africa), Chaminda Vaas (Sri Lanka), Shane Bond (New Zealand), Muttiah Muralitharan (Sri Lanka), Glenn McGrath (Australia); 12th man: Michael Hussey (Australia)

no time for me to check-in or even have a shower before I joined my team-mates in the ballroom.

On the flight, I'd done plenty of stretching, drank gallons of water, and managed a little kip, but for all that, by the time the last award had been handed out, it had been 24 hours since I'd last slept in a bed. But before I had time for some much-needed shut-eye, I had to cast an eye over the notes Tim Nielsen had made concerning the performances of the boys in the practice matches and what tactics he believed were most important when playing the Twenty20 form of the game. A key to batting well, Tim argues, is that we need to be mentally prepared if two or three wickets fall quickly. That's when the batting team needs to hold its nerve, stick to the game plan and not panic. It could be that there is an advantage in batting second in Twenty20, because then you know what you're chasing; otherwise, there could be a natural inclination to think that you're not going quick enough.

These sort of debating points really had me thinking, and despite my weariness it still took a little to get to sleep. When finally I woke up, I was genuinely excited that the 2007–08 season is about to get under way.

THURSDAY, SEPTEMBER 13

ICC World Twenty20 Group B match, at Cape Town (September 12):
Australia 9–138 (20 overs: A Symonds 33, BJ Hodge 35; E Chigumbura 3–20) lost to **Zimbabwe** 5–139 (19.2 overs: BRM Taylor 60*) by five wickets

The Australian team might not have played any competitive cricket since the World Cup, but even so a series of injuries has meant that our preparation for the World Twenty20 has hardly gone smoothly.

Stuey Clark had stayed in Sydney for a couple of days after the bulk of the team departed, so he could be with his sick daughter. Watto and I also missed that first flight to South Africa, Michael Clarke suffered a lower abdominal strain at training, which ruled him out of both the practice matches, and then Matthew Hayden's back stiffened over the weekend. We needed a positive, and it came in the form of Brett Lee, who by all accounts was very impressive in the Twenty20 rehearsals against New Zealand and South Africa. Bing had missed the World Cup because of injury, so this tour is hopefully the start of a big comeback for him. I've been told that Ben Hilfenhaus also looked good, bowling outswingers that apparently had a real zip about them. He took 3–11 against New Zealand, not a bad effort in a 20-over game.

Our other man in form was Andrew Symonds, who hit 45 from 26 balls against the locals, a day after smashing 70 from 43 against the Kiwis.

These sort of performances meant that, while there was cause for us to be a little concerned going into our first match, against Zimbabwe, there were also plenty of reasons for us to be optimistic. Consequently, I came out of our opening game with no excuses, just very disappointed and even a little embarrassed by the way we played and the result.

I can't remember walking off a cricket field feeling that way in quite a while, and the rest of the team felt similarly aggrieved. I told the boys straight after the game that it was as bad a loss as I've been involved in with the Australian team. We didn't respect the game or our opponents as much as we needed to. The thought was, *We'll go out and smack these blokes all over the place, make 250 and that'll be it.* All of a sudden, we were 4–48. Cricket can bite you if you go into it with an attitude like that. But there is no sense within our squad that this is a 'second tier' tournament, that it doesn't really matter; rather, we want to win

A BREAK CAN BE A BONUS

I must admit I haven't added them all up, and it is true that some parts of the cricket world are in turmoil at the moment, but over the next 18 months we will be playing a hell of a lot of cricket — something like 25 Tests, more than 50 one-day internationals, who knows how much Twenty20. During that time there will be discussions — among our leadership group and, inevitably, in the media — about subjects such as player burnout, squad rotation and the pressure to blood young players so we don't get caught out by senior guys retiring or losing form.

There is no doubt that we have to be careful with the way we manage our top players, especially those who are playing both Test and limited-over cricket. And this applies not just to playing time, but also to the way we go about preparation and recovery, so no one gets 'over-loaded' with cricket.

Occasionally, players will need to rest — whether they like it or not — because being mentally sharp is as important as being in good physical shape. It's amazing how many injuries occur when the mind is a little frazzled. That's also when bad habits can develop, and then enthusiasm can be a little hard to find. At the same time, this can never be an excuse to ease off for too long, because one of our strengths in recent times is that we have done all the work, got our preparation right, and been ready for the next challenge. I think some lessons will be learned along the way, and while we will always be keen to have our best team playing as often as possible, there will be days when guys will be rested, simply because they need to have a break. And we'll treat injuries carefully. That is why Michael Clarke missed the game against Zimbabwe; he'll be back in the team for our second game, against England.

A major problem is that there is a not one bloke in our squad who doesn't want to play for his country as often as possible, and I for one never want to see any change in that attitude. Playing for Australia is an honour, and feeling a little 'tired' doesn't sound like much of a reason to give someone else a chance to take your spot. Yet I have learned myself, during the Commonwealth Bank Series in Australia over the past couple of years, that a break can be a bonus. It's all about balance, and being aware that you'll never be able to please all of the people all of the time.

and are filthy that we let ourselves down. All credit to Zimbabwe, who clearly deserved their victory. We were outplayed, and what is most frustrating was that they did the basics and handled the critical moments better than we did. Doing the simple things right is something we'd prided ourselves on throughout the 2006–07 season.

There wasn't much else I could say after the game, other than to remind everyone that the past 12 months is now part of cricket history. It was a great year — winning the Champions Trophy for the first time, reclaiming the Ashes and then winning the World Cup so decisively — but we must refocus on the cricket in front of us. Against Zimbabwe, we didn't perform as true professionals. This was especially true of the top of the batting order, and I was as guilty as anyone. In both practice matches we lost three cheap wickets at the start of our innings, and at our pre-game team meeting we'd talked about these ugly starts. But it made no difference. Hopefully, we'll play a lot smarter tomorrow when we face England; if we don't, our tournament will be over.

SUNDAY, SEPTEMBER 16

ICC World Twenty20 Group B match, at Cape Town (September 14):
England 135 (20 overs: A Flintoff 31; NW Bracken 3–16, MG Johnson 3–22) lost to **Australia** 2–136 (14.5 overs: ML Hayden 67*, AC Gilchrist 45) by eight wickets

England's Kevin Pietersen is a dangerous player, but he says some silly things. He was at it again before our game here against the Poms, saying he didn't just want to beat us; his aim was to 'humiliate' us. Here we were, extra keen to make amends for the

WHAT NOW FOR FREDDIE?

A sad aspect of our game against England was the way Andrew Flintoff felt for his ankle at the end of his fourth and final over. Less than a year ago, 'Freddie' was the England captain looking forward to an Ashes series, but now his career appears to be in jeopardy. He's only 29, so he should have plenty of cricket ahead of him, but it appears that the poor bloke is struggling to get his body right. There have been many cricketers over the years whose bodies haven't been able to stand up to the stresses of fast bowling, and I just hope Freddie is not one of those, because he is a terrific player, a fantastic competitor and a great person to play against. I still remember how, at different times in Australia last season, he was very good, most notably on the first day of the series in Brisbane, when, thinking back to England in 2005, we all thought, *Here we go again.*

Now, though, he seems unable to get through even four overs without developing a limp and a grimace. If he's not right for the 2009 Ashes series, it will be a huge setback for the Poms. Freddie might not be irreplaceable, but he's close.

loss to Zimbabwe, and a bloke we handled pretty well last summer is trying to sound like Muhammad Ali. He is a good batsman, so there was always a chance he'd back his words with some runs, but instead Nathan Bracken knocked him over for 21 (from 20 balls), we kept them to 135 all out from their 20 overs, and then Haydos and Gilly took us to victory with more than five overs to spare. That's a massive victory, akin to winning with 20 overs remaining in a 50-over game.

I've been around long enough to know that, more often than not, when someone starts talking in such a way before a game, it comes back to bite them. My preference is simply to get on with what I have to do. Of course, there have been exceptions — Shane Warne and Glenn McGrath were quite capable of backing up big statements they made before a match or a series, but they were champions. My understanding is that England captain Paul Collingwood wasn't too thrilled with Pietersen's pre-game comments, but all he said publicly after the game was, 'Kevin's obviously Kevin.'

I think I know what he means.

Bracks' effort to win the man of the match award was superb. Unless they change the rules to make the game kinder for them, Twenty20 will rarely be a bowler's game. But here he managed to take three wickets and concede only four runs an over. As a team, there was more intensity and intent about our cricket, and we played smarter, too. The England players are coming to the end of their home season, so they've been playing a lot more cricket than many of our guys, and they are much more experienced than us in this form of the game. That we handled them so comfortably reassured me that the first-up loss to Zimbabwe was a one-off rather than a sign of potentially awkward times ahead.

It also emphasised for me that we are a group who enjoy playing under pressure, that the stress of *having* to win is something we can handle.

FRIDAY, SEPTEMBER 21

ICC World Twenty20 Group F match, at Cape Town (September 16): Bangladesh 8–123 (20 overs: Tamim Iqbal 32, Aftab Ahmed 31; B Lee 3–27) lost to **Australia** 1–124 (13.5 overs: ML Hayden 73*, AC Gilchrist 43) by nine wickets

ICC World Twenty20 Group F match, at Johannesburg (September 18): **Australia** 7–164 (20 overs: MEK Hussey 37, BJ Hodge 36; Sohail Tanvir 3–31) lost to **Pakistan** 4–166 (19.1 overs: Shoaib Malik 52*, Misbah-ul-Haq 66*; SR Clark 3–27) by six wickets

ICC World Twenty20 Group F match, at Cape Town (September 20):
Sri Lanka 101 (19.3 overs: SR Clark 4–20) lost to **Australia** 0–102
(10.2 overs: ML Hayden 58*, AC Gilchrist 31*) by 10 wickets

Beating England meant we qualified for the 'Super Eights', the 'second round' if you like, as the top team in Group B (the 12 teams involved in the tournament had been divided into four groups of three, with the top two in each group gong through to the Super Eights). The draw meant we needed to beat two out of Bangladesh, Pakistan and Sri Lanka to reach the semi-finals, and we achieved that reasonably comfortably in the end, though on a personal level I wasn't feeling too flash after straining my left hamstring during our loss to the Pakistanis in Jo'burg.

NO FEAR

The arguments that batting second in Twenty20 is a big advantage grew louder as the tournament progressed, and the effort of Shoaib Malik and Misbah-ul-Haq for Pakistan against us, when they went from 4–46 after 6.4 overs to 4–165 in 19.1 overs to win the game, seemed to offer more evidence in that direction. I must admit I can't think of too many circumstances where batting first would be helpful, but I do wonder if in fact what is happening in Twenty20 is just mirroring something that was already happening in the 50-over game. Think of South Africa's effort against us in Johannesburg in 2006, when they successfully chased 434, or perhaps New Zealand's performances in the Chappell–Hadlee series earlier this year, when we scored 336 and 346 but that wasn't enough.

Teams used to be intimidated by big totals, but not any more. So many things — helmets, better bats, flatter wickets, shorter boundaries — have worked to the batsmen's advantage, and meant that fear is less of a factor in cricket these days. Further, as the game has become more professional, a batting order has more direction as a group these days. Each player knows his role, and thus the path to achieving a big run chase doesn't seem so steep.

It is never fun being stuck on the sidelines while your team-mates are competing. Of course, I would have felt a lot worse if the boys had lost to Sri Lanka, but instead they performed magnificently — reducing what is usually a very good batting line-up to 7–43, taking the 10th wicket in the final over, and then Gilly and Haydos scored at nearly 10 runs an over to win in a canter. The way everyone has responded after our disappointing start has been terrific, and we have earned our place in tomorrow's second semi-final against India in Durban.

I'm happy that we've made the final four, but I'm still not quite sure what to make of Twenty20 cricket. There have been some exciting games and some spectacular sport. India's Yuvraj Singh smashing six sixes from one over by England's Stuart Broad (during an innings of 58 from 16 balls in 14 minutes) would be most people's No. 1 standout. The crowds here have been substantial and vibrant, and everyone who has turned up — including, I sense, most of the players — has enjoyed the experience. So even the strongest critic has to concede that the event has been a success so far.

I'm not as cynical about the game as I once was, but some negatives still nag at me. There is so much luck involved in this shortened form of the game; it's not always going to be the best team that wins. I guess that's true of all sport but it seems to be accentuated here, almost like having a golf tournament decided purely by a sudden-death play-off, without having the first 72 holes. Teams that are outclassed in five-day matches and even 50-over games are much more competitive in Twenty20. India offer a good example of this. The shorter the format of the game, the more dangerous they become. Some of their batsmen — Yuvraj and MS Dhoni are classic examples — can hurt you more in shorter games, because there is less opportunity to find ways of picking apart their techniques. Little wonder, then, that the tournament has been unpredictable, with many locals stunned that the previously unbeaten South Africa was eliminated so comfortably by India last night. Form in Twenty20 really doesn't count for all that much.

It is inevitable that we'll be playing much more Twenty20 as the seasons roll on. The economics of sport will see to that, and just as one-day cricket evolved through the 1970s and 1980s, so too will this form of the game change and improve. My guess is that by the end of 2008 we will have a much clearer view of the new game's pros and cons, and where it should fit in 21st-century cricket.

There is no doubt that a whole new breed of spectator (and plenty of old ones, too) love watching Twenty20. As a top-order batsman, if you get on a roll, swinging away successfully with little if any thought for 'building' an innings, it can be exhilarating. There's certainly no reason to fear a bowler and unless there is an immediate batting collapse there is no need to worry about protecting your wicket for the final overs. Matthew Hayden was having the time of his life against Sri Lanka, smacking the bowling all over the place. But I wonder if the balance of the batsman-bowler confrontation is tilted too much in the batsman's direction in Twenty20 cricket. For every personal highlight by a bowler — such as Brett Lee's hat-trick against Bangladesh — there are 10 or more by batsmen, usually involving a colossal six or a series of sixes. I also worry about the future for traditional middle-order batsman, and for 'support' bowlers. Take Michael Clarke, for example, who in four games here has faced one ball (from which he was run out) and conceded nearly 10 runs an over. Cricket is an 11-a-side game, but in a way the 20-over game takes me back to schoolboy games when it was two or three stars in a side who scored all the runs and bowled all the overs, while the others were there to make up the numbers.

Sadly, my dud hammy has ruled me out of the rest of this tournament, and I'm not sure at this point if I'll even be going to India for the seven one-dayers Australia will be playing there from September 29. But I'm keen to travel with the boys, even if I can't play in the first two or three games.

Over the past few years, I've had some problems with my back, and the doctors are telling me that as a result of a chronic weakness there, I'm probably going to have some more trouble with my hamstrings in the future. This is not ideal, of course, but it is manageable. The particular strain I'm recovering from now came about in unusual circumstances. I had a long net at training the day before the Pakistan game, about an hour and 20 minutes, and at the end of it I could feel a sore spot in the back of my leg, which I assumed was the result of me strapping my pad or thigh pad a fraction too tight. It was still there during our warm-up on game day, and once I started moving in the game it deteriorated to the point that I knew I was in trouble.

One thing the experience showed me was how familiar the guys in our team are with the way each of us goes about our business. We know each other's games pretty well. After the game, a few of the boys remarked that, even before I had faced a ball, I just didn't look right. I wasn't conscious of it myself at the start of my innings, but apparently I was stretching more than usual and not moving as freely as I normally do. With hindsight, I guess, I shouldn't have played, but the truth is that there was no way I was going to be forced out by something as minor as a slight sore spot in my leg. In the past few years, we have grown used to battling on with little niggles like that, and it rarely leads to major setbacks. If we dropped out of games because of these sorts of things, we wouldn't play much cricket at all.

TUESDAY, SEPTEMBER 25

ICC World Twenty20 Second Semi-final, at Durban (September 22): India
5–188 (20 overs: RV Uthappa 34, Yuvraj Singh 70, MS Dhoni 36) defeated
Australia 7–173 (20 overs: ML Hayden 62, A Symonds 43) by 15 runs

I can only imagine the buzz throughout India after their cricketers became the Twenty20 world champions by beating Pakistan in the final last night. Good luck to them — MS Dhoni's team played really well in the semi-final against us and then followed up with a brave effort in the decider, successfully defending 157, which is no mean effort. I guess we'll find out soon enough just how much the win means to them, because we are about to head to the airport to fly to Bangalore for the start of our tour there. I hear the Indian Board have paid their team a US$3 million bonus, which suggests that everyone in that part of the cricket world is more than a little excited.

I've never really worried too much about one-off Twenty20 games before, but the one scheduled for Mumbai at the end of October has suddenly taken on a whole new meaning. I'm sure the Indians will be keen to confirm their status as Twenty20's top dogs, and we'll be eager to show them that we're still the No. 1 nation in the world, whatever form of cricket you're talking about.

While I'll be flying with the team to India, Mike Hussey and Shane Watson, who have also suffered hamstring injuries, will not. I'm expecting to play in most of the games in India, but the expectation is that Huss and Watto will take longer to heal, hence the decision to send them home. Much has been made of the injuries we suffered during the Twenty20 tournament (Brad Hodge has also strained a hamstring), with theories blooming that this sudden susceptibility to soft-tissue injuries is proof that there is something wrong with the way we prepare, or maybe it

ICC WORLD TWENTY20 TABLES

Group A

Team	Played	Won	Lost	Tied	NR	Points	Run-rate
South Africa	2	2	0	0	0	4	+0.97
Bangladesh	2	1	1	0	0	2	+0.15
West Indies	2	0	2	0	0	0	-1.23

Group B

Team	Played	Won	Lost	Tied	NR	Points	Run-rate
Australia	2	1	1	0	0	2	+0.99
England	2	1	1	0	0	2	+0.21
Zimbabwe	2	1	1	0	0	2	-1.20

Group C

Team	Played	Won	Lost	Tied	NR	Points	Run-rate
Sri Lanka	2	2	0	0	0	4	+4.72
New Zealand	2	1	1	0	0	2	+2.40
Kenya	2	0	2	0	0	0	-8.05

Group D

Team	Played	Won	Lost	Tied	NR	Points	Run-rate
India	2	0	0	1	1	3	0.00
Pakistan	2	1	0	1	0	2	+1.28
Scotland	2	0	1	0	1	1	-2.56

Super Eights: Group E

Team	Played	Won	Lost	Tied	NR	Points	Run-rate
India	3	2	1	0	0	4	+0.75
New Zealand	3	2	1	0	0	4	+0.05
South Africa	3	2	1	0	0	4	-0.12
England	3	0	3	0	0	0	-0.70

Super Eights: Group F

Team	Played	Won	Lost	Tied	NR	Points	Run-rate
Pakistan	3	3	0	0	0	6	+0.84
Australia	3	2	1	0	0	4	+2.26
Sri Lanka	3	1	2	0	0	2	-0.70
Bangladesh	3	0	3	0	0	0	-2.03

Semi-Finals

At Cape Town (September 22): New Zealand 8–143 (20 overs) lost to Pakistan 4–147 (18.5 overs) by six wickets

At Durban (September 22): India 5–188 (20 overs) defeated Australia 7–173 (20 overs) by 15 runs

Final

At Johannesburg (September 24): India 5–157 (20 overs) defeated Pakistan 152 (19.3 overs) by five runs

shows just how old we're all getting. However, Alex Kountouris got out his calculator and did some maths on the rate of hamstrings torn or strained by Australian cricketers during a normal international season — including Tests, one-dayers, Twenty20 and Pura Cup games — and the answer is a grand total of five a year. We experienced four in less than a week, so at least the numbers are now in our favour. I have a lot of faith in our staff, the way we prepare and the way we manage muscle injuries, so it will take a lot more than just one bad run before I'll start thinking we have a major problem.

So what did we learn from our time in South Africa? We knew going in we were a bit 'underdone', compared to other teams, but that was not a fault of attitude, but a reflection of the fact that we were coming off our winter break. Any tournament staged in September is going to be difficult for us, whatever form of cricket is involved. If we made a mistake it was to underrate the importance of the competition — to us, Twenty20 was still the 'exhibition' class; to others; it's already much more than that. Before the Champions Trophy last year, we played a series of one-dayers in Kuala Lumpur, and I think that we have to ensure that prior to the next Twenty20 world championship we play some serious trials, to get us in full working order before the tournament begins.

And there will definitely be another World Twenty20. The popularity of this one guarantees it. We didn't play well enough to win on this occasion, but we did learn things and we will do things better next time.

In fact, there was quite a bit to like about the way we played. Matt Hayden was outstanding with the bat, and I was thrilled with the way Brett Lee came back after missing the World Cup. For anyone to miss an event like that, to have to sit on the lounge at home and watch your mates win a trophy you had set your own sights on, must be so difficult. But instead of feeling sorry himself, Brett worked really hard to get back to his best. With the likes of Glenn McGrath and Shane Warne gone now, he is going to be so crucial for us in the future. Here in South Africa, he has bowled really quick from the first game, and he's demonstrated that just because there are only 20 overs in an innings, there is still a place for an out-and-out wicket-taker. As captain, whenever I thought, *we need a wicket right now*, my natural reflex was to try to get Brett on to bowl.

Given that everyone, me included, is calling Twenty20 a batsmen's game, it is somewhat ironic that it was mostly our frontline bowlers who performed up to expectations. Besides Brett, I was also very happy with the form of our two left-hand quicks, Nathan Bracken and Mitchell Johnson, and Stuart Clark was excellent, too. Stuey took 12 wickets in the tournament, including three against Pakistan and four against Sri Lanka, managing to put the pressure back on the batsmen in a way few other bowlers in the competition were able to do. Bracks and Mitch's competition figures were almost identical — eight wickets in six games, with Bracks conceding 6.35 runs per over and Mitch 6.37. Of course, Bracks is already established as a key member of our one-day squad, while Mitch left me convinced that he's a big chance to make his Test debut before the season is over. I'm sure he'll be keen to follow up his good form here with some big performances in India.

Another bloke who I imagine can't wait to spend some quality time in the middle is Michael Clarke. I'm sure he thinks the whole adventure was a waste of time, given that he hardly faced a ball, but even in his experience we can gain something. We needed to acknowledge that in the normal course of a Twenty20 game, not everyone is going to play a part, but in the next game that player might suddenly be required to do something special. We needed to mix up our batting orders a little in the early games, to try to give everyone a hit. Instead we stuck rigidly to the same line-up, which was good for Haydos, Gilly and me, but not so good for Pup. In the semi-final, we needed him to come out and slog straightaway (33 to win with 20 balls remaining), but he hadn't had a decent hit while he's been here. The end result was that he was bowled by Harbhajan Singh for 3 from the third delivery he faced. A few minutes later, we'd come up 15 runs short, India was in the final, and we could start looking forward to part two of our season. There's a long, long way to go.

PART TWO
THE AUSTRALIANS
IN INDIA

*'When the Australian team talks about playing
aggressively, we are committing ourselves to playing
hard. There's nothing given and there's nothing
asked to be given.'*

— Ricky Ponting, October 6, 2007

THURSDAY, SEPTEMBER 27

We landed in Bangalore yesterday, flying into a country that is absolutely mad for Twenty20 cricket and their new 'world champions'. I reckon we'd been on the ground about five minutes when someone told me that a survey had just been undertaken asking Indians what was their favourite form of cricket ... and Twenty20 had won easily!

We sensed a new-found confidence in their cricket community, which wouldn't have been there six months ago when they failed to make the second stage at the World Cup. Apparently, winning a Twenty20 World Cup can do that for you.

On the surface you'd have to think the locals have an advantage over us, given that the buzz in their group is so positive, whereas our preparation has been confused somewhat by a run of injuries. The latest thought is that I'll miss at least the first game of the series, on Saturday, and probably the second game as well. Wicketkeeper-batsman Brad Haddin and all-rounder James Hopes have come into the squad, while Adam

Voges, who had been captaining Australia A in Pakistan, will travel with us as cover in case my leg doesn't improve.

Nathan Bracken is also going to be absent for a while, as he has been granted leave to return home and be with his wife Haley as she prepares to give birth to their first child. Our expectation at this stage is that Bracks is unlikely to miss the whole series, so we don't feel the need to call up another replacement at this point.

I must say I'm sick of the thought of missing games. It was tough watching the semi-final in Durban and it's going to be just as difficult watching these early games in India from afar. But while I'm a little agitated about my predicament, it's nothing compared to the stir-crazy mentality of Brad Hogg, who had a very frustrating time of it in South Africa. Hoggy is a hyperactive guy by nature, a bloke who has to be training or playing, but the way the World Twenty20 tournament was structured he got to do neither. Losing that first game against Zimbabwe meant we never had a chance to pick anything other than our strongest XI, and while he was unlucky not to be selected, given that he had played such an important role for us at the World Cup, someone had to miss out. His consolation is that, given the nature of Indian pitches, he is likely to play a big role for us in the upcoming matches, as he has done before in one-dayers on the sub-continent.

Another bloke super keen to get out there is Brad Hodge, who we intend to bat at No. 3 while I'm on the sidelines. It will be a good opportunity for him to get some solid time in the middle, which might sound a bit strange given that I'm writing about a one-day match, but after the frenzy that was the Twenty20, the idea of a 50-over innings sounds like a lifetime. Hodgey has talked to me about the idea of opening the batting for Victoria when we get home, on the basis that with Justin Langer having retired, the top of the order might represent his best chance to gain a permanent spot in the Test team's batting line-up. To me, this concept has some merit, and I know that there are precedents in Australian cricket history of guys turning themselves into openers and launching long and highly successful careers. Bob Simpson, Keith Stackpole and Lang are three who readily come to mind. This said, the competition for that position has already become red-hot: Phil Jaques (who played Test cricket when Lang was injured in 2005–06) scored a couple of hundreds for Australia A in the unofficial Tests in Pakistan, while Western Australia's Chris Rogers made a couple of half-centuries and also scored a century in the third one-dayer on that tour.

James Hopes was another to make a big 'Test' hundred in Pakistan and he was also very effective bowling first change. The man known as 'Catfish' sends them down at a lively fast-medium and is a good striker of the ball in the middle order. Although he didn't play any one-day international cricket in 2006–07, I still remember how we threw him the ball in Bangladesh in late April 2006 and he tied them down during a vital part of the game, finishing with 1–8 from five overs. I love the idea of him being in the side, because he gives us balance and a variety of bowling options that I'm very comfortable with. Back at the World Cup, we played four quicks — Glenn McGrath, Shaun Tait, Nathan Bracken, Shane Watson — plus a spinner, Brad Hogg, with Michael Clarke and Andrew Symonds also very capable of chipping in with the ball. Here, we might be without all four of those pace bowlers, because of retirement, injury or personal circumstances, but in Hopes, Stuart Clark, Ben Hilfenhaus, Mitchell Johnson and Brett Lee we're still very well-armed for this upcoming series.

I first visited India way back in August–September of 1993, as part of a Cricket Academy side that was captained by Justin Langer. There were a few other future international players in that squad: Michael DiVenuto, Murray Goodwin, Simon Cook,

Shane Lee, Glenn McGrath and Jon Davison. Our two keepers were Queensland's Wade Seccombe and Tim Nielsen, the current Australian coach, and among the players we faced on the tour were Sourav Ganguly, Rahul Dravid and Anil Kumble. We also visited Sri Lanka on that trip, and this was where I had my weirdest cricket moment of the tour. I was 99 not out at the end of the 48th over of a 50-over game in Colombo when the umpires suddenly decided there wasn't time for the final 12 deliveries. So much for that century!

Of course, the Indian people have always loved cricket — I knew that from my first day in this extraordinary country — but the sense I got back in the early 1990s, even the mid '90s when I made my international debut, was that many people based outside India didn't like playing there. They were intimidated by the pitches, the heat and the cultural differences. Few people like being out of their comfort zone, and many Australian teams struggled when they toured the sub-continent. We didn't win a Test series here between 1969 and 2004.

Fortunately, things have changed over the course of my career. Those Indian pitches that were so foreign back then are familiar to us now. I believe that every time we've toured India we've improved, which means we are learning. Our results in one-day matches have been excellent, and we've done well on our past two Test tours as well. We probably should have won in 2001, when VVS Laxman and Rahul Dravid inspired that famous fightback in Kolkata, and then we did win the first three Tests out of four in 2004.

As a team, we have been very good at adapting to different conditions; it is a challenge we enjoy. I put this down to the fact that over the past decade we have always had experienced guys in the squad, all of whom are willing to share their knowledge with the newer blokes in the side.

On a personal level, though, I've rarely been happy with my form over here. My record is not so good in this part of the world, especially in Test cricket, where I've averaged only 12.29, with one half-century (though I've only played one Test in India in the past six years). Growing up in Tasmania, I almost always batted on hard wickets (in junior and club cricket we mostly used synthetic wickets) and then I've been spoiled by all the good batting tracks I've seen in Australia since my first-class career began. It is true, too, that while we have had Shane Warne and Stuart MacGill, there have been very few other dangerous spin bowlers about, especially finger spinners, because they struggle to get anything out of our wickets. So I when I come to India, I am suddenly in unfamiliar territory, and while I believe I've adapted much better in recent years, the first couple of tours were tough.

Our tactics have evolved, too. There was a time when we came here with teams full of spinners, but that strategy was flawed because the Indian batsmen play the slow men so well. I remember their opening bat, Navjot Sidhu, smashing our off-spinner Gavin Robertson to all parts in 1998, but gradually we realised that he wasn't so good against the quicks, even when the wickets were slow. They don't have fast bowlers in their ranks, so it makes sense to have our attack dominated by the quicks, especially when we are so rich in this department. In the Champions Trophy last year, even though we played on wickets that were always going to spin, we went into many matches with four quicks and Shane Watson, and we won the tournament. My view is that whatever the conditions, if you've got guys in your team who can execute and are adaptable, then most times you'll be better off playing those guys rather than automatically picking a spinner just because that's the way it's always been done in the past.

MONDAY, OCTOBER 1

Game One, at Bangalore (September 29): Australia 7–307 (50 overs: MJ Clarke 130, BJ Haddin 69; S Sreesanth 3–55) versus **India** 1–9 (2.4 overs). Abandoned due to rain

There was a stage where we didn't think Michael Clarke would play in the first game of the series. He didn't look too flash in the dressing room before the game, and he hadn't had a thing to eat and had been up most of the preceding night because his stomach was too temperamental. But after a being put on a remedy of antibiotics and rehydration he didn't just play, he batted for more than three hours and managed to peel off his third ODI hundred. The only pity was that because rain washed out India's reply, his gallant effort counted for nothing (at least from a result point of view), and we headed to Kochi on the southwest coast of India with the rubber, in a sense, still to get underway.

The biggest wrap Pup received came from Brad Haddin, with whom he shared a 144-run partnership. 'He was in a better state than me at the end,' Hadds reckoned.

Maybe it was the fact that this was where Pup scored 151 on his Test debut three years ago that so inspired him. 'I think I'll have to buy a house here,' he laughed afterwards. For me, the thing I like best is that it's something of a reward for the hard work I know he put in during the off-season. There might have been a time during the Twenty20 in South Africa when he was wondering why he'd bothered.

I was also interested to hear how he feels his approach has changed since he scored that maiden Test hundred. 'My batting has improved since then,' he told reporters. 'I know a little bit more about the way I need to play to be successful.

'I give myself more of a chance now when I start the innings. When I was young, I was keen to score straight away, but when the conditions don't suit, you can't do that. Generally, you need to give yourself a little more time … in cricket and in life.'

I had to learn that lesson, too. Once I did, I never forgot it.

WEDNESDAY, OCTOBER 3

Game Two, at Kochi (October 2): Australia 6–306 (50 overs: ML Hayden 75, A Symonds 87, BJ Haddin 87*; S Sreesanth 3–67) defeated **India** 222 (47.3 overs: RV Uthappa 41, MS Dhoni 58; GB Hogg 3–40) by 84 runs

I think we were as surprised as anyone when the game in Kochi turned a little nasty. My guess is that the home team decided — after we made such a positive start in Bangalore — that the way to match us was not just to talk more on the field, but to be antagonistic, as if that would then mean they were matching us in the 'aggression stakes'. The result, in my view, was that they just looked a bit silly, both in their actions and on the scoreboard. They're a good team and they can compete with us, but not by trying to be something they're not.

For me, aggression is about being proactive and maintaining your skill when the going gets tough. In response to India's 'tactics', we resolved to work as a team and aim to play our best cricket, because we are confident that that they'll struggle to stand up to the pressure that can be generated by simply playing good hard sport.

The 'fun' in Kochi yesterday came about after their pace bowler, Sreesanth, and Andrew Symonds started up a series of verbal exchanges, the subject of which none of us in the dressing room could quite work out. Sreesanth (who back in South Africa had been fined for excessive appealing in our semi-final in Durban) had been jibbering away throughout the innings, while

DON'T FORGET THE CRICKET!

One very unfortunate aspect of the unhappy incidents on the field in Kochi was that it took a lot of attention away from what was an excellent Australian performance. To recover from 2–8 (after 3.1 overs) and 3–66 (after 15.3 overs) to make 7– 306 from our 50 overs was a tribute to the quality batting of Matt Hayden, Symmo and Hadds, and then the bowling and fielding was superb. The wicket was awkward early on, but our trio of big-scorers crashed eight sixes and 22 fours on the way to a match-winning total.

When it was our turn to bowl, Mitchell Johnson was fast and dangerous early on, Stuart Clark was smart and typically accurate while achieving figures of 2–14 from six overs, and James Hopes was also economical and snared the important wicket of Yuvraj Singh. Our two spinners, Brad Hogg and Michael Clarke, were both among the wickets, and a couple of brilliant catches — one by Mitch, the other by Pup — was the icing on the cake.

It is possible Nathan Bracken will be back in time for game three, and I'm 99 per cent sure I'll be available, which will leave us with a couple of tough decisions to whom might be left out. There are a number of ways of identifying a very good cricket team, and the quality of the players who are unlucky to miss out on a place in the starting XI is one of the best of them.

Symmo was on his way to a crucial 87 from 83 balls, which set up our big total, and the chat reached its peak in the 45th over, after Sreesanth came down the pitch to within a couple of feet of Brad Haddin, after a delivery bounced off Hadds' pad and landed a few metres down the pitch. Symmo appeared to suggest it might be time for the young bowler to grow up, and then, though the play had clearly stopped, Sreesanth thought this would be a good time to try to run Symmo out at the bowler's end. The skirmish ended with Indian captain MS Dhoni having to push his charge away to prevent the clash getting any uglier.

I think Sreesanth was trying to prove a point to the more senior guys in the Indian team, that he was able to stand up to the Aussies, that he was capable of leading their attack. I thought his actions were childish.

In a flurry of runs during the final overs, Sreesanth dismissed Symmo, caught and bowled, after an attempted pull shot went straight up in the air, and made plenty of fuss about it, but chiefly through Hadds' hitting we managed a further 38 runs from the last 19 balls of the innings. And we certainly made a telling point when the home team struggled in their run chase, finishing 86 runs short.

One bloke who found this scenario a little hard to handle was India's spinner Harbhajan Singh, who tried to create a scene after he was stumped in the 31st over, a dismissal that left his team needing more than seven-and-a-half runs per over with just three wickets in hand. Harbhajan took ages to leave the wicket, and then he slowly, sadly and a little grimly started walking from the crease. He'd said a few words before he left, and then, he stopped, turned around, and said to Michael Clarke, 'Do you want to fight?' There were 11 Australians out there in a huddle, and as one they replied, 'Yep! Drop your bat. Let's go!' Of course, there was never any prospect of a blue. It was all a bit ridiculous.

Harbhajan is a bloke who has plenty to say on the field, but when someone says something back to him he can carry on a little. Maybe on this occasion he didn't like the fact that Haydos had belted him for six earlier in the game, or that the same fans who had been cheering them wildly at the start of the encounter were now leaving the stadium early. I can't help thinking that, along with an ill-conceived game plan, part of the problem for guys like Sreesanth and Harbhajan was simply a result of all the acclaim the Twenty20 champions have received in the past week. A big loss wasn't supposed to be part of the plot, and they didn't cope well with this blow to their ego. My hope is that it will be a one-off, and by the time the media have published a few more negative reports and we get to Hyderabad for game three everything will be sweet.

My view with these sorts of incidents is that if they aren't part of a sequence then there isn't a problem. There's a lot of pressure in one-day international cricket, with packed frenetic crowds and national pride involved, so it's inevitable that occasionally tempers will fray. But if a pattern emerges, then that's a different matter. So the people involved in these stoushes have to be smarter next time; and people such as myself in leadership positions have to be aware of our responsibilities, to our team, the country we represent and to the game.

When we were in camp in August, preparing for the long 'season' in front of us, we had a discussion about the concept of 'there is no truth, only perception', and how it applies to many things we are involved in, because of the blanket media coverage

WHAT IS SLEDGING?

There is talk on the field; of course there is. When we say something to a rival, what we're trying to do is infiltrate that player's head, make him think about something other than his own game. I read a quote recently by the great Argentinian golfer Roberto De Vicenzo, who said, 'He who thinks on the backswing makes himself harm. He who thinks about the follow-through, helps himself.' I want our opponents to be thinking about the things that will do their games harm. We might quietly suggest a batsman's back-lift doesn't look right or their feet aren't moving properly. This is part of the game, has been since Test cricket was invented. Have a look at some of the things WG Grace or Warwick Armstrong got up to. If that is what people call 'sledging', then I have no problem with it.

However, if 'sledging' is making a personal attack on somebody, I am dead against it. We don't do that. I think people outside the game's inner circle who have been fed unsubstantiated tales of vicious verbal assaults would be astonished to know how rarely that sort of crap surfaces in modern cricket.

of top-level cricket. After the game in Kochi, the match referee, England's Chris Broad, stressed that there were some things that occurred on the field that he wasn't happy with, but the umpires didn't report anyone and Chris opted not to discipline anyone after the game. But given the media storm the confrontations created, everyone knows we nearly crossed the line and that the time for second chances is over.

My guess is that the Indian team will eventually come out of this a better, tougher side. Both teams can still play aggressively, but that doesn't involve jumping up and down, sledging, giving people send-offs, that sort of stuff. To me, that's exactly the opposite of what aggressive or positive cricket is all about. I'm not sure if some of the Indian players understand this, and I guess if a few fellows on the field are confused then it's inevitable a number of spectators, whether at the ground or watching on television, are going to be confused, too.

I know that over the past 10 years, probably longer, a notion has developed that the Australian team walks out onto the field intent on getting in faces and having a few words. But I can't recall a team meeting where we've talked about doing that. We have got where we are in international cricket through a mixture of skill, hard work, good planning and tough, hard-nosed cricket. Most of the teams that have beaten us have played bravely and aggressively. That's the way the sport should be played.

Unfortunately, as soon as a spectator or a commentator spots one of my team chipping an opponent, they assume it is a premeditated attack. After the game in Kochi, we heard allegations along these lines. Most of the time, as occurred this time, the Australian player is actually responding to something that was said that was out of line. The most laughable aspect is when I hear former players complaining, as though they never put a toe out of line in their day. I still have a vivid image of Sunil Gavaskar angrily trying to take his opening partner off the MCG with him in 1981 after he was given out lbw in a Test match, but to hear him today you'd think he was positively angelic when he was the best opening batsman in the world. Frankly, I'm not concerned by what others say so long as I believe in the integrity of our players. I spend more time with my team-mates than any of the critics, and know them much better than anybody else does.

The members of the Australian cricket team set the bar high when we made a pledge to adhere to a set of principles we call 'the spirit of cricket', but we are not perfect and we don't claim to be. We sincerely want to be good role models for young people. But if you look at any major sport — Australian football, rugby league, baseball, football — there is usually banter between competitors, because that's a part of the psychological battle that is sport at the highest level. I know cricket fans prefer to see a high-class, aggressive battle, and I know I certainly enjoy playing such contests. They are the best games to play.

SUNDAY, OCTOBER 7

Game Three, at Hyderabad (October 5): Australia 7–290 (50 overs: ML Hayden 60, MJ Clarke 59, A Symonds 89) defeated **India** 243 (47.4 overs: SR Tendulkar 43, Yuvraj Singh 121; B Lee 3–37, GB Hogg 3–46) by 47 runs

It was good to finally get back on the park for the third game of the series, but I must confess I felt a little guilty coming into the side for Brad Haddin, given that he was averaging 156 for the series at better than a run a ball. However, we took the attitude that Brad Hodge had been chosen for this tour as a specialist batsman, whereas Hadds was more a wicketkeeping/batting

UNDER ATTACK

The on-field acrimony that received so much publicity after our game in Kochi had an unfortunate sequel here in Hyderabad when a local threw a missile of some kind at the team bus after the one-day international.

We were about 15 minutes from the ground, on the way back to the team hotel in central Hyderabad, when a young bloke emerged from a hiding spot to chuck something at the bus. I was on the phone, talking to Rianna, when ... bang!!! The sound was like a gunshot. The result was a broken window that left shards of glass on the vehicle's floor, and our security guards took off into the night looking for the offender. My understanding is they never found him.

There was no insignia or banner on the bus to say it was carrying the Australian cricket team, and I'm almost sure they couldn't have seen me or anyone else inside the bus through the tinted windows. It was just a random attack, I reckon. It scared the life out of me.

allrounder, so it wouldn't have been fair to drop Hodgey after just two innings over here. We also gave consideration to bringing Nathan Bracken back into the side after he arrived yesterday, but the bowlers were excellent in Kochi so there didn't seem any reason to rush Bracks in.

In Hyderabad, there was none of the verbal that spoiled the game in Kochi, but off the field it was hard not to notice how much time the Indian players were spending in the lead-up to this game attending World Twenty20 victory parties and sponsors' events, which hardly seemed the ideal preparation for a ODI they needed to win. Yuvraj Singh hit a spectacular century, but all he did was give the home team's scorecard some respectability, while I thought our performance was pretty clinical. The top-order built a platform, Andrew Symonds provided the fireworks in the final overs, and then our bowlers all contributed, with Brett Lee in outstanding form.

Their opener, Gautam Gambhir, must be absolutely sick of the sight of our opening bowlers. In Kochi, the left-hander was knocked over by an absolute beauty from Mitchell Johnson that pitched on a length and fizzed in between bat and pad. Here, Bing beat Gambhir for pace, trapping him lbw in the third over.

The only fault I could find in the team performance came right at the end, when we took the foot off the accelerator a fraction, instead of truly burying them. We got a bit lazy, but that can happen in one-day games when you get the opposition on the back foot so early.

After the game, at the captain's media conference, MS Dhoni revealed that he had complained to the umpires about what he called 'harsh' language that I and some other Australian players had reputedly used on the field. I really don't know where he was coming from. The umpires didn't have a problem, match referee Chris Broad didn't have a problem, and I wonder whether Dhoni was trying to somehow square the ledger after the controversy that engulfed Sreesanth and Harbhajan in Kochi.

I actually sat on the plane yesterday right behind Chris Broad, and he made a point of turning around and congratulating me for the way our team approached the game.

I had spoken to the press before the Indian skipper, and spent most of my time talking about the new rule that makes a change of ball mandatory after 35 overs of a 50-over innings. During the home team's reply here, the umpires decided the ball had to be replaced by a newer, harder ball after 27 overs, because the old one was scuffed and difficult for the batsmen to pick up, which was fine, but then they got *another* ball eight overs later, which was ridiculous. A major flaw had been exposed in the new rule, and in my view this sort of thing shouldn't be happening in international cricket.

'It is fine for people to come up with these rules,' I told the assembled reporters. '(But) I would like to see them used somewhere else first.

'Something like that can really determine the outcome of the game. It might be something little like that that can have a major influence on the game.'

To me, commonsense suggests that if a team gets a new ball earlier, then there shouldn't automatically be that second change. Why not trust the umpires' judgment? If they think there is a need for a third new ball, that's fine; otherwise, let the game run its natural course.

WEDNESDAY, OCTOBER 9

Game Four, at Chandigarh (October 8): India 4–291 (50 overs: SC Ganguly 41, SR Tendulkar 79, MS Dhoni 50) defeated **Australia** 7–283 (50 overs: ML Hayden 92, A Symonds 75) by eight runs

Our innings totals in this series have been declining slightly with each match: 307, 306, 290 and now 283, and this fourth score, made batting second, was not quite enough to win the game. On a wicket that lost pace and bounce from the first ball to the last, the home team's spinners, Harbhajan Singh and Murali Kartik, were just that little bit too hard to get away, and we finished up eight runs short. At 5–268 late in the 47th over and with Andrew Symonds still at the crease, I thought we had a great chance of pulling off a memorable victory, but then Symmo and Brad Hogg were dismissed off consecutive deliveries, and we came up short. It was a terrific game that brought the series back to life, but the loss ended a run of 14 consecutive ODI victories for us that went back to the start of the 2007 World Cup.

My innings ended in rather controversial circumstances, when I was given out stumped by the video umpire. My score was on 29 at the time, and we were travelling okay at 1–122.

I was facing Irfan Pathan, and it was one of those moments when — as the bails were taken off by MS Dhoni — my gut instinct said I was just okay. But the umpire upstairs ruled otherwise, even though there were quite a few people who were prepared to argue that the evidence was inconclusive. I've studied the film a few times and I'm not sure, which makes me wonder if I was entitled to the benefit of the doubt. Of more concern to me, though, were the 39 extras we conceded during India's innings, and the 30 runs the home team smashed in their final two overs. Both were a result of a sloppiness that entered our play, and they cost us the game.

Perhaps the most bemusing episode of the game came from our old mate, Sreesanth, who wasn't in the Indian starting XI but was still involved, as 12th man. He was keen to talk to us whenever he ran on the field, and chipped me when I walked out to bat. When I had an opportunity to ask him about that a bit later, when he brought some drinks out for his team-mates, he claimed he wasn't talking to me. But as I said to an AAP journalist after the game, 'He is doing it for a purpose, because he wants a response. We are all aware of it.'

Probably the main thing that disappointed me about what happened was that Sreesanth wasn't playing, so there was no chance of us getting 'revenge' on him during the game. But we have a few months of cricket left to play against these guys, and if he does get selected again, we'll be looking for an opportunity to prove our point.

FRIDAY, OCTOBER 12

Game Five, at Vadodara (October 11): India 148 (50 overs: SR Tendulkar 47; MG Johnson 5–26) lost to **Australia** 1–149 (25.5 overs: AC Gilchrist 79*) by nine wickets

It's amazing how some days you just have a good feel about the way a game will go. I was confident about the result yesterday from before the match even started, mainly because our preparation had been so good and also because there seemed to be heaps of pressure on MS Dhoni's team. This was the first time Australia had played a ODI in Vadodara and it was also Sachin Tendulkar's 400th ODI, so there was pressure on to suitably mark the twin occasions. Their win in Chandigarh had rebuilt expectations, yet I think deep down they know they're not as good as their recent Twenty20 triumph implied they might be. Pressure can be a terrible burden when you don't think you can handle it. The Indians played like a team dreading the worst.

Of course, it's one thing to have a psychological advantage, another to exploit it, and we were brilliantly served by Brett Lee and Mitchell Johnson, who performed superbly with the new ball. Our bowling and fielding was excellent throughout, and the vibe we created during the Indian innings, the pressure always on, was fantastic. And I was really thrilled with the clinical way in which Gilly, Haydos and I chased the small target down — on a pitch that was tough to bat on and against spinners who actually bowled really well. It was one of the most efficient, skilful and satisfying one-day wins we've ever had.

One thing I've come to realise over the years is that you often learn more from a loss than from a win. Quite often, if you win a few in a row, naturally enough all you talk about is keeping on doing the little things right, keep working for each other. But if

ZERO TOLERANCE

The big negative to come out of the game in Vadodara was the behaviour of a small part of the crowd, who racially abused Andrew Symonds when he was fielding on the boundary during the game. It was cheap stuff. The booing when Symmo touched the ball was repetitive and mindless, the water bottles and other junk lobbed from the crowd on to the field were stupid, but the racist stuff is different. I hated it when it happened a couple of summers back in Australia, and I hate it now.

I actually didn't learn about the 'monkey' chants that came from a small section of the crowd until after the game. I was fielding in 'the ring', inside the circle, and Symmo was on the boundary on the other side of the ground from me, maybe 100 metres away. Those fans' behaviour has received some media attention — none of which was instigated by us — and the story is brewing.

The Baroda Cricket Association has expressed its disappointment, with one of its officials being quoted as saying, 'Like any cricket centre, we cannot tolerate this sort of behaviour.' It will be interesting to see how the wider cricket administration reacts to the situation. In my view, the onus in this case is on the Indian officials to try their best to ensure it doesn't happen again, but the truth is that there is a responsibility on all our shoulders to make sure this is a problem that disappears rather than festers.

For now, we'll move on. There was little talk in the dressing room about what happened, and Symmo was reasonably philosophical though I can tell he is upset about it. It's been a pretty difficult tour, with one controversy following another, and most of us have come to the conclusion that we'd just like to get the remaining matches out of the way as quietly as possible, so we can all go home.

you lose, you just as naturally stop and reassess the way you are going about things. We had a couple of really good meetings on Wednesday — the bowlers got together, then the batsmen and finally the full squad. We spoke at length about the areas where we were deficient in Chandigarh, such as all the wides we conceded, the lack of spark with the new ball, the way we lost wickets, rather than consolidated, at crucial times. We didn't do any of those things yesterday.

On a personal level, I was happy that I got most aspects of my preparation right. As soon as I saw the wicket, I knew I'd be most likely be facing some left-arm spin at some stage during my innings, so I worked on that in the nets on the day before the game. When Dhoni opened the bowling with Harbhajan Singh and then had the left-handed Murali Kartik on after six overs, I felt I was ready for them. I finished 39 not out, while Gilly, who'd taken six catches earlier in the day, crashed his way to an unbeaten 77.

Normally, that double by our champion keeper-batsman would have been good enough to snare the man of the match award. But not this time, as the judges preferred Mitch's outstanding five-wicket effort. Maybe, there should have been a shared award. One thing for sure is that, as we get closer to our first Test match of the summer, it's getting harder and harder to come with an argument against the Queensland left-armer earning his first baggy green cap. He's been super impressive on this trip, especially with the way he gets batsmen jumping at the start of the innings. He's dismissed Sachin twice in four innings. It takes a bowler with rare ability to extract life from these grassless pitches, and Mitch has consistently managed to do just that.

I know Mitch really impressed Troy Cooley, our bowling coach, during the off-season when they worked together, and he has shown the benefits of all that effort here. There aren't too many left-arm fast bowlers around who can swing the ball at 150k like he can.

I am sensing that Mitch understands the mechanics of his bowling action more now. He can run in and bowl fast with confidence that the ball will leave his hand right and go in the correct area. Before, he didn't like to let himself *really* go, but now — because he's in control of things — he'll bowl even faster. My prediction is that one or two years from now he'll be one of the quickest bowlers going around. I've faced him in the nets a few times and he hits the bat as hard as anyone in our squad.

THURSDAY, OCTOBER 18

Game Six, at Nagpur (October 14): Australia 8–317 (50 overs: AC Gilchrist 51, RT Ponting 49, A Symonds 107*) defeated **India** 7–299 (50 overs: SC Ganguly 86, SR Tendulkar 72, RV Uthappa 44; GB Hogg 4–49) by 18 runs

Game Seven, at Mumbai (October 17): Australia 193 (41.3 overs: RT Ponting 57; M Kartik 6–27) lost to **India** 8–195 (46 overs: RV Uthappa 47; MG Johnson 3–46) by two wickets

We travelled a lot of kilometres on this trip, but now we find ourselves in Mumbai, a vast and vibrant city that I think of not just as the 'heart of India', but also as one of the focal points of international cricket. Of course, tradition has it that Lord's is the 'home' of the game, and nothing, for me, will ever diminish the history of that place or the significance of Ashes Tests. But in the 21st century, for me India has a similar status as England when it comes to influence in world cricket.

So much of the game's revenue comes out of this part of the world, and as I believe is being demonstrated by the rise of Twenty20, the people here are responsible for trends that will shape the future evolution of our sport. The way Mumbai has reacted to their team's triumph in South Africa is extraordinary — it is the talk of the town, with the news, sports and business pages all dominated by conjecture over what new competitions will now be played, how much money might be involved, and

FLYING HIGH

We travel so much these days that we tend to take things like check-in lounges, customs and window or aisle seats for granted. If we stopped to think about the potential dangers of plane travel we'd probably go mad, but flying out of Nagpur we did have a reminder that very occasionally it can be a hazardous business.

Both teams were on the same flight, from Nagpur to Mumbai, and apparently what happened was that the plane hit a bird during take-off, it lost power in one engine, and we were required to make an unexpected early landing back where we'd just left. Everyone lived happily ever after, so I can laugh about it now, but it will take a while for me to forget the chill in my spine when the engine trembled and the plane shuddered, and how I quickly made some calculations and realised that we were going too quickly to abandon the take-off.

Someone with a window seat near the damaged engine muttered, 'Check that out!' And the news quickly spread that the engine was vibrating in a way engines shouldn't do. A few rotor blades appeared to be missing. Eventually, the pilot explained that he had some 'bad news' … the plane had to turn back … and as we slowly descended towards the airport the sight of fire engines and ambulances, lights blazing next to the runway, did not fill me with a lot of confidence. The time from take off to emergency landing was probably about half an hour, but it seemed like a hell of a lot more than that.

what this revolution means for Test and 50-over cricket. The Indian players are being feted as rock stars, even though they have lost the one-day series, and I can't help but think that we are on the threshold of a flashy new cricket era. I just wonder if the people back home full comprehend this.

Mumbai is a terrific city to be in, as a cricketer and a tourist. In the first two weeks of the tour, we were based in towns where cows roamed the streets and shamiana canopies provided shade for the spectators at the small grounds; the contrast to the bustling metropolis we now find ourselves in — with its streets packed with people, flash hotels, terrific restaurants and huge, packed stadiums — is vast and exciting.

The last two games of this series were very different affairs. In Nagpur, a belligerent Andrew Symonds century, 107 runs from 88 balls, was the main feature of a game dominated by the batsmen, while the final game of the series, here in Mumbai, was played on a less placid pitch and as a consequence produced a thrilling contest where, for the most part, the bowlers were in the ascendancy.

Symmo has been under the microscope throughout this series — from the clash with Sreesanth in Kochi to the racism controversy of Vadodara — and it seemed to me that he set out to respond in the best way he knew how: with his bat. One spectacular blow off Murali Kartik sailed high over the press box, smashing the windscreen of a car that had been innocently parked in a street outside the ground, and I've rarely seen him as animated as he was after he reached his hundred, leaping in the air and running towards the Aussie change room to wave his bat towards his mates.

Symmo has been cast as the villain by the Indian media during this tour, but that doesn't change the fact that he has been the key batsman of the series, easily scoring the most runs and at better than a run a ball. Batting is all about good habits and Symmo is making all the right decisions with his one-day cricket at the moment. He's reacting well, whatever the situation, which he didn't always do earlier in his career. In years gone by, the pressure of the situation he found himself in at Nagpur — when at 4–129 in the 22nd over one more wicket might have been the end of us — may have been too much for him, but now he has faith in his ability and understands his own game really well.

First of all, we needed to get a partnership going. There was no need to take unnecessary risks; Symmo knew that if he batted normally, the runs would accumulate, the innings would get back on track, we'd have wickets in hand, and then he could mount his counter attack. He reached his 50 from 54 balls, which sounds pretty quick, but 15 came from one over bowled by the part-timer Yuvraj Singh. A few years back, in the same circumstances, if Symmo wasn't 30 from 20 balls, in his eyes he wasn't doing any good, and he'd get out trying to do more than was necessary.

We were without an injured Matt Hayden for this game and India were able to get a new ball in the 27th over of their innings, which was as ridiculous here as it had been in Hyderabad. But I thought we were in control for most of the game, even though some big hitting by the Indians got them a bit too close for my liking near the end. One colossal blow by MS Dhoni off a Brett Lee slower ball ended up way back in the crowd behind long-off, but the Indian captain was eventually outdone by Mitchell Johnson, whose effort in producing a double wicket maiden in the 49th over was very impressive.

The crowd was making an unbelievable amount of noise when it appeared Dhoni and Robin Uthappa might pull off an unlikely victory, but gee they were quiet after the pair were finally dismissed. One moment, you couldn't hear yourself think; the next, you could hear your footsteps. I enjoyed the contrast for two reasons. One, obviously, the silence meant we'd won the game. Two, it reminded me about the genuine love so many people here have for the game. It's unrelenting, sometimes it can almost overwhelm you, but I've always loved and respected India's passion for cricket. At Nagpur and especially in Mumbai there were mugs in the crowd giving Symmo a hard time, and when I saw them at their worst I was really disappointed.

It actually got so bad that when we walked out onto the field in Mumbai it felt like most of the stadium was chanting,

'Symonds is a monkey! Symonds is a monkey!' It was so unfair. Symmo is one of our sport's great entertainers; at the start of the series he was being cheered because he is such a dynamic cricketer, yet by game seven he was being booed every time he went near the ball — because of prior incidents he was involved in, but were not his fault. As I understand it, some spectators were thrown out of the ground in Mumbai for what they shouted. It's hard on occasions like this, but I have to make sure that I don't let those mindless idiots cloud my respect for all the genuine cricket fans of India.

I'm sure they enjoyed their win in Mumbai, when Dhoni's men fought back after we reduced them to 6–64 and then 8–143 chasing 194. The wicket wasn't easy to bat on, so I thought we

SACHIN'S TOWN

Mumbai is Sachin Tendulkar's home city, and every time he plays here the locals turn out in huge numbers to see him bat. I remember the first time I fielded to him here — it was the 1996 World Cup and he scored a magic 90 in a game we won. The noise was seriously deafening that night; it was on this tour, too, though the silence was palpable when Bing knocked him over for 21 with an absolute beauty.

Back in February 1998, Sachin scored his maiden first-class double century here in a tour match against us, and played beautifully throughout. For me, right at the start of my Test career, it was a great experience just to see such a champion player going about his business in *his* conditions. I have always maintained that he at his best was fractionally ahead of Brian Lara at his best, and they are the best two batsmen I have played against. As I write this, he has scored 14 international hundreds against Australia during his career (seven in Tests, seven in ODIs), and I have been on the field for many of them, so I have had plenty of opportunities to gauge just how magnificent and complete a batsmen he is. We have tried a wide variety of schemes and strategies, but he's usually had the answer to all of them.

were in control, but Zaheer Khan and Murali Kartik rode their luck and played intelligently to claim a notable victory. Unfortunately, James Hopes (1–13 from five overs) strained a hamstring and was unable to bowl at the death, when I think he would have been very hard to get away.

There was also an incident on the field in Mumbai that involved Symmo and Harbhajan, which might have led to some trouble for the Indian spinner if we'd gone on with it. However, Symmo decided to fix it by just talking to the bloke, and getting a guarantee that it won't happen again. I imagine that's the end of it — Symmo is the sort of bloke who if you tell him you're going to do something and you don't follow through then you're the worst in the world, and I'm fairly sure Harbhajan is aware of that.

Sadly, some local cricket officials are now trying to suggest that we imagined the racist taunts from the crowds during this series. The least effective way to fix a problem is to pretend it doesn't exist, but this is the path which some people are now travelling down.

It wasn't until photographers actually captured some people in the stands mimicking a monkey as they hurled their abuse that the administrators were forced to acknowledge that things weren't good.

Equally frustrating has been learning that a few former Australian cricketers, including Allan Border and Mark Waugh, have apparently been suggesting that Symmo was being 'precious' and 'melodramatic' when he talked about the crowd's behaviour. (Symmo has emphasised the point that he never complained; rather, he responded honestly to reporters' questions as to whether he heard the spectators' taunts.) The trouble is that these ex-players are thinking back to when they were touring, when the crowds were just as loud, but there wasn't the spiteful element we've seen a few times on this trip. If Allan and Mark were here, I reckon they'd think differently.

We now have just one match remaining before we can head home — a Twenty20 clash in Mumbai with the reigning world champions in this form of the game. I imagine this game will be quite a party, hopefully without that nasty edge that infiltrated parts of the crowd last night.

MONDAY, OCTOBER 22

Twenty20 International, at Mumbai (October 20): Australia 5–166 (20 overs: RT Ponting 76) lost to **India** 3–167 (18.1 overs: G Gambhir 63, RV Uthappa 35, Yuvraj Singh 31) by 18 runs

As we come to the end of this tour, I am being asked quite a few questions about how different life is in the Australian team now that we have a new coach in Tim Nielsen, who, of course, came into the job after John Buchanan retired after the World Cup. 'Buck' had been in the role since November 1999, overseeing an era in which Australia was just about unbeatable, losing only two Test series (in India in 2001 and in England in 2005), and winning two World Cups (2003 and 2007).

Buck did a great job, there is no doubt about that, but I can't see why Tim can't do an even better job. I like the fact that because he was once Buck's assistant coach he has worked with all the senior players in the team.

When he worked at the Centre of Excellence, Tim had the drive to develop and run his own program, and he got to know the next generation of younger players who are now coming into the Australian side.

A WHOLE NEW BALL GAME

I reckon I'm starting to learn a few things about this Twenty20 caper. When I'm batting, I always feel under pressure — if I face just a couple of 'dot' balls, then I have to fight the urge to try to hit the next ball for four or six, no matter what. The truth is, I don't think you need to be too concerned if you get held down for a couple of deliveries. Not everyone has to get 50 from 15 balls, especially in the first half of the innings. If you lose three or four wickets early, it can be hard to work your way back into the game.

It might only be 20 overs a side, but there is still time for a top-order batsman to build some sort of innings. If I can get myself in and hit a couple of boundaries with normal cricket shots early on, then I can feel 'set' and then start improvising and playing the big shots. In these circumstances, I reckon I can get anything off the final overs. The perfect example of this is actually the first Twenty20 international we played, against New Zealand in Auckland in February 2005, when we lost four wickets in the first six overs, but I settled in, scored only 10 runs from the first 11 balls I faced, and ended up 98 not out, from 55 deliveries.

For bowlers, a key is for them not to think of themselves as 'fodder' for slogging batsmen. They have to think they're way through, stick to a plan, and bowl to their field placings. A couple of boundaries conceded is only a disaster if the bowler loses his rhythm or composure; then he'll go for 15 or 20 in an over and the game will be lost.

These are the type of things we have to get right if we want to be the world champions in this form of the game as well.

When it comes to technique, I need a coach who understands my technique inside out, so when something goes awry he can come and tell me what is going wrong and suggest ways to fix the problem. All of us are confident that Tim understands our games, and also the techniques of the young blokes coming through, which is a skill Buck did not have to the same degree.

It was inevitable that there'd be some pressure on Tim coming into this tour, because he would have known that had we lost, critics would have been wondering if the change of coach was a reason for the defeat. Of course, that would have been ridiculous, but it was still nice to win for his sake, as well as our own. He sent each of us a short note after the one-dayer in Mumbai, thanking us for what we had done, which suggested to me that the series win had taken a little weight off the new coach's shoulders.

AS FOR THE TWENTY20 international we played last Saturday evening in Mumbai, I could pretend that it didn't really matter, that it was only Twenty20, and that after the turmoil of the one-day series all we wanted to do was get home. But the truth is that we really wanted to win. It's disappointing to finish any tour with a loss. In this case, it was two losses, which took a little of the icing off the fact we won the one-day series comfortably.

We wanted to finish the tour on a high and we wanted to avenge the loss of the World Twenty20 semi-final, so losing those two games was definitely disappointing. But we arrived in India knowing they're a good one-day side and it was going to be hard work, and Mike Hussey wasn't there, so to win the way we did is very satisfying. Still, we are very proud of our status as the No. 1 team in both Tests and one-day international cricket, and it's a little disconcerting that following the recent tournament in South Africa we have to acknowledge India as the world Twenty20 champions.

On the night, though, the home team was too good for us. They won with 11 balls to spare, which in 20-over cricket is an easy victory, as they responded better to the incredible buzz that filled Brabourne Stadium before the game, an explosion of interest that was reflected by the kilometre-long queues that snaked away from the turnstiles as we entered the ground.

The 2007–08 season started with the inaugural ICC World Twenty20 tournament in South Africa. Here I'm in Cape Town, rehearsing shots I might not practise too often during a Test series.

Above: Sachin Tendulkar hits Brett Lee for six in Kochi, the start of a thrilling, high-quality battle between the two that would continue throughout the summer.

Above left: India's Sreesanth gives Andrew Symonds a 'send off' in Kochi.
Above right: Umpire Steve Bucknor guides Harbhajan Singh towards the dressing room later in the same game.

Above: Matthew Hayden at the Brabourne Stadium in Mumbai. Left: Andrew Symonds after reaching his century in Nagpur. Below: Michael Clarke during his gallant hundred in Bangalore.

Left: Mitchell Johnson has Sourav Ganguly caught behind for a duck in Mumbai.

Below: MS Dhoni and me, the Indian and Australian one-day captains, in Nagpur. We saw plenty of each other in 2007–08, in all forms of the game.

Above: Sreesanth and I have a quick 'dance' during the Twenty20 international in Mumbai.

Below: Later in the same game, Brett Lee is on the ball in a flash as Virender Sehwag (left) and Gautam Gambhir attempt a very quick single.

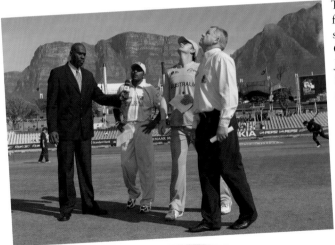

Three 'postcards' from the first half of our long season: Top: Adam Gilchrist and Mahela Jayawardene toss before the Australia–Sri Lanka game at Cape Town during the ICC World Twenty20. Mike Procter, the match referee, is next to Gilly. Middle: The light towers loom over the stadium at Kochi. Bottom: Beautiful Bellerive during the Test against Sri Lanka.

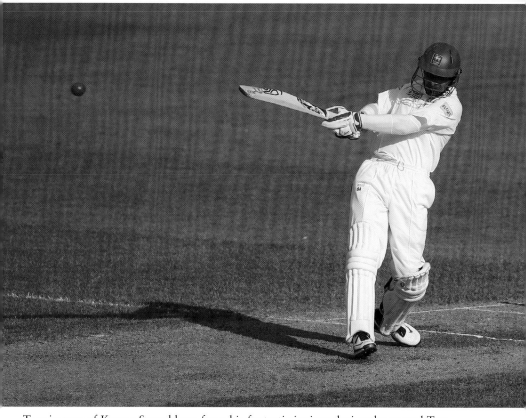

Two images of Kumar Sangakkara from his fantastic innings during the second Test. Above: He smashes Stuart MacGill down the ground to reach his hundred. Below: Adam Gilchrist, Stuart Clark, me and Matthew Hayden immediately after he was controversially given out for 192.

Above: Adam Gilchrist hits a ball clean out of Bellerive Oval. This was the 100th six of his Test-match career.

Below: Phil Jaques in Hobart, where he made his second Test century of the Australian summer.

Right: I've just scored a one-day hundred on my home turf, against New Zealand during the Chappell–Hadlee series.

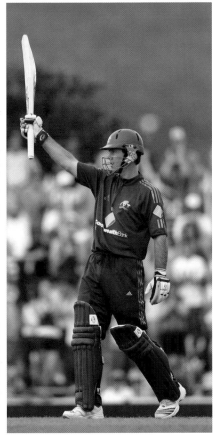

There was little we could do as Uthappa and Yuvraj Singh hit their way to victory. The crowd got stuck into us a bit, Symmo every time he went near the ball, but I didn't hear anything untoward and the general mood was more akin to a carnival, or a nightclub, with music blaring and lights flashing, than a cricket ground.

So many things were different to what we've come to expect: there was no ground announcer, just a DJ; the scoreboard was used purely to display advertisements for the many sponsors; one fan even held aloft a sign reading, 'Sorry Symonds'; and Sreesanth actually applauded when I reached my fifty.

Afterwards, it wasn't easy watching MS Dhoni and his men celebrating with their supporters, because I'm never a happy man after a loss, but such was the mood there was no way you could think that Twenty20 cricket isn't here to stay. I'm sure a momentum is building for this new game that will be impossible to stop, and while I'm still not convinced that it's a great game to play, I do know I'm going to have to get used to it.

The loss was an unfortunate last memory to take away from this tour, but as I said to the guys in the dressing room after the game, in terms of performance we've had an excellent tour. We have every right to be proud of what we've achieved, because it is never easy to win on the subcontinent, and some things that happened could have distracted us if we hadn't stuck together and stayed disciplined. Much of the cricket we played was very, very good, and I think that some of our younger guys learned a lot about themselves and about one-day cricket in this part of the world. In this regard, I was especially impressed by the way Mitchell Johnson and James Hopes contributed. But because of all the controversy, their efforts, all our efforts, have been pushed into the background.

Just a few hours after the game we were on our way to the airport, ready to fly home. It was late and mentally I felt a bit fried, as if I'd been under a spotlight for all of the time we'd been away. Being India, there were plenty of people about on the sides of the road, though few stopped to notice the Aussie team bus. Four weeks earlier, they reckon there were a million people lining the route when the home town heroes returned from South Africa with the World Twenty20 trophy.

Exactly where such mania will take the cricket world is very hard to tell.

PART THREE
AUSTRALIA v SRI LANKA
TEST SERIES

*'There's a lot of hard work that goes into winning
any Test match.'*

— Ricky Ponting, November 20, 2007

MONDAY, NOVEMBER 5

I was sitting next to Matthew Hayden on the flight home from India a couple of weeks back and can remember clearly how excited we both were when we talked about how we'd soon be hitting and catching red balls again. Late October/early November is always a really exciting part of the year for us. I always start thinking about the Gabba, the lead-up to the first home Test, all the hopes and dreams that the season will work out well for us. Brisbane is a great place to play and we have a sensational record there (I've played in eight wins and three draws in 11 Tests at the ground since 1996). Inevitably, we've done a heap of work and the expectations are that all that effort will be worthwhile. Over the past few years, it usually worked out that way.

In this case, the sense of anticipation was accentuated by the fact that we hadn't played a Test match since the first week of January: the end of the 2006–07 Ashes series. In the meantime, we'd played 32 one-dayers and eight Twenty20 internationals. At first glance, this would suggest that the schedule was out of kilter, but last season did involve a World Cup, and then we had an extended break, from the end of the World Cup to the start of the World Twenty20.

The first Test against Sri Lanka begins on Thursday. So what has been happening in the past two weeks?

First up, I had to respond to questions from the Australian media concerning the racism we'd seen in India. Did I expect the Aussie fans to respond in kind? 'I'd like to see the Australian fans and public treat the Indian team the same way they would any other team,' I said at Sydney Airport. 'I don't think they should be treated any differently because of what's happened over there.'

It is true that in past seasons, some outstanding cricketers have been cast as 'public enemy No. 1' during an Australian season. I can remember as a boy how everyone had it in for Richard Hadlee and Ian Botham, but while they copped a bit of barracking, the fans never lost respect for them. 'I'm sure that at different times Sreesanth and a few of the guys will cop a hard time from the Australian fans,' I said. 'That will generally happen at some stage to most teams that tour here. But I just hope — I'll keep my fingers crossed — that no racial stuff comes up at all through the summer.'

Gradually, the focus moved away from that controversy and on to the upcoming Test series. Naturally, with Sri Lanka involved, much of the talk was about Muttiah Muralitharan, who is on the brink of breaking Shane Warne's Test wicket-taking record. Murali has played 113 Tests, but only three in Australia: two for Sri Lanka in 1995–96 (when he was called for throwing) and one for the ICC World XI in 2005–06. We should be thrilled that he is finally coming back to play some more Test cricket here, but I can assure you that we will be trying our utmost to deny him the nine wickets he needs to break Warney's record.

THE INDIAN PREMIER LEAGUE

On October 28, the *Sunday Age* revealed that I and a number of other members of the Australian team had signed to play with the newly-established Indian Premier League (IPL). Among the names mentioned were Nathan Bracken, Brad Haddin, Mike Hussey, Mitchell Johnson, Brett Lee and Andrew Symonds, and also on the paper's list were the recently retired Shane Warne and Glenn McGrath, who had actually committed to the new project a little while back.

Within a couple of days, the organisers of the IPL had added a few more high-profile Aussie names to the list: Michael Clarke, Adam Gilchrist and Matthew Hayden.

It is true that I have agreed in principle to be involved, but I have done this on the basis that some issues between the IPL, Cricket Australia and the ICC will be satisfactorily resolved. I never discussed the matter with Cricket Australia before I put pen to paper, mainly because a potential clash between the IPL and the international cricket program isn't an issue for me. I do want to be a part of this new competition — the concept is fascinating, most of the game's best players will be involved, and the money is great — but only when it doesn't interfere with my Australian commitments.

At the moment, it seems that the inaugural matches will happen next April, when we are scheduled to tour Pakistan and then the West Indies, so it is possible that my involvement will be limited or nil, at least in the first year.

Of course, Shane was our spinner during last season's Ashes series. I am fully aware that Stuart MacGill has been troubled by a knee injury over the past few months, but throughout the break between Tests I was also firmly of the view that, if he could prove his fitness, he was still the man to take over. After all, he's taken 198 Test wickets and he's taken them as rapidly (40 Tests) as just about anyone in the history of the game. If Warney hadn't been around for the past 10 years, Stuart might be remembered as one of our greatest ever bowlers. Consequently, I was delighted when he came through a Pura Cup game for NSW against Queensland to confirm he was right for the first Test. As a precaution, the selectors also named Brad Hogg in the first Test squad, but Stuey will play if his fitness holds.

Ben Hilfenhaus is also part of our squad, having come in a couple of days back after Shaun Tait was ruled out because of an elbow problem. Given Mitchell Johnson's terrific form in India, I was expecting him to make his Test debut in the opening Test, and now that Shaun is out I think that is a

BACK TO THE PURA CUP

My first Pura Cup game of the season was the match against South Australia played at Bellerive Oval in Hobart from October 29 to November 1.

For me, the game provided a good hit out, as I made 96 in our first innings and 126 in the second. I was keen for the first-innings hundred, but Shaun Tait did me with a good lifter that I edged through to the keeper. Unfortunately for Shaun, that was his only wicket of the innings, but it was a batsman's game, with South Australia's Graham Manou and Jason Gillespie and Tasmania's Michael Di Venuto making big first-innings centuries, and Michael Dighton and George Bailey playing key knocks as we sped to victory with six wickets in hand.

It was a game that needed a couple of declarations, one from me when we were 119 behind on the first innings, and then a response from the Redbacks, who closed their second innings just before lunch on the final day, leaving us 349 to get in 74 overs.

The way this Australian season is structured, there is a chance I will play at least one more Pura Cup game and maybe a couple of Ford Ranger Cup one-dayers for Tassie. It's a strange set-up this year, with little international cricket in late November or the first three weeks of December — the option will be to take a break from all cricket on the basis that there is a lot of cricket to be played in the first half of 2008, or to keep going as I would most seasons. It won't be a hard choice — I'll just let my body and the Australian team's support staff advise me as to what's best in the long term.

certainty. That said, if Ben was chosen, I know he'd do an excellent job. He's impressed everybody in the Australian set-up over the past 12 months — he works hard, he's strong, he can swing the ball and I love the smart way he uses his bouncer and slower ball.

Sri Lanka have some fitness concerns of their own, with their vice-captain Kumar Sangakkara a doubtful starter because of a hamstring tear he sustained in his team's first tour game. His absence would be a cruel blow for them, because in the past couple of years he has established himself as arguably the second best keeper-batsman in world cricket, behind only Adam Gilchrist and in front of South Africa's Mark Boucher and India's MS Dhoni. The Sri Lankans are a very good side — it was no fluke they made the World Cup final — but they haven't got a lot of depth in key positions (most notably with their pace attack and at the top of their batting order), and can't afford to lose any of their genuine top-liners.

In contrast, Stuart MacGill's inclusion in our squad means that — even though there is no Warne and no Glenn McGrath — we will go into the first Test with a potent and well-balanced attack: A right-hand fast bowler, Brett Lee, who has taken 231 Test wickets; a right-armer in the McGrath mould, Stuart Clark, who has taken 47 wickets in nine Tests; the left-arm pace, bounce and swing of Mitchell Johnson; and Stuey MacGill's leg-breaks. Furthermore, the middle order — Ponting, Hussey, Clarke and Symonds — is locked in, and Phil Jaques is fully entitled to first crack at the opening position left vacant by Justin Langer. In saying this, I am aware that Brad Hodge would do a great job if he was chosen. As Lang said when asked if Hodgey could handle opening the batting in a Test match, 'Talent is about making runs, and he knows how to do that.' I like our current Test line-up ... I like it a lot.

TUESDAY, NOVEMBER 6

Brad Hogg stayed with the squad until today, when it was confirmed that Stuart MacGill would be our spinner for the first Test. The media have enjoyed describing a net session the two had yesterday as a 'bowl off' for the spot in the side, but I didn't see it that way. It was more a case of making sure Stuey is going all right, because he hasn't had a lot of cricket lately because of some injuries. We feel he'll be okay, though we have kept Ben Hilfenhaus in camp, just in case the pitch is so seamer-friendly that we opt to go into the game with an all pace attack. I would say such a move is extremely unlikely, though if we did go that way I know Ben wouldn't let anybody down.

Today is, of course, the first Tuesday in November: Melbourne Cup Day. My intention had been to watch the Cup with the rest of the boys in the team room at our hotel, but Phil Jaques and I were late back from training because we enjoyed a little extra batting practice, so we ended up watching the race in my room. I was keen on the English horse, Purple Moon, and Zipping, who ended up running second and fourth (Zipping's stablemate, Efficient, was first home), and because I backed both of them each way I collected just about enough to finish square.

As always, we had a team sweep, and as always it was won by a 'ring-in'. This time it was Ray McLean, a trainer with the RAAF who has built a reputation working with some of the top AFL, rugby league and rugby union teams. Ray has been talking to us about motivation and leadership, and he was lucky enough to land the Efficient ticket. Tim Nielsen had Purple Moon and Michael Clarke got a small return from the third-placed Mahler.

In the lead-up to the Test, some journalists and commentators have been keen to highlight some comments from my diary of the 2006–07 season, when I wrote that the Sri Lankans 'feared' us at the last World Cup in the West Indies, where we beat them twice, in the 'Super Eights' and the final. I know my opposing captain, Mahela Jayawardene, has rejected this idea, but I still believe it. Their body language in those two World Cup games wasn't very positive, and we thought their selection policy in the first encounter, the way they 'rested' blokes, was strange and self-defeating. The squad of players here is essentially the same as they had in the Caribbean, for this first Test they'll be without one of their most confident men, Kumar Sangakkara, and their record against us isn't flash (just one Test win from 17 starts), so I'm sure they'll go into the game feeling at least a little intimidated.

I sensed by the way the media was reacting to my answers that they felt I was engaging in some kind of 'mind games' with the visitors. But I'm not; I'm just trying to respond to their questions as honestly as possible.

We only know one way to play, and that won't change because of whom our opponents are, or because we've lost some great players to retirement in the past 12 months. As always, we'll be playing to win. We built an imposing record with the likes of Shane Warne, Glenn McGrath, Justin Langer, Damien Martyn and John Buchanan, but those blokes aren't here now. We have to find ways to win games without them, and I believe we will. One example: when Glenn and Shane were in their prime, they were absolute masters at dominating other teams through constantly building up pressure; now, with Brett Lee and Mitchell Johnson at the forefront, we might have to look to sheer pace to get our breakthroughs. I see the coming months as a real opportunity for this group to create its own identity.

EVEN THOUGH WE'VE ALREADY played a Twenty20 'World Cup' and been to India for seven one-dayers and a Twenty20 game, for me this still feels like the start of the summer. The

Brisbane Test is always a fantastic occasion, the Gabba wicket is usually the best track we play on all year, and this time we have some new players in our line-up — from the XI that played in the last Test we'd played (the fifth Ashes Test last January), McGrath, Warne and Langer, veterans of a combined 374 Tests, had been replaced by Johnson, MacGill and Jaques. Stuey might have been around for a while, but Jaquesy has played only two Tests and Mitch will be making his Test debut. Ben Hilfenhaus, still to play a Test, has also been with us, as has the young-at-heart Brad Hogg, who played one Test in 1996 and three in 2003. Understandably, there is a feeling about that this is the start of new era in Australian Test cricket.

I have always believed that younger guys have a vital role to play in a team environment, simply by expressing themselves and using their natural energy and enthusiasm to boost the entire group. This is especially true for us now. Guys who have been around a long time can get settled in their ways, so a new approach can sometimes have an astonishingly positive impact. I don't want the new fellas to be arrogant or to assume they know it all, but neither do I want them to stay in their shells and just try to be like everybody else.

I played cricket for Tasmania when I was 17, for Australia when I was 20. Earlier than that, in junior representative teams, I was usually younger than anyone else, which meant that leadership roles never came my way, simply because those jobs are inevitably going to go to the 'senior' players. But in my mind I always felt like I was a leader around these teams, even if it was only by being the most enthusiastic at training, or by trying to lift things up and drag the older guys through the difficult times. I was young, I was keen and I wanted to improve all the time. I wanted to work harder then everybody else and I think that had a positive impact around the group. A good attitude is worth catching.

These days, I always try to pass on tips I've learned from the great captains I've played under, such as David Boon, Mark Taylor and Steve Waugh. At the same time, I'm smart enough to realise there are plenty of things I can learn — from team-mates young and old. An act of inspiration or leadership from an unexpected source can be extremely powerful. Of course, I don't expect every new guy to have a major impact in this way, because being assertive at an early age is not for everybody. But the ones who are natural leaders will do it — Michael Clarke is a great example — and we'd be crazy to try to diminish them in any way.

One thing I say to any bloke who comes into the team for the first time or after an extended spell out of the line-up is that I want him to be himself *all the time*. Whatever new guys do for their state team, I want them to do that for Australia, too. Such behaviour will help us to get to know them, and it will add something fresh and positive to the group. The way new players — young and not so young — have blended into the Australian team in recent seasons is one of the reasons we've managed to stay on top for so long.

TUESDAY, NOVEMBER 13

First Test, Australia v Sri Lanka, at Brisbane (November 8–12): Australia 4–551 dec (PA Jaques 100, RT Ponting 56, MEK Hussey 133, MJ Clarke 145*, A Symonds 53*) defeated **Sri Lanka** 211 (MS Atapattu 51; B Lee 4–26) and 300 (MG Vandort 82; B Lee 4–86) by an innings and 40 runs

This was one of our most systematic Test-match victories, achieved through a combination of ruthless batting and excellent, consistent pace bowling. If this is representative of what the new era for Australian cricket is going to be all about, it's going to be a very enjoyable one to be involved in.

It is true that the Sri Lankans played like a team short of a gallop. They are a much better team than what they showed here. Further, they were without Kumar Sangakkara and I think they made a mistake at the selection table when they left out Lasith Malinga. Maybe he's carrying an injury, or is out of sorts; whatever, with him not there and Chaminda Vaas well below his best, their attack had a sameness that not even Murali's off-breaks could overcome.

The game was a triumph for Phil Jaques, who marked the start of his career as a first-choice opener by scoring his maiden Test ton. It was also a big game for Michael Hussey, who scored a hundred and took his Test batting average into the eighties, and Michael Clarke, who justified the talk from a number of people (including me) who have suggested he is a future Australian captain, by scoring 145 not out. Brett Lee was the pick of the bowlers, taking four wickets in each innings and demonstrating conclusively that his recent ankle operation has not slowed his bowling one iota. At times, I wondered if he might even be quicker than ever.

The first day of the series started with Glenn McGrath striding onto the Gabba to present Mitchell Johnson with his first baggy green cap. Then Mahela Jayawardene made what I always think is a mistake at the Gabba ... he sent us in! Phil Jaques then had to face 34 balls before he could hit his first run, and I'm not sure who was most relieved, Phil, the people in the crowd or his team-mates in the dressing room, when he finally found a run behind square leg. I ventured out to the middle in the 23rd over — after our openers had done well to survive and score runs on an awkward pitch and some rain delays — and was happy with the way I played, but frustrated when I became Murali's first wicket of the series, stumped for 56. Of course, there is no shame in being beaten by the champion off-spinner, but I was very disappointed when he got me out. I know that if we can prevent him from taking too many wickets, we'll be a long way towards winning the series.

MUPPETS AND JOKERS?

Everyone in the Australian camp was a bit bemused when we read comments reputedly offered by Sri Lanka's Marvan Atapattu at the end of the third day of the first Test. Atapattu, a bloke who was playing in his 89th Test, has captained his country and scored more than 5000 Test-match runs, was referring to the Sri Lankan team's selection committee when he said, 'Sri Lanka cricket at this moment of time is not going in the direction it should be going, especially with a set of muppets headed by a joker. I don't give credit to the way they have handled selections.'

This Test at the Gabba was Atapattu's first for nearly two years, and my guess is that by making comments like these he won't be playing too many more. His beef appears to be that, in his view, there is not a lot of planning going on when it comes to team selections, which meant he had to be recalled for the tough Australian tour. He did play well here, gutsing it out for 51 in their first innings before Mitchell Johnson did him for pace.

Inevitably, comments like these suggest that there are problems in the Sri Lankan team, but I haven't seen evidence of that, either from watching them play and train, or from talking to their Australian coach Trevor Bayliss. Atapattu also addressed this issue, being quoted on *Cricinfo* as saying, 'We are a happy dressing room at the moment. A section of people has been trying to say that it is divided, but it is not so. We don't have problems inside the dressing room, but people from outside are trying to create unpleasantness through the media and by statements made by ex-cricketers to displease us. I don't think they have succeeded.'

You learn pretty quickly as an international cricketer, and especially as a captain, that there is rarely much to be gained by making such comments. I'm sure Atapattu would have much preferred to have stayed quiet on the issue, so he must really believe there is a major problem, and that going public in the way he did is the only way it is going to be addressed.

One of my favourite memories of this Test will be of the second afternoon, after we'd declared, when Brett came out and showed there was actually something in the wicket for the pacemen. He took two wickets in that period, both caught behind. Replays suggested Sanath Jayasuriya might have been unlucky, but there was no doubt Bing was fast and dangerous; it was one of those fabulous situations for a captain when I was very happy to be at second slip waiting expectantly for an edge rather than facing what Bing (and Mitchell Johnson, too) was dishing up. Of course, it's way too early to be sure we'll be able to handle the loss of McGrath and Warne from our attack, but these signs were very good. I think it reflected the fact that we're not thinking about just sustaining the status quo in the Australian camp. As Mike Hussey put it when he was interviewed after his hundred, 'We're still trying to raise the bar and that comes down to the guys working collectively to raise their own games and our team to keep growing.'

Another thing I liked about Brett's performance was the maturity he brought to his bowling. Not only was he very quick at times, he also had spells where he dropped his pace and relied on getting his line and length right. He still looked like taking wickets when he did this, and the Sri Lankans could never relax against him. Then on the final morning, when bowling against their tailenders, he ran in fast, unsettled them, and took three wickets.

On past occasions when we've batted first and then established a big first-innings lead, we've tended not to enforce the follow on, usually because it is in the best interests of our bowlers to give them a break rather than make them bowl 150 or more overs in succession. This policy has worked extremely well for us, but on this occasion we ran through the Sri Lankans so efficiently in their first innings, with the quicks each bowling less than 20 overs, that

I thought it was worth the risk of a long couple of the days in the sun to try to rip through their batting order again. My view is that the psychological damage a huge innings win for us would have achieved could be telling, and not just for this series but into the future, because I really feel we have a bit of a mental grip over these guys. Even though they batted well in their second dig, getting to within 40 runs of making us bat again, I still feel the decision was the right one. We only had to bowl 21.2 overs on the final day, so our attack should be okay for the second Test, in Hobart, which starts next Friday.

A couple of notable landmarks in the game were Mitchell Johnson's first Test wicket and Stuart MacGill's 200th. Mitch's moment came on day three, in his eight over, when Thilan Samaraweera edged a catch through to Adam Gilchrist, giving our keeper the first four wickets on the innings. Stuey's first Test wicket of the season was Chaminda Vaas, bowled near the end of Sri Lanka's first innings; his second came late on the fourth day, when he was too good for the visitors' top-scorer, Michael Vandort. He was clearly very keen to become the 13th Australian to take 200 Test wickets and the ball that allowed him to reach that landmark was a beauty, a sharply turning leg-break that fizzed between Vandort's bat and pad and struck the off-stump. I read later that only Australia's Clarrie Grimmett and Dennis Lillee and Pakistan's Waqar Younis have got to 200 wickets quicker than Stuey's 41 Tests.

I gave him a couple of really long spells during the Test, hoping he'd bowl himself into form, and maybe he did to a degree — though the truth is he was only good in parts. He was still able to bowl the big leggie or a wrong 'un that is all but unplayable, but there was too much loose stuff, and against a more aggressive batting line-up he would have been expensive. He's got some work to do — we all know that — but I'm still

FASTEST TO 200 TEST WICKETS

Bowler	Career	Date	Time	Tests
Clarrie Grimmett (Aust)	1925–1936	15/2/36	10y 353d	36
Dennis Lillee (Aust)	1971–1984	1/2/80	9y 3d	38
Waqar Younis (Pak)	1989–2003	8/12/95	6y 23d	38
Ian Botham (Eng)	1977–1992	27/8/81	4y 30d	41
Stuart MacGill (Aust)	1998–	8/11/07	9y 282d	41
Shane Warne (Aust)	1992–2007	8/12/95	3y 340d	42
Allan Donald (SA)	1992–2002	27/3/98	5y 343d	42
Muttiah Muralitharan (SL)	1992–	27/8/98	5y 364d	42
Alec Bedser (Eng)	1946–1955	25/6/53	7y 3d	44
Richard Hadlee (NZ)	1973–1990	25/8/83	10y 204d	44
Joel Garner (WI)	1977–1987	23/11/84	7y 279d	44
Imran Khan (Pak)	1971–1992	23/12/82	11y 203d	45
Curtly Ambrose (WI)	1988–2000	17/3/94	5y 349d	45
Glenn McGrath (Aust)	1993–2007	2/1/99	5y 51d	45

In this table, 'Career' indicates the span of the bowler's career, from first Test to last; 'Date' indicates the date the Test in which the bowler took his 200th wicket began; 'Time' indicates the number of years and days it took the bowler to reach 200 wickets, from Test debut to the start of the Test in which he took No. 200; 'Tests' indicates how many Tests it took the bowler to reach 200 wickets.

The thing that stands out about this table for me is the sheer quality of the cricketers featured. In my opinion, Stuart MacGill is fully entitled to be included among them.

sure he's our best spinning option. Bowlers such as Stuart MacGill don't come around too often.

This win was our 13th in a row, which means we are closing in on the record set by the team captained by Steve Waugh that won 16 straight between 1999 and 2001. My attitude is that we take this sort of thing one game at a time — to get ahead of ourselves and think about the record would be crazy. I'm more focused on us trying to get better. This might have been a comprehensive victory, but I reckon we'll be letting ourselves down if we just try to maintain standards. As I said in the media conference after the game, 'This is one Test win. We hope the end result of this group over the next 12 months is that the gap does widen [between us and the other Test-playing teams]. The overall plan is we stay a good step ahead of the rest of the pack.'

THURSDAY, NOVEMBER 15

Recent events have shown just how dynamic and occasionally tempestuous the modern cricket world can be. In the past week, we have heard news that Cricket Australia will be sending a team of security people to Pakistan to determine if our three-Test, five-ODI tour that is scheduled for early next year can go ahead. I don't pretend to be an expert in this area, nor do I see myself as an authority on world politics, but it does seem to me that the region is extremely unstable at present.

Australia has not played a Test in Pakistan since 1998. In 2002, Tests that had been originally programmed for there were played on neutral venues in Sri Lanka and Sharjah due to security concerns. It is true that Australia A and the Australia under-19 team both travelled to Pakistan in September and October, but that was before a state of emergency was declared, as the country prepares for general elections in early January. For the moment, I will be guided by Cricket Australia and the Australian Government as to what we should do, but I would be pretending if I said that the thought of missing the tour, even if it goes ahead, has not crossed my mind. As Andrew Symonds said when he was interviewed on the subject, 'At the end of the day it is only a game of cricket.'

In a very different part of the world, it was announced that when we tour the West Indies next year we will be part of the inaugural Twenty20 international to be played in the Caribbean. The match will be played under lights in Barbados, between the third Test and the first of five one-day internationals. It was a natural, given the buzz the Twenty20 has created in other parts of the cricket world, that this would happen in the Windies; my only fear at the moment is that during the next couple of years, tour itineraries might get overloaded with Twenty20 games. I'm starting to really warm to the idea of the Indian Premier League, which will feature teams that include players from all the Test-playing nations representing cities or regions, a kind of 'club' competition, if you like, but the idea of the 20-over game coming to dominate international cricket doesn't excite me at all. If that was to happen, I'm sure cricket would suffer in the long run, because then we'd be ignoring our traditional base and competing with other forms of entertainment that come and go on the public's whim, like soap operas and reality TV shows.

As far as our current series is concerned, the major issue for the Sri Lankans is whether Kumar Sangakkara will be right to play. Based on the press reports we have been reading, he is optimistic his damaged hamstring will be okay, and the competitive side of my brain is keen that he does play, because there is always something extra satisfying about beating an opponent who is at full strength. We will field an unchanged XI, and I can't imagine the selectors talked for very long before deciding that this would be the case.

Another slightly bizarre storyline being run in some places is that the size of the crowds at the recent Test in Brisbane is evidence that people are losing interest in Test cricket. To come to this conclusion, the cynics compared this season's Gabba attendances to last year's Ashes series, an event that we all know attracted unprecedented interest. To me, that's a case of using

A NEW PRIZE

The 'Warne–Muralitharan Trophy' — which will become the prize for Australia v Sri Lanka Tests — has been unveiled by the two great spinners in a ceremony in Hobart. It had been announced a couple of weeks ago that the new trophy would carry their names, but unfortunately there was a bit of trouble in the lead-up to today's event, after Warney was quoted in the papers suggesting Murali's action should be re-examined in a Test match and Murali responding by describing Shane as a 'miserable man'. The two great bowlers seemed happy enough in each other's company as the trophy was being showed off for the first time, and the problem has been blamed on a 'miscommunication'.

I just think the new trophy is a fantastic idea, a worthy 'brother' to the Border–Gavaskar (versus India) and Chappell–Hadlee (versus New Zealand) trophies that the Aussie teams play for.

After Warney made his original comments, Murali wondered if he was upset because he was about to lose his Test wicket-taking record, but Shane has put that straight. 'I'm happy to pass it [the record] on to Murali. I think he'll take a thousand,' he said.

He might be right about Murali eventually getting to four figures, but we're still keen to prevent him from getting the record here!

stats to twist an argument the way you want it to go. Someone from Cricket Australia pointed out that the first Test crowd this season was actually the third biggest in Brisbane since the 1970s, but by then the story had taken on a life of its own. When I spoke to the media today, I was quickly asked if the 'disappointing' first-Test crowds and the rise of Twenty20 meant Test cricket was dying. I said that was ridiculous, but I did take the opportunity to challenge other countries — especially those where Test-match crowds have been down for a number of years — to play the sort of attacking cricket that will sustain interest in five-day games.

'That is one thing we've done particularly well over a long period of time,' I argued. 'If you look at the way we score our runs, the way we have been able to bowl in Test cricket, we have made the overall game a lot more attractive than other teams have.

'The other countries have to start looking at not playing as many drawn games, at maybe challenging themselves a bit more to start winning and having results in Test matches.'

WEDNESDAY, NOVEMBER 21

Second Test, Australia v Sri Lanka, at Hobart (November 16–20):
Australia 5–542 dec (PA Jaques 150, MEK Hussey 132, MJ Clarke 71, A Symonds 50*, AC Gilchrist 67*) and 2–210 (PA Jaques 68, RT Ponting 53*) defeated **Sri Lanka** 246 (KC Sangakkara 57, DPMD Jayawardene 104; B Lee 4–82) and 410 (MS Atapattu 80, KC Sangakkara 192; B Lee 4–87) by 96 runs

For a bit more than three days this match was mimicking the Test in Brisbane, but then Kumar Sangakkara strode out to play one of the best Test innings I've seen in a long time. The only shame was the way it ended — with a controversial umpiring decision — but I hope that doesn't cloud any of the memories of Sangakkara's superb display.

His was one of four hundreds scored in the Test, after impressive innings by Phil Jaques, Mike Hussey and Mahela Jayawardene, and it was unarguably the best of them. And I write this not trying to diminish the quality of the other three guys' innings. They all played beautifully, but Sangakkara was something else. I know, because of his hamstring injury, that he didn't keep in this Test, but he usually does and I think of him as a keeper-batsman. It wasn't so long ago that men such as the West Indies' Jeffrey Dujon and Australia's Ian Healy were showing that keepers couldn't survive in modern Test cricket by the quality of their glovework alone; they needed to average in the 30s with the bat as well. By the time Adam Gilchrist emerged at the end of the 20th century, just about every Test team had a keeper who was also a very good batsman. But then Gilly, and now Sangakkara, too, have taken the concept of a keeper-batsman to a whole new level. For a while, when Gilly was averaging 60 as a Test batsman and also keeping to a high standard, I wasn't sure I'd see an all-rounder capable of making the same impact as him. But the truth is Sangakkara is not that far behind. He showed us here that, once he gets going, he is probably as good as anyone going around.

As always for a Test in Hobart, I received a stack of goodwill from the local fans and felt a lot of pressure to succeed because I was playing in front of my family and so many good friends. A Test in Hobart has always meant a lot to me, going right back to the very first one, which was played against Sri Lanka during the 1989–90 season. I turned 15 during that game, which was played from December 16 to 20, dates I know off by heart, and I can vividly recall racing home on my BMX bike from high school in Launceston, last week of the school year, to watch my uncle, Greg Campbell, open the bowling for Australia. Disappointingly for me, for my fourth Test in Tassie out of five I struggled, though I did manage to get past 50 in our short second innings. In six previous Test innings in Hobart I'd only made it past 17 once (157 not out v New Zealand in 2001–02); this time, I scored 31 and 53 not out, so at least my home supporters did get to see me out in the middle for a little while. This was the third Test win I've been a part of at Bellerive, with two draws.

There were many ways our first innings matched what happened at the Gabba. We batted first (though this time I won the toss), Jaques and Hussey scored centuries, Matt Hayden was dismissed by a paceman, I fell to Murali. We lost three wickets on the first day, but on this occasion we lost five in all, one more than in Brisbane. I was impressed by the way Jaquesy went on with it this time, going all the way to 152, whereas last Test he was out as soon as he reached three figures, as if the excitement of reaching his first Test century cost him his concentration for a critical moment. I'm sure he feels very much part of the Australian team now, and it wouldn't surprise me if he is part of the side for years to come. Huss just continued on the way he has been going for two years now. He scored his maiden Test century here against the West Indies two years ago, when if he'd failed he might have been dropped before his Test career had a chance to get going. Since then, he's hit another six hundreds in 16 Tests, and in all has scored nearly 2000 Test runs at an incredible average of 86.18.

Huss rushed to his hundred late on the first day, and then he, Michael Clarke, Andrew Symonds and Adam Gilchrist continued the carnage on day two. Gilly hit three sixes — taking him past 100 sixes in Test cricket, the only man to achieve this feat — including two massive back-to-back legside blows off Murali, one of which led to a replacement ball being required, the old one having being lost.

The Sri Lankans had Lasith Malinga — he of the unusual, slinging action that generates plenty of pace — back in their side, but left Chaminda Vaas out to make room for him. This would have been Vaas' 100th Test had he played, and we did hear that he's carrying a shoulder injury. The change made little difference, except that the ball came off the Australian bats a bit quicker. When Sri Lanka batted, Brett Lee was fantastic again, taking four wickets in each innings, just as he'd done at the Gabba. Despite Jayawardene's excellent hundred, once again we could have made them follow on, but this time I resisted that temptation, almost on a gut instinct — I just felt that it would be too big an ask for our bowlers, not so much in terms of this game but because asking the guys to bowl two innings straight for two Tests straight might impinge on one or more of them in the weeks and months to come.

Of course, our quicks are all big, strong blokes who look like they could bowl for ever, but don't forget that Brett is coming back from a significant layoff with that ankle injury that cost

SUPER SUB

One bloke who won't forget this Hobart Test in a hurry is 24-year-old Rhett Lockyear, a member of the Tasmanian squad, who spent the best part of three days not just as a 'backroom' member of the Australian team, but who also spent plenty of time in the field after Andrew Symonds twisted his ankle while batting on the second day. By the time the Test was over, Rhett was walking off Bellerive as the proud owner of two Test run-outs, one catch, a Test stump and a match ball.

He handled himself brilliantly throughout the game, and then there were some personal highlights. On day three, in Sri Lanka's first innings, Farveez Maharoof was batting with a runner, Chamara Silva, when there was a mix-up between that pair and the batsman at the non-striker's end, Mahela Jayawardene. Our man picked up the ball, fired it to Gilly and Maharoof was run out. On day four, he took a fairly easy catch (if there is such a thing for a rookie) to dismiss Michael Vandort, and then on day five he chased and then threw the ball from out near the boundary to run out Dilhara Fernando.

A week ago, Rhett was playing for the Tassie Second XI against the South Australian Second XI at the Adelaide Oval No. 2. And now here he was trying to work out what to do after the final wicket fell in the second match of the series between Australia and Sri Lanka when Adam Gilchrist, a veteran of 92 Tests, strolled over and said, 'Mate, take a stump.'

At the same time, I was asking umpire Rudi Koertzen for a ball from the game, which I then gave to our super sub. When I asked him afterwards what he'd do with his souvenirs, he replied with a grin, 'I'll probably give them to Mum and Dad. They will look after them.'

him the World Cup. I am absolutely delighted with the way he's come back, especially impressed with the skill and common sense he is bringing to his bowling, and it would have been silly to test his endurance too much at this stage of the summer.

'The more you play the smarter you become and that is where it is with Brett at the moment,' I said at the media conference after the Test. 'He knows if he bowls enough balls in the right area and uses his skills — which are great pace, a great bouncer and some good outswingers with the new ball — then he will keep the batsman under pressure and give himself the best chance of taking wickets.'

'That is what Glenn McGrath did over the years,' I continued. 'He didn't do anything special; he just got the ball in the right area and built enough pressure to force the batsman to play a bad shot.'

The Sri Lankans began their fightback on day four, led by Sangakkara and Marvan Atapattu, who took the score to 1–158 before Bing struck a crucial double blow. First, he induced Atapattu into an ill-advised hook shot, which finished up in the hands of Phil Jaques at deep square-leg. Next ball, Bing produced an absolutely magnificent delivery to dismiss Jayawardene — out of the hand, the line was just enough outside off to convince the batsman to let it go, but then it began to dip and swing … and hit the off stump. It was a stunning moment, and though Jayasuriya stayed with Sangakkara while a further 107 runs were added, batting into the final day, from the time the Sri Lankan captain was knocked over I was confident we were going to win. This was true even though the wicket had flattened right out, and our attack was a little short-handed, with Symmo unable to bowl and Stuart MacGill hampered by arm and knee problems. When Stuey did bowl, his line and length were ordinary, and Sangakkara got into him. I had been reasonably impressed with Stuey's efforts in Brisbane and even in the first innings here (when he took 2–81 in

HUMAN ERROR

Kumar Sangakkara's second-innings dismissal happened this way. Stuart Clark pitched one short, Sangakkara went for a pull shot, and we heard two noises as the ball ballooned to me in the slip cordon. Later, after watching the replay, we saw clearly that the ball hit him on the shoulder and then the helmet. He shouldn't have been given out, but there shouldn't have been a problem with us appealing. My first reaction was that he was out, which is why I went up. Soon, my instincts were telling me that maybe it wasn't quite right, but that didn't mean I knew he shouldn't have been given out. I just wasn't sure.

At the time, and even when I think about it now, it sounded like it was either glove or bat and up into his helmet. It might have just been the way Sangakkara reacted that put doubt in my mind. Sometimes you can tell from a batsman's instinctive reaction that he's been hard done by.

As soon as umpire Rudi Koertzen saw the replay he made a point of apologising to the unfortunate batsman, which I saw no problem with. To me, it was a classy thing to do.

25 overs), but he struggled on the fourth and fifth day. He really needs to get his body right and until he does I'm not sure we can rate him as our first-choice spinner.

When Jayasuriya fell to Bing early on the fifth day, Sangakkara was 115 not out and Sri Lanka were 4–265. Ten overs later, they were 8–290, but Sangakkara wouldn't be denied, and he began a one-man assault on our attack that only ended when he was the victim of an undeniable umpiring error that most likely cost him a Test double-century. He dominated a ninth wicket stand with Malinga, hitting Lee, Clark and Johnson for fours to all parts of the ground. One Johnson delivery went sailing over the cover boundary for six. I said straight afterwards that I thought it was some of the best batting I'd ever seen by a batsman who was running out of partners, and I still think that now. The way he worked the second new ball around the ground — something that is never easy to do against a good bowling attack — was superb. By the time he was finished, he'd achieved the highest Test score by a Sri Lankan against Australia, and the highest Test score made in Hobart. And he did it in style.

It was strange in the dressing room afterwards, thinking about the fact that it will be more than a month before we'll be playing Test cricket again. It's almost as if the season started, and now we've got to put everything on pause for a while before we can get going again. I know we have some domestic cricket and then the Chappell–Hadlee series to play over the next four weeks, but for the past 10 years in Australia once you commenced a Test series during a home season, you kept going and then played the one-dayers. This year, we have to readjust, but I'm highly confident we can. It's just another challenge we have to conquer.

We have to start the Melbourne Test in the same manner we kicked-off in Brisbane. Hopefully, we'll be able to get on top of India from the jump and stay there throughout the series. But it won't be easy, and if the experience of the recent one-day series in India is any guide, there might be a bit of an edge to the games as well. Frankly, I don't mind the sound of that, so long as things don't go silly. I rate India a stronger side than this Sri Lankan team that gave us a few tricky moments in Hobart, and I have strong memories of the Indians' last series in Australia, Steve Waugh's last summer, when they led the four-match series after two Tests and played very well against us. Their World Twenty20 triumph was built around younger cricketers, suggesting they have plenty of talent coming through, but they still have some outstanding players who have years of experience. Rahul Dravid, Sourav Ganguly, VVS Laxman and Sachin Tendulkar have done well against Australia in the past and we all know how dangerous they can be.

PART FOUR

CHAPPELL–HADLEE TROPHY SERIES

'It's not about what you say; it's what you do.
And I think right at the moment we're doing
things really well.'

— Ricky Ponting, December 20, 2007

THURSDAY, DECEMBER 13

Twenty20 International, at Perth (December 11): Australia 6–186 (20 overs: MJ Clarke 33, A Symonds 85*) defeated **New Zealand** 132 (18.3 overs: JDP Oram 66*; AA Noffke 3–18) by 54 runs

What do you do during an Australian summer when there's suddenly no major international cricket for 23 days? I know this sometimes happened in the good old days — I mean, up to the mid 1960s there were entire seasons devoted solely to domestic matches. But since the days of World Series Cricket, the Australian season has usually been full on from November to February, and for players such as me who play for both the Test and one-day teams (in years to come, I guess, it will be guys who play Tests, one-dayers and Twenty20) there has been little respite between matches. In previous years, India would have arrived earlier, and played one or two Tests before the Boxing Day encounter, but this year they are playing a three-game series against Pakistan (which they won 1–0, the final match ending last night, our time, in a draw), so the opening Test of our series won't begin until December 26.

CAREFUL WITH THE ROPES

I managed to grab a headline or two after the Ford Ranger Cup game at North Sydney Oval by putting forward my view that the boundary ropes at many grounds are being brought in too close to the pitch for some limited-over games. 'A ground like this does create a nice little carnival atmosphere,' I explained, 'but to tell the truth I'd really like to see our playing arenas be a bit bigger.'

This tendency to 'rope off' the grounds has been growing in popularity across Australia in the past few years. To me, the practice takes away a little of the character of the grounds and gives too big an advantage to the batsmen. North Sydney Oval usually provides an excellent batting wicket, and it's not a big playing area anyway, so why do the officials make it any smaller than they have to?

It's the same at some major international games. The boundaries at the MCG and the Adelaide Oval have been reduced significantly for one-day games over the past couple of years, but I don't believe that needs to happen. My understanding is that two reasons for the boundary ropes being used are for security purposes, to create a small area between the field of play and the crowd, and also to prevent a fieldsman hurting himself by crashing into the boundary fence. Fair enough on both calls, but I've seen the straight boundaries in Adelaide and the square boundaries in Melbourne roped in by up to 30 metres. Somehow I don't think anyone is going to slide that far into a boundary fence.

The ideal scenario for major matches is that the playing area is as big as possible, with the wicket somewhere near the centre of the ground. Cricket should never be just about fours and sixes.

Over the past three weeks, one subject that has captured the attention of the pundits has been leadership. For me, this started when, before Tasmania played its Ford Ranger Cup match against New South Wales on November 25, I made the decision to stand down as state captain. It wasn't a hard call, although part of me hated doing it. Really, I'd been captain in name only for the past five years, having played the grand total of two four-day games and three one-dayers in that time. Daniel Marsh had led the team to the Pura Cup last season, and it seemed to me that this was the right moment for Dan to take the job on a permanent basis.

'To captain Tasmania is a great honour and something I'll always cherish,' I said in a statement. 'Naturally I'll continue to play with Tasmania and assist the leadership group as much as possible.'

I made this call knowing I'd be playing in two Ford Ranger Cup one-dayers, against NSW and Western Australia. As it turned out, I had a really good time in both games, especially at North Sydney where I scored 111 not out as we beat NSW by nine wickets. During that game, Michael Dighton (146 from 138 balls) and I combined to add 263 for the second wicket, which we learned later was Tasmania's highest ever one-day partnership.

I enjoyed playing without being captain. It was almost a relief not having to worry about things such as the coin toss and the official media conference after the game. Before today, bar for a few games I played in England with Somerset in 2004, I've been captain of every game I've appeared in since Steve Waugh's final Test.

My time with the Tasmanian side for this season almost certainly ended with the game against WA in Perth, in which I scored 10 and we won by three wickets. Initially, I was intending to play in the Pura Cup game at the WACA, but after discussions with Cricket Australia I decided it was better to rest a bit and make sure my body was right for the Chappell–Hadlee matches. This meant that I also missed the Australia-New Zealand Twenty20 game that launched the Black Caps' short Australian tour. This game was staged in Perth on December 11, with the captaincy handed to Michael Clarke — further evidence of this impressive young man's rising status in the game.

It's been an incredible 12 months for Pup, when you think that a little more than a year ago he wasn't in the original

Australian Test squad chosen for the first Ashes Test. But then Shane Watson dropped out, Pup came in, he scored a half century in the opening Test, hundreds in the next two, and he's been spoken of as a possible future captain ever since.

I thought it was a good idea giving Pup some leadership experience, yet at the same time I don't think he has been automatically anointed as our next captain. It is true, though, that in a few years, he should be perfectly positioned, age-wise and experience-wise, to claim the leadership roles, but there are other guys in the Australian set-up with genuine leadership credentials, most notably Mike Hussey, who led the team when I missed the short tour to New Zealand last February. I should also add that I have no intention of stepping aside in the near future anyway, so hopefully any conjecture about the short-term is unnecessary.

I guess there'll be people now saying we should be promoting Pup into the vice-captaincy for the Test and one-day teams, but I don't see the need to rush. I'm not sure if people quite realise how much the deputy's job means to the people in that position — it's not something that should be swapped around as if it's just a token. I remember clearly how proud I was when I was first named vice-captain, what it meant to me. I would have been filthy if they'd taken it off me, because it was someone else's turn.

As long as Pup is thinking like a vice-captain when he is around the group, then he'll get as much experience doing that as he would being vice-captain. One of the main jobs of a vice-captain is to be a sounding board, someone who can come up with a possible new direction, or whom I can bounce an idea off. If I can do that with Pup, too — with any of the guys — then the team will be all the better for it.

The Australian squad for the twenty20 game read this way: Michael Clarke (captain), Adam Gilchrist, Brad Hodge, Mike Hussey, Andrew Symonds, Adam Voges, Brett Lee, Ashley

THE ENTERTAINER

Australian cricket won't ever be quite the same following the news Darren Lehmann revealed last month that he was going to retire from first-class cricket. Whenever I played with Darren, better known to us as 'Boof', we seemed to have this unbelievable knack for being able to build some really good partnerships. For example, I was at the other end for every ball of his first Test century — 160 against the West Indies at Port-of-Spain in 2003 — when we added 315, still the Australian record for the third wicket. We added more than 100 during his last Test century, too, when he made 153 against Sri Lanka in Colombo in 2004.

I remain very grateful Boof was around when I became Australian captain. To have someone with his knowledge and experience around the team was invaluable. He has a great cricket brain, was a great competitor and is a great bloke. He never got too serious about his cricket, always saw the fun side of the game and thoroughly enjoyed playing it. This was refreshing attitude to have around a team full of ambitious, committed professional cricketers, because he never went too far the other way. He kept us balanced, never a bad thing.

As a batsman, he was brilliant. Talk to any of the first-class bowlers who tried to knock him over, even during the last couple of seasons when he was past his best, and they'll remember a day when he just embarrassed them by the way he batted. He was a genuinely great player of spin bowling, something he demonstrated again in his farewell to Adelaide, a Ford Ranger Cup game against WA on November 21, when he scored 126 not out from 104 balls and made Brad Hogg look like someone who has never played cricket before.

When he announced his retirement, Boof was asked how he'd like to be remembered. 'As one who entertained everyone, one who always played for the team,' he answered.

That, mate, you most surely did.

Noffke, Nathan Bracken, Stuart Clark, Mitchell Johnson and Shaun Tait. I was pleased to see Tait, Voges and Hodge back in Australian colours, and also delighted that Ashley Noffke had been rewarded for some superb bowling in interstate cricket. It's hard to believe that it's more than six years since he joined us a replacement on the 2001 Ashes tour. Injuries have hampered his progress, but I've never had any doubts about his talent. The end result was a comprehensive victory for the good guys, with Symmo in imperious form and Noffers (three wickets) and Taity (two) both doing good things with the ball.

I watched the game while lying on the lounge at home in Sydney, and enjoyed especially the story of how exciting WA batsman Luke Pomersbach received the phone call most people only dream about as he was parking his car at the WACA. Luke's intention was to watch the game as a spectator, but he was quickly told that Brad Hodge had hurt his back in the dressing room and he's been nominated as Hodge's replacement. The new man dashed for the home team's dressing room, his brother set off to get his gear, and not too long afterwards he was out in the middle, scoring 15 from seven balls including a big six over midwicket.

I didn't mind watching the action from a different angle, and enjoyed hearing from Adam Gilchrist and Andrew Symonds as they were 'miked up' during the play. With the guys explaining field placings and even successfully predicting outcomes, I reckon the blokes up in the commentary box might be just about redundant!

THE AUSTRALIAN OPEN GOLF Championship is being played at The Australian in Sydney from December 13 to 16, and two days back, the same day the Twenty20 international was played in Perth, I ventured out to the course to catch up with a good mate of mine, two-time Australian Open winner Aaron Baddeley, who was playing in the 'pro-am' that precedes the tournament.

I first met Aaron maybe five years back, when I went out to Melbourne's Capital Golf Club with Dean Jones and Allan Border for a round. Aaron happened to be there, we played together that day, and have stayed in touch since. He loves cricket and I love golf, so it is a natural partnership.

As I read yesterday's papers, I was taken by a quote in a story where Aaron talked about our friendship. I thought it was revealing that he specifically highlighted an aspect of my approach to cricket that I've always seen as a crucial ingredient in the recipe for success. 'He is always struggling to get better,' Aaron said of me. 'It does not matter how good he is or how good the team is, he is always looking to improve.

'You can relate to that in golf. It does not matter how good you get, you always want to improve.'

One thing Aaron and I have in common is that we both hit the big time early in our sporting careers. Aaron won the 1999 Australian Open as an 18-year-old amateur, beating a field that included Greg Norman, Colin Montgomerie and Nick Faldo, and then won again in 2000. Huge things were predicted of him, but success on the biggest golfing stage, the PGA Tour, didn't come easily. His first win in America occurred in 2006, and he's followed that up with a great 2007, winning once and playing in the last group with Tiger Woods during the final round of the US Open. All up this year, he's earned more than US$3 million.

Because Aaron spends so much time in the States and I'm often away on tour it's hard for us to catch up, but we often send each other text messages or give each other a call. Inevitably, all he wants to talk about is cricket and all I want to discuss is golf, but we usually manage to find a compromise.

At The Australian, I watched Aaron and his fellow pros closely, trying to pick up little things that might help my own game. And when I got the chance I talked to him about the swing changes he's implemented over the years and different techniques used by other players I've seen from week to week as I devoured

TV coverage of the PGA Tour. I really am a golf tragic. It was a terrific day, my idea of perfect relaxation as I sought to freshen up before the international cricket season got back into full swing.

FRIDAY, DECEMBER 21

Chappell–Hadlee Trophy

Game One, at Adelaide (December 14): New Zealand 7–254 (50 overs: BB McCullum 96, LRPL Taylor 50; SW Tait 3–59) lost to **Australia** 3–255 (42.3 overs: AC Gilchrist 51, RT Ponting 107*, MJ Clarke 48) by seven wickets

Game Two, at Sydney (December 16): New Zealand 3–30 (six overs). Abandoned due to rain

Game Three, at Hobart (December 20): Australia 6–282 (50 overs: RT Ponting 134*, A Symonds 52) defeated **New Zealand** 168 (34 overs: SB Styris 75; B Lee 3–47, GB Hogg 3–49) by 114 runs

In the lead-up to this December's Chappell–Hadlee series, there were any number of Kiwis who were keen to talk about how last season's matches had gone. Remember them? Because we won the World Cup so decisively, a lot of Aussies have forgotten that just before we left for the Caribbean we were defeated 3–zip in New Zealand. When people from our side of the Tasman are reminded of those games, their perception is that we were thrashed, but the fact is that it wasn't quite like that. Yes, game one of that series was one-sided (New Zealand won by nine wickets) but the last two games went down to the wire, after Australia made big totals batting first.

NIGHT MOVES

On the eve of the Chappell–Hadlee series, Cricket Australia boss James Sutherland threw one from left field when he suggested that day-night Test matches could be being played 'within a decade'.

James' comments quickly took me back to the 1994–95 season, when some day-night Sheffield Shield matches were played without generating any great crowd support. Everyone I've spoken to who was involved in those experiments said it was difficult to pick up the ball they used, which was a shade between yellow and orange. It was hard for the batsmen, bowlers, fieldsmen and fans. Soon after the idea was raised this time, a spokesperson from Kookaburra, the ball manufacturer, explained that they'd been trying to come up with a ball that would behave like the traditional red one, last as long, and could still be picked up at night, but they still have not found the answer.

James argued that a day-night Test would attract four times the number of TV viewers, because the final session of each day's play would be televised in prime time. While I don't believe the game should ever be a slave to ratings, it would obviously be a positive to have so many more people watching what I still believe is clearly the 'showpiece' of our game. However, one of the subjects constantly raised at captains' meetings I've sat in during the past four or five years has been the difficulties created by playing Test cricket when the light starts to fade. A move to day-night Tests would accentuate that problem, with questions constantly being asked about whether play could continue during the 'twilight' period when the floodlights aren't as effective as they are at night.

I'm not saying the idea should be dismissed out of hand, but there remain a number of major hurdles to be overcome before it could be instigated.

However, as I've said before, perception can spin into reality. Such was the furore created by those shock defeats, I had to spend the first week of our World Cup campaign reminding many members of our squad, including most of our support staff, that our form wasn't as ordinary as what many sceptics were saying. Coach John Buchanan was especially gloomy, but I knew that we had played some good cricket without winning. The memory of those team discussions has stayed with me, and it definitely served as a source of extra motivation for this series. I wanted us to set the record straight.

As it turned out, the 2007–08 series started brilliantly for us on the field, but there was a disappointing aftertaste because someone in the Kiwi camp decided to question the legality of Shaun Tait's bowling action. I think if anything the controversy spurred us on, but after I'd finished answering questions on the subject I was left wondering why they'd decided to discuss the issue publicly. If they were trying to unsettle Shaun, it didn't work. I knew Taity was still going all right because I'd had the 'pleasure' of facing him in the nets between the first and second match of the series, and it hurts just thinking of the ball jarring on the bat. There's no doubt he's fit and bowling quick. If the New Zealanders were attempting to deflect attention from their own performance, I don't think that worked either.

As I said at the media conference, to suggest Taity's bowling action is crooked is absolute rubbish. The Kiwis haven't made any sort of official complaint; I guess someone in their camp just decided to put the idea 'out there' to see if it would make an impact. The whole concept of 'mind games' in big-time cricket is so overrated, and I'm sure the people from across the sporting world who try to get involved do more damage to themselves than to anyone else. Can you imagine the hours these amateur psychologists spend coming up with their latest ploy? If they devoted as many hours to the actual playing of the game I'm sure they'd be better off.

Shaun attacked a little too much at the start of the innings and was hit about a bit by Brendon McCullum, but he got his line and length right in his second spell and finished with three wickets. Then Adam Gilchrist launched our reply in spectacular

OUR TEAM FOR THE FIRST TEST

Two days before the third Chappell–Hadlee game for 2007–08, the Australian selectors named our squad for the first Test against India, which starts on Boxing Day. There were no real surprises: with Stuart MacGill out because of wrist surgery, Brad Hogg took the spinner's spot, while with Shaun Tait restored to full fitness he returned to the squad at the expense of Ben Hilfenhaus.

Hoggy has had one of the more unusual Test careers: one Test in 1996, three in 2003, and now he seems likely to play a key role in this upcoming series. At the same time, up to the end of this series against New Zealand, he's played 116 ODIs. I am really happy that he's getting this opportunity in Test matches, I know he deserves it, and I'm sure he'll do the job.

In announcing the team, chairman of selectors Andrew Hilditch left the possibility open that we'd go into the first Test with a four-man pace attack, and Andrew Symonds and Michael Clarke providing the slow stuff. I guess that's possible, but you know what a fan I am of having a balanced attack. I'd want the MCG wicket to be very green and lively before I'd be backing such a move.

I've read quotes attributed to India's captain, Anil Kumble, and their off-spinner Harbhajan Singh in which they've said Hoggy isn't up to Test cricket. This has led to some commentators wondering if they're trying to con us into playing four quicks in Melbourne. But a lot of international players have had a lot of trouble trying to read Hoggy in one-day cricket — he's brought a number of batsmen undone with his variations in that form of the game — and I can't see why he can't do the same in Tests.

style, smashing 51 from just 29 deliveries. 'Pretty fantastic and pretty brutal,' was how Kiwi captain Daniel Vettori described it. 'I won't lay all the blame on my bowlers, just sit back and admire that innings.' Gilly and Matt Hayden were scoring at 13 runs an over for the first four overs of the innings, 10 an over for the first seven, creating a platform that I was happy to exploit. Not for the first time in my one-day career, I was left feeling a little inadequate because I could 'only' score at a run a ball. Still, we cruised home with seven-and-a-half overs to spare, going part of the way to erasing the memory of last year's series, when they swept us in New Zealand.

Game two, in Sydney, was a washout, which meant we had to win in Hobart yesterday to regain the Chappell–Hadlee Trophy. But, more and more, as Boxing Day draws closer, the talk was not about that deciding game, but about the upcoming Test series. The Indians arrived last Tuesday, the same day the Australian selectors announced our squad for the opening Test. One subject the home critics and the arriving Indian press pack have jumped on is our possible bowling line-up for the five-day games, focusing on the fact that we've preferred Shaun Tait to Mitchell Johnson in the latest one-day matches. Is this an indicator to who we might go for in Melbourne? I don't think it is. Shaun was close to being our best bowler at the World Cup, but then injury cost him a trip to India in October. Now he's fit and ready to go again, it was fair and natural that he'd come back into the one-day team.

For me, this scenario with Shaun and Mitch is the same as the situation that occurred last season, when Andrew Symonds missed some one-day matches, Brad Hodge replaced him and did very well, but when Symmo was right again he was straight back in the side. I'm not saying that decision or this one with Shaun and Mitch was easy. Selectors have to make tough calls at different times. Luckily for us, the Australian selectors have got most of their difficult ones right over the past few years.

They will make the final call, but when we have a chat about the final line-up I will argue that Mitch is the current 'front-runner' for the Test matches. I thought he was outstanding against Sri Lanka, seemingly getting better by the over, and his form is evidence of a growing trend within the team set-up. I love

THE HOBART THOUSAND

I love the greyhounds, and over the years I've had a lot of fun racing dogs. This has been especially true in recent months, mainly because one of my bitches had a litter of nine pups about two-and-a-half years ago and eight of them have gone on to win races in Tasmania.

Modern technology being what it is, I can tour the world and still keep track of how my dogs are going. I can get on the internet and listen to race replays, and in some places I can set up my mobile so I can watch the races on Sky Channel. They race two nights a week, Mondays and Thursdays, plus Tuesday afternoons in Tassie, which means during an Australian season I'm often watching races after training or a day's play. I find it very helpful to have such an outlet, something away from cricket, to take my mind off the game. Ask any punter and they'll tell you one of the appeals of the horses or dogs is that when your fancy is running, whether you're an owner, punter or both, all your other worries fade into to the background. People who don't follow the races will never quite understand this.

One of the benefits of the third Chappell–Hadlee game finishing early was that we could have a couple of celebratory beers in the Bellerive Oval dressing room and still have plenty of time to get to the Elwick track for the running of the Hobart Thousand, Tasmania's only Group One greyhound race. The favourite for the race was a fawn dog by the name of First Innings, which I race in partnership with Tim Quill, one of my best mates going back to primary school, and Tim's father, John. There was a big crowd on hand for the race, and many of the boys from the Aussie team joined me at the track.

Prior to this race, my biggest success as a greyhound owner was with My Self, which won the Tasmanian leg of the National Sprint Championship at Launceston in 1995, and Ricky Tim, a Devonport Cup winner I raced with Tim and John. Had First Innings snared first prize in the $50,000 race last night, those successes would have been pushed firmly back into the minor placings. He'd run the fastest time in the heats and was jumping from the one box, but he missed the kick, copped some interference as he tried to rail through, and couldn't recover. It was an unlucky end to what had been a long, draining but very exciting day.

the fact that the competition for pace-bowling spots is very strong. From the day he was appointed, we knew bowling coach Troy Cooley would do an amazing job with the younger brigade of fast bowlers across Australia. Just as importantly, he's having a major impact with the more established guys as well.

This was shown again in the game in Hobart, where Lee and Tait played leading roles. After we scored 6–282 from our 50 overs, Bing came out and knocked over their openers in his first 14 deliveries and then came back later to dismiss their top-scorer, Scott Styris, as well. Taity took two wickets, and went for less than four an over, as we won with 16 overs to spare.

It was a great win for us, one I enjoyed immensely, but with the contest so one-sided I guess it wasn't surprising that an on-field exchange between Daniel Vettori and me during our innings — which occurred after the Kiwis accused Brad Haddin of deliberately running up the middle of the pitch during the 40th over of our innings — would become the lead in many media reports. I'm sure Vettori and his men would have known there was nothing in Hadds' behaviour, but they decided to try to create a scene anyway by crying to the umpires. Coming on top of the New Zealand camp's comments in Adelaide about Taity's bowling action, I thought their complaint was provocative and unnecessary, and after the game I was happy for the world to know that. It was, I told the journos, an 'ordinary pot shot'.

'They had a go at Hadds for running on the wicket; it was about the third ball he faced,' I explained. 'He turned one off a spinner and took a couple of steps down the track. It was as if it was some pre-conceived idea, or a plan of ours to run down the wicket because we were batting first.

'It's quite often that the New Zealanders will point the finger with those little sorts of things in the game towards us, as if it's things we've thought about and planned. I was a bit disappointed to hear some of that stuff and I just returned a little bit back.'

Countering any bitterness I felt over that episode was the joy I experienced from scoring a big hundred in Hobart. Of course, I went into the game knowing Bellerive has not been my most productive venue, which I blame on the fact that I simply try too hard whenever I come here, put too much pressure on myself to get some runs and thus do the right thing by family and friends. Early on in this innings I thought it would happen again, as I struggled against some excellent bowling, but I dug in and on the day was good enough to get through that tough period and then go on to bat through the innings. It's taken me a long while to score a ODI century on my home track (previously, I'd scored a total of 74 runs in five digs), so there was a sense of relief as well as pleasure in my reaction to finally getting this one on my résumé.

After the game, someone told me that of all the major cricketing countries, I have scored more runs, hit more centuries and half-centuries, and have a better batting average against New Zealand than any other team. 'Why is that?' I was asked. The truth is that it's mostly a quirk in the stats. I don't think my game is more suited to their bowlers than others, or that they are inferior to other teams. Their record in recent seasons, especially in one-day cricket, hasn't been too bad. But there is something in the fact that they are our near-neighbours, and also the fact that whatever the circumstances and whatever the sport there is always at least a little spice to Trans-Tasman encounters ...

'It's probably got something to do with the rivalry we have,' I responded. 'We always want to play well against New Zealand.'

PART FIVE

AUSTRALIA v INDIA TEST SERIES

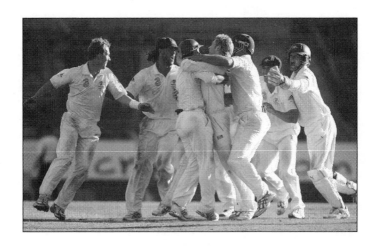

*'We've coped well since we lost four
players last summer and now we've
lost one more ...'*

— Ricky Ponting, January 28, 2008

MONDAY, DECEMBER 24

Christmas won't be quite the same this year. The departure of fathers such as Justin Langer, Shane Warne and Glenn McGrath hasn't just had an impact on the way we go about things on the park, it's changed the machinations of the team off the field as well. One day when this will be very obvious will be tomorrow, when, for one thing, there will be fewer young 'uns running around than in previous years. Lang has four children, Warney three and Pigeon two, so I don't think Santa's sack is going to be quite as heavy as it's been in previous years. This said, Brad Hogg's two children will be with us after his well-deserved selection for the first Test, so that'll balance things up a little bit.

Over the past few years, Cricket Australia and team management have made a real effort to build a strong family environment around our playing group, with wives, partners and children made to feel welcome whenever they travel with the team. Just about everyone who's ever been connected with the team reckons this has worked really well, and no one could argue that our performance has been harmed. Christmas always has a

FROM PLAY TO PRESS

It was interesting how the media played up an alleged 'spat' between Adam Gilchrist and Shane Warne in the lead-up to the Boxing Day Test. This allegedly major story started when Warney had a shot at former Aussie coach John Buchanan and escalated when Gilly responded to a question about Shane's comments by talking about the broader subject of former team-mates being critical of the Australian team.

I am with Gilly 100 per cent when he says of the guys who wear the baggy green cap: 'It's an elite club and we've always felt that a major characteristic of being in that club is respect, and it just seems that maybe some guys in retirement have just lost that.'

Gilly is not the only member of the Australian team who has become a little exasperated by the fact that a number of ex-players have gained a ticket to the pressbox and now feel an obligation to sledge the current squad. I seem to be bringing this up more and more lately, maybe because some guys are having to say increasingly outlandish things to get noticed. The funniest thing about this situation is that these critics are sometimes guys who, when they resided in the dressing room, complained loudly about this very practice.

I have come to accept, albeit reluctantly, that there is a price we have to pay for winning and playing attractive cricket. If our knockers ever see or perceive a weakness, they're going to come down extra hard on us. Of course, they have a right to be critical, but I would have thought they also have an obligation to be perceptive and even-handed, too. Sometimes I don't think they manage that. That some of those commentators are ex-players makes this imbalance so much harder to take.

buzz about it, we have a pretty fair record in the Boxing Day Test over the past eight seasons (eight wins out of eight!), and then we will head to Sydney as a group and enjoy New Year's Eve on the harbour. It's a great week, one of my favourite times of the year.

As a kid, I used to lap up every ball of the Melbourne Test. Christmas Day was fantastic, and then the next day I'd be perched in front of the television the moment Nine's coverage began. As a teenage cricketer, one of my biggest ambitions was to play in a Boxing Day Test, to experience the huge crowd and play at one of sport's great stadiums. Having done it once — in 1995–96, the Test in which Muttiah Muralitharan was no-balled for throwing by Darrell Hair — I wanted to do it again and again. The thrill has never been diminished, and I've been lucky enough to have had a bit of success, too, most notably the last time we played India here, in 2003–04. I made 257 in that game, my highest Test score. Last season there was nearly 90,000 there on day one, even though the weather was ordinary.

I think every Aussie cricketer who's played a Test in Melbourne experiences the same adrenalin rush. To walk on to a packed MCG with thousands of fans clapping and cheering sends tingles up and down your spine. I heard Hoggy say that he's been dreaming about it all his cricket life, and that he wouldn't care if he was 12th man, just so long as he was a part of it. I'm confident he'll be playing, and that he'll do a good job for us.

My two favourite Tests in a cricket year are the first one of the Australian summer at the Gabba and the Boxing Day Test at the 'G'. I love the build-up to the Brisbane Test. We usually have four or five days, with the sun on our backs, to work hard and sharpen our skills before the first ball is bowled. Melbourne is, almost invariably, the biggest game of the year. This season, because of the unusual schedule that has meant we haven't played a Test for a month, I feel as if I'm getting the best of both worlds. In a way, this upcoming Test has the same start-of-the-summer atmosphere I usually associate with Brisbane. I've had a couple of weeks off when all I did cricket-wise was some fitness work at home, then I scored some runs in the Chappell–Hadlee Trophy, and now I'm really keen to enjoy another big Test match.

The Indians will go into the match battle-hardened after a tough series at home against Pakistan, but maybe their preparation was thrown out just a little by the fact that the one tour game before the first Test was abandoned due to rain. Because of lousy weather, their match against Victoria involved just 48 overs, during which they scored 4–133 (Sourav Ganguly 59, Rahul Dravid 38 not out). Other than that, their cricket time in Australia has been restricted to the indoor nets.

On paper, India's batting order — starring as it does Sachin Tendulkar, VVS Laxman, Dravid, Ganguly and Virender Sehwag (if he's selected) — will be the strongest we've faced in a while. As I said to the media today, if we can restrict the top half of their batting order I think we will have gone a long way towards winning the series. Furthermore, there has again been some talk from their camp about how they are going to be aggressive and how they won't back down against us. When I was asked about this, I avoided the issue a little, though not entirely. I looked back to the last time we played a series in Australia, 2003–04, when the first Test was drawn, then they beat us at the Adelaide Oval before we squared things up in Melbourne.

'We did over-attack some of their players just the little bit,' I conceded. 'Back to Adelaide, in particular, we probably let them score a few too many runs.'

Being aggressive is usually a good thing, though not always. We are aware of that; it will be interesting to see if our opponents are similarly savvy. They didn't always get it right when we beat them in those one-dayers a couple of months ago.

One bloke who might be on edge on Wednesday will be Sourav Ganguly, who is about to play his 100th Test. I can remember how I felt going into my 100th Test, how I was quite nervous and put a bit more pressure on myself. But he's a class player more than capable of making a big score to mark his special milestone. The century he made at the Gabba four years ago, on a wicket with a bit of seam and bounce in it, was proof of that.

We'll be doing all we can to ruin his party. These days, England, South Africa and India are the big Test series for me. It is very satisfying to play against and beat any one of that trio, and I truly don't know if one is more satisfying to beat than another — it really depends on the circumstances. After the Ashes loss in 2005, we certainly enjoyed thrashing England next time around, and because it was the first time in 35 years, it was exhilarating to win in India in 2004. Right at this moment, I'd say that in some ways, our rivalry with Kumble's team might even be more intense than that which we've had with Poms. The memory of playing in front of those big crowds on the sub-continent a couple of months back, with all the emotion and tumult, is quite a spur — and it's a shared memory for us, which accentuates the bond of mateship that has for a long time been a feature of our group. We're determined, once again, to get the job done. Our aim is to get on top of them early, put the pressure on, and be relentless for the rest of the summer.

SUNDAY, DECEMBER 30

First Test, Australia v India, at Melbourne (December 26–29): Australia 343 (PA Jaques 66, ML Hayden 124; Z Khan 4–94, A Kumble 5–84) and 7–351 dec (PA Jaques 51, MJ Clarke 73) defeated **India** 196 (SR Tendulkar 62; B Lee 4–46, SR Clark 4–28) and 161 by 337 runs

The weather wasn't flash leading into this year's Melbourne Test, which meant that when we arrived at the ground on Boxing Day morning we knew the wicket would have some moisture in it and that, as a consequence, batting wouldn't be easy for at least the first hour or two. The curator told us that the square had been covered for three of the five days going into the game, but we could see some pretty significant cracks in the pitch even before a ball was bowled, which made me wonder if it would hold up once the moisture dissipated. However it might play, the wicket didn't look so potentially dangerous that it induced us to play four quicks; nor did it convince me that I should do anything other than bat first if I won the toss.

I'm a captain who usually likes to bat first if the coin lands my way. My biggest problem is that I haven't been too good at winning Test-match tosses. In the 37 Tests in which I was captain before this game in Melbourne, I'd been successful at the toss only 14 times, a 'success' rate of 38 per cent. I'd only twice sent the opposition in: New Zealand at Christchurch in 2005, when we won by 10 wickets; and controversially at Edgbaston later that same year, when we lost by two runs after England made 407 on the first day.

It's not that I'm blindly opposed to asking the other team to bat first, more just a case that I need a really good reason to do so. While scoring runs might be difficult on the first morning, if you get through that period you can usually exploit the best batting conditions of the match. Here in Melbourne, there was every indication the wicket was going to deteriorate as the game went on, and I certainly didn't fancy batting fourth against the spinners on a wearing fifth-day pitch. All reports were that the square had been below its best all season, and we had a fair idea, even though there was a fair amount of moisture in it on the first morning, that the track would play lower and slower as the game went on. And while it had no impact on my thinking, I did note that India had selected two slow men, so I had no doubt they

A TOUGH DECISION

An appalling sidelight to the first Test was the dreadful news from Pakistan that their former prime minister, Benazir Bhutto, was assassinated on December 27 while campaigning for the country's upcoming general election. This, of course, is a human tragedy that goes far beyond sport, but it does have ramifications for us in a cricketing sense because the Australian team is scheduled to play three Tests and five one-day internationals in Pakistan from next March. Reading of the murder and then seeing images of the rioting and security clampdown that followed showed clearly how at least parts of Pakistan have become seriously unstable.

I have absolutely no idea what impact the assassination of Mrs Bhutto will have on the total security situation in Pakistan, but it is understandable, surely, that I should have serious doubts about touring there in the current circumstances. Part of me will never easily relinquish an opportunity to play for Australia, and another part is comfortable with accepting whatever guidance we receive from cricket authorities, security experts, the Australian Cricketers' Association and the Australian Government. Such advice has never let us down in the past. If we have to play at a neutral venue, as we did in 2002, then so be it.

There is, however, another part of me that keeps asking whether touring Pakistan in the current climate is worth it. It is easy for those who won't be going to say we have an obligation to the game and to Pakistan, but I have obligations to those close to me — and to myself — that I also must consider. I have enjoyed touring Pakistan in the past and I would hate to see Pakistani cricket diminished because of something over which the cricket people there have no control, but if I can't be comfortable in my own mind that we'll be okay, then there's a chance I won't be going even if the tour in March proceeds. I'll listen to all the advice, but in the end the final decision over my involvement will be mine.

would have batted first if their captain, Anil Kumble, called correctly.

He didn't, and then Matthew Hayden and Phil Jaques strode out to win us the game. I really don't think it's too big a statement to suggest that our domination of this Test was built on the first 142 minutes of day one, when Haydos and Jaquesy put together a brilliant opening partnership of 135 despite the surface playing awkwardly. Even though India fought back to have us 9–337 at stumps, thanks largely to Kumble's five wickets, we had an advantage we never looked like relinquishing.

Haydos' hundred was his sixth century in his past seven Melbourne Tests, and might have been the best of them. Since 2001, the only time he failed to score a hundred in an MCG Test was in 2004, when he made 9 and 56 not out against Pakistan. He was aggressive and decisive in his shot selection and running between wickets, taking every single and turning the strike around so the Indian bowlers could never get into a groove. To the quicks, he focused on playing straight, and when the spinners came on he went straight for his trademark sweep shot, getting the ball down to backward square no matter what length his opponents bowled. Jaquesy was a terrific foil, efficiently putting the bad ball away and never getting ruffled if a delivery misbehaved. Phil has ended up playing five innings in Test cricket in 2007, for scores of 100, 150, 68, 66 and 51.

Day two was the Brett Lee and Stuart Clark show, as the pair ran through the Indian batting line-up to give us a first-innings lead of 147. Both finished with four wickets, Bing through his pace and bounce on a track that two years ago wouldn't have suited him, and Sarfraz through his typically relentless accuracy. Sure it's popular, but I have always been hesitant to label Sarf as 'McGrath-like', because it's a tough call inviting anyone to cope with the pressures of such a comparison, but I have to concede that his methods are similar and similarly effective. He gives the batsmen no breathing space, and on a pitch such as this, where it was impossible to ever feel that you were truly 'in', his skill and bowling nous were wonderful assets.

The key wicket, as always against India, was Sachin Tendulkar, and in the first innings Sarf did the job after the maestro had played superbly to score 62. Tendulkar's clash with Bing was fantastic sport, as he showed an innovative streak that his colleagues couldn't match, and he was immediately aggressive when Brad Hogg came on to bowl. But the mood changed when Sarf came back for his second spell. Eleven consecutive deliveries from the big quick went scoreless, and then he bowled exactly the right line and length, Tendulkar went for a shot that wasn't on (even for him), and all he could do was chop the ball back on to his stumps. It was a memorable moment: big MCG crowd, two great cricketers going head to head in a battle that could well decide the game, and our man came through.

Another big dismissal for us on that second day was that of Sourav Ganguly, who fell to a superb Brad Hogg delivery just when it seemed he might be going to mark his 100th Test match with an important innings. Early on, Hoggy copped a fair amount of stick from the Indian batsmen, who had clearly decided at their pre-Test team meeting to attack our 'new' spinner from the moment he came on to bowl. But while his final bowling figures in this innings (2–82 from 21 overs) might not have looked too flash, I was reasonably happy with the way he went. The sheer joy he exhibited when he took any of his four wickets was a big buzz for us in itself. After Hoggy's first six overs went for 40 runs, Adam Gilchrist and I discussed the way the Indians were playing him, and we agreed that the best tactic was to persevere with him, in the hope that he would get a wicket or two and gain some confidence. If you've only played a handful of Tests in 12 years it would have to be impossible, initially at least, to feel overly comfortable when finally called upon. The fact that when Hoggy finally got his chance he found

THREE OF A KIND

There were three significant milestones passed during the first Test that in each instance highlighted the cricket ability and magnificent durability of the men involved. The sheer numbers, and the fact few players in the game's history have managed to achieve them, help explain why the Australian team has been successful in recent years ...

Matthew Hayden became the fifth Australian to score 8000 Test runs, after Allan Border, Steve Waugh, Mark Waugh and me.

Brett Lee became the sixth Australian bowler to take 250 Test wickets, after Dennis Lillee, Craig McDermott, Shane Warne, Glenn McGrath and Jason Gillespie.

Adam Gilchrist completed his 396th Test dismissal, breaking Ian Healy's Australian record for most keeping dismissals and moving him into second-place all-time behind South Africa's Mark Boucher.

All three guys are winners, no doubt about it. They want to be the best they can be, and leave no stone unturned with their preparation. Over the past two years, for example, Brett has paid a lot of attention to the way he gets ready for matches, through things such as ice baths and massage, and the way he uses his time between games to get away and relax. Life has changed a lot for him since he became a father on the eve of the Ashes series last year, and he really enjoys spending time with his family away from the game, especially because he knows he can do that without compromising his cricket.

Matty is a batsman who doesn't have to hit a thousand balls at every training session to feel like he's fully prepared. He would rather walk out to the middle, sit on the pitch, and visualise what he hoped would happen the next day rather than spend another hour in the nets just for the sake of it. Gilly, in contrast, is someone who needs a lot of volume. This is especially true with his wicketkeeping. Despite his extraordinary success with the bat, Gilly has always seen himself as a keeper first and is very proud of his record with the gloves. Even on the rare occasions when he is finding runs hard to find, he believes that if he works hard on his keeping his batting will come good as well.

The trio's common trait is that they are all super competitive cricketers who are constantly seeking ways to improve. That philosophy has been a key factor in their success — and in Australia's success as a team, too.

himself bowling to Tendulkar, one of the greatest players of spinners in history, only added to the challenge. The more this game went, the better he bowled. Knocking over Ganguly with one of the best flippers you'll ever see must have helped him, and two days later he snared Ganguly again and Yuvraj Singh, too, which I'm sure will boost his confidence even further going into next week's Sydney Test.

I enjoyed the way we batted the Indians out of the game on the third day, with everyone bar the captain making a contribution as we set them 499 to win. Obviously, I didn't enjoy having a twin failure — the first time for more than six years, I'm told, that I failed to reach double figures in either innings of a Test — but at least I picked a good time to do it, when the rest of the batting order performed superbly. It's been one of the strong characteristics of this team in recent times, how if one player is off his game his mates cover for him. In this instance, Haydos and Jaquesy were excellent again and then Michael Clarke was especially impressive as the boys set up a declaration that gave us six sessions plus eight overs to bowl them out. We didn't get a wicket before the close of play on day three, but I went to bed that night knowing that only an unexpected change in the weather could prevent us going one-up in the series. On that wicket, against our bowlers, no team in the world was going to last two days or get 500.

It was all over midway through the final session of day four, the result of a superb bowling and fielding performance that had commentators using words such as 'demolition' and 'suffocation' to describe the manner of our win. In Tests in Australia, we've become used to being able to blast teams out, using aggressive fields including plenty of slips and one or two gullies, but here we had to do things differently. The ability of our bowlers to adapt was excellent — an example of this is how Mitchell Johnson took a string of wickets at the end of the second innings by bowling around the wicket and using reverse swing to move the ball away from the right handers — and the support they got from the fieldsmen was very important. This was perhaps best captured by Mike Hussey's dive and throw to the non-striker's end from cover to run out of Harbhajan, who didn't face a ball in their second innings.

Afterwards, everyone was quick to bag the way Rahul Dravid batted for the tourists, and it is true he struggled, but I wish more had been made of the way we bowled to him. The thing with Dravid (a man who has scored nearly 10,000 Test runs) is that when he is out of touch he looks as bad a player as anyone going around, so he can become an easy target. Virender Sehwag, one of the best openers in the game when he's on song but out of the Indian team for this Test, is the same. Dravid was fighting himself all time, while we were relentless, never giving him an opportunity to sneak a cheap single. If a class player such as Dravid can only score 21 runs from 180 balls in the game then obviously our bowlers were doing a few things right. Going into the series, there had been a few doubts raised about our attack, given that we are without Warne and McGrath, and also Stuart MacGill and Jason Gillespie, but the guys responded exceptionally well.

This was especially true of Brett Lee, who right at this moment is a bowler completely on top of his game. Bing now has an extraordinary ability — whenever we talk about a specific tactic we need him to implement — to deliver exactly what we're after. Throughout the summer so far, if we spoke about unsettling a batsman with bouncers, or setting him up this way or that, then Bing was good enough to do exactly what we asked.

Of course, when you're confronting an outstanding batting line-up like this Indian side, no matter how well you implement a game plan it won't always come off. But Brett does have the golden touch. In the first innings of this Test, VVS Laxman ducked a bouncer that was quick but didn't quite lift as the startled batsman expected; it hit him on the gloves and I was able to snare the catch. In the second, Bing produced some genuinely fast bowling that unsettled Sachin Tendulkar, and finally nailed his man when Tendulkar flashed at a quick one that pitched just short of a length, just outside the off stump, and edged a catch to Gilly. We'd talked about getting him out that way, and it was so beautiful to see the plan come true.

It was certainly a comprehensive Test victory, one of the most clinical over a top-level opponent that I've been involved in — and especially satisfying given that it was achieved on a slow pitch that wouldn't have been out of place if it had been transplanted to the subcontinent. After the game, I described the surface as 'the hardest to bat on of any of my Tests in Australia'.

That was no overstatement. Sure, it was possible to survive, but the lack of pace and bounce in the track from as early as the second hour of day one was alarming, far removed from what I used to think of as a 'typical' MCG wicket. In 21st-century cricket, where a dynamic new 20-over form of the game is coming into vogue, it can't be good playing a showpiece Test on a pitch that just doesn't make for attractive cricket, and I hope that something can be done to put more speed into it for future matches. To me a deck that prevents fast men from bowling decent bouncers and results in edges not carrying through to the slips is not what Test cricket is about. I appreciate that the groundstaff had their troubles in the lead-up because of the rain, but this is not the first slow wicket I've played on in Melbourne in recent times. It seems to me that the decline in the MCG square dates back to when they started using 'drop-in' pitches, and my fear remains that the use of such drop-in pitches will continue to diminish the unique character of the major

Australian grounds where they've been used. It's a problem that needs to be addressed.

As was inevitable, ever since the final wicket fell yesterday afternoon, there has been a lot of talk outside the Australian dressing room about the fact that we're now just one short of the world record 16 consecutive Test-match victories achieved by the Steve Waugh-led Australians between October 1999 and March 2001. Our run started in the Boxing Day Test against South Africa two years ago, and has involved Tests against South Africa, Bangladesh, England, Sri Lanka and India. Our last Test defeat occurred at Trent Bridge in England in August 2005.

We know we're close to a special achievement, something that reflects a spell of sustained excellence, but we didn't talk about it at all in the lead-up to this Test, and I'll be doing my best to see that embargo continues as best as possible between now and Sydney. Of course, 17 or more would be a record we'd be extremely proud of, if we manage to make it, but if we get ahead of ourselves the opportunity will surely slip away. It sounds like a cliché, I know, but we have to take things one game at a time. Otherwise, even though they might not have shown their best form here, a good team such as India will jump all over us.

TUESDAY, JANUARY 1

Ever since the second wicket fell in Australia's second innings in Melbourne, much has made of the fact that I have been dismissed a few times in Test cricket by India's Harbhajan Singh. When I was caught by Rahul Dravid at slip off a ball that held its line

THE WILL TO WIN

The freshness of youth can be terrific but in many circumstances you can't beat experience. A great player knows that if he plays a certain way for a long period of time he's going to get runs. Very few young players can resist the temptation to play the big flashy drive when they're on 20; their thought process says, *If I let that go and don't try to hit the four will I get another opportunity?* They might get away with it for a Test or two, maybe even a series, but eventually this precociousness will catch up with them, then the confidence will drop, the runs will dry up, luck will desert them and the selectors will give them a spell. Young bowlers are the same: they can only bowl their way.

When the rookies come back, though, they'll be wiser, and if they have the talent they'll develop the champion's qualities they used to think they had from the start. Brett Lee, Michael Clarke and Andrew Symonds were all rough diamonds at the start of their international careers. If you've been in the fire and successfully come out the other side, you do so armed with confidence, patience and the will to win. As a team, for a few years now, I believe we've had that will to win to an extent other teams have not. Our new challenge is to sustain that advantage, even without our recently retired warriors.

Part of this involves the pure joy we bring to our cricket. Simply put, we love being out there, in the heat of battle, playing the game we love. Training is a buzz, too. So is the realisation that we are constantly learning as we go.

This happy, positive mindset is a feature of the Australian team, and it's a trait carried by the successful state teams across the country. Our coaches enjoy working with us. Cricket is fun. We know how lucky we are to be wearing the baggy green.

One thing I keep reminding the boys about is that we have to keep working harder than the other teams in world cricket. At the same time, we must never forget that while the work we do to sustain our ranking as the world's No. 1 team is hard and long, it's never a chore. When we stop enjoying what we're doing is when we'll come back to the field. There are plenty of worse things we could be doing, for far less reward.

and bounced a bit, it was Harbhajan's 250th Test wicket, and the sixth occasion in seven Tests that I've fallen to the off-spinner.

I've actually had a few experiences during my career when bowlers have had some decent spells against me. Sri Lanka's Chaminda Vaas got me out in three of my first four Test innings, back in 1995–96. In a sequence of four straight Ashes Tests for me, one in 1998–99 then three in 2001, Darren Gough knocked me over six times in a row. New Zealand's Shane Bond was too good for me in six successive ODIs against New Zealand in 2002 and 2003. When I've been in the middle of one of these sequences, I tried not to let it bug me, and I don't think it really has, but I will confess that I have got a little irritated every time I've been reminded that during the Test in Melbourne, after that second-innings dismissal, Harbhajan had a bit of a dig when he was interviewed by the media. 'Is there a deficiency in Ricky Ponting's technique that you can exploit?' he was asked.

'He hasn't batted long enough against me,' he replied. 'So I don't know.'

That was good. 'He got me first ball last week,' I replied when I was asked if he had my measure. 'So I have got some improving to do.' What Harbhajan didn't mention is that five of those six dismissals in Tests occurred in the one series, back in 2001, when I was out of nick and he was amazing, taking 32 wickets in five innings. So he hadn't got me out in a Test for more than six years before Melbourne. And he's only dismissed me twice in 19 one-day internationals, one of which was the 2003 World Cup final when the pressure was really on and I made a big hundred.

There is no doubt he's a very good off-spinner, and it looks like we've now got another good little battle on our hands. I find him awkward to play, because like Murali but unlike just about everyone else, he's an offie who can spin the ball the other way.

We've certainly never had such a bowler in all the years I've been playing in Australian cricket, so to face a bowler of this kind at Test level is always going to be a challenge. That Harbhajan is enigmatic as well as exceptional only adds to the adventure.

At least Harbhajan was talking himself up, unlike Anil Kumble, who came up with the Indians' 'limited preparation' before the Test as the reason for their defeat. India's one practice match was a washout, and this led Kumble to say that he and his men 'certainly require more acclimatisation when we come to Australia'.

I think this is an ordinary excuse. India played three Test matches against Pakistan between November 22 and December 12, so it's not as if they hadn't played any competitive cricket leading into the tour. Furthermore, the MCG wicket was a slow one, so they could hardly say they were the victims of unusual bounce. But it's become the norm in Australia for visitors to blame a dud preparation if they struggle in the first Test of a series. I remember England last year saying something similar even though they actually arrived in Australia before we returned from the Champions Trophy in India. The thing is, your skills don't suddenly leave you at the start of a new tour. It's a fact of modern cricket that you won't get weeks to settle in before a series or tournament starts, and it has become a skill to be right and ready when the first ball is bowled.

We have decided to announce early that we'll be going into the second Test with an unchanged XI. India, meanwhile, are apparently pondering whether to recall the dangerous Virender Sehwag to open the innings. Sehwag has been out of form, but after Rahul Dravid's uncertain display as an opener in Melbourne, it wouldn't surprise me if they made that call. That would allow Dravid to bat at No. 3, where the likelihood is he'd be much more comfortable. The experienced Indian batting line-up has come in for some criticism from their media, who thought they were too defensive, but I think they should be giving more credit to our bowlers, for the way they stuck to their plans and kept the pressure on throughout the game.

The weather forecasts aren't particularly promising, but I'm still certainly looking forward to this Test. I love batting here in Sydney, and I've had a lot of luck when I've captained Australia at the SCG: four Tests for four wins. I'm training hard and even though I had those twin failures in Melbourne I feel like I'm batting well. Hopefully a big score is just around the corner.

TUESDAY, JANUARY 8

Second Test, Australia v India, at Sydney (January 2–6): Australia 463 (RT Ponting 55, A Symonds 162*, GB Hogg 79, B Lee 59; RP Singh 5–124, A Kumble 4–106) and 7–401 dec (ML Hayden 123, MEK Hussey 145*, A Symonds 61) defeated India 532 (R Dravid 53, VVS Laxman 109, SR Tendulkar 154*; B Lee 5–119) and 210 (S Ganguly 51) by 122 runs

For now, I'm going to keep this post to the cricket, because you don't have to be Einstein to know that the controversy the second Test generated — through India's loss, the ordinary umpiring, the incident on day three that led to Harbhajan Singh's three-Test suspension and then Anil Kumble's comments at the post-Test media conference, in which he said Australia doesn't adhere to the spirit of the game — has some way to run. Right at this moment, I can't be sure the series will be completed, because yesterday the Indian camp threatened to go home unless Harbhajan's ban was overturned. The suspension came as a result of a complaint I submitted following an on-field comment

Harbhajan made to Andrew Symonds during the third day's play that we believe to be racist. It was a great Test, our 16th win in a row, but the victory has been substantially squeezed into the background. I won't dodge the controversies but, as far as this diary entry is concerned, I'll leave them for another day.

It's such a huge shame that the Test ended so bitterly, because amid all the drama and animosity there was some genuinely outstanding cricket moments. On the opening day, the Australian dressing room revelled in the batting of Brad Hogg, who came to the wicket when our score was 6–134 and turned things around in a sensational partnership with Andrew Symonds. I doubt there was an Australian fan anywhere in the world who would have begrudged Hoggy a hundred, such was the clear joy he got from his success, but behind that animated body language were a cool nerve and a lot of commonsense.

Symmo did get a couple of fortunate breaks with the umpiring, but he was good enough to take advantage of his luck, and scored his second Test century. A lot of cricketers get umpiring decisions that go their way in Test matches; the 'lucky' players are the ones good enough and smart enough to take advantage. Symmo's total faith in his natural game was on full display, and the way he maintained his concentration was magnificent. He admitted later that he never looked at the scoreboard until late in the day, and was pleasantly surprised when he did look up to see just how many runs he and the team had scored. Hoggy wasn't dismissed until the total had reached 307, and Symmo was unbeaten on 137 and we'd reached 7–376 by stumps. I doubt there have been too many more entertaining first days in the history of Test cricket in Sydney.

India were well served by their chief wicket-takers — RP Singh and Anil Kumble — and also by their new young quick, Ishant Sharma, who was the unlucky bowler when Symmo was

MR CRICKET'S STATISTICAL ADVENTURE

Mike Hussey's remarkable Test career continues to go from strength to strength, as here in Sydney he completed his eighth Test century in just his 20th Test.

The cricket statisticians must love him. My co-author tells me he has now scored a Test hundred at each of the six major Australian grounds, a good trick considering he only made his Test debut a little more than two years ago. This is a feat I've managed, along with Mark Taylor, David Boon, Mark Waugh, Justin Langer and Matt Hayden. Even more impressive is the fact that Huss has now scored 2120 runs in Test cricket, at the incredible average of 84.80. To put that stat in perspective: of all batsman who have played 10 or more Test innings, only Sir Donald Bradman, who scored 6996 runs at 99.94 in 52 Tests, is in front of Huss. Third spot is taken by a New Zealander, Charles Dempster, who averaged 65.73 in 10 Tests, followed by Australia's Sid Barnes, with a 63.06 average from 13 Test matches.

Of batsman who played 30 Test innings, South Africa's Graeme Pollock (2256 runs at 60.97) is third, with the West Indies' George Headley (2190 runs at 60.83) and England's Herbert Sutcliffe (4555 runs at 60.73) the only other men to average more than 60. Huss really is mixing in some very special company.

given his reprieve. Harbhajan did get me out again, but he was lucky to do so, and he also trapped Michael Clarke, but he also conceded a lot of runs. Hoggy played him beautifully. 'It was just fantastic to have a partnership with my good mate Andrew and to knock a couple of records out during the day,' he said to the press gallery after he was invited to the first day's media conference. Their stand was a record for the seventh wicket in Australia–India Tests and for all Tests at the SCG, the third highest seventh-wicket partnership made in Tests in Australia, and the fourth highest seventh-wicket stand made in Tests by an Australian pair.

On day two, Symmo went on to 162 not out, Brett Lee got within five runs of his highest Test score, and we totalled 463. By stumps, India were 3–216, VVS Laxman had made another beautiful century in Sydney (it was his third, after 167 in 1999–2000 and 178 in 2003–04), and Sachin Tendulkar was 9 not out. Bing had started the Indian innings by bowling an absolutely brilliant yorker to Wasim Jaffer, and then he thought he had Laxman lbw when the batsman was only 17. But as Symmo had done the day before, Laxman was good enough to exploit the tight decision that went in his favour. One five-ball sequence from Mitchell Johnson went for 18 runs — 4, 4, 2, 4, 4 — the first four shots through the covers, the last one a glorious flick off his pads to deep backward square. Late in the day, about 10 overs before stumps, India were 1–183, with Laxman past his hundred and Dravid going along slowly but seemingly entrenched, but then Mitchell Johnson got Dravid to edge a catch to Matt Hayden in the slips. Six balls later, Laxman fell to Brad Hogg and we went to bed that night with the Test intriguingly poised. I was pleased we got those two late wickets, which I saw as a reward for our fitness and tenacity.

One thing I constantly remind the guys about is that our body language and our intensity need to be exactly the same regardless of the time of day or what the scoreboard says. We know how just a couple of balls can change a game. Belief is such a virtue in elite sport — if your preparation and game plan are right and you keep believing in what you're doing then things can work for you. Maybe not immediately, but eventually. I think the pressure we exert on opposition teams, which comes from our relentlessness, is one of the main reasons we win so often. We put teams under pressure for longer periods of time than they put us under pressure. That period late on the second day, when we dismissed Dravid and Laxman, was a very important ingredient in our ultimate victory.

Day three, however, belonged to Tendulkar, who batted for almost the entire day, finishing up unbeaten on 154 when the Indian first innings ended just before the close of play. His defensive play from the first ball of the day was immaculate (reviving memories of his double hundred here in 2003–04, when he never played a cover drive for the best part of two days), and we knew quickly he was planning to bat for as long as possible. For me, if a great player looks balanced and water-tight when he keeps out the good deliveries early in his innings then the likelihood is that he's going to produce an important knock, and that was certainly the way Sachin operated during the first hour. His partnership with Harbhajan was a crucial one, because when we had them 7–345 we felt we were just one more wicket away from nabbing an important lead.

That stand evolved after Adam Gilchrist grabbed his 400th Test dismissal (in his record-breaking 94th consecutive Test), and it was one of those situations where, on a good batting track, we felt our best strategy was to give Tendulkar singles to get at the inferior batsman. But Harbhajan, who we know can bat, played pretty well. It was during this partnership that the confrontation between Symmo and Harbhajan occurred, which led to the report of alleged racial abuse being lodged with match referee Mike Procter. At stumps, we were 0–13, behind by 56, and with rain predicted it seemed that a draw was the most likely result. While we hadn't ruled out a 16th straight win, my message to the boys that night was that our first objective was to bat the Indians out of the Test. We'd give them nothing. My No. 1 priority was to win the series, and if we came out of this game one-up with two to play, one of them in Perth, then I was confident we'd achieve what we most needed to do.

Of course, the lead news story to come out of the third day was the reporting of Harbhajan, but once that was done and the decision was made that an inquiry would be held after the Test was completed, we had to forget about it as best we could and get on with the game. Inevitably, the media wanted us to talk about it, but we'd been advised by Cricket Australia to stay quiet for the moment, which we all knew was the right thing to do, at least in the short term.

Before I could think too seriously about a declaration we had to bat well in our second innings. Both teams had made big totals in the first innings, but only because of crucial late-order partnerships, so we had plenty to do. Fortunately for us, Matt Hayden and Mike Hussey both batted superbly, making big hundreds. I managed only a single, before Harbhajan got me first ball again, this time when I indecisively pushed forward and managed only to lob an easy catch off the leading edge to Laxman close in on the offside. It was an ordinary shot, a miserable lapse in concentration, and my mood wasn't helped when I saw later how the bowler had marked my dismissal — with a long sprint and an old man's roll on the ground which I guess was his version of a footballer's celebration after an important goal. Most people got a chuckle out of Harbhajan's performance and if he wants to do that sort of thing then fine. He got me out again; he could do whatever he wanted. But strangely the people who thought his reaction was terrific later got into us for 'over celebrating' after we won the Test. Why the double standard?

After I was dismissed, I spent a significant part of the day acting as Haydos' runner after the big fella hurt his thigh while he was batting. I guess the exercise was good, and it was nice to get a close-up view of our two left-handers dominating the game, but at least once or twice I couldn't help thinking, *I wish it was me*. Still, I enjoyed being back out there again. I guess I just love the game — the competition, the one-on-one battles. When I'm batting, I love the idea of it being two against 11. In this case my mindset was that I was definitely a part of it, three against 11, if you like, and I resolved to do everything I could to help Haydos and Huss bat us into an impregnable position.

While we do practise running between the wickets at training, we never rehearse running for someone else. Once I got out there, the first thing the three of us clarified was exactly who was calling when, and the system we adopted was simple: when I was at square leg, with Haydos on strike, the striker and non-striker did the calling. When I was at the non-striker's end, with Haydos resting his injured leg at square leg, Huss and I worked together. It can be hard being a runner, maintaining a concentration you're not used to, and I found it extremely nerve-racking. It's a little weird, too, when you stand at square-leg, waiting to run — your perspective of the ground is different to if you were at the batting crease. You're forever thinking that a ball has been hit into a gap … or maybe a fieldsman has it covered … you have to back the call the blokes in the middle have made, even though your instinct might think otherwise. We seemed to get it right, at least most of the time. Haydos' century was his 29th in Tests, level with The Don.

BECAUSE THE WEATHER HAD held up on day four, we went into the final day pretty confident we could win. Again, there were concerns about the rain, but it stayed away and after we took the first six wickets in 40 overs I thought we were going to continue our winning run. Laxman, out lbw, and Tendulkar, bowled off an inside edge, both fell to Stuey Clark. Throughout the day, the blokes who'd been with me throughout my time as Test captain — Gilly, Haydos and Symmo — kept reminding us about the third

Test against Sri Lanka in 2004, my first series as skipper, when we won on the last day with eight deliveries to spare, Shane Warne taking the ninth wicket in what could have been the third-last over, then Michael Kasprowicz getting the winner seven balls later. Here, into the last hour, Kumble and Dhoni defended really well during a seventh-wicket stand that lasted about 90 minutes, and none of our frontline bowlers could break through.

I know my nickname is 'Punter', but early in the day I'd thought it was best to be conservative with the declaration (closing 15 minutes before lunch, leaving India needing 333 in 72 overs) and then I felt an obligation to give our leading bowlers every chance to get the key wickets during the dramatic final session. It wasn't until there were 30 or 40 minutes remaining that I went into gambling mode, backing Andrew Symonds and then, famously, calling on Michael Clarke to get us home. Symmo had been as dangerous as anyone when he bowled some overs earlier in the innings, and my faith in him was rewarded when he broke through with 10.4 overs to go, trapping Dhoni lbw when the batsman didn't offer a shot.

Harbhajan and Kumble mostly stonewalled for the next eight overs, while I tried Hogg and Lee and then Clarke from the northern end. When I invited Pup to have a crack, it was his first over of the innings and he cheekily muttered, 'Thanks mate, you've given me just enough time to win a Test match.'

My instincts said otherwise, that we weren't going to be quite good enough to get there. But Pup is a good bowler, in part because he backs himself every time. 'Give me a bowl, skipper, give me a bowl,' he's always saying. 'I'll get us a wicket.' I'll never bag a bowler for wanting to bowl all the time. Like Darren Lehmann, who also bowled left-arm, Pup is a smart cricketer, and just as 'Boof' did, I think that in the future Pup will develop into a reliable Test and one-day support bowler.

We'd identified Kumble as a late-order batsman who handles the quicker stuff better than the spinners, but throughout this dramatic afternoon he proved us wrong. With our spinners firing the ball into the bowlers' footmarks and catchers around the bat, I thought we were a big chance for a bat-pad, but his defence was very good, and he concentrated superbly. If they'd held out for a draw, he would have been a hero, the man who saved the day, and maybe the fact he missed out on that played a part in his reaction afterwards.

Pup was on to bowl the 69th over, probably the fourth-last of the Test, unless we bowled quick enough to squeeze a fifth over in (or, less likely, the wickets all fell before then). We knew India would try every tactic imaginable to make sure there were only four.

Afterwards, it was largely forgotten that Pup bowled this first, uneventful over. It was as if he came on and waved his magic wand pronto. Kumble was on strike, and he had no worries with the first two deliveries, and then cut the third for four to take him to 42. With three balls left in the over, we were keen to keep the Indian skipper on strike, so Symmo could have a decent shot at Harbhajan, but after Kumble defended the fourth ball, he pushed the fifth into the offside, backward of point and ran a comfortable single. There were no dramas from the final delivery of the over; with three overs to go we still needed three wickets. The atmosphere, on the field and in the crowd, was pretty tense, though I sensed a resignation among the spectators that the game would end in a draw.

Symmo was bowling around the wicket, slanting the ball across the right-handed Kumble, but though he tried a well-flighted delivery, then a faster, flatter one, the Indian captain was composed. His concentration and dedication to the task of batting out the day were very impressive. When he drove the third ball through mid-wicket he saw the chance for two, to keep the strike, and took it, but for the rest of the over there was no chance for a single, so although time was beating us, at least Pup would be bowling to Harbhajan. All we could do was put a pack of fieldsmen around the bat … and hope for a miracle.

I knew that if we took just got one wicket everything would change. Suddenly, the pressure on the incoming batsman would be enormous, as the fear of defeat would loom horribly large. Pup's first ball pitched perfectly, just short of a length, too close to the off stump to be left alone, and instead of keeping low as most of its predecessors had done, this one kicked up, hit Harbhajan's bottom hand, and speared to first slip, where Mike Hussey grabbed it joyfully. It was Pup's first Test wicket in Australia, and the mood in the group was all about, 'We can win this now!' I started thinking, *He's a lucky bugger, we're a chance here!* And the crowd was right into it, which for us was an exhilarating feeling.

Pup's body language was from the Shane Warne school. He wanted the ball. The new batsman was RP Singh, who'd bowled so well on the first day and had probably spent most of the day hoping desperately that he wouldn't be needed. He walked to the middle like he was following a funeral, took guard, listened to his captain, studied the pitch earnestly and finally faced up … and the ball pitched on the line of off stump, straightened a fraction as Singh played half-forward. His bat was well outside the line, and umpire Benson ruled the ball wouldn't have cleared the bails — it was one of those lbw decisions that umpires in the old days didn't give because the batsmen was a fair distance from the stumps, but more often than not they give them nowadays. I've seen the replay a few times and it sure looks out to me. India were nine-for, the crowd was roaring, Pup was on a hat-trick!

If you'd asked me beforehand if I'd have been thinking about the winning streak if we'd found ourselves in this situation, I would have said that it was definitely in the back of mind. But the truth is I'd forgotten about it. I was 100 percent focused on this game, this victory. We were so close. Out stumbled Ishant Sharma with his two right-handed gloves ... he waited, we waited ... and eventually, slowly, he continued his saunter to the middle. We were absolutely buzzing, knowing that our best chance of victory lay in what was left of *this* over. Kumble had been batting so well; he was odds on to see out the final six balls if the game got to a final over. First ball, Sharma was rapped on the pads, and we stifled an appeal. It was missing leg stump and he was a *long* way forward. Second ball was too short, again on leg-stump line, and the batsman nudged it nervously back up the pitch. Pup walked across and nonchalantly fielded the ball in front of the non-striker. Two balls to go. No way would Kumble take a single. He'd be on the strike for the next over ... if there was a next over.

Sharma patted down the pitch, then looked up and saw his captain coming down to talk to him. He turned around and looked at us, as if he needed permission to leave his crease. We didn't say a word. There were four men close in on the offside, plus a short leg and a short cover. I can't imagine Kumble would have said anything more than just some standard encouragement for his young No. 11; maybe logic behind the chat was about chewing up a little more time and ensuring Sharma was thinking reasonably straight. Then Sharma came back to us at the striker's end, took his stance, and Pup was at him as quickly as he could ...

This one was slightly quicker, and well-pitched up. Sharma's first instinct was to play well forward, hoping to smother the ball, but the delivery was aimed slightly outside off and he had to straighten himself and lean over slightly, bat a fraction from his pad, to reach it. Maybe he should have let it go, but he was committed, and the ball took the outside edge on the half volley

THE CORRECT CALL

Sourav Ganguly's dismissal in India's second innings of the Sydney Test caused a lot of controversy. It came soon after he'd reached his half century, when an edge flew low to Michael Clarke at second slip. Pup caught the ball at ground level, and as he jumped to his feet he flung the ball in the air — in his mind, the catch had definitely been completed. Ganguly stood his ground, umpire Benson walked towards us, and I signalled to him that the catch was good. I did this because Anil Kumble and I had agreed before the series began that we'd take the fieldsman's word on such chances. To me, that is a much more effective system than relying on the video umpire, who — because the TV images are invariably inconclusive — in 99 per cent of cases is obliged to give the batsman the benefit of the doubt.

In this instance, before I gestured to the ump I asked Pup if he was sure he had caught the ball. 'Yes,' he said firmly, 'I'm sure.' Benson gave Ganguly out, and the former Indian captain was clearly unhappy as he walked away. For me, whatever Ganguly's reaction, Pup's call should have been the end of the matter, but instead some commentators tried to make an issue of it, and then at his media conference Kumble used this incident as his main example of how Australia didn't play within the spirit of the game. Apparently, he intends to review our agreement before the next Test in Perth.

Kumble is wrong on this one. I'll take Michael Clarke's word every time. There were a number of umpiring mistakes in this Test, but the Ganguly dismissal was not one of them.

and went smoothly, waist high, to slip. Huss grabbed it, and the party started. Pup ran off towards cover, arm in the air, triumphant; soon we were together in a mass team embrace. Sharma stood his ground for a moment, not quite sure what had happened to him, before the umpire confirmed the inevitable. I'd been fielding in a helmet, close in on the offside, and there was no time to remove it before I was engulfed by jubilant team-mates. As I said, we were bagged by some people for over-celebrating but I really think these critics didn't have a clue. In those few ecstatic moments immediately after the final wicket fell, after five draining days, I reckon we were entitled to get excited, to revel as a team in the moment. It was a huge victory, unexpected because, just 10 minutes earlier, the game was heading towards stalemate. Furthermore, we'd been through quite a bit emotionally in the previous two-and-a-half days, much of it related to the racism row. We'd still come through. When we came out of our scrum, adrenalin pumping through our systems, there were high fives, we hugged some more and a few of us, me included, gestured exuberantly to the Aussie supporters in the crowd, who were almost as excited as we were. As quickly as I could, I'd taken off my helmet and donned the baggy green. Gilly and I, captain and vice-captain, two old pros, had a long embrace mid-pitch. Then we went over and shook hands with our opponents, who had sportingly come out onto the ground. No one had a dig at us about the way we played the game.

Quickly, Mark Taylor, known throughout his cricket career and now as a Channel Nine commentator as 'Tubby', grabbed me for an on-field interview ...

Mark Taylor: 'I've got Ricky Ponting with me. Ricky, you got it dead right ... what a declaration!'

Ricky Ponting: 'I think I told you this morning, Tubby, we were going to have a pretty good game on our hands today. We got about the amount of runs that we wanted in about the amount of time that I thought was going to be right on that wicket. As we saw right through the game, it was a hard wicket to score on, but if you had partnerships going it was a pretty hard wicket (for the bowling team) to defend on as well ...

'Michael Clarke's got the golden touch, hasn't he? The boys are calling him "golden bollocks" at the moment ... he's come on and got three late ones ...

'All the guys today just hung in there and stuck in there, and we knew if we kept them under pressure then we'd be a good chance of winning the game. It was an unbelievable win. That's almost as good as any I've been in.'

Mark Taylor: 'C'mon mate, eight minutes to go ... that's cutting it a little bit fine?'

Ricky Ponting: 'Yeah, the first series I was captain, in Sri Lanka, we won one in the last (sic) over and that came out a few times today. The boys mentioned that a few times ... we knew, you know, we knew we were the only ones who could win the game. When I declared, I thought we were the only team who could win the game, which is what I wanted today. To have to try and survive, to bat out 70 overs on that wicket, was going to be hard work ...'

The interview continued with me giving a big wrap to Symmo's bowling and then Tubby remarked, 'You've retained the trophy ... 16 in a row ... does it get any better than that with this crowd behind you?'

Ricky Ponting: 'I haven't even thought of that 16th one, actually. I haven't had a chance to think about that yet. Just being so wrapped up in that there today. This crowd today has been amazing, as it has been right through the game.

'We go into Perth now with, as you say, a record just around the corner ... a venue we love playing on. I think our bowlers play very well over there and our batsmen are obviously used to those sort of conditions ...

> '*After the two venues we thought the Indians would probably be most dangerous — Melbourne and here — we go to one now that should suit us more …*'

After a little more talk about Pup's incredible last over, Tubby ended the interview with this comment:

> '*Well, mate, congratulations. It's been an unbelievable Test match. There's been a bit of controversy, but you've got through all that. You've got a great win out of it. Well done!*'

I knew we still had the Harbhajan inquiry ahead of us, and I knew if he was found guilty that there'd be considerable debate in the media and the cricket community over the outcome. But if you'd told me at that moment, when we were still out on the field, that within the next 36 hours my integrity and that of the Australian team would be brutally questioned, and that relations between the two camps would apparently deteriorate so much that the rest of the Test series would be in jeopardy, I would have thought you were coming from a different planet. We learned quickly that some of the TV and radio commentary had been negative towards us, but things began to change from the moment Anil Kumble had his dig at the post-game media conference. Then Harbhajan was suspended by Mike Procter, and as a result the Indian authorities posted their threat to abandon the rest of the tour. Fanned by some provocative local reporting and a storm of protest from India, the mood has turned incredibly ugly. Right now, I feel as if the quality and excitement of our win have already been largely forgotten, and that the biggest job ahead for me is not to win the series and 17 Tests straight, but to defend my reputation and the good name of my team.

SATURDAY, JANUARY 12

The media has been calling the controversies of the past week 'the biggest cricket crisis since the match-fixing scandal'. I'll leave it for others to decide just how dire the events have been, but I have to say I've been staggered by some of the more strident criticism we have received, and have also been as much bemused as angered by some of the actions and accusations coming out of the Indian camp. Where it's got really silly was the reaction of the mugs who forced my parents to change their home phone number after they received a series of abusive calls.

Again, I'd like to keep most of my thoughts on the controversy for later. I know it's a huge story that's been page one in newspapers on two continents, and I'm thinking the whole story, from start to however it finishes, will be the obvious chapter one for this book. Let me assure you that it's been a trying time for me, as I became something of a target, with some commentators calling for my head and reports emerging from India that people were burning effigies of me. I never thought I'd arouse this sort of passion. At the same time, I've been reassured by the mountain of support I've received from a wide variety of people — on the street, at the newsagents, the bakery, the golf club, phone calls, texts and emails — many of them from individuals not involved in cricket. It's always good to be reminded who your friends are.

The day after the Test, the tourists were due to visit the Bradman Museum in Bowral on their way to Canberra for a match against an ACT Invitation XI, but instead they stayed an extra 24 hours in their Sydney hotel while their team hierarchy and senior officials met to decide if they wanted the series to continue.

CAUGHT OUT

I want to come back to the whole question of ground-level catches. One talking point to come out of the second day of the Sydney Test concerned my decision to withdraw our appeal over a chance Rahul Dravid nicked to me at second slip during India's first innings. I was sure the ball got to me on the full, but I sensed that as I caught it, with my fingers outstretched, that the ball might have grazed the ground. Because I couldn't be sure that no part of the ball touched the ground as this 'catch' was completed, I motioned to the umpires that the decision should be 'not out'. Afterwards, though, as I quickly looked at the laws of cricket, I wondered if, by the rules of the game, I'd done the right thing. Law 32 (Caught) states that a batsman is out if a fielder holds a 'fair catch' *before* it touches the ground.

So what is a 'fair catch'? I'm no physics expert, but I would imagine that in this situation the force of the ball as it crashes into the hands would compress the fingers and make it at least likely that ball would make contact, however, slight, with the turf. Law 32 states that 'the act of making the catch shall start from the time when a fielder first handles the ball and shall end *when a fielder obtains complete control both over the ball and over his own movement.*' I have deliberately italicised that last part, because I reckon I could argue that if the ball hits my fingers on the full, and the ball only grazes the ground between my fingers, then I have control over it and that the ground has played no part in me achieving that control. However, the law also states that, for

My attitude was that it was up to the Indians to do what they saw as appropriate, but it did seem to me that going home would be an extreme response, no matter how aggrieved they were at the guilty verdict against their man. I also concede that they are entitled to their opinion over the way the second Test was played, but as I keep going back over the game I still can't see how we did anything wrong by the spirit of the game. We played it tough, sure, but as Cricket Australia CEO James Sutherland said, 'It is not tiddlywinks.' The only major incident to come out of either of the first two Tests, the only matter deemed to be worthy of a report, was the Harbhajan incident. Or at least it

a catch to be fairly made, throughout the act of making that catch the ball cannot 'touch the ground, even though the hand holding it does so in effecting the catch'.

So my question is, when did I obtain *complete* control over the ball? If the ground played no part in me controlling the ball, and the ball hit my fingers on the full (that is, I didn't scoop it up on the half volley), then I think I can argue that I had control before it grazed the ground. But I realise you could just as easily argue the other way, that the ball grazed the ground before I had control of it, so maybe the doubt should go — as it did in this instance — to the batsman. Maybe.

There will always be a grey area with ground-level catches, and I know there will be rare instances when a fieldsman will genuinely believe he has made a catch but the video evidence will prove otherwise. But I'm sure the best solution is to take the fieldsman's word. And if a player is subsequently shown to have cheated, then let's make an example of him, rub him out for a while. The game would be better off without him.

Later in the Test, on the final day, there was some debate about a 'catch' I claimed off MS Dhoni, when I caught the ball cleanly and then it touched the ground as I used the hand that was holding the ball to cushion my fall as I dived to the ground. Our appeal was turned down, because the umpire ruled the ball had only hit Dhoni's pad, not his bat, but I can't see how it wouldn't have been ruled a fair catch if he had hit it, because surely I was in control of the ball and my own movement by the time my hand (and the ball) came into contact with the ground.

was until India decided to make a formal complaint against Brad Hogg, who they allege called one of their players a 'bastard' during the game in Sydney. Whether Hoggy said that, and whether it's a crime under the ICC's code of conduct, are things I'll leave for the administrators to work out. It did occur to me, though, not for the first time in this saga, that if that was the worst thing our accusers could come up with, then why were they so put out by our on-field behaviour?

That other members of the Australian team were thinking the same way was underlined by something Stuart Clark said when he gave a press interview last Wednesday. 'Most of the talk (on the field) in the Sydney Test was all pretty light-hearted, anyway,' Sarf remarked. 'And that has been one of the reasons we have all been taken by surprise with what's gone on after.'

I also saw a quote on the internet last night which for me adds further perspective to what happened in Sydney. 'Sometimes things happen at the heat of the moment, but I also admired how desperate they were to win,' Sourav Ganguly said of us in an interview with India's *Star Sports*. 'That's not a bad thing in sport.'

However, I do want the guys in my team to be remembered as being good people as well as great cricketers, so I can see why there is value in us going over the video of some of the incidents from the Sydney Test. We'll be doing that before the first ball is bowled at the WACA. As we keep learning, perception can become reality, and we have to acknowledge that it is possible for observers beyond the boundary rope to misinterpret what is happening on the field, and for those misconceptions to cause trouble. Positive, assertive body language, the way we carry ourselves, working as a 'pack' — these are features we've seen as important parts of our make-up over the past decade, and there's no way we're going to change that. We can't lose that edge, now or ever. But we have to take the opportunities away from the snipers who like to sit back and fire shots at us. Staying at the crease too long after you've been given out never looks good, whatever the emotions going through your head. And in certain circumstances a harmless on-field chat can be misconstrued as a slanging match; in the current climate, we have to try our best to prevent that from occurring.

Coinciding with their protest over the Harbhajan verdict, the Indians were adamant that umpire Steve Bucknor wouldn't be umpiring in the third Test in Perth, because of the mistakes he had made in Sydney. Bucknor was due to stand in Perth with

Asad Rauf from Pakistan, but given the scale of India's protest it came as no surprise to anyone when the ICC announced last Tuesday that Bucknor would be replaced by New Zealand's Billy Bowden. This decision was part of a package that ensured that the tour would continue. The ICC ruled that Harbhajan could keep playing until his appeal before Justice John Hansen of the New Zealand High Court was heard, with the indications being that the hearing won't be staged until after the series is completed. And it was also announced that cricket's No. 1 match referee, Ranjan Madugalle of Sri Lanka, would be at the WACA to chair a pre-Test meeting between Anil Kumble and me, and to support Mike Procter throughout the match.

TUESDAY, JANUARY 15

We know now that Harbhajan's appeal will be heard immediately after the fourth Test, in Adelaide, and we learned yesterday that the Indians have withdrawn their charge against Brad Hogg. That latter development hardly shocked us — I don't think anyone ever really believed that Hoggy was going to be in any trouble. Within the group, we have tried to talk as little as possible about the incidents from Sydney, other than in a special team meeting organised by Cricket Australia that was conducted three days ago, not long after we landed in Perth, but that has been difficult because that is all the media and much of the public wants to talk about. I'd much prefer to focus on the cricket, we have a Test match to win, but I'm constantly being asked about matters unrelated to the game at hand. A number of guys in our line-up have been trying to avoid the same inquisition. One irony is that, because the expectation is that the WACA pitch will help the fast bowlers, neither Harbhajan nor Hoggy is expected to play in this Test.

Another meeting I was part of in the lead-up to the Test was the one at the Hyatt Hotel two days ago that also involved Ranjan Madugalle and Anil Kumble. During the course of what I felt was a fairly amiable chat, Madugalle made the point that we have to always consider the bigger picture, that the game is bigger than any individual, and that as captains we have to make sure we are doing the right thing by the game. There is no harm in re-emphasising these goals. Straight afterwards, we kept our public comments to a minimum but eventually, at the WACA, we two captains did answer the media's questions. 'It's good that Anil and I sat down like two grown men yesterday and had a good chat,' I said. 'I feel a lot happier after yesterday's meeting and I am sure Anil does the same. Both of us have been under a lot of pressure this week.'

Was there any bad blood between the teams?

'I can only go by the word of Anil who said there wasn't,' I replied. 'I said the same thing. No doubt you will see this game played in terrific spirit, like the Melbourne Test and the majority of the Sydney Test as well. We are happy to leave everything behind us and with India withdrawing their charge against Hogg last night, they have shown that they really want to move on with things as well.'

Later, I was asked about the agreement between the two teams to take the fieldsman's word on ground-level catches.

'It's been scrapped, as of yesterday,' I said as dispassionately as I could. 'That wasn't the way I wanted to play. But the feeling through the Indian team, and probably not just Anil's thoughts on it, was that they would like it to go back and be in the hands of the on-field umpires.

'I've just had a chat with the umpires out on the ground now about the whole thing and they'll be endeavouring to make the call between themselves on the field rather than referring everything. That's the way it's going to be, I think, for the rest of the series.'

SUNDAY, JANUARY 20

Third Test, Australia v India, at Perth (January 16–19): India 330 (R Dravid 93, SR Tendulkar 71; MG Johnson 4–86) and 294 (VVS Laxman 79; SR Clark 4–61) defeated **Australia** 212 (A Symonds 66, AC Gilchrist 55; RP Singh 4–68) and 340 (MJ Clarke 81, MG Johnson 50) by 72 runs

Test teams from the subcontinent have a terrible record in Perth. It started in 1977–78, when an Australian team weakened by World Series Cricket defeated India by two wickets. In the following season, a still below-strength Aussie team beat Pakistan by seven wickets. In 1981–82, Australia beat Pakistan by 286 runs; two years later, the winning margin over Pakistan was an innings and nine runs. In 1987–88, Sri Lanka were thrashed by an innings and 108 runs, then in 1991–92 India lost by 300 runs. In 1995–96, my Test debut, Sri Lanka were beaten by an innings and 36 runs, and then in 1999–2000 Pakistan lost by an innings and 20 runs. In 2004–05, we beat Pakistan by 491 runs. And then, in January 2008, India beat Australia by 72 runs.

So what happened? It is true that the pitch for this Test was not your typical WACA wicket, which meant that our strategy of going into the game with four pacemen — Brett Lee, Mitchell Johnson, Stuart Clark and Shaun Tait — was far from being as destructive as we had hoped. But the reality is that we were

THE 600-WICKET CLUB

When Anil Kumble dismissed Andrew Symonds in our first innings, caught at slip by Rahul Dravid after the ball deflected off keeper MS Dhoni's gloves, he became the third man to take 600 Test wickets, after Shane Warne and Muttiah Muralitharan.

Kumble made his Test debut back in 1990, and his feat in reaching this milestone is a tribute to his remarkable durability. The ability to succeed at the highest level for an extended period is something I admire greatly, because it requires a certain toughness, mental strength and a persistent streak that few sportspeople possess. You need to be smart, too. He is a very good bowler on the subcontinent, where — even though he doesn't spin the ball away from the bat very much — his top spinner, almost a flipper-type delivery, gets him lots of wickets. A quarter of his wickets have been lbws, and he also has a lot of victims who tried, like Symmo in Perth, to cut a ball that fizzed through too quickly, or who fell to a bat-pad catch.

In Australia, we sometimes felt we had Kumble's measure (his Test bowling average here is eight-and-a-half runs higher than his career mark of 28.72), though he has never been a bowler you could relax against. He always keeps coming, and started this Test series by snaring a five-for in the first innings in Melbourne and then taking four wickets in each innings in Sydney, which suggests he might be getting even better with age. Glenn McGrath and Courtney Walsh, the two pace bowlers with more than 500 Test wickets, both did that. It's an exclusive group, the 500-plus Test wickets club, and the Indian captain fully deserves to be a member of it.

simply outplayed by a team that, over the four days of the game, was more switched on than we were.

India went into the game bent on vengeance, and they won the toss on a pitch that fooled a lot of us. I had Justin Langer in my ear before the Test, telling me I had to field first if we won the toss, the mail from the groundstaff was that it'd be quick, and we had strong memories of the Twenty20 game Australia played against New Zealand in December, when the ball was jumping all over the place and Taity had a real night out, bowling like the wind. One member of the WA squad told me the pitch was like 'a sheet of glass'. But as it turned out the Test wicket might have been the slowest Perth pitch in history, not a bad batting track at all, and the tourists' batsmen went pretty well on the first day, and then their bowlers shattered our top-order on day two. My understanding is that the entire square was re-laid recently, except for one wicket, and that all the new pitches are super-fast, just like the WACA used to be. The one old wicket was the one they prepared for the Test.

Our first innings started terribly. We were 3–14 (in the eighth over) and then 5–61 (midway through the lunch-to-tea session) in reply to 330, and though Andrew Symonds and Adam Gilchrist batted well to limit our first-innings deficit to 118, when we bowled again we couldn't quite get through the Indian batting line-up quickly enough. We went into the fourth day at 2–65 chasing a huge target, 413, to win, but I really thought we were a chance. However, I couldn't quite get through a fantastic spell of bowling from Ishant Sharma, and while Mike Hussey and Michael Clarke batted well and Mitchell Johnson smashed his first Test fifty at the death, we came up short. We might not have been as inspired as we've been at other times, but our effort was still first-class — all you can do in such circumstances is tip your baggy green to your opponents and concede that on the day they were the better side.

We went into the game without Matthew Hayden, who was forced out by the hamstring strain that restricted him during his second-innings century in Sydney, and we miss him in a number of ways, not least his skill, strength and his stature in the game. Over the past few years, he has developed a commanding presence which leaves some opponents beaten before a ball is bowled. He had scored a century in each of the first two Tests, and given the pressure we were under I knew we'd miss his

OVER RATED

The question of slow over-rates in modern cricket was a major talking point during the third Test, not least because there was a stage when it looked like I, as captain, might be suspended because we fell too far being the prescribed rate. There was much criticism of the players, and some of it was justified, but I can assure you we weren't bludging and that in 21st-century cricket it isn't always easy — if your attack features four quicks — to bowl the 90 overs Test teams are required to send down in a day.

'It's something we're very wary of,' coach Tim Nielsen said after stumps on day three, when he was probed about our problems with the over-rate. Then he was asked if the regulations would lead to the demise of pace quartets in Test matches.

'It's something different and is really good to watch,' Vin responded. 'We don't see it a lot in Australia and I hope it's not pushed out of the game because of the conditions.'

There are at least a couple of things about modern cricket that can make it difficult to stick to the required over-rate. Our tactics are more specialised these days, with fields often changing for different batsmen. Even 15 years ago, there was much less video analysis of individual opponents, which meant a captain was less likely to order a field change in the middle of an over. I accept that this shouldn't be used as an alibi — we need to fit our strategies to the rules and regulations — but I found here in Perth that it was more time consuming than I'd previously realised. Because we've always had Shane Warne or Stuart MacGill in the side, I just wasn't used to having four pacemen to choose from. More significantly, I think, more often than not runs are being scored at a faster speed these days, and if fieldsmen are being required to frequently chase balls to the boundary rope, or more fielders are being stationed in the deep, it has to slow the game down.

Further, a captain is more likely to talk to his bowler mid-over when the batsmen are on the attack, or he'll want to tweak the field a little, maybe even a lot. It has to take a team longer to bowl its overs if the opposition is scoring 370 runs in a day, instead of 250, or 330 in a 50-over game, instead of 200. Even the fact that spectators aren't allowed onto the ground to get the ball and throw it back in can slow things down a fraction.

strong character and great experience. He desperately wanted to play — to do his bit to win the series and get us to the record — and he was bitterly disappointed when he was ruled out. He hadn't missed a Test since he came back into the Aussie side in 2000. Into the side came Chris Rogers, who was handed his first Australian cap by Lang, one left-handed WA opener to another, in a brief ceremony on the morning of the game. Unfortunately, Chris didn't have a very productive game — the highlight being a great catch he took, diving full-length to his right at cover point, to dismiss Kumble on the second morning — but it's no fluke he's scored a truckload of runs in first-class cricket and I doubt this will be the last Test cricket sees of him.

India got plenty out of this game, and not just the result. Ishant Sharma showed that he has the potential to be an exceptional Test bowler, while the return to the side of Virender Sehwag and the return to form of Rahul Dravid adds plenty to their batting order. Dravid seemed much more comfortable at No. 3; he didn't come in on day one until the total had reached 57 and he was helped when Pup missed a regulation catch at first slip when he was just 11. His foot movement improved the longer his innings went and it looked like he had a hundred there for the taking until he tried to swing Symmo away but only managed to top-edge a catch into the covers. Sachin Tendulkar was in good nick, too — his battles with Brett Lee are superb theatre — Irfan Pathan did enough to be named man of the match and Kumble took his 600th Test wicket. For all of India, it was a memorable four days.

We had some problems maintaining a reasonable over-rate, and this became a major issue in India's second innings, when I had to give Pup and Symmo extended spells to avoid me, as captain, being suspended. That's the penalty meted out if a team's over-rate falls more than six overs behind the 90-over-a-day stipulation — the skipper pays the price — so I had to decide whether we kept chasing wickets with the quicks, or bowled the slows to hopefully still take wickets but also avoid punishment. I was on and off the field a few times, to find out exactly where we stood, and at lunch on day three, we estimated we'd fallen at least eight overs behind schedule. India went to lunch at 5–158, a lead of 276, and then we conceded 87 runs in the middle session while taking three wickets. Of course, the critics wanted to argue that the quicks would have done better than that, but they conveniently forgot that Laxman and Dhoni, who batted for much of the session, are not mugs with the bat. The biggest negative to all this was that Shaun Tait was struggling for rhythm and the ideal would have been to give him an extended spell at the bowling crease. But I couldn't do that and avoid a suspension, so Shaun only bowled six overs for the day. This wasn't about putting myself ahead of the team; rather, it was a judgment call about what we felt was best for the side long-term, and while I know that didn't help Taity at all, and I didn't like doing it, I'm sure, all things considered, it was the right thing to do. It was a good batting deck, and India only managed 9–242 for the day, so it's not as if things went catastrophically wrong for us.

It did mean, however, that we had to chase 413 to win, which would have been the second highest target ever achieved in Tests had we been successful. We'll never know what the target would have been had I been able to keep the quicks on, but I was proud of the way we kept fighting all the way to the line. To come up just 72 short, with no one making the big score we needed, showed that the game was still there to be won when we began our second dig, and we were a little unlucky with the umpires, who could have been kinder to Huss and Symmo. Ironically, given the events of the previous day, Sehwag's part-time off-spin

SIXTEEN STRAIGHT

Our run of 16 consecutive Test victories stretched back to the Boxing Day Test of 2005–06, when we defeated South Africa. Before that (going backwards), we had drawn a Test with the South Africans in Perth, swept a three-Test series against the West Indies and beaten the ICC World XI in Sydney. Prior to that match, we'd won the opening Test of the 2005 Ashes series in England, but failed to get another win in that five-match rubber. So the second-Test win in Sydney was our 20th victory in our previous 21 starts.

The 16 victories were:

Date	Opponent	Venue	Result
Dec 26–30, 2005	South Africa	Melbourne	Australia won by 184 runs
Jan 2–6, 2006	South Africa	Sydney	Australia won by eight wickets
Mar 16–18, 2006	South Africa	Cape Town	Australia won by seven wickets
Mar 24–28, 2006	South Africa	Durban	Australia won by 112 runs
Mar 31–Apr 4, 2006	South Africa	Johannesburg	Australia won by two wickets
Apr 9–13, 2006	Bangladesh	Fatullah	Australia won by three wickets
Apr 16–20, 2006	Bangladesh	Chittagong	Australia won by an innings & 80 runs
Nov 23–27, 2006	England	Brisbane	Australia won by 277 runs
Dec 1–5, 2006	England	Adelaide	Australia won by six wickets
Dec 14–18, 2006	England	Perth	Australia won by 206 runs
Dec 26–28, 2006	England	Melbourne	Australia won by an innings & 99 runs
Jan 2–5, 2007	England	Sydney	Australia won by 10 wickets
Nov 8–12, 2007	Sri Lanka	Brisbane	Australia by an innings & 40 runs
Nov 16–20, 2007	Sri Lanka	Hobart	Australia won by 96 runs
Dec 26–29, 2007	India	Melbourne	Australia won by 337 runs
Jan 2–6, 2008	India	Sydney	Australia won by 122 runs

It is team records like this one, or winning World Cups without losing a game (as we did in 2003 and 2007) that rank highest with me when I'm comparing different things I've managed to achieve during my career. Of course, with any extended winning sequence in cricket you need the weather to be kind, but you also need to have the skill to overcome adverse pitch conditions, injuries and retirements. Inevitably, you need some luck as well. All things considered, that I was a part of this winning streak will remain one of my favourite memories from my sporting life.

took two key wickets, including Adam Gilchrist just when we were thinking Gilly might be able to produce another miracle. Johnson and Clark put on 73 for the ninth-wicket, and again we started to hope that a sensational comeback might be possible, but then Sarf nicked Irfan Pathan to the keeper. Mitch went on to his first Test half-century, but our winning streak was over.

When we set the 16-game record back in 1999–2001, we honestly felt it wouldn't be broken for ages, if ever. To win one Test is hard work, so to perform at a high standard consistently enough to win 16 straight is something quite special and I hope

---

THE MAGNIFICENT 29

Given the retirements that occurred last season, I imagine many people would have expected this current Australian team to have used more players in its 16-Test winning run than Steve Waugh's team did between 1999 and 2001. In fact, both sequences involved the same number of Aussies. Eleven men played a part in both efforts:

1999–2001 (20 players)
16 Tests: Michael Slater, Justin Langer, Mark Waugh, Glenn McGrath; *15*: Steve Waugh, Adam Gilchrist; *13*: Ricky Ponting; *11*: Shane Warne; *9*: Greg Blewett; *8*: Damien Fleming; *7*: Colin Miller, Brett Lee, Matthew Hayden; *5*: Jason Gillespie; *4*: Damien Martyn, Stuart MacGill; *2*: Scott Muller, Michael Kasprowicz, Andy Bichel; *1*: Ian Healy.

2005–2008 (20 players)
16 Tests: Matthew Hayden, Ricky Ponting, Mike Hussey, Adam Gilchrist, Brett Lee; *13*: Stuart Clark; *12*: Andrew Symonds, Shane Warne; *11*: Michael Clarke; *9*: Justin Langer; *7*: Glenn McGrath; *6*: Phil Jaques, Stuart MacGill, Damien Martyn; *4*: Mitchell Johnson; *3*: Michael Kasprowicz; *2*: Brad Hodge, Jason Gillespie, Brad Hogg; *1*: Dan Cullen.

none of this is overlooked when people look back on the season. I have sensed that the magnitude of our achievement was lost somewhat in all the fuss that engulfed the game in the time between the Sydney and Perth Tests.

This was my first defeat as a Test captain in Australia. For many of the team — Jaques, Rogers, Hussey, Symonds, Clark, Johnson, Tait and coach Tim Nielsen — it was their first Test loss anywhere. The real measure for all of us, as leaders, cricketers and men, will be how we bounce back. I'm very confident we'll be okay.

TUESDAY, JANUARY 29

Fourth Test, Australia v India, at Adelaide (January 24–28): India 526 (V Sehwag 63, SR Tendulkar 153, VVS Laxman 51, A Kumble 87, Harbhajan Singh 63; MG Johnson 4–126) and 7–269 (V Sehwag 151) drew with **Australia** 563 (PA Jaques 60, ML Hayden 103, RT Ponting 140, MJ Clarke 118)

If you look solely at the scorecard, you'd think the fourth Test was something of a run-fest, a batting-dominated game that was hardly the most exciting way to end such a headline grabbing series. However, it was actually a damn fine Test match, a good old-fashioned clash where India took full advantage of typically excellent Adelaide batting track to go past 500, and then we did the same, under pressure with the series at stake. At stumps on day four, India were 1–45 — essentially 1–8 once their first-innings deficit was factored in — which for those with good memories was similar to England's position with a day to go in last season's Adelaide Test. The Poms had been 1–59 then —

essentially 1–97 — but we bowled them out for 129 and then got the runs with six wickets and 19 balls to spare.

This time, Virender Sehwag stood in our way, completing the fifth individual century of the match and scoring more than half the Indians' second-innings total.

Without a big finish, the game will now be remembered as possibly Sachin Tendulkar's final Test match in Australia (maybe the last, too, for Laxman, Dravid and Ganguly) and definitely, and in some ways sadly, Adam Gilchrist's last Test anywhere. I say 'in some ways' only because I sense, as I did with the guys who retired last year, that Gilly has found, for him, the right time to go. We'd all like to go on for ever, and I'd especially like Gilly to continue a while longer because I love his cricket and treasure his friendship, but it seems to me that eventually you lose that 'one per cent' that leads to training, touring, maybe even playing occasionally becoming a grind. I also imagine it becomes harder and harder to farewell your family again, especially when your kids are old enough to say they're going to miss you.

Gilly announced he was going to retire after stumps on day three. Two days earlier, Tendulkar took 18 balls to get off the mark, 77 balls to reach his fifty, and another 56 to get his 39th Test century. He went from 86 to a 100 in four balls: 4, 2, 6, 2. He batted beautifully, but though he was in good form and the pitch was a belter, when Brett Lee was at him we always felt we were a chance. At other times, though, there seemed no way we'd dismiss him.

Throughout the series, the clash between Lee and Tendulkar has been superb, and I think it reached its peak here. And though Sachin got a hundred, I refuse to concede that he won the battle. He might have scored nearly 500 runs during the series, with two hundreds and two fifties, but I reckon the judges got it right when they named Bing player of the series.

THE AUSTRALIANS, 2007–08

Above and below left: Adam Gilchrist (above left), Matt Hayden (above right) and Brad Hodge during the ICC World Twenty20.

Right: Nathan Bracken after our aborted flight out of Nagpur.

Ben Hilfenhaus (above) and James Hopes
(right) in Mumbai.

Two images from the Test against Sri Lanka in Hobart. Left: Mitchell Johnson
bowls late on the fourth day. Right: Phil Jaques (right) with Rhett Lockyear, our
Tasmanian 'supersub'.

The Australians, 2007–08

Above and below left: Ashley Noffke (above left), Luke Pomersbach (above right) and Shaun Tait during the Twenty20 international against New Zealand in Perth.

Above: Stuart Clark knocks over Sachin Tendulkar in Melbourne during the first Test.

THE AUSTRALIANS, 2007–08

Above: Two of the key players from the final day of the second Test against India in Sydney — Andrew Symonds (left), after he trapped MS Dhoni lbw, and Michael Clarke, after dismissing RP Singh in what proved to be the final over.

Left: Brett Lee with the Border Medal.

Below: Chris Rogers with his first Australian cap.

THE AUSTRALIANS, 2007–08

Left: David Hussey (centre) with Michael Clarke and Adam Gilchrist after he dismissed MS Dhoni during the Twenty20 international in Melbourne.

Below: Adam Voges tries for a hat-trick later in the same game.

Bottom: Mike Hussey celebrates his brilliant catch of Robin Uthappa during the first Commonwealth Bank Series final.

Above: Fellow retiree Adam Gilchrist, between Stuart Clark (at back) and Brett Lee (far right), acknowledges Brad Hogg at the Gabba, at the conclusion of the Commonwealth Bank Series.

Left: Beau Casson in Barbados, with his new baggy green.

Below: Stuart MacGill in Antigua, nearing the end of his highly successful Test career.

THE AUSTRALIANS, 2007–08

Right: Simon Katich scored two Test centuries in the West Indies.

Below: His NSW team-mate, Doug Bollinger, was part of our Test squad in the Caribbean.

A third 'Blue', keeper Brad Haddin, seen here trying to stump Shivnarine Chanderpaul, made his Test debut in Jamaica. I'm at first slip, not my favourite fielding position to a spinner.

THE AUSTRALIANS, 2007–08

Luke Ronchi (top left), Shane Watson (top right), Shaun Marsh (bottom left) and Cameron White all wore Australia's colours during the one-day series in the West Indies.

Brett finished with 24 wickets at 22.58, but beyond those raw figures, his effort was remarkable — he captured those wickets on pitches that didn't suit him, and he got them through a mixture of pace, adaptability, relentlessness and reverse swing. No doubt, he enjoys being the leader of our attack, and I love the way he can bowl to a plan now, something he couldn't always do four or five years ago. Perhaps it was the fact he dismissed Sachin four times in the series that most impressed the pundits. Over the past 12 months he has matured into a genuinely great bowler; in my mind, right at this moment, the best fast bowler in the world.

Unfortunately, for the second game in a row our catching wasn't as good as it could have been, with seven chances going down. That was unacceptable, even though it didn't reflect any drop in effort. The final frustration was having Kumble and Harbhajan add 107 for the eighth wicket, to push their innings total past 500, batting into the sixth session of the Test.

We had to be careful on day three, Australia Day, and as he's done many times in the past, Matt Hayden showed the way, becoming the sixth man in Test history (after Sachin Tendulkar, Brian Lara, Sunil Gavaskar, Steve Waugh and me) to score 30 centuries. For the fourth time in the series, Hayden and Jaques compiled a substantial opening stand, and as we'd done each of the previous three occasions, the rest of the batting order capitalised on that good start.

The first wicket didn't fall until the second over after lunch on day three, when Jaquesy was bowled by Kumble for 60, leaving us 1–159, and though Haydos couldn't survive a terrific spell of seamers and reverse-swing by Ishant Sharma (who took 1–10 from nine overs straight after lunch), and Mike Hussey was also dismissed before stumps, Michael Clarke and I combined in a long fourth-wicket partnership that took us within 75 runs of India's score.

I was determined to do well, but while I was proud of the way I persevered, it was not one of my more fluent knocks. I felt like I was fighting myself, my stance didn't feel quite right, the bat handle felt funny, my grip was wrong, I had to keep reminding myself to concentrate, to keep going. It was a war of attrition, with the Indians bowling a defensive line for much of the innings, waiting, it seemed, for us to make a mistake. *Don't they want to square the series?* That's what we kept thinking. It took me 53 deliveries to find the boundary, and 114 balls to reach 50, one of the slowest digs of my career, but after my struggles against Harbhajan in Melbourne and Sydney, and the duel with Sharma in Perth, I enjoyed the fact that I prevailed against them here. Second last over of the day, I hit Sharma for two fours — a pull and a leg-glance — which helped set the mood for day four, when we sought to build a big enough first-innings lead to make things awkward for them. If Pup had held a hot chance off Sehwag just before stumps on day four, we might even have won.

Though Pup and I both went on to make hundreds on day four, the headline act was Gilly, who played what proved to be his last Test innings. He made only 14 from 18 balls, but a fierce straight drive that nearly cleaned up umpire Billy Bowden and a deft late cut gave the crowd a nice reminder of his glory days, and the two standing ovations he received, on the way out and the way back, will stay in the memory.

My second fifty came from 69 deliveries, and I felt I was running into some decent form until my back seized up and I had to call Huss out to run for me. Pup batted superbly, and I was glad I was able to survive long enough to be there when he reached three figures. Unfortunately, his 100th run was the last gasp of our partnership, because three balls later I inside-edged Sehwag back onto my stumps.

THE REBUILDING PHASE

I was in a bit of a mellow mood in the dressing room at the end of the fourth Test, and not just because my back was aching and we had the Harbhajan appeal hearing to attend the following morning. I was reflecting on the series, trying to gauge exactly how we'd gone, and where the team was at. It was here in Adelaide last season that Damien Martyn played his final Test, and it was in the rooms afterwards that Shane Warne asked for a quiet word and told me he was going to pull the pin. Now Gilly has retired as well. A few of the great players who opposed us in this series are near the end of their careers; soon India will be entering the rebuilding phase we're currently going through.

All things considered, I rate our cricket this summer as being terrific, especially the way we've covered for the guys we lost last season. Nobody can say they're not impressed with Phil Jaques or Mitchell Johnson. Brett Lee, Michael Clarke and Andrew Symonds are now exceptional Test cricketers. The reality is that Sri Lanka and India are very good Test teams and we've had to play very well to beat them.

But then I looked over at Brad Hogg and could see he was disappointed with how this Test had gone. I don't think Hoggy let anyone down in the three Tests he played in this series, but both here and in Sydney there was a chance for him to take some wickets on a pitch that might have suited him and it didn't happen for him. At age 37, there's still a chance for him to play some more Test cricket over the next couple of years, but he'd be the first to admit he certainly didn't do enough to lock up the spinner's spot in our side.

Overall, I still think we've got enough talent in our ranks to maintain our No.1 ranking in Test cricket, but there's no doubt the next couple of years are going to be challenging. As I said at the post-game media conference ...

'Test cricket is about big moments and we've won those through the summer. (But) how we do from here on will determine how good a group we are.'

On the final day, the match petered out to a draw, and I guess you'd have to say the honours for the game were about even. Sehwag was the undoubted star as the series drew to its conclusion — no other Indian batsmen made it past 20 in their second knock — and he played beautifully, almost taunting us by the way he'd hit the ball into a gap, we'd cover it, and then he'd hit the next ball to where the fieldsman had previously been. Sehwag really is an amazing player — when he is out of touch he is the worst batsman in the world, quite capable of missing the most innocuous of deliveries, but when he's 'on', even though you always think you can get him out, he's as dangerous as any batsman I've ever seen. Given the quality of his effort here, it was somewhat appropriate that when he was finally out for 151 it was Gilly who took the catch. That was the 416th dismissal of Gilly's career, which puts him three clear of South Africa's Mark Boucher at the top of the Test wicketkeeping dismissals list. He'd equalled Boucher when he caught Harbhajan on day two of this Test, and moved clear when he caught Anil Kumble soon after. I know, barring unforseen circumstances, that Boucher will get the record back soon, but it was nice and fitting that Gilly went out as No. 1.

I write this diary entry having just learned that Harbhajan has been cleared by Justice Hansen of the racist abuse charge, but found guilty of a lesser charge. I can't say I'm happy with the way this has played out, but as with all the controversies of the past three-and-a-half weeks, I'm going to sit on what's gone on for the moment, then write about it at a later time. For now, I've got to look after my back, and try to get myself right for the Commonwealth Bank Series, which begins on February 3. I'm next to no chance of playing in the Twenty20 match in Melbourne two days before that, and I can cope with that. My main ambition over the coming few days is to do my best to ensure I miss as little cricket as possible. I sense the Indians are pretty keen to get square for the beating we gave them on their turf last October, and I don't want to give them that pleasure.

PART SIX

COMMONWEALTH BANK SERIES

'You can't blame any of the issues for our performances in the last two games because there really hasn't been anything that's happened in the last couple of games.'

— Ricky Ponting, March 4, 2008

THURSDAY, MARCH 6

I began my column in *The Australian* on February 29 with the following line: 'In the dozen years I have been playing international cricket, this season has been the most frustrating by the length of the straight.'

A week on, now that we've lost the Commonwealth Bank Series finals 2–0 to India, my feelings on this summer haven't changed one iota. Controversies have come up all over the place, and as I'm the captain — whether the issue involves me or not — I'm the one who has to answer the questions that flow as a consequence. Always, there is pressure on me to be honest and, at the same time, not say the wrong thing, in an environment where some people are sweating on me making a mistake. It almost doesn't seem to matter how we play, or what we do, someone will find an issue, usually something they can beat us over the head with.

Escaping the scrutiny has been just about impossible. Coming on top of the 'natural' stresses that are a feature of the annual one-day series in Australia — most of them a consequence of all the frequent-flyer points we rack up as we crisscross the country — it made February '08 a very awkward month.

Furthermore, it was, in many ways, the same for just about all of us, because the manner in which the Test and one-day squads have evolved over the past couple of years, most of us are now in both teams. From the Adelaide Test, 10 Australians — Hayden, Ponting, Hussey, Clarke, Symonds, Gilchrist, Hogg, Lee, Clark and Johnson — appeared in the one-dayers, while only six of the Indians — Sehwag, Pathan, Tendulkar, Dhoni, Harbhajan and Ishant Sharma — did likewise. The trend towards having separate Australian teams for the two forms of the game has turned full circle. This is not necessarily a bad thing, I need to stress that, but it has created a new set of challenges that we have to manage better in future seasons.

Until the eve of the finals, I felt that as a group we had managed to sustain our effort pretty well. We weren't in our most imposing '2007 World Cup' form, but we lost only one of our first six completed games, gaining a bonus point in four of them, with the match against India in Brisbane washed out. However, for the second season in a row, our performance was below standard in the games of this competition that really matter, and a team that we'd dominated in the early games came back and beat us two-zip in the finals.

We've been left wondering if it is possible to play at our best throughout a long Australian summer. Of course, it must be, and we have to find out how. For me, the reality is that, as much as we try to convince ourselves that because we're athletes and we love the game we can be fit and fresh for every game we play, we're not always as fit and fresh as we need to be. This is not because we play too much cricket. Cynics like to have a shot at us whenever we claim we're tired, sneering that we're happy to play IPL, we're happy to play county cricket, and so on, so how can we moan about schedules? But they miss the point. Like so many things in modern cricket, the answer is about balance. Some of this, I believe, is on the men who create the playing schedules — they need to allow sufficient travel and recovery time between games, because when players haven't got that time, their minds and bodies become weary and performances suffer. But most of it is on us, as a team and as individuals within the team set-up — we have to be able to step back and take a break before we reach 'breaking point'; in other words, we have to accept international cricket's playing schedules for what they are and respond pragmatically to them.

No elite player wants to give up his place meekly, even for one game, and that's not just because he is worried that his replacement will do so well that the decision to have a short break will have long-term ramifications. He also thinks, *If I take a day off and we lose the game, how bad am I going to feel?* However, he has to get over that mindset, to take the attitude: *What ever is going to be best for the team, that's what I'll do.* Sometimes, we've all just got to take our foot off the pedal a little bit. That's what we in the Australian set-up have to get better at, rather than simply deciding to classify some players purely as Test cricketers, others as one-day cricketers. Doing that would be self-defeating.

The fact we haven't won the Commonwealth Bank Series for the past two years is extremely disappointing (the only other time that has happened, since the annual one-day tournament was instigated to Australian cricket in 1979–80, was in 1983–84 and 1984–85). That we will no longer be sharing an Aussie dressing room with Adam Gilchrist and Brad Hogg is even sadder. I'll never forget the moment at training in Melbourne, on the day of the Allan Border Medal presentation, when Hoggy attempted to tell us he was calling it quits — he has always been an emotional bloke, and on this occasion he had trouble getting the words out. It was a cogent reminder of just how lucky we are to be playing cricket for Australia. A couple of times during the previous month, some of us might have forgotten that a fraction.

Here is a summary of just some of the things that have been part of my cricket life over the past five weeks ...

FEBRUARY 1, 2008:
TWENTY20 INTERNATIONAL V INDIA IN MELBOURNE

I missed this game to give my back a rest, not the first time it's caused me to take a short break. It was the same type of injury as the previous problems I've had with my back, but this time the spasms occurred in a different area — down near the small of the back rather than about halfway between my neck and my waist. The remedy was the same: rest until the muscles in the inflamed area revert from their 'protective' mode, a reaction caused when a disc in my spine catches on a spur on one of my vertebrae and becomes inflamed. I'd been sweating while I was batting in Adelaide, a breeze blew in and I could actually feel my back getting cold, and then I started to bend down ... and as I did, I felt it starting to go. *Oh no, I'm gone!* I anguished. I tried to straighten up, but it was too late.

My absence gave Michael Clarke his second run as Australian captain, and he took his record to two from two, as the boys crushed the Twenty20 world champions by nine wickets with 52 balls to spare. The crowd was an amazing 84,041, only Irfan Pathan (26 from 30 deliveries) reached double figures for India, and the tourists hit a grand total of three boundaries, the last of them in the sixth over. Pup added his own touch to the game by putting eight men around the bat — hardly your conventional Twenty20 field — when Adam Voges was on a hat-trick late in the Indians' innings.

The way the team approached this game, like the game against New Zealand at the WACA in December, reflected the fact that we are now treating Twenty20 cricket seriously. The game has grown on all of us. 'How good is this?' asked Adam Gilchrist in his dual role as keeper-batsman and on-field Channel Nine commentator. While it might still be a fraction too early to say Twenty20 will always be with us, the size and energy of the crowd and the huge television ratings (a peak figure of more than 2.7 million people nationally) had me thinking once again, more strongly than ever before, that it is so much more than just the latest fad.

FEBRUARY 3: GAME 1,
AUSTRALIA V INDIA IN BRISBANE

My back was probably about 90 per cent right when I played in the Commonwealth Bank Series opener, a washout that ended with us 3–51 in the eighth over chasing 194. Although this game didn't end in a result, it did begin a trend towards lower scores that continued pretty much unabated for the rest of the competition. Brett Lee was the chief catalyst on this occasion, taking 5–27 from nine overs, including Sachin Tendulkar, back in their side after missing the Twenty20, who was out hit-wicket trying to fend off a fast one.

The following day, I was obliged to field some questions on the upcoming Indian Premier League, after it was suggested Cricket Australia might still exercise its veto power over its contracted players participating in the new venture if 'competing sponsorship' issues arise. I didn't expect there to be a problem, and I knew if there was any hassle it would be sorted out by Cricket Australia and the Australian Cricketers Association, but it was still a distraction to be probed on the subject. At this point, the IPL 'player auction' was still a few days away and a final decision on the tour of Pakistan had not been made.

Little did I know just what a huge story this would become before the one-day series was through. More than once, I'd need someone from Cricket Australia to interrupt the journos during a media conference and ask them if they had any questions about the game at hand.

FEBRUARY 8: GAME 3, AUSTRALIA V SRI LANKA IN SYDNEY

I was out for a duck in our rained-out game in Brisbane, so I didn't have a chance in that encounter to see if my back would hurt my batting, so before the game in Sydney against Sri Lanka I purposely had an extended hit-out in the nets to get a bit more confidence in my movements and to try to iron out a little bit of the stiffness that was still bugging me. I was confident at the time that I could get through the one-dayers, but I also knew I needed to be cautious, and most of all I had to work on increasing my core strength.

Part of my problem is that I spend so much of my time on the field in a crouched position. When I'm batting, I'm crouched. At second slip, I'm crouched. Close in on the offside, I'm crouched. I'm forever putting stress on a part of my body that would much rather be lying straight on a bench.

Our big win against Sri Lanka at the SCG was made possible by important innings by Adam Gilchrist, Matt Hayden and Michael Clarke, and excellent bowling performances by Nathan Bracken and Mitchell Johnson. Having made what we thought was a match-wining total on a pretty slow deck, we deliberately limited Bracks to three overs in his opening spell,

MORE PERSPECTIVE

In the dressing room following the last day's play of the Adelaide Test, as we reflected on our series victory and Gilly's retirement, and at the same time tried to get our minds prepared for the Harbhajan appeal the following morning, Tim Nielsen pulled me to one side and said quietly, 'Mate, Taity's feeling pretty low at the moment. He's decided to take a break from the game.'

I wasn't sure how to react. 'Is he OK?' I asked. Vin explained that the long-term outlook was positive, but for the next few months, at least, we'll have to do without the big fella.

I had never noticed anything about Shaun in the weeks before that might have indicated he was anything other than the fun-loving bloke I've known for a few years now, the bloke who is always ready for a laugh. Maybe, with hindsight, he was a little down during the Perth Test, but I would have assumed that was the result of the nerves that come with making your home debut combining with the reality that his form in that game wasn't up to his best. Maybe his run with injuries had got to him a little. It was as if he was fighting himself a bit, but I thought he was just searching for his rhythm, and once he rediscovered that he'd be okay. When we talked about the fact he didn't get much bowling in their second innings, he seemed philosophical about it. He certainly wasn't angry.

When I spoke to him a few days after the Adelaide Test, we didn't talk about cricket at all; rather, we chatted about how important it is that, if he does come back to international cricket, the team set-up has the structures in place to help him out. I sensed that for the moment he just wants to step away and reassess if big-time cricket is what he really wants to do. I'll be thrilled if, down the track, he gets some good solid cricket for South Australia under his belt and ends up having the career for Australia his talent undoubtedly deserves.

so he could come back and attack their middle order with his range of cutters. He ended up taking 5–47 as the last seven Sri Lankan wickets fell for just 51 runs, while I rated Mitch's effort (1–9 from five overs) as close to anything he'd ever done in Australia.

FEBRUARY 10: GAME 4,
AUSTRALIA V INDIA IN MELBOURNE

Our third game of the competition was our first loss, and it was a bad one for us, the result of a feeble batting effort — apart from Mike Hussey, who made 65 not out — that saw us bowled out for 159 in the 44th over. Our bowlers worked hard to try to get us an unlikely win, and we reduced India to 5–102 in the 29th over, but Rohit Sharma and MS Dhoni got them home.

I never enjoy media conferences after a loss, and I sat down for this one and waited to be asked a series of questions about our ordinary display, but quickly the subject turned to the IPL, and whether we Australian players would be involved. The reason the journos were keen to talk Twenty20 was because Andrew Symonds had written in his newspaper column that we players were upset at what he described as Cricket Australia's negative stance to us playing in the IPL. I knew there were sponsorship issues that needed to be addressed, but I was content for the ACA and the administrators to try to sort them out (and was genuinely confident they would). So I kept my answers short. For the moment, I was trying my best not to think about Twenty20, and wanted everyone else in the Aussie dressing room to do the same, on the basis that, as things stood, we wouldn't be playing, that we'd be touring Pakistan. It was only after I explained that philosophy that the discussion finally, slowly turned back to the cricket.

FEBRUARY 15: GAME 6,
AUSTRALIA V SRI LANKA IN PERTH

This was Gilly's WACA farewell, and he said goodbye with another stunning century. He did so in front of a sell-out crowd, scoring exactly half of our innings total of 236, and then taking his final international catch at the WACA (off Brad Hogg) as we sailed to a decisive 63-run victory. It was Gilly's 16th one-day hundred, giving him 33 in international cricket, a total more than double the next best (Zimbabwe's Andy Flower, who scored 12 in Tests and four on ODIs), and the irony was that he actually played the way I've always wanted him to play. He got off to a flying start, got to 40 at better than a run a ball, but then played sensibly rather than go looking to score at eight or 10 an over. As he went to 50 from 57 balls, 70 from 74, 80 from 86, I got the impression he was fighting himself, wanting to go faster, so I was sending messages out to him, to keep going the way he was, pace yourself, get a big score for us. The atmosphere as he approached three figures was tremendous, and Gilly was very emotional when he reached the landmark, leaping and punching the air, then acknowledging all corners of the ground.

To have all his family and a lot of his closest friends there, and to be able to give them a final memory like that was terrific — for him and for them. Any international game is hard, and home games (such as Perth for Gilly, Hobart for me) and 'milestone' games (50th Test, 200th ODI, and so on) can be harder. I imagine 'retirement' games, one last chance to leave an indelible mark, must be harder still.

Meanwhile, the debate of how the IPL might impinge on international cricket continued, in part because Cricket Australia did not agree to its players being involved until the day of the Perth game. This resolution came about, as I understand it, after there was a bit of give and take on both sides, most significantly in that we will not be required to actively promote IPL franchise sponsors, if those sponsorships conflict with existing Cricket Australia deals. Until the situation was resolved, however, the questions kept coming, partly because a deadline for Aussies confirming their interest, so we could be involved in the player auction, had been set for February 17, and also, I guess, because the media smelt the possibility of a major split in the sport. When I met the press the day before the Perth one-dayer, I was quickly asked if there was a chance players would desert the traditional game. I responded this way:

'If there are guys approaching the end of their international careers anyway, the thought of being able to play 44 days of cricket and maybe still have the chance to play just one form of the game I'm sure is really attractive for them.

'Especially if they have families and they're starting to get sick and tired of the amount of travel that you do as an international cricketer. I'm sure that's appealing to some, but not to me right now.

'I really cherish every opportunity I get to play for Australia, but there are some programming issues which the ICC and the home boards have to look at as far as maybe carving out a window each year where this (IPL) tournament can sit.

'Otherwise there will be guys making the decision of whether they're playing both forms of the game for their country, or have a bigger break each year and play 44 days of Twenty20 cricket and probably make more money than they are making internationally.'

I was certain then, even before the matter was resolved, that members of the current Australian team, bar Gilly because he had retired, would not play in the IPL until they received permission from Cricket Australia. Though, as I kept explaining, if we went to Pakistan in March-April, and then to the West Indies in May, none of us would be involved in year one. (At this time, we were receiving updates on the situation in Pakistan every day, but a final decision was still weeks away.) The international program for 2009, as it presently stands, would rule us out of the second season of IPL as well.

The one laugh I got came when a scribe suggested Symmo and I would go for plenty at the upcoming IPL player auction. 'That amazes me after the last couple of weeks,' I chuckled, as I thought back to the burning effigies and the cheating allegations of the previous month. 'I thought our prices would have gone right down.'

Meanwhile, after four games in the Commonwealth Bank Series, my runs aggregate stood at 43, at 10.75. But I'd been heartened a little by my cameo in Perth. I only scored 25, but I hit four boundaries and felt I was running into a little bit of form when I edged Chaminda Vaas to first slip.

FEBRUARY 17: GAME 7, AUSTRALIA V INDIA IN ADELAIDE

This game was described as 'highly charged', but in any other year I don't think there would have been any controversy at all. But this summer people are looking for incidents, so when I was spotted exchanging a few words with our old mate Harbhajan inevitably that became the lead in many newspaper reports. The game, which ended in a comfortable 50-run win for Australia, featured some excellent batting by Michael Clarke, three more wickets to Mitchell Johnson (spearheading the attack in the absence of the rested Brett Lee), and five dismissals to our retiring keeper, including a one-handed screamer to end the night. But afterwards, the first thing they wanted to know about was what Harbjahan and I had said to each other.

The Indian spinner has a knack of making something look a whole lot more confrontational than it actually is. I hadn't enjoyed a great Test series with the bat, I was struggling big-time in the one-dayers, and from the moment I got out there he was into me. *Here we go again!* I thought to myself. It was fine, though; while I was batting I just ignored him. We finished with 9–203 from our 50 overs, but that looked like it was going to be enough when India's top-order batsmen struggled. They were 6–134 when Harbhajan came out to bat in the 35th over, with Robin Uthappa, a good player, at the other end, so there was still a big chance they could win. Inevitably, he had to walk straight past me on his way to the middle, and I said, 'Rightio champ, we'll see how good you are now.'

'How many runs did you get today?' he replied.

I'd managed to keep to my tournament average, scoring 10 from 14 balls before I hit a soft catch to Rohit Sharma at point.

'Don't worry about how many runs I've made, mate. Let's see if you can win this game for your country.'

These sort of on-field 'chats' happen often in the hard-nosed world of international cricket, but the way Harbhajan reacted you'd have thought this was the first time such a discussion had ever occurred. He kept staring at me, as if I'd gravely insulted him, presumably because he wanted the umpires (and, I guess, the pressbox) to know I was talking to him. Quickly, Mitchell Johnson fired in a short one, Harbhajan hooked at it, it went straight up in the air and Adam Gilchrist grabbed the catch. 'On your bike, champ!' I shouted as the ball fell into Gilly's gloves. He took a couple of steps towards the pavilion, and then he stopped, half turned around, and then slowly walked off. When the teams shook hands after the game, he tried to start an argument, but after a couple of words I was on my way. Later, he told the press I swore at him when I farewelled him out in the middle, but that was not true. It was good to win.

Andrew Symonds was in a similar batting rut to me. After being dismissed for 3 in Adelaide, Symmo was averaging 9.5 from his first five innings in the competition. Over the past few years, it has been rare for two or three of the batsmen to be out of nick at the same time, and on this occasion it didn't overly worry me because the team was still winning. Some people wanted to blame the run droughts Symmo and I were going through on the off-field pressures, on the IPL, Pakistan, Harbhajan, everything. But I took solace in the reality that the rest of the team had been confronted by the same issues and they were going okay. And I'd always prided myself on being able to separate off-field business and playing the game. 'When it's cricket time, it's cricket time,' has become a personal mantra.

I did find it a bit awkward, however, talking to the rest of the batsmen, as their captain, when I asked them to get their heads down and work hard for their runs. We weren't scoring as many as we had in the past and I was hoping we could reverse the trend. But it's pretty hard to tell everyone to pick up their games if I'm not doing the job myself. And if I want something to change, I've always felt that the best way to make that happen is to go out and show how it's done.

FEBRUARY 22: GAME 9,
AUSTRALIA V SRI LANKA IN MELBOURNE

The IPL player auction took place on February 20, and two days later we were at the MCG beating Sri Lanka in a rain-affected game to confirm our place in the finals. On game day, it must have been a little incongruous for some of our blokes, as they gazed over at the opposition and thought, *I'll be sharing a*

AUCTION RESULTS

These were the players who were bought for US$300,000 or more at the IPL player auction conducted on February 20. All amounts are in US dollars. 'Icons' receive 15 per cent more than the next highest paid player at their franchise ...

Bangalore: Rahul Dravid (icon), Jacques Kallis (South Africa) $900,000, Anil Kumble (India) $500,000, Cameron White (Australia) $500,000, Zaheer Khan (India) $450,000, Mark Boucher (South Africa) $450,000, Nathan Bracken (Australia) $325,000, Dale Steyn (South Africa) $325,000.

Chennai: MS Dhoni (India) $1.5m, Jacob Oram (New Zealand) $675,000, Albie Morkel (South Africa) $675,000, Suresh Raina (India) $650,000, Muttiah Muralitharan (Sri Lanka) $600,000, Matthew Hayden (Australia) $375,000, Mike Hussey (Australia) $350,000, Stephen Fleming (New Zealand) $350,000, Parthiv Patel (India) $325,000.

Delhi: Virender Sehwag (icon), Gautam Gambhir (India) $725,000, Manoj Tiwary (India) $675,000, Mohammad Asif (Pakistan) $650,000, Daniel Vettori (New Zealand) $625,000, Dinesh Karthik (India) $525,000, Shoaib Malik (Pakistan) $500,000, Glenn McGrath (Australia) $350,000, AB de Villiers (South Africa) $300,000.

Hyderabad: Andrew Symonds (Australia) $1.35m, RP Singh (India) $875,000, Rohit Sharma (India) $750,000, Adam Gilchrist (Australia)

dressing room with that guy in a few weeks. There are no Kolkata players in the Sri Lankan side, so I didn't have that experience, but Haydos will soon have Muttiah Muralitharan as a team-mate at Chennai, Binga will have Mahela Jawaywardene and Kumar Sangakkara cheering for him in Mohali, and Gilly and Symmo will be introducing themselves to Chamara Silva in Hyderabad.

I was at home in Sydney when the auction took place, and then flew down to Melbourne the next day. One thing the big money that was paid by the IPL franchise owners did was to give us an opportunity to get into the blokes — Symmo (US$1.35m), Bing (US$900,000) and Gilly (US$700,000) — who received the most cash. It's the Australian way to have a good-natured shot in

$700,000, Shahid Afridi (Pakistan) $675,000, Herschelle Gibbs (South Africa) $575,000, VVS Laxman (India) $375,000.

Jaipur: Mohammad Kaif (India) $675,000, Graeme Smith (South Africa) $475,000, Yusuf Pathan (India) $475,000, Shane Warne (Australia) $450,000.

Kolkata: Sourav Ganguly (icon), Ishant Sharma (India) $950,000, Chris Gayle (West Indies) $800,000, Brendon McCullum (New Zealand) $700,000, David Hussey (Australia) $625,000, Murali Kartik (India) $425,000, Shoaib Akhtar (Pakistan) $425,000, Ricky Ponting (Australia) $400,000, Ajit Agarkar (India) $350,000.

Mohali: Yuvraj Singh (icon), Irfan Pathan (India) $925,000, Brett Lee (Australia) $900,000, Kumar Sangakkara (Sri Lanka) $700,000, Sreesanth (India) $625,000, Mahela Jayawardene (Sri Lanka) $475,000, Piyush Chawla (India) $400,000.

Mumbai: Sachin Tendulkar (icon), Sanath Jayasuriya (Sri Lanka) $975,000, Harbhajan Singh (India) $850,000, Robin Uthappa (India) $800,000, Shaun Pollock (South Africa) $550,000, Lasith Malinga (Sri Lanka) $350,000.

Among the players who sold for less than $300,000 were Australia's Simon Katich and Justin Langer, Pakistan's Younis Khan and Umar Gul, South Africa's Makhaya Ntini, Sri Lanka's Chaminda Vaas, Chamara Silva and Tillakaratne Dilshan, West Indies' Shivnarine Chanderpaul and Ramnaresh Sarwan, and New Zealand's Scott Styris.

these situations, so quickly, for example, Symmo was being asked where his bodyguards were, and then, when we were kicking a footy at training and he couldn't jump up high enough to claim a mark, it was suggested his pockets were too heavy because of all the gold in them. Someone asked if the disparity between the money different blokes are getting might cause some friction in the dressing room, but I sensed exactly the reverse. Everyone is happy for the blokes who did well, and I think everyone is now looking at the IPL as a really exciting venture — an opportunity to make some big money, sure, but also a potentially important and dynamic competition we want to be involved in.

An irony of our innings in this game against Sri Lanka was that our two chief scorers were Mike Hussey (64 not out), who didn't receive a bid in the first stage of the IPL auction (he was later signed by Chennai), and Michael Clarke (50), who chose not to get involved in the IPL at all. Gilly, Haydos, Symmo and me — worth a combined US$2.8m — managed 44 runs between us.

FEBRUARY 24: GAME 10,
AUSTRALIA V INDIA IN SYDNEY

This was the best game of the competition to this point, and not just because I managed to finally come good with a hundred and

---

PRACTICE MAKES PERFECT

I went to the SCG early on the day of the game against India, because I wanted to get up to the indoor nets and have a good, long hit. There was plenty I needed to work on. Tim Nielsen was there to meet me, but when we arrived at the practice area we were greeted by a pre-game corporate function in full swing. The nets had been set up on one side of the indoor centre, and the rest of the area was filled with tables of 10, with a small stage set up with lectern and microphone. I think entrees had just been being served.

So Vin and I went about our business, and it was a bit weird trying to focus on my footwork and my techniques knowing that many of the people at the function were more interested in what I was doing, rather than what was now happening on stage. At one point, the bowling machine speared a 'delivery' into my pads and instinctively I stepped across and lifted it into the legside net. Unfortunately, though, the ball cleared the net and sailed up dangerously close to the guest speaker, who by this stage was in the middle of his routine.

And who was that guest speaker? Peter Roebuck. I looked up as he stopped in mid-sentence, recalled the column he had written straight after the Sydney Test, and thought, *He's going to think I'm aiming at him.* And then I got back to trying to get my batting right.

Andrew Symonds and Matthew Hayden also made decent scores. Chasing 318 to win, India had a real go at it, with their No. 3 Gautam Gambhir making his second century of the series and Robin Uthappa hitting 51 at better than a run a ball to get the tourists a little closer than we would have liked. Brett Lee's 5–58 was very important, as were Adam Gilchrist's six keeping dismissals (five catches and a stumping).

This was the 10th time a keeper had completed six dismissals in a ODI. Six of those instances are by Gilly. Ironically, that night we received word from South Africa that Mark Boucher had made his 417th Test keeping dismissal, meaning he'd taken back the top spot from our man, this time for good.

I was lucky during our innings when Rohit Sharma misjudged a catch off Ishant Sharma's bowling when I was just 13. But even if that chance had been accepted I would have felt better about my batting, because I felt more comfortable at the crease from the first ball I faced. In our previous game in Melbourne I'd deliberately tried to get settled in before I played any big shots, but all I did was scratch around for 11 from 34 balls, so this time I resolved to be positive from the jump, to just see the ball and instinctively react to it. Sreesanth had been bowling some pretty good outswingers at a fair pace but immediately I went forward and half-pushed, half-drove him between cover and mid-off for three runs. It got me going; it's amazing how much confidence a positive, well-timed defensive shot can give you. I always felt that what I needed was some quality time in the middle and I got plenty of that during this knock. It was nice to once again feel good about being at the batting crease.

One intriguing episode concerned MS Dhoni, who was told to change his keeping gloves during our innings after it was suggested that the webbing in the pair he started the game with might have been illegal. Soon after, Dhoni complained to the umpires that Matt Hayden and I were 'bullying' the Indian players on the field, and this received some media coverage after the game. Later in the innings, after Andrew Symonds was bowled by Ishant Sharma, Symmo muttered, 'Well bowled, champ,' as he left the middle and they complained about that as well, saying our man was being provocative. Next day, there was a story on the back page of one of the papers claiming I'd had *another* run-in on the field with Harbhajan. In fact, we'd never said a word to one another. We were happy to accept that if there was anything wrong with the Indian captain's gloves it was a totally innocent error, but to come up with these sledging gripes straight afterwards was, in my view, pretty pathetic.

FEBRUARY 29: GAME 12, AUSTRALIA V SRI LANKA IN MELBOURNE

India's defeat of Sri Lanka in Hobart on February 26 assured them of a place in the finals, and turned our last qualifying game — a 13-run loss to the Sri Lankans — into something of an exhibition. Even so, I was disappointed to lose the game, as I felt it stifled a little of our momentum going into the deciders.

Before that, though, we had to deal with another media 'storm', after news broke that Haydos had described Harbhajan as an 'obnoxious little weed' during an interview on Brisbane FM breakfast radio, one he'd been asked to do to promote the second one-day final, which was to be played at the Gabba. I wish Matt hadn't said it, and he does too, but it was hardly the 'stinging verbal attack' that one Australian newspaper writer called the remark, or a 'new low' as the *Times of India* described it. It was a light-hearted interview, in which a number of matters were talked about, and then Matty was asked about Harbhajan's

BING CLAIMS THE BORDER

Brett Lee might have been a little surprised to be named the Allan Border Medal winner for 2007–08, but no one else was, as we all felt he was a standout after his brilliant performances this summer.

Having taken 40 wickets at 20.58 in the six Tests we played this summer, the only way he could have been beaten would have been if his absence from last year's World Cup worked against him. But after giving Matt Hayden a start, he charged through the field by gaining votes in so many of the matches we've played in India and then at home in the past three months, and won going away from Haydos, with me a long way back in third place. Andrew Symonds, Michael Clarke and Stuart Clark rounded out the top six.

The full list of winners were:

Allan Border Medal: Brett Lee
Test cricketer of the year: Brett Lee
One-Day International cricketer of the year: Matthew Hayden
State cricketer of the year: Ashley Noffke
Women's international cricketer of the year: Lisa Sthalekar
Bradman young cricketer of the year: Luke Pomersbach

On the day of the medal presentation, Rianna and I had told a few people beyond our tight family circle that she was 14 weeks pregnant. The baby is due in August, and we couldn't be happier. Word spread much quicker than we expected, and on the red carpet, walking into the function, Michael Slater, who was working for Nine, asked me if the mail was true. Then on stage host Mark Nicholas wanted to talk about it as well. I didn't want the world to know, not that night, but once they asked me there was nothing I could do but confirm the news and hope the conversations would turn to cricket as soon as possible. With hindsight, I guess we were a bit naïve thinking the information would stay private until after the medal presentation was completed, and initially I was disappointed our good news was publicised in this way, at that time, because I didn't want even a skerrick of attention to be taken away from Bing's win. Fortunately, in the end, I don't think that happened.

latest complaints, relating back to the game in Sydney when the Indians claimed we'd acted like 'bullies'. A hearing had to be called, lawyers were briefed, Haydos was reprimanded, and afterwards he released a statement which read in part, 'My intentions were never to denigrate cricket or anyone. That said, the umpire has made his decision. In the spirit of our own code of behaviour and our great game of cricket, I respect and accept this decision.'

Harbhajan reacted by giving an interview with an Indian paper in which he claimed Matthew Hayden was 'one of the most disliked figures in world cricket' and that not only were we constant sledgers on the field, that we went to great lengths to hide the fact so we wouldn't get caught. As far as I know, no one called him in for a hearing. I didn't care. He could say whatever he liked.

What was most upsetting was that the furore took away some of the attention from the game at the MCG, which was not only the last Melbourne appearance for Adam Gilchrist and Brad Hogg, but also, quite possibly, for a couple of great Sri Lankan champions: Muttiah Muralitharan and Sanath Jayasuriya.

MARCH 2: FIRST FINAL, AUSTRALIA V INDIA IN SYDNEY

I was shattered by our performance in this game, which was one of the sloppiest I've been involved in since I became Australian captain. And I let the boys know it, giving them a bit of a spray in the SCG dressing room after the match. I did so even though I know this sort of tirade rarely works. All the guys were hurting as much as I was, and I know they are quite capable of identifying for themselves the things that had gone wrong. I think in this instance there was a little bit of me that wanted to remind them that winning this tournament meant a great deal to me, that I still cared, that we had standards of excellence that I wanted us to maintain. And, I'll freely admit, part of me hated the idea of India going home with even one trophy.

I hadn't liked the way we played against Sri Lanka in Melbourne, and this was worse. We pride ourselves on the way we play in the big games, and there are plenty of examples of where we have risen to the occasion, but this was a million miles from that. The kind of mistakes we made in the final were ones we don't usually make in important games. Experienced players were dismissed playing big shots to the wrong deliveries at an inappropriate time of the innings. We got off to a poor start, worked our way back into the game with some good partnerships through the middle of the innings, but then threw away some key wickets which left us unable to have a real red-hot go in the final few overs. We forgot we were playing a good and determined side and were never really in the hunt. Sachin Tendulkar's first ODI hundred in Australia set up India's victory with 25 balls to spare.

And then, the next day, Pakistan's cricket coach Geoff Lawson came out and bagged Cricket Australia over its failure to confirm unequivocally that we'd still be touring at the end of March. The trip had been delayed by three weeks, with a final decision still to be made.

'Henry' suggested one of the reasons the tour might be abandoned was so the Aussie players could participate in the inaugural IPL. Suddenly, I was being asked questions about Pakistan and Twenty20 again, which right at this moment was all I needed. There was precious little time available to try to get our team back on track for the second final and that's what I had to focus on, if only I could.

MARCH 4: SECOND FINAL,
AUSTRALIA V INDIA IN BRISBANE

All things considered, we should have lost this game by more than we did, but we showed a lot of fight in the latter stages of both innings. India batted first, and seemed destined for a huge total, but we took 5–54 from the last 11 overs; and after we collapsed to 3–32 in the ninth over, we came back to make it very interesting. At least we went down with a fight, and I was especially impressed by the way James Hopes fought all the way to the finish line to almost get us home. He was out for 63 off the fourth delivery of the 50th over of our innings, with Australia still needing 10 to win, nine to tie. Earlier, Gilly's final innings was way too brief, out for 2 off the third ball of our innings, so with that and the loss, the beers straight after the game were pretty flat. But we picked up eventually, and gave him and Hoggy a reasonable send-off. I just wish we could have put them on the plane to Adelaide, for the third final, rather than to Perth, for retirement. I treasure every game I played for Australia with them; one more would have been nice.

The controversies in this game were relatively minor. Andrew Symonds gave a streaker a decent old shoulder charge when the dill made the mistake of trying to flash past Symmo as he ran across the ground. And there was a weird moment when a caught behind appeal against Mike Hussey was referred to the third umpire. We assumed he was checking on whether the catch carried, but that seemed so clear-cut we wondered if the umps were confirming if the ball had been nicked. I think the right decision was made, so I had no problem with it, but as I said it looked a bit strange. I still don't think the game has worked out how to best use the video replays.

Last year, after we lost the Commonwealth Bank Series finals to England, we came back and won the World Cup in emphatic fashion. This year, the opportunity for redemption is not immediately available, and though we will be determined to win the one-dayers in Pakistan, if we tour, and the West Indies in June it probably won't be until the Champions Trophy in November that we have a real chance to get our stellar reputation back.

THAT WE WON'T HAVE Hoggy to help us in this quest only adds to the challenge. It's impossible not to like Brad Hogg. Throughout his time with the Australian team, from our tour to India in 1996 through to the Commonwealth Bank Series in 2008, he was a great trainer, working as hard on his game and his fitness as anyone I've met. Even better, everything he did was achieved with a smile on his face. When he scored 79 on the first day of the Sydney Test this year, in the process rescuing our first innings with Andrew Symonds, he was obviously having the time of his life. At the same time, he was a really tough competitor — he couldn't have done as well as he did and lasted as long as he did without that grit.

Year after year, training session after training session, he'd spend an extra half hour or more working on his bowling. He'd usually be up early for a morning run, or to get to the gym. I reckon he got the absolute maximum out of himself as a cricketer, and to have someone with that drive as part of our group was very good for the rest of us. Because he came along at the same time as Shane Warne and Stuart MacGill, he never had a chance to build a regular Test career, but as a one-day bowler he was tremendous, as clearly Australia's second-best one-day spinner ever as Warney is the No. 1. His effort at the 2007 World Cup, when he made a lot of good batsmen look very ordinary, was simply superb.

At around the same time Hoggy announced his retirement, those two great warhorses, Jason Gillespie and Michael

Kasprowicz, also pulled the plug on their first-class careers in Australia. Both were outstanding international bowlers, especially 'Dizzy' Gillespie, who in my view is one of the greats. When you talk to some of the English and New Zealand batsmen who tried to counter him, they rate him as highly as any fast bowler they ever saw. Same with the guys who shared an Aussie dressing room with him.

Dizzy was tall, quick when he wanted to be, could swing the ball away from the right-hander and he could generate McGrath-like bounce. Because his action was so strong through the crease, he could get a lot of energy on the ball, and when it all came together, such as at Headingley in 1997 when he took 7–37 on the first day, he was genuinely awesome. 'Kasper' was a different sort of bowler, not as explosive, but what I really admire about him was the way he sustained his career for 19 first-class seasons. He started as a 17-year-old who bowled fast outswingers and eventually turned himself into a real stayer who could bowl 20 or 30 overs in a day. He had some great days as a Test cricketer, including a couple of seven-fors, but for me his finest performances occurred in India in 2004. That was when we came up with a radical game plan that was totally dependent on our frontline bowlers going against their natural instincts, being more defensive than they would have liked, relentlessly keeping to a persistent line. Kasper, alongside Dizzy and Glenn McGrath, was magnificent, and we had the series won in three Tests, without the crack Indian batsmen ever dominating on their home turf.

Over the past 15 months, many of the blokes that I've played with during my international career, people who taught me so much in so many different ways, have retired from Test and ODI cricket. You can actually make a pretty fair side from them: Justin Langer, Matthew Elliott, Jimmy Maher, Damien Martyn, Darren Lehmann, Adam Gilchrist, Brad Hogg, Jason Gillespie,

Shane Warne, Michael Kasprowicz and Glenn McGrath. Some have just quit international cricket, while others are focusing on Twenty20, either in the Indian Premier League or the Indian Cricket League. All those familiar faces I played and trained with, shared so many good times and a few not-so-good times ... they're no longer around. Matthew Hayden, Stuart MacGill and I are the only blokes in the Australian team going to the West Indies in May who played a Test match with Mark Taylor. Brett Lee is the only other guy in the squad who appeared in Test cricket before 2000, and he made his debut on Boxing Day 1999.

All this change doesn't mean my life as Australian captain will be any less rewarding. In fact, as I've said many times in the past 12 months, because of all the fresh faces the next two or three years could turn out to be among the most exciting I experience during my time in charge.

PART SEVEN
GILLY

*'Every wicketkeeper around the world is expected
to make runs now, and expected to get them fairly
quickly as well.'*

— Ricky Ponting, January 28, 2008

SATURDAY, MARCH 8

I discovered Adam Gilchrist was retiring from international cricket in the middle of the Adelaide Test. It was the night of day two, a day in which Gilly had dropped VVS Laxman, a fairly straightforward catch, one that hit the dead centre of his gloves and just bounced out. When he made that blue, we all thought at once ... *What's happened there?* ... and Gilly's reaction was revealing, one of exasperation more so than anger. It was the sort of mistake he simply didn't make. I was back at the hotel after play, having dinner, when I received a text message from him: 'Are you in your room? Would you mind coming to my room to have a chat.' As soon as I read that I thought, *Something's up here; this isn't good.* I dodged dessert and went up to see him as quickly as I could.

'What's going on, mate?' I asked as soon as he greeted me at the door.

'I'm out,' he replied a little tiredly. 'The time has come.'

He explained that he felt his game, and particularly his wicketkeeping, had slipped to a level where he realised that to get it back to where it needed to be he'd have to do a stack of work. There'd be no short cuts. But he didn't have the desire to do all of that. Not at this time of his life. I thought briefly about trying to talk him out of it, to maybe suggest he give the one-dayers away, to focus on the Tests, but I knew it wasn't my place to say that, and that it wouldn't have made any difference anyway. I can't imagine an elite sportsperson retiring without first going through all the alternatives, again and again and then just one more time. I didn't stay with my mate long; instead, I headed back to my room, pondering cricket life without him, while Gilly began inviting a few senior players and chairman of selectors Andrew Hilditch up to his room, while at the same time chasing family and friends, hoping that as many as possible could get to Adelaide for the last couple of days of the Test. Things moved quickly. He told the rest of the guys the next morning, the media heard whispers about the story during the day, and there was an official announcement at the close of play. By the time Gilly walked out to bat on day four the whole world knew, and there were a few tears about. The crowd at the Adelaide Oval did itself proud, the way they cheered him — it was a special time for a special cricketer.

The first time the boys were together after he'd made his mind up, on the team bus at the start of our short journey from the hotel to the ground for the third day's play, he stood up and confirmed he was retiring. He did so in a pretty matter-of-fact manner, emphasising that we had a Test to win. But later, in the dressing room, talking to us as a group, he choked up as he explained how much he'd loved every minute of his time playing cricket for Australia. I'll never forget his show of emotion. 'The thing I'm going to miss most,' he said, 'is the time in the change rooms, the time I've spent with my mates, you guys, the blokes I've played with.' He didn't talk for long, but every word counted.

His decision surprised me. I had sensed a few times during the season that he'd been thinking about giving the one-dayers away, but continuing on in Test cricket for another 12 months, maybe longer. I'll always wonder if — before he missed a few chances in the Tests against India — that was his original intention. I have never given a thought to how or when my career might end, but at the same time I could definitely understand why he was giving it away. He's been in the game at the highest level for a decade, and I know how hard he has worked on his game, particularly his keeping, throughout his career. That hunger, real hunger, was no longer there to drive him to work as relentlessly as he needed to do to get his greatness back.

He just didn't feel he was sharp enough, wasn't moving well enough, and he was finding it difficult to concentrate *all* the time, which wicketkeepers have to do. But we only needed to watch how he played in some of the Commonwealth Bank Series games, especially during that wonderful farewell century at the WACA, to see that he is still very capable of playing high-class international cricket.

I'M SURE THERE WERE many things that would have weighed into Gilly's decision. He is a very devoted father, and I could see occasionally on tour how the time away from his family was frustrating him. There are a lot of day-to-day pressures we international cricketers face that others aren't aware of ... most of them relating to the reality that we are away from home so often. Being an elite cricketer can be a glamorous business, no doubt about it, but at the same time some of the locations we head to are not necessarily the easiest places to pack your family up and take them with you, particularly if you've got two or three young kids, one of whom might have just started school. You can go a couple of months without seeing your wife and

MATCH WINNER

As well as being one of only four keepers to have completed more than 300 Test dismissals, and one of two to have completed 250 ODI dismissals, Adam Gilchrist hit 33 hundreds in international cricket — 17 in Tests and 16 in ODIs. Thirty of these centuries helped Australia to victory, including every one of his one-day hundreds ...

TESTS

Season	Score	Opponent	Venue	Result for Australia
1999–00	149*	Pakistan	Hobart	won by four wickets
2001	122	India	Mumbai	won by 10 wickets
2001	152	England	Birmingham	won by innings & 118
2001–02	118	New Zealand	Brisbane	drawn
2002	204*	South Africa	Jo'burg	won by innings & 360
2002	138*	South Africa	Cape Town	won by four wickets
2002–03	133	England	Sydney	lost by 225 runs
2003	101*	West Indies	Port-of-Spain	won by 118 runs
2003–04	113*	Zimbabwe	Perth	won by innings & 175
2004	144	Sri Lanka	Kandy	won by 27 runs
2004	104	India	Bangalore	won by 217 runs
2004–05	126	New Zealand	Brisbane	won by innings & 156
2004–05	113	Pakistan	Sydney	won by nine wickets
2005	121	New Zealand	Christchurch	won by nine wickets
2005	162	New Zealand	Wellington	drawn
2006	144	Bangladesh	Fatalluh	won by three wickets
2006–07	102*	England	Perth	won by 206 runs

ONE-DAY INTERNATIONALS

Season	Score	Opponent	Venue	Result for Australia
1997–98	100	South Africa	Sydney	won by seven wickets
1998	118	New Zealand	Christchurch	won by seven wickets
1998	103	Pakistan	Lahore	won by six wickets
1998–99	131	Sri Lanka	Sydney	won by eight wickets
1998–99	154	Sri Lanka	Melbourne	won by 43 runs
2000	128	New Zealand	Christchurch	won by 48 runs
2000	105	South Africa	Durban	won by eight wickets
2002–03	124	England	Melbourne	won by 89 runs
2003	111	India	Bangalore	won by 61 runs
2003–04	172	Zimbabwe	Hobart	won by 148 runs
2005	121*	England	The Oval	won by eight wickets
2005–06	103	World XI	Melbourne	won by 55 runs
2005–06	116	Sri Lanka	Perth	won by six wickets
2005–06	122	Sri Lanka	Brisbane	won by nine wickets
2007	149	Sri Lanka	Barbados	won by 53 runs
2007–08	118	Sri Lanka	Perth	won by 63 runs

kids, phone conversations being as close as you get to a kiss and a hug.

Since I came into the Test team in 1995–96, David Boon's last international season, I've seen different team-mates retire for a wide range of reasons, and it's never been simply a reaction to a drop in form or how they were playing at the time. There are always what I call 'external' pressures — which can vary from case to case — that can impact on a bloke's call to keep going, or to give it away.

The widely different manners in which Mark and Steve Waugh ended their careers provide examples of this. In 2002, there was a lot of media speculation about how much longer they could keep playing for Australia. Neither twin was in the best of form, and every time they failed to post a big score, it was always trumpeted by the media as further evidence that they were past their best. Mark grew sick and tired of reading all the negative stuff about him, so he retired. Stephen used the criticism as motivation. The same media pressure that forced Mark out of the game kept Steve going for longer than might otherwise have been the case.

I don't think I've ever seen anyone retire just because they've have had enough of the game itself. They might quit because of all the other things that go with being an international cricketer — the travel, the training, the scrutiny, the pressure — but they still love the game and the on-field contest. The impression I get, from seeing other guys give it away, is that gradually other things become as important, or even more important, than life as an international cricketer. For the other guys in the Australian set-up, especially the blokes who are building their careers, there is nothing in the world more important than playing for your country as often as you can and doing it as well as you can. People might put all sorts of barriers in front of you, but they won't stop you. They'll hardly slow you down; they might even inspire you. But playing as often as we do can gradually start to wear you down a little, and eventually, I assume, maybe without too much warning, it starts to wear you down a lot. Getting up and going to training becomes hard work. And then that hunger and passion that you've always had for trying to improve yourself every day is not there anymore.

With Gilly having retired, on top of the four guys going last season, and with Rianna and I expecting our first child, it was natural, I guess, for people to ask me if I have started looking towards the end of my career. Gilly turned 36 last November; I hit 33 a month later. The truth is that retirement is one thing I haven't pondered.

Maybe I will when our young baby grows to school age, or we have more children, but from what I've seen cricketers rarely truly plan their retirements. My hope is that I can go out at the top of my game, with the same sense of dignity that has marked the retirements of Shane Warne, Justin Langer, Glenn McGrath and now Gilly. Before that, a few great Australian cricketers felt that they were forced out before they were ready, which was unfortunate. Would I rather play one game too many or one game too few? Definitely, one game too few, but I realise that is not an easy thing to achieve.

I clearly remember something Steve Waugh once said: 'The day I don't think I can go to training and make himself a better player is the day that I think it'll be time to pull up stumps.' Right now, I feel there are lots of ways I can make myself a better player and a better leader. Furthermore, there are voids in my cricket résumé that I'd like to fix, such as my record in India, where I've never made a Test hundred. There's plenty for me to achieve and right at this moment I'm razor keen to work hard to try to make it all happen.

I FIRST GOT TO know Adam Gilchrist well during the 1991–92 season, when we were at the Cricket Academy in Adelaide. We went to South Africa with an AIS team in March '92, Gilly as captain, me as the 17-year-old 'young punk'. He already had a reputation as a special kind of cricketer, and to my young eyes he seemed so much more advanced in his cricket and the way he thought about the game than I was. I realised I could learn a lot about the game by observing how he went about things. In this regard, nothing ever changed.

Even in those days, he always saw himself as a wicketkeeper/ batsman, not a batsman who also kept wicket. Playing purely as a batsman, as he did for his native NSW until he went to Perth in 1994, was never going to satisfy him. In the years that followed that move west, I could never understand when his keeping was criticised, and I often wondered if it came back to the fact that he was such an explosive, high-scoring batsman the knockers found it hard to acknowledge that he was also an excellent gloveman. In my view, he's as good a wicketkeeper as I've seen.

You know the thing they always say about keepers — if you don't notice them, then they're doing a great job. Gilly went better than that, doing all the fundamental things right but also making people stand up and take notice when he did things out of the ordinary. He is tall for a keeper, and athletic, capable of taking some unbelievable one-handed catches. Other keepers would never have gone that wide, or if they did they would have spilt the catch and been rightly criticised as a 'shark', but Gilly made it look natural and inevitable. People used to rave about Ian Healy's work behind the stumps when Shane Warne was bowling, and it was always outstanding, but I don't remember Gilly making too many mistakes off Warney either, and he completed a substantial number of dismissals off the great leg-spinner, too: 59 to be exact, in 70 Tests (Heals had 49 dismissals off Warney's bowling, in 74 Tests).

In all, Gilly averaged 4.33 dismissals per Test (416 in 96 matches), a notable stat because he is the only keeper with even 100 dismissals in Tests to have averaged more than four dismissals per game. Maybe a little of these numbers highlight the fact that he was part of a successful side, which meant we were getting all 20 dismissals in most of the games he played, but it also suggests he was doing plenty right behind the stumps. As the focus of our fielding team, he was superb and aggressive; the batsmen always knew he was there, sweating on a mistake.

For all that, it was as an all-rounder that Gilly changed the game. We always viewed him that way, because he did two of the disciplines — in his case, batting and keeping — exceptionally well. Through the years, the great batting or bowling all-rounders — men such as Sir Garfield Sobers, Keith Miller, Ian Botham, Imran Khan and Kapil Dev — have been vibrant cricketers. Logic says that the way Gilly went about his batting was not always going to come off — you can't try to take apart the opposition attack every time and hope to get away with it — but he succeeded so often that there were periods during his career when he made what he did look easy. It never was.

In my opinion, it was his courage — the totally fearless way he went after the bowling — that set him apart. He took the game on, ignored conventions, and specialised in attacking one-day opening bowlers at seven, eight or nine runs an over, and turning an innings score of 5–200 in a Test match into 5–350 or 5–450 at better than a run a ball. He *always* wanted to ram home an advantage, or rip the game away from the opposition. He must be the best No. 7 Test cricket has ever seen, and I'm sure the judges were right when last November they named him Australia's greatest ever one-day cricketer.

The way we look at the overall role of the wicketkeeper in modern cricket has changed as a result of how successfully he played our game. Every team is now searching for a 'Gilly-like' keeping all-rounder. This has resulted in some sides using keepers who weren't up to Test standard; in doing so, they proved just how rare are players who come even close to matching Gilly's unique all-round ability. Gilly played his 96 Tests consecutively — he never missed a game from November 1999 to January 2008. That's not just a record for wicketkeepers who are always squatting, putting all sorts of pressure on their knees and back; that's the record for consecutive Tests for *all* cricketers. In the same period, England used five keepers in Test matches, India selected 10. Lately, India have had MS Dhoni, who is an excellent cricketer, but he averages about 33 with the bat in Tests, whereas for the first half of his international career Gilly averaged almost double that. South Africa's Mark Boucher, the other keeper to make 400 Test dismissals, scores his runs at about 30 runs an innings; perhaps Sri Lanka's Kumar Sangkkara is closest, as he averages more than 50 as a Test batsman — but his average drops much closer to 40 in Tests when he is also asked to keep wicket.

It was no accident that so many of Gilly's big scores in Tests and especially in ODIs led to Aussie victories. He mightn't have pioneered the concept of a one-day opening batsman attacking from the jump (Sri Lanka were doing it when they won the World Cup in 1996), but he took the concept to a new level. It didn't matter if he scored a hundred, a fifty or maybe even less; so often, he set the mood and in the process made life so much easier for the guys who followed him in the batting order. The bowling team was under pressure from the very first ball, and the batting team could aim for 300, even 350, without having to take too many risks. The 2003 World Cup final against India is a perfect example of this. When Gilly was dismissed for 57 from the last ball of the 14th over, we were 1–105, the perfect platform for us to go all the way to 2–359 without ever really slogging.

There were so many memorable on-field moments with Gilly. One that captured how special he was occurred in the Twenty20 international against England last season, when Channel Nine 'miked' him up and then had the commentators in his ear as the bowlers were running in to bowl. 'Where are you going to hit this one, Gilly?' they'd ask … he'd nominate a particular part of the field … and no matter where the ball was bowled Gilly would crack it to where he wanted. Unbelievable.

His ability to pick up the length of the ball early must be as good as anyone who has ever played the game. Because of this, he was able to make it seem as if he was premeditating some of his shots — this was especially evident when he pulled knee-high deliveries or drove through the line, over the top, balls that pitched well short of a length. These are shots we mortals can't play if you misjudge the length. Gilly's eye was good and his reflexes were fantastic, so he could adjust in an instant and be perfectly balanced as he dispatched the ball to all parts. His ability to concentrate on the task at hand was brilliant, too; out in the middle, he had a rare ability to clear his head of everything bar what really mattered.

There's no shortage of drive in Adam Gilchrist, and he was always very motivated to do the utmost for his team. He won't mind me saying this, but I occasionally got disappointed with him in one-day games, when he'd hit 40 runs from 20 balls but then get out. If I could get 40 from 20, then in my mind I was going on to 100, and unless we were chasing a colossal target it wouldn't worry me if I slowed down a bit to get there. In my pragmatic world, that is what is best for the team. Gilly's mindset was always to keep flying, that if he was 40 from 20 then he should aim for 80 from 40, but if he'd been a fraction more conservative he might even have been more prolific. He could have scored more hundreds than he did. But it wouldn't have been so much fun, and his attitude summed him up — it wasn't about how many hundreds he made or what his batting average might have been, it was looking at might be possible and going for it. He aimed for the clouds and often got there.

GILLY WAS A SENSATIONAL cricketer and is a better bloke. His demeanour and manner around the dressing room, in particular his ability to make time for his team-mates, and especially guys who were new to the team, was always superb. And he enjoyed a celebration as much as anybody I've ever played with. If we won a Test bowling last, come one or two o'clock in the morning he'd still be in the change rooms with his wicketkeeping pads and spikes still on, maybe even his box still on. It wasn't impossible for him to finally head back to the hotel still clad in his playing gear, for one last beer, another story, more laughs.

We shared in plenty of great victories, but the first one that comes to mind when I think of Gilly is India in 2004, when I was injured and he took over as captain. Winning that series, the first Australian victory on Indian turf in 35 years, meant so much for all of us, but it was an especially special moment for him. In the lead-up, coach John Buchanan, Gilly and I had decided to change the way we played — primarily the bowling tactics and field placements we'd employ against the excellent Indian batsmen on their pitches — and as captain there was a lot of pressure on him to implement that game plan effectively. He delivered magnificently. I also think of the 2007 World Cup final, not just because he batted so brilliantly but also because the win was — for him, Glenn McGrath and me — the third Cup final victory in a row. And there was the five-zip Ashes triumph in 2006–07, when immediately I think of Perth ... and not just because he smashed an awesome hundred in our second innings from just 57 deliveries, one ball off the Test record.

Gilly was always a loyal and determined supporter of mine. It was his style to care, and he was very aware that life can sometimes be difficult if you're the Australian skipper. I remember when we took the last wicket at the WACA, the one that regained the Ashes — Panesar, bowled Warne — I was fielding at bat-pad on the offside and when the ball crashed into the stumps I just

JOSIE'S JOY

One thing that always stood out for me with Adam Gilchrist was his ability to share his own time with his team-mates. If a new man came into the squad, Gilly was keen to get to know him, and then, having learned a bit about the bloke, he wanted him to feel part of the group. He had a range of methods for doing this; one day, we were at training, in a circle doing stretches, when out of the blue he shouted, 'Righto everyone, tell us all one thing about yourself that we don't know.' Over the next half hour I saw how an interaction such as this can bond a team just that little bit tighter.

A couple of blokes really opened up. Me? I fell back on an old greyhounds story, of how on the eve of the 1997 Ashes tour I travelled down to Hobart in the back of the ute with a dog named Josie's Joy. She was the outsider of the field but she won and paid $26.30.

I'm not sure if this was exactly the kind of yarn Gilly was after, but then I don't think he was after my inner-most feelings either. I did notice that he quickly moved the discussion on to the next bloke. Still, I'll never forget that journey from Launceston to the old Hobart Showground, a couple of good mates in the front and me in the back, talking to her and patting her every kilometre of the trip. She was jumping up and down and barking all the way to the start, and even in the boxes she kept barking and barking … then the bunny came around and she exploded out, charged to the front, led by six or seven lengths coming into the bend, and hung on to win by a couple. Maybe all the attention I gave her helped. I fed her KitKats all the way home, which we all agreed was the least I could do. We'd made a fortune!

took off running across the wicket. I wasn't sure where I was going. Gilly chased me, jumped on my shoulders, grabbed me around the neck and shouted something like, 'I'm so bloody proud of you!' He knew how much the criticism I'd copped after the Ashes loss in 2005 had impacted on me, and how I'd set about turning things around, as a cricketer and a leader.

He and I will always keep in contact. I intend to talk to him and text him regularly during the West Indies tour, and I'm sure his media and sponsor commitments will see him spending a fair amount of time in Sydney, so there'll be plenty of chances to catch up in the years to come. But there'll still be times when I'll rue the fact he's not there, when I need his advice, his optimism, his humour. We talked so often, as mates over a beer or a coffee, as captain and vice-captain, as second slip and keeper, sitting together in the dressing room after play, as batsmen during a partnership. All of it was about sport. A lot of it was cricket, but any sport would do. He used to say this was my fault, that I was the 'sport tragic', but he was kidding. I have trouble recalling exactly what happened in many games I played in, whereas Gilly can remember details about any Test match involving Australia from the past 30 years. He's got total recall in all manner of sports, and if he works in the media he'll end up not just as a cricket commentator but a sports media all-rounder, and a good and fair one, too.

I remember one thing he said to me while we were batting together during the one-dayer against Sri Lanka in Sydney on February 8. I'd only been in for a couple of overs, when during a mid-pitch chat he suddenly looked at me and said, 'I'm going to miss this.' I thought he meant playing in front of a big crowd, representing your country, but he went on. 'I'm going to miss all the good times we've had on the field. I'm going to miss batting with you.'

'Mate, let's not talk about that now,' I replied. 'We can talk about that later.'

We never did continue that conversation later, but we didn't need to. Everyone knows I loved batting with him.

I don't think Gilly liked the spectacle that was created through February and early March, when every game during the Commonwealth Bank series was promoted as being a part of his 'farewell'. Forever the team man, he tried to get away from that as much as he could, but such is the public's regard for him that was very, very difficult. It was certainly disappointing that we couldn't do the right thing by him and win the last international tournament he played in. That would have been a fitting end for him, because — in my eyes and the eyes of all his comrades and supporters — Adam Gilchrist was always a winner.

PART EIGHT

INDIAN PREMIER LEAGUE

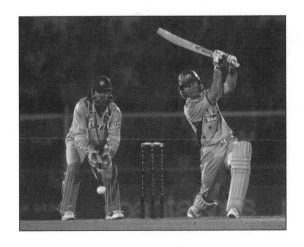

*'It will be good getting a chance to know
and play with some of these guys that I have
spent most of my life playing against. It will
be fun playing against some of my
Australian mates, too.'*

— Ricky Ponting, April 18, 2008

FRIDAY, MAY 2

I guess it's too early, after I've played only four games, for me to make a final judgment on the future of the Indian Premier League, and even on Twenty20 cricket in general. To me, we're in a situation now where there are a lot of players still trying to come to grips with the game, how it's played, its status compared to Tests and one-day internationals. The public and big business, however, seem to have made up their minds. They've taken to it in a big way; they're sure it's here to stay.

What I now know is that Twenty20 is an enjoyable game to play. I'm a convert. Its rise is being driven by the fans, who flocked to it from day one, when national teams played the occasional game, usually at the start or end of a Test or one-day series. They've made it matter. Big money in India saw an opportunity, and cricket officials in that country jumped on for the ride, while elsewhere officials were still thinking about it. The IPL has given 20-over cricket a real competitive edge, and a definite point of difference from 50-over matches and Test cricket. While I was in India, I felt like I was in a genuine competition, not part of a series of made-for-television exhibitions. I want the IPL to work, and I really want the Kolkata Knight Riders, my team, to win.

The IPL has put an extraordinary amount of money into the game, which has certainly got the players' attention. This is especially true for Test players from teams who are unable to reward their stars as well as we are paid in Australia, for veteran players who might not want to endure the long haul that is modern Test and ODI cricket, and — perhaps most ominously for the game's future — for young players who have not yet reached the top. This is the danger for the game as a whole, that some in it might decide that the IPL riches are more attractive than 'traditional' cricket. That's what I fear. That is what everyone in the sport must guard against.

BRENDON McCULLUM, NEW ZEALAND'S outstanding keeper-batsman, who was a team-mate of mine at the Knight Riders, found himself in a similar situation to me in that he had to leave Kolkata after just a handful of games, in his case to join the Black Caps' tour of England. Purely from a monetary perspective, that was the last thing in the world he wanted to do, because the money he was earning in India was substantially more than he would get for playing in the UK. Brendon is a passionate New Zealander who wants to build as good a record as he can in international cricket. He also has only a limited time as a professional sportsperson — these are probably the best earning years of his life. He doesn't want to miss out financially on what he'll otherwise never get.

The best cricketers in the game want to keep representing their country, but if it's going to be costing them *that* much money then there are tough decisions ahead — for players and also for administrators. We cannot afford to lose teams such as

New Zealand and the West Indies from international cricket, but my fear is that this could happen if the game cannot strike a balance between Tests and ODIs and the IPL's riches. Unless such a balance can be achieved, I could see some countries' cricket teams declining in the way Zimbabwe's sides have struggled over the past few years.

Personally, I think a solution can be found, provided the IPL fights the temptation to expand its competition. To do so would be a mistake on two fronts: it will put too much pressure on the players to choose between employers, and it will unnecessarily test the public's appetite for Twenty20. In my view, one annual six-week IPL season works best, and hopefully the international game can set its schedules around that. There might be the occasional overlap, and players and franchises will have to accept in those circumstances that country must always come before club, but within that framework the IPL can become an exciting constant in cricket's calendar. This year, the IPL runs from the opening ceremony and first game on April 18 through to the final on June 1. In my view, if a future IPL competition goes longer than six weeks, or if they try to stage 'back to back' leagues, even two competitions in the same year, then players will resent the pressure they'll be under to pick one form of the game over another, it will be tougher to retain the public's interest, and eventually the golden goose will be no more.

I can't see a scenario where I would play IPL instead of international cricket. But I might be 'old school'. I'm not sure if all cricketers from all Test-playing nations will always feel as I do, and it could be that if the IPL keeps growing or even more money becomes involved, then the next generation of players might opt for franchise over country. Everyone in the game should work towards ensuring that never happens.

TWENTY20 CRICKET HAS grown on me, a consequence of me playing the game more and understanding it better. It is not just 'hit and miss', as I first feared. I never thought it would get to where it is right now, and one reason for that was that I couldn't see where it was going to fit into the international program. I couldn't see where the game was going to find an extra window in every year when the players of all the major countries would be available at the same time. Sure, the Australian team has had extended breaks in 2006 and 2007, but other teams were fully booked out at the same time.

My first game of Twenty20, played in early 2005, was no more than a promotional tool for a one-day series in New Zealand. It was about getting new fans to the game. In England, Twenty20 gained a foothold because in summer you could start a game in the late afternoon and finish it before the sun set. With sports television always searching for content, it caught the attention of business executives and cricket officials on the subcontinent. Quickly, certainly in India, it became the game of choice for many who don't have traditional ties to cricket. It's possible that these new audiences will now start playing and watching other, older forms of the game. If that happens, it's possible for everyone to win. That's why I think if it's managed right, Twenty20 can be very good for cricket, because it will broaden our overall fan base.

Further, Twenty20 should end up being good for 50-over cricket and even Test cricket, in the way 50-over cricket eventually boosted Test cricket through attacking batsmen using their limited-over methods in Test cricket without damaging their batting averages. The overall run-rate in five-day cricket increased, games were won rather than drawn, fans loved it. This is certainly what happened in Australia. These days, the middle overs in a 50-over innings are often boring, as batsmen are happy to score at four or five runs an over and the bowlers are content to let them, but I reckon Twenty 20 will prove that such conservatism is unnecessary. We've seen a little of this already, through the efforts of players such as Andrew Symonds; as Twenty20 grows I think we'll see more bold batsmen take to ODIs in the same manner.

MY ORIGINAL AGREEMENT IN regards to the IPL was with the Board of Control for Cricket in India (BCCI). From there, because I am a contracted player with Cricket Australia, it was a case of officials in India and Australia coming to an agreement that I could play, and then I had to wait for the 'player auction' to find out which franchise I would be representing.

Because my availability over the first two years was going to be limited, I was tempted not to be involved at all. I was offered a sign-on fee and then I would be paid a proportion of the money bid for me at auction (that percentage being based on how many games I played). The 'carrot' was just big enough for me to want to be involved from the start. Being involved in the auction was one of the stranger experiences of my sporting life. There were all sorts of rumours buzzing as to what players might go for ... my name came into the sales ring ... US$400,000 was bid ... and that was it! It was late at night, Sydney time, and I was watching FoxSports News, when across the 'ticker' bar at the bottom of the screen came the news that I was going to Kolkata. Some people suggested there was something sinister about the fact I received less than a number of other top-level cricketers, but when you look at the overall list there were some weird bids, high and low. It didn't really worry me. Australia's tour of Pakistan was still on when the auction happened (it was eventually cancelled on March 11), so there was a distinct possibility I wouldn't be available for the IPL in 2008 and it seemed likely that my international program in 2009 would stop me playing the second season of IPL, too. So I could understand why I wouldn't have been at the top of any of the franchises' shopping lists.

By the time the IPL came around, I was very enthusiastic, though this wasn't because I felt as if I was going on some great adventure or that we were revolutionaries or anything like that. It's just that I love playing cricket. Having had a good break from the game since the Commonwealth Bank Series, I was taken with the idea of getting in some good solid training and playing some serious sport before our Test tour of the West Indies. Because I live in Sydney but play for Tasmania, I can't train with the NSW squad, so I'm always searching for ways and means to get my batting and fitness work done. I was in India for a fortnight before the first IPL game, working on my game every day, and for two weeks before that I was training my backside off at home, whether it was priming my cricket skills or sweating in the gym. By the time the first Twenty20 ball was bowled, I was really excited about cricket again.

SHARING A DRESSING ROOM with blokes from different countries is something I haven't done a lot of during my career. It was good fun, not so much because I was suddenly confronted with a variety of cultures and different senses of humour; more because I was able to work with and support my new colleagues, blokes I hardly knew. I love the team environment, and being able to help people. As I did when I played with Somerset in 2004, I especially liked working with some of the young blokes from the local domestic set-up, and also, as a senior player, I enjoyed trying to build a genuine team spirit. As it turned out, I hardly scored a run in the four games I played, but I still received plenty of 'whispers in my ear' about the value of my contribution. I found this feedback a little strange, in the sense that I felt like I was stepping into *their* dressing room, rather than them into mine, but my natural inclination is to try to boost the team I am a part of, get us all working as one. That's what happened here.

The Knight Riders captain is Sourav Ganguly, and sharing a dressing room with him gave me a chance to see from a slightly different angle the kind of suffocating pressure the top Indian players are under. Sourav is very driven in the way he trains and prepares, a bloke who will get into a net and bat and bat and bat. There were a couple of times when I was due to use his net straight after him but I was left standing there, waiting 20 or 30 minutes with my pads on, before I finally had my hit. On other occasions, I had young team-mates, bowlers in particular, after games or at training sessions, asking me questions about how they were going or what they should be doing. I don't know if the skipper felt threatened by me getting involved in this way, but it might have been a catalyst for one funny episode, which happened when I was fielding at slip in our game against the Mumbai Indians at Eden Gardens ...

One thing I've learned in Twenty20 cricket is that you have to be always thinking a few balls, even a few overs ahead. If you don't, the game will pass you by, you have no time to ponder or to think, *We'll see how things are going in 10 or 20 minutes.* For a Twenty20 captain in the field, the job is in many ways very similar to a 50-over game, except you have to do things by the ball rather then by the over. If you have a hunch something is going to happen you have to make sure you react to it — change the field, talk to the bowler — before the ball is bowled, not at the end of the over. I've always felt that I'm pretty good at reading a game in this manner, so a couple of times in this game, as we sought to defend 137, I suggested a field change. Then, when I couldn't get my captain's attention, I quietly made a change myself. Big mistake. Suddenly, Sourav was looking at me and pointing down to third man. I'd been 'banished' to the boundary!

Probably the biggest frustration for me in the short time I was there was that our bowlers weren't quite able to respond to suggestions I made about competing with Aussie batsmen such as Adam Gilchrist, Andrew Symonds and Matthew Hayden. I spoke at team meetings about what tactics we could adopt against them, and my main message was that because they are special players we needed to do things a bit differently. But that didn't happen, and while Gilly (who scored 23) and Symmo (32) didn't do us too much harm in our game against Deccan Chargers, Haydos (70 not out) smashed us in Chennai. I'm not sure exactly what the boys said about me in their team talks, but it must have been on the money, because I was out for a first-ball duck in both matches. They never even had a chance to sledge me! Not that there's any time for that in Twenty20 anyway.

I DID ENJOY BEING able to play cricket without any of the extra responsibilities that come with being captain. I certainly never saw Sourav at a media conference and thought, *Gee, I wish that was me.*

I quickly came to feel as if I was a home-town Kolkata cricketer, a Knight Rider. I don't think it's reached the stage yet where hundreds of local schoolchildren have Ricky Ponting posters on their walls, but there is a real fervour about our home games, and the people I ran into on the street or at and around my hotel seem genuinely excited that I am 'one of them'. I especially liked the fact that when we were playing at home, if the crowd had a choice between cheering for me or supporting an Indian Test player from another franchise, they backed me every time. Aussies at other teams had the same experience.

I also enjoyed having the chance to work with former Australian head coach John Buchanan again. Buck is the Kolkata coach and he'd recruited current NSW coach, Matthew Mott, fresh from the Blues' success in the Pura Cup final, as his assistant. Initially, it was hard for them because they were coming into an environment where they didn't know anything about most of the local players, and with Sourav playing Test cricket in South Africa, it was left to Buck, Matty, Brendon McCullum and me to work out which of the locals were going to get into our squad. I found this aspect of our preparation rewarding, and it led to what, for me, was one of the best stories to come out of the IPL.

In our squad were pace bowlers such as Pakistan's Shoaib Akhtar and Umar Gil and India's Agit Agarkar and Ishant Sharma, but for a variety of reasons we couldn't get them on the park together for the start of the competition. Instead, we turned to Ashok Dinda. 'Ashok Who?' I hear you ask. As we'd prepared for the first game, a few net bowlers came down to help us out, one of whom was Ashok, a fast-medium bowler who'd just turned 24 and who has played 20-odd first-class games, but hasn't had any success at that level for a couple of seasons. He hails from a village about three hours out of Kolkata. We were impressed by what he did in the nets, but sensed that the Knight Riders weren't going to sign him. However, with Shoiab and Umar out of the team for the first game, we insisted that not only should he be included in our squad, he should be in the starting XI, too. Then, out in the middle, I learnt for the first time that Ishant Sharma doesn't like bowling the first over of an innings, so Ashok was handed the new ball. One week, he was a mere net bowler; the next, he's bowling the opening over for Kolkata in the first game of one of the most revolutionary events in cricket history. He is still in the starting XI and going well. Throughout the time I was in India, he had three or four of his family staying in his hotel room with him, because things were much plusher there than back in the village from where they came.

Playing at Eden Gardens in Kolkata is always a great experience, but right at the moment, unfortunately, the square is below standard. This was especially true for our home opener against Deccan Chargers, when the ball was exploding through the pitch's surface. The floodlights also failed in this game, which led to some confusion because the officials weren't sure if you can apply the Duckworth-Lewis method if the lights don't work. Though I assume it was never the intention, it is possible, after a reading of the regulations, to conclude that Duckworth-Lewis only applies to matches interrupted by rain. Fortunately, they found the right switch, the lights came back, and my Aussie team-mate David Hussey played a terrific innings to get us home.

Two days before that, I was at the opening ceremony in Bangalore, an event that featured plenty of Bollywood, music, lasers, fireworks and even the Washington Redskins cheerleaders. I wondered, at times, if the off-field razzamatazz went over the top. There were times during the games I played when they had to hold up the cricket because the disc jockey was still rocking. But for better or worse 20-over cricket lends itself to that. Part of it is about seeking points of difference — from other forms of cricket and even other forms of entertainment. The opening ceremony was such a massive event that the game between the Knight Riders and the Bangalore Royal Challengers was delayed for something like 45 minutes, but when we finally got underway Brendon McCullum produced a spectacular show of his own: 158 from 73 balls with 10 fours and 13 sixes, one of the best exhibitions of pure hitting I have ever seen.

I scored 20 from 20 balls in this game, playing a supporting role, and doing my best during a series of mid-wicket chats to ensure that Brendon didn't throw his dig away after he got off to a flying start. He actually didn't score off the first six deliveries he faced, but then hit the next four balls from Zaheer Khan for four, four, six and four. He was 40 from 19 balls when the first wicket, Ganguly, fell in the sixth over, but if he'd got out then all the early momentum would have been lost. 'Let's make sure we get another partnership going,' I said. For the next six overs, we scored at nine runs and over; after that, he went crazy, smashing his last 99 runs from a freakish 35 balls. As I said to him out in the middle, in Twenty20 you have more time than you think. Sometimes, the right batting strategy is to pull back a little, hit the ball into the gaps, make sure you don't lose the momentum.

I saw over the next 11 days how Twenty20 can be a very unfair game. For middle order batsmen, it's pretty hard work — your job is to go in with an over or two to go, when there's not much to be gained. Meanwhile, bowlers can do a lot of things right and have nothing go their way — top edges falling safe, that sort of thing — while another bowler can send down three bad balls in a row and take a hat-trick. The teams around the world that play the game well will feature a lot of skilful Twenty20 players, but there is still a lot of luck involved. I know 'sky balls' happen in 50-over games, too, but you usually have time to make amends. In 20-over cricket, you rarely do.

After we won our first two games, the Twenty20 buzz around Kolkata was incredible. The talk was about how the team would go once it reached the semi-finals, but I suspect we're more a 'middle of the road' side. This was borne out in our next two games, when he lost to Chennai and Mumbai. However, our principal owner, Shahrukh Khan, a major Indian film producer and founder of Red Chillies Entertainment, the Knight Riders' franchisee, remains very excited. Shahrukh is a terrific bloke, and a man who I quickly discovered is incredibly passionate about his cricket team, to the point that it is now not unusual for me to receive extraordinarily lengthy and always friendly text messages from him.

I was sad to leave when I did — one, because I was having such an enjoyable time; two, because it was a seriously exciting event; and three, because I felt as if I owed them a little, given that I'd scored only 39 runs in my four innings.

I enjoyed getting to know better blokes who had previously only been opponents — men such as Ajit Agarkar and Murali Kartik. And I especially enjoyed my time with a team-mate named Laxmi Shukla, the captain of Bengal in Indian domestic cricket.

Back in the late 1990s, Laxmi was one of the most promising young cricketers in India, and he made his ODI debut as a 17-year-old in March 1999. Unfortunately, he didn't have any immediate success, and he was cast aside after just three matches. He came to be regarded as a reasonable middle-order batsman and a steady bowler, one of those all-rounders who is not quite good enough in either skill to be successful at the highest level. I quickly learned, though, from watching him in the nets, that he is one of the purest hitters of a cricket ball, especially against slow bowling, that I've ever seen.

However, one day, not long after I arrived in India, he told me that he struggled with the pull and hook shots, to the point that in games, his opponents would constantly pitch the ball short at him, and wait for him to get himself out.

'I think I can fix that,' I said.

I grabbed a tennis racquet and a dozen tennis balls and we went into a vacant net. Laxmi was padded up, bat in hand, as if this was a normal hit, and after I showed him a few technical things about playing cross-bat shots properly I started smacking the tennis balls into the wicket so they'd bounce up around his helmet. His reflex was to try to whack the ball as high and as hard as he could, but I wanted him to strike with more control, and not necessarily hit it in the air. When we played Matt Hayden's Super Kings in Chennai, Laxmi batted seven, going out to bat in the 10th over, and sure enough, first ball, they bounced him and he ducked out of the way. Soon after, Jacob Oram dropped it short ... and Laxmi rocked back and creamed a pull shot forward of square for four. On the sideline, we all roared our approval, and he was looking for me, grin from ear to ear, eager to let me know how proud and happy he was that he'd got the stroke exactly right.

I came out of that cosmopolitan Knight Rider dressing room with some new friendships, and with a better understanding of some guys, too. One of those was David Hussey, Michael's younger brother, who I suspect I will be playing with again soon, in an Australian side. Another was Ishant Sharma, with whom I'd had a couple of interesting battles in Australia, but (as we joked about a few times during the IPL) this doesn't mean we're going to be giving each other a cuddle in the middle of the wicket next time we face each other in a Test match.

An irony of the tournament was that, while the Australian players all seemed to get on really well with their Indian counterparts, the same wasn't always true of the Indians themselves. It was impossible for me not to have a quiet chuckle when I saw the replays of Harbhajan and Sreesanth having a blue in a match between the Kings XI Punjab and the Mumbai Indians, which left Sreesanth in tears. For Harbhajan to do that to a guy with whom he has played plenty of international cricket was, in my view, quite dismal.

In one sense, it is disappointing that I won't be able to play in the IPL next season, but for me it's just part of the 'swings and roundabouts' of international cricket. England's players couldn't play this year, we can't play next year, but we'll get our chance in the years to come. I'm very comfortable with that scenario. I'll always want to wear my Australian cap first. As I've said from the start, I want to play international cricket for as long as I can and as well as I can, but if, like Shane Warne, Adam Gilchrist and Glenn McGrath, I can play more IPL when my international career is over, then that will be a bonus.

PART NINE

THE AUSTRALIANS IN THE WEST INDIES

*'It's a really good time in my career,
to have some of these younger guys
coming into the team now.'*

— Ricky Ponting, May 10, 2008

THURSDAY, MAY 15

If you'd told me last August, on the flight to South Africa for the World Twenty20, that I would have felt as good at the beginning of this Caribbean adventure as I do right now, I would have laughed at you. My expectation would have been that I'd be a little weary by this point, after eight months of cricket, but the way the season has worked out, with that extended break between the end of the Commonwealth Bank Series and the start of the IPL, I felt really good when we landed in Jamaica last Monday.

Prior to the IPL, I'd put the bat away for a couple of weeks, and played a heap of golf before flying to Kolkata. As I've already explained, I then got caught up in the excitement of the Twenty20 matches, and was feeling very positive about life when I returned to Oz for a pre-Windies tour camp in Brisbane. Now we are here for the start of the post-Gilchrist era, arriving with plenty of challenges to respond to, not the least of them being: 'Can the captain regain his most productive form?'

I guess if I was looking for somewhere to get back to my best it would be the West Indies. My first major tour with the Australian team was to the Caribbean, for the famous series in 1995 when Mark Taylor's team finally regained the Frank Worrell Trophy. I didn't play a Test on the trip, but in five Tests from two tours, 1999 and 2003, I've averaged 98.71, with four hundreds. It was here in 1999 that I regained my Test place after losing it during the Ashes series in Australia that was played earlier that season, and I've been in the side ever since. In 2003, I scored a century in each of the first three Tests before missing the fourth through illness. In 25 one-dayers from four tours — 1995, 1999, 2003 and the 2007 World Cup — I've averaged 42.80, with six fifties and a hundred last year against Scotland in St Kitts. I love the place.

We landed in Kingston without a vice-captain, because Michael Clarke, just appointed to replace Adam Gilchrist, has stayed in Australia for personal reasons. Brad Hodge replaces him. We're not sure exactly when Pup will arrive — the instruction to him was simple: stay home for as long as you need. The strong likelihood is that he will miss the first Test, but he could be back with us in time for the second Test, in Antigua, which beings two weeks today.

Before we began the long flight to the Windies, the questions from the media about the upcoming tour were drowned out by those concerning the IPL, with one inquisitor pointing out that there could be a clash for TV viewers: the Twenty20 on one station, the West Indies Tests on another. 'I'd like to think that most people in Australia will be watching their national team represent their country over a couple of the other guys — retired guys most of them now — representing an Indian franchise,' I replied. 'I know if I was sitting back in my lounge room, being the cricket traditionalist I am, I would certainly be watching Test cricket over the IPL.'

As I tried to get comfortable in my seat I couldn't help thinking that our time in the Windies would serve as an escape from the stresses of what had been such a turbulent Australian summer. It was funny, when I was asked about this I replied, 'Everything to do with last summer is long behind us now, it's up to all of us to move on and get on with things.' And then I added, '*Last year* for me was a little bit different than what I've been used to for the last six or seven years. It was one of those years where I had a few high moments but the majority of it involved pretty low scores.'

I italicised 'last year' deliberately. I guess you could argue that this Windies tour is still part of the 2007–08 season, but for me it's like a new beginning.

Our squad includes a couple of new faces, NSW left-arm wrist-spinner Beau Casson and Queensland quick Ashley Noffke, while Brad Haddin, of course, is the natural successor to Gilly and Stuart MacGill has proved his fitness. Reflecting the fact that we're a team in transition, four of the 15 players on the plane — Casson, Noffke, Haddin and NSW left-arm quick Doug Bollinger (who has come in for the injured Ben Hilfenhaus) — have not played a Test; two more — Hodge and Mitchell Johnson — have not appeared in a Test outside Australia; and a seventh, Phil Jaques, has played just one Test outside Australia, against Bangladesh in 2006. Only four of us — MacGill, Hayden, Lee and Ponting — have made a Test tour of the West Indies before.

At the same time, things are happening that highlight how exhilarating change can be. For example, when I faced Mitch in the nets in Brisbane during our pre-tour camp, I couldn't help but think how much he's improved since we got together at the same venue last November, before the Sri Lanka Tests. He was a real handful, a lot of the guys commented on that, and I was also taken by how vibrant our net sessions were. More and more, I've come to realise how good a barometer that can be as to the on-field competitiveness of a top-level cricket team.

Another instance of this occurred here in Kingston today, painfully for me, when Bing gave me a good working over. The quality of the Sabina Park practice wickets wasn't great, the leader of our pace attack was charging in … and one pitched just short of a length and spat up at me, striking me on the gloves. By the time I was finished my net, the pitch had more divots in it than a driving range and though I don't think the session did too much for my timing, it certainly made me concentrate. I enjoyed that. I always want to face Binga in the nets, and I want him charging in. Same with Mitch, Sarf, all the quicks. I know I'll cop a few bruised fingers, but that's a small price well worth paying. Who cares if I get out four or five times during the net session? Since the 2005 Ashes tour, when I felt our training sessions often lacked intensity, I've demanded that my batting practice is always competitive, that I'm in 'game mode' and the bowlers are, too.

One of the anomalies of this relatively short Test tour, which involves just one preliminary game (against a Jamaica Select XI) and three Tests, is that a couple of guys probably won't get a game, because we have to play close to our likely Test XI in the warm-up. Chairman of selectors Andrew Hilditch arrived here yesterday, and we'll sit down tonight to discuss exactly what side we should put on the park for the tour opener. The likelihood is that Matt Hayden, still struggling with an Achilles tendon problem, won't play, in the hope that he'll be ready for the first Test. This will give Simon Katich and Brad Hodge chances to press for a Test recall.

SCREEN TEST

While we were in camp in Brisbane, I took advantage of the absolute latest in technology, by batting in the practice nets with a giant plasma television positioned in the next net. One of the coaching staff put a video camera on me, and the footage was immediately played on the TV screen, so that I could see exactly how I was playing my strokes.

I'd never done anything like this before, and I found it invaluable. It's great to have a coach who knows your game watching you in the nets or during a match, but to see what you're doing for yourself, to be able to identify your own flaws and then be able to rectify errors immediately is a fantastic aid. I've often studied game footage over the years — a split screen showing when you're going well and when you're not can be very useful — but this was different, so much more immediate, and I came out of the session genuinely excited about the way I was hitting the ball.

I'm not sure how difficult it will be to take the big screen away with us on overseas tours in future, but if it's possible, I'd be all for it. Straight afterwards, I described it as the best training device I'd ever used, and more than a week later I still think that. It was brilliant.

TUESDAY, MAY 20

Tour game, at Trelawny (May 16–18): Jamaica Select XI 297 (CS Baugh 111*; SCG MacGill 4–79) and 194 (SM Katich 4–15) drew with the **Australians** 396 (SM Katich 97, A Symonds 86, BJ Haddin 64) and 1–65

From the cricket perspective, this game went very well for us, with a number of guys who needed to score some runs or take some wickets doing exactly that. However, much of this good work was overshadowed by the controversy that came about after we wore caps bearing the name of our tour sponsor, Victoria Bitter, rather than baggy greens when we fielded in the Jamaica Select XI's first innings.

The feedback we received, most of it generated from comments made by past players, was all negative. We never realised we'd upset so many people by doing what we did. It was a situation where, placed in an awkward position, we made a choice that was the easiest in the circumstances, though I am happy to concede that perhaps we should have gone looking for a different solution. The irony is over the past couple of generations of Australian cricketers, the regard for the baggy green has grown enormously — I would argue that there has never been a time when it was more respected. When I started my Test career, caps were handed out at the start of a tour in what now seems to be a ridiculously blasé fashion, in the same way you received the rest of your tour gear. That doesn't happen now. Instead, the legend of the cap has grown enormously. Because of this evolution, our decision to wear the sponsor's caps has struck a nerve in a way it might not have done 20 or 30 years ago.

Just before the game, Brad Haddin — the one bloke in our starting line-up who has not played a Test — told me that he didn't want to wear the Test cap until he made his debut. 'I don't want to wear a baggy green until I've earned it,' he said. Hadds might be the only keeper in our squad, but he is the sort of bloke who never takes anything for granted, and he won't think of himself as a Test cricketer until he actually walks out on the field on the morning of the first Test. As a team, we didn't want to go into the game wearing an assortment of caps, and not everyone wanted to field in a white 'floppy' hat. The least-worst option, we felt after I discussed the situation with team manager Steve Bernard, was for us to wear our blue training caps, the ones that carry the VB logo. With hindsight, we should have done what we did in the second innings — the guys with baggy greens wore them, while Hadds kept in a floppy (though he'd much rather keep in a cap) — but it is a scenario I'd prefer to avoid altogether in future. It could be that a new cap needs to be created, one to be worn in tour games. Already, Cricket Australia has floated the idea of every player being given a baggy green-like cap without an emblem on the front, or perhaps the Cricket Australia logo, to wear if the same circumstances come up again.

I must say I was bemused by some of the more vitriolic criticism that came our way, most notably from one former Australian player who was quick to say in the media that what we'd done was disgraceful. This was coming from a bloke who a few years ago felt so highly of his own baggy green that he sold it at auction to the highest bidder.

THERE WERE A NUMBER of positives to come out of the match. The value of Simon Katich's man-of-the-match performance (97 and 37 not out with the bat, 2–51 and 4–15 with the ball) was accentuated by the news that Matt Hayden is still struggling and is no good thing to play in the upcoming Test, while Stuey MacGill's four wickets in their first innings was encouraging, especially his first spell of 3–22 from 12 overs. After the game, there was some talk that Shane Warne might be planning a comeback for the 2009 Ashes series — conjecture prompted by Warney's good form bowling four overs at a time in the IPL — but my view is that Stuey is the best candidate at present. 'If his body stays right there is no doubt that he is the best wicket-taking spinner in Australia,' I said when the subject was raised. 'If he keeps himself fit and has the desire and passion to keep playing cricket then I'm pretty sure he will be good enough to get the Ashes job done.' Not long after, I received a text message from Warney, expressing his disappointment that the story had got some traction.

Two of Stuey's wickets in this game involved Brad Haddin, a catch and a stumping, as our new keeper completed five

THE BAGGY GREEN

Today, the baggy green is a Test-match cap, and for all the players in the Australian squad it is a much cherished item. In former days, if you wanted another cap you just had to ask for one, but times have changed — Matthew Hayden, for example, has had one baggy green throughout his entire career, and if he needs a new one he'll have to sign a form that says the old is worn out and won't be going anywhere (such as a public auction). Surely, this shows how seriously we regard the cap.

I have had two baggy greens in my career. The first was stolen on the way home from our tour of Sri Lanka and Zimbabwe in 1999, when I'd played 28 Tests (going into this Windies series I'm up to 116). The one that's shared the rest of my career with me is very precious: it never travels in my kit or my suitcase; it stays in my hand luggage or close to me at all times. At home, it is stored in a safe and special place.

My ambition is this cap will stay with me for the remainder of my career. It's been through so many adventures with me, all the ups and downs, that it wouldn't feel the same if I had to play a Test match without it.

dismissals on the first day. Jaquesy, Symmo and Hadds all made some good runs in our first innings, while our pace attack had a good hit-out. I scored 17 in the first innings, and wasn't very happy, and then 20 not out in the second, when I felt that my feet were starting to move in the right directions. A couple of shots off the back foot — one a pull shot through mid-wicket, the other a hook shot just backward of square — were much more like it, and left me thinking that a big score is just around the corner.

For most of the last day it looked like we were going to prevail. However, a 10th-wicket partnership held us up for a while and then a storm blew in over Montego Bay and that forced us off the field 90 minutes before the scheduled time for stumps, when we were 31 runs away from victory.

WEDNESDAY, MAY 28

First Test, West Indies v Australia at Kingston (May 22–26): Australia
431 (RT Ponting 158, MEK Hussey 56, BJ Hodge 67, A Symonds 70*) and
167 (A Symonds 79; DJ Bravo 4–47) defeated **West Indies** 312 (RS Morton
67, S Chanderpaul 118) and 191 (SR Clark 5–32) by 95 runs

It's amazing to think that, prior to this Test match, the last time
Australia had played a day of Test cricket overseas was on April
20, 2006, a fraction more than 25 months ago. With Matt
Hayden ruled out, Simon Katich was duly chosen as an opener
and Brad Hodge came into the middle order. This left me the
second oldest member of the team, behind only 36-year-old
Stuart MacGill.

As a Test side, we were coming off that hard-fought victory
over India, while the West Indies went into the game on something
of an upswing. Amazingly, they didn't win a Test between the end
of May 2005 and late December 2007, but in the last five months
they've won Tests against South Africa and Sri Lanka, which
prompted stand-in Windies skipper Ramnaresh Sarwan to speak
with a little confidence at the pre-game media conference. 'It's a
great time, actually,' Sarwan said when asked if this was a good
time to be meeting us. 'Obviously, they've got quite a lot of new
faces as well. The players that are there are very good, and you
obviously can't take anybody for granted. But it's a great
opportunity for us as a team to continue to play well.'

We felt it was important to stifle as quickly as possible any
optimism they might have felt, which was one reason I was
delighted with my first-day hundred.

Another cause for joy was the fact that I played extremely
well — a welcome change after my struggles in Australia and
lack of runs in the IPL. I didn't do a lot wrong, my concentration
was strong and I felt my feet were moving in all the right

THREE 'NEW' MEN

There were three changes for this Test from the top seven in the batting order that played in the fourth Test against India four months ago. With Matthew Hayden injured, Michael Clarke absent and Adam Gilchrist retired, the new men are Simon Katich, Brad Hodge and Brad Haddin.

Here are three guys with a few things in common. All have been waiting patiently on the sidelines, hoping for an opportunity and doing plenty right so that if a chance did come up they'd be there to take it. Hadds has been obliged to wait for Gilly to finish his career, just as Gilly had to wait for Ian Healy, and now that the NSW gloveman has his chance I'm certain we'll quickly be acclaiming him as an accomplished Test keeper-batsman. Gilly was a once-in-a-lifetime cricketer, so it will be hard following in such a unique champion's footsteps, but Hadds has the ability and strength of character to quickly forge his own path. Not many people realise just what a natural athlete he is — if all the Australian players on this tour had a sprint over 20 or 25 metres, I reckon Hadds would win every time. He becomes Australia's 400th Test cricketer.

Kat lost his Test place soon after the 2005 Ashes series, and then he lost his Aussie contract, too, but he has fought his way back through the sheer weight of runs he has scored in domestic cricket during the past two seasons. I see his return as a great tribute to his ability, determination and tenaciousness, and a real lesson for others who might find themselves in the sort of position he was in two-and-a-half years ago.

The way Hodgey has returned to Test cricket is another terrific story. He was very unlucky to lose his place in the top side when he did, so soon after he scored an unbeaten double century against South Africa in 2005–06. He was born 10 days after I was in 1974, on December 29 (David Boon's 14th birthday), and we've known each other since our days at the Academy, when I quickly learned that he is a batsman with an enormous amount of natural talent. Right now, as captain, it's reassuring to know that there are gifted blokes like him around who we can call on whenever things get tight. Over the next two or three years, it wouldn't surprise me if he enjoyed an extended run in the Test and one-day line-ups.

directions. It was nice to feel comfortable at the crease. Physically, I felt terrific, and the only downer was that I was dismissed just before stumps, out to a brilliant one-handed catch by Brenton Parchment after I thought I'd pulled Dwayne Bravo forward of square for four. Having been 2–37, it would have been quite an achievement to lose only one more wicket for the rest of the day, and I would have liked to come back on day two and tried for a really big score. Fortunately, Andrew Symonds and Brad Hodge allowed us to post an excellent first-innings total, and then our bowlers produced a quality all-round effort to give us a 119-run lead.

It was one of those wickets where once the hardness went out of the ball it was hard to score runs, and it got more difficult in this way as the game progressed. I was confident 350 would be an impossible fourth-innings target, but when we could only make 167 in our second innings — with Symmo getting almost half of them after we collapsed to 5–18 — I thought we might have opened the door for them. There were times during Symmo's dig when I thought, *That's as good as I've ever seen you bat.* It wasn't the boundaries he hit or even the shots he played, it was more the solidity of his defence and the way he managed the situation. He kept us in front, Brad Hodge offered terrific support, and then Stuart Clark completed the best innings bowling figures of his Test career — 5–32 from 20 overs, including the first three wickets of the innings — and the game ended just before the scheduled time for tea on day five.

This was Sarf's second major bowling contribution of the game. On day two, after Parchment and Devon Smith began the West Indies' reply with an opening stand of 47, he took three wickets in 16 balls, giving us an advantage we never really handed back at any stage. He has become a bowler with a happy knack of getting us a wicket, or a clutch of wickets, when we really need them. The latter two wickets in this spell, Sarwan and Parchment, were both caught behind, the first dismissals of Brad Haddin's Test career. At the start of day five, Sarf took 3–11 in a spell of 10 overs, an effort that went a long way towards winning him the man-of-the-match award, the third of his career in his 16th Test.

The way he and his pace-bowling comrades, Brett Lee and Mitchell Johnson, went about their business on day five was super impressive. As you can tell, I'm sure, from the positive tone of my writing, I am really excited by this win. The Windies started the day at 1–46, chasing 287, and they must have given themselves some sort of chance, even though the pitch was wearing. But the way we went about things during that crucial first session was superb, really high-class Test cricket. We didn't give them any easy runs, the bowlers stuck to their jobs manfully, and we took five wickets in the first two hours for just 71 runs. The thing is, these pitches are vastly different to what we're used to in Australia, and our bowlers have to find different ways of working batsmen over and getting them out. The adaptability of our bowlers is a vital part of their makeup, a real tribute to their skill and their cricket brains, and also to the nous of our support staff, who are forever pointing us in the right directions.

MICHAEL CLARKE HAS ARRIVED in the Caribbean, and it will be good to have him back, because we're playing a pretty fair side, who look like having their first choice captain, Chris Gayle, and pace spearhead, Jerome Taylor, returning to their line-up for the second Test in Antigua. We suspected before the game that they could be dangerous, but now know that if we relax for a moment, the Windies are good enough to get over the top of us. I'm not sure all the people at home realise what a good Test match this was.

A SCARY MOMENT

The moment Shivnarine Chanderpaul collapsed to the ground after he was hit in the back of the helmet trying to duck a Brett Lee bouncer, we sensed the tough little man from Guyana was in serious trouble. He didn't move, just lay there, and we rushed to him, thinking the worst, with Bing the first man to reach him. He seemed to be unconscious for a few seconds, or paralysed, maybe, and a doctor dashed to the middle with stretcher bearers close behind. The silence around Sabina Park was palpable. But then Chanderpaul was helped to his feet, stood there and nodded he was right, and after a re-jig of his helmet and an adjustment to his armguard he took guard again.

Chanderpaul was on 86 at the time, the Windies were 8–276, and he went on to be last man out for 118. Throughout, he played really well, especially at the end when he fought on while wickets fell around him, and the unflappable way he continued after that frightful blow was remarkable. He's as well organised at the crease as anyone currently playing. His method is unorthodox, sure, with his pronounced 'squared up' stance, but when the ball is not bouncing, it's very, very hard to get him out. He goes back in front of his stumps, and either squirts the ball backward of point or whips it through the legside. We do think, however, that he's a little vulnerable when the fast bowlers can get the ball bouncing, and that's what happened here, when Brett, great bowler that he is, somehow got a ball to lift more than expected on the dead surface.

After Chanderpaul was dismissed, they took him to hospital for some precautionary scans, which gave him the all clear. With Brian Lara gone, Chanderpaul is now the key West Indies wicket; it wasn't until Bing got him, caught and bowled, in their second innings, that we felt truly confident the first Test was ours.

The prognosis on Matt Hayden's injury, unfortunately, is negative. He had some scans done while we were playing the warm-up game against the Select XI, and these were sent back to Australia so the experts at home could have a good look at them. Their verdict is that the damage is so severe he won't be right until after this tour is completed, so he'll be heading home, to try to get his leg right for the games against Bangladesh in August-September, and the Champions Trophy after that. Typical Haydos, he put himself through a 30-minute net session and some sprint work with team physio Alex Kountouris on the last day of the Test, hoping to disprove the inevitable, but it was no good. Brad Hodge had originally come over as cover for Pup, but he'll now stay with us for the remainder of the Test series. A decision as to who might take Haydos' place in the one-day team will be made later.

WEDNESDAY, JUNE 4

Second Test, West Indies v Australia at Antigua (May 30–June 3):
Australia 7–479 dec (SM Katich 113, RT Ponting 65, MJ Clarke 110, B Lee 63*) and 6–244 dec (PA Jaques 76) drew with **West Indies** 352 (XM Marshall 53, RR Sarwan 65, S Chanderpaul 107; B Lee 5–59) and 5–266 (RR Sarwan 128, S Chanderpaul 77*)

My primary ambition, going into this Test, was to either win or draw, as I knew that either result would mean we'd retain the Frank Worrell Trophy. I am very aware that we are a team in transition, especially with Matthew Hayden now on his way home, and the last thing I wanted was to give the knockers any opportunity to chip away at us. This doesn't mean that we were playing for a draw, far from it, just that I'd made retaining the famous trophy a priority. After the stresses of the India series, our defeat in the Commonwealth Bank Series finals and the loss of Adam Gilchrist (permanently) and Haydos (temporarily), I was concerned that some of our aura of impregnability was fading. That is a worry we need to arrest quickly. Losing the series here would have set us back in that quest.

So the final result of this Test was a long way from a disaster, though having got ourselves in a position on the final day where it looked like we were going to win, it was disappointing in the end not to take a 2–0 series lead.

Many critics have continued to assume that because we've lost a number of top-class players that we are beginning to slump, but there are many positive aspects to the way we're going — most notably Brett Lee's fantastic form and Andrew Symonds' batting. Stuart Clark's excellent efforts have minimised any impact we might have felt by Glenn McGrath's departure, and Mike Hussey and Michael Clarke give us plenty of punch in our middle order. There is plenty to like about this current line-up. In my view, all it will take is for some of the new guys in the squad to really take to Test cricket and we'll sustain our No. 1 rating.

It is true, though, as I conceded after this Test, that our bowling attack has 'come back to the pack a little bit in Test cricket'. And it will stay that way until we find a spinner who can fill the void left by Shane Warne's departure from international cricket and now Stuart MacGill's retirement (something Stuey made official on day three of this Test). Beau Casson will almost certainly get first shot at that opportunity in Barbados.

We all knew that losing the greatest spinner the game has known last year was going to take something away from the team, and our experience on the fifth day here reminded us of that. 'It certainly is a challenge when you haven't got some of the other guys who have been around,' I said after the game, as I answered a range of questions about the all-round quality of our bowling attack. 'It's a great challenge for me and the rest of the guys but, more importantly, it's a challenge for the bowlers to stand up and make a name for themselves as very good Test bowlers. Brett's done a very good job of standing up in Glenn's absence over the last 12 months and will continue to lead the attack well. The next spinner is the interesting one for me. We'll see how that pans out.'

I DON'T THINK ANYONE was happy about the way Stuart MacGill's Test career ended. It certainly wasn't perfect, but nor was it as sinister as some made out. The problem for us started when the hotel we were originally booked into didn't meet all of our needs. Our manager organised for the squad to switch hotels, but in the meantime, unbeknown to us, Stuart had made a change of his own, and was consequently not staying with the rest of us. Of course, we weren't happy with that, and to make matters worse, he then missed the team bus for the trip to the ground for the second day of the Test. There were stories about that he was hung over, but that wasn't true. He just slept in, which he blamed on a dud alarm clock.

What we didn't know as we made our way to the ground without him was that Stuart had already decided to quit Test cricket, as of the end of this match. From what I understand, he'd made an emotional call to wife Rachel straight after the first day's play to tell her he was retiring, then spoke to his father and then informed the team following stumps on day two. The news was made public on day three, while we were waiting for the ground to dry after some heavy overnight and morning rain.

Stuart hasn't been bowling well, and I guess he's lost that crucial piece of enthusiasm you need to keep going at the highest level. He was fielding like a bloke who didn't want the ball to come to him. It would have been great if he could have spun us to victory in this Test, but it wasn't to be, though it was good to seem him trying his heart out all the way to the end. We're going to miss him, on this tour and beyond. He was an outstanding bowler, good enough to take 208 wickets in Test cricket and unlucky at the same time, in that his career coincided with that of Shane Warne. Who knows how many wickets he might have taken if he'd had an extended run as Australia's No. 1 spinner? Ironically, at the same time Stuart was announcing his decision to quit, Shane was leading the Rajasthan Royals to a dramatic victory in the IPL final. Even on his retirement day, Stuart was forced to live in Warney's shadow.

FOR THIS TEST, THE selectors chose to stick with Simon Katich at the top of the batting order, which meant Brad Hodge was unlucky again, as Michael Clarke came back into the middle order. This worked out beautifully for us, with Kato making a hundred on the opening day and then Pup doing likewise 24 hours later, which produced an emotional moment as he dedicated the ton to his fiancée Lara's father Graham, who had passed away three weeks ago in Sydney.

Kato played very sensibly, reflecting the fact that for the past 12 months he has been as prolific in first-class cricket as just about anybody on the planet. A few people had written him off a couple of years ago, but he's shown plenty of ticker to come back, especially to return with such confidence in his game and his mental make-up, and I'm really happy for him. He's become a very disciplined batsman who sticks to what works for him. Most importantly, he just loves batting. He's one of those blokes who doesn't just love hitting fours, he also loves playing a good forward defensive shot, loves watching the ball, loves making the right decision to let a ball go, loves judging a quick single right. He's also a great character to have around the team.

Pup was sensational, considering that he has hardly picked up a bat since the end of March. Unlike the rest of us, he didn't play in the IPL. Such is his character, it wouldn't have surprised me if

A TEST OF TIME

After I scored 158 in the first innings of the first Test, Lachy Patterson, our media manager, informed me that I needed another 66 runs to reach 10,000 runs in Test cricket. 'You'll be the seventh player in history to do it,' he said, 'and the third Australian after Allan Border and Steve Waugh.'

Normally, personal stats don't interest me too much, but this one did — primarily because it shows that I've been playing at the top level with some success for a long time. When I went into bat in our second innings at Kingston the fact I needed another 66 was prominent in my thoughts ... and when I was dismissed I still needed 61. Here in Antigua, that number was at the back of my mind, and I did get a little nervous as the milestone approached. Finally, I went down the wicket and pushed a delivery from Sarwan through the covers for a two to get me to five figures, but any joy I felt was soon tempered by my dismissal in the very next over.

It was funny when I did get to 10,000, how the whole crowd started applauding. *How do they all know?* I thought to myself. I learned later that they'd put my stats up on the big screen at the ground just a few minutes earlier. Kato knew, too, and he was quickly down the pitch to shake my hand. And here I was thinking

he'd come out and battled his way to a big score, but instead he was relaxed, fluent, almost flawless from the get-go, playing some cracking shots and making the century almost seem a formality. We were helped by the fact that the Windies struggled without a front-line spinner. I think their strategy was to use Chris Gayle as their main slow bowler, but when Gayle dropped out again because of his groin strain, they were left with a posse of fast and medium-pace bowlers and lacked the variety you need on the slow wicket we were playing on.

Our objective on day two, as it always is if we have a good opening day with the bat, was to bat our opponents out of the game. Whenever we win the toss and bat the whole objective for us is to try to bat once in the game, or at least to get enough runs

it was going to be a private little moment. Later, I was told that the record for fastest to 10,000 Test runs, in terms of number of innings played, is jointly held by Sachin Tendulkar and Brian Lara. They each took 195 innings to get there. This was my 196th innings. I would have loved to have shared that record with them — that would have looked very nice on my CV.

As at June 4, 2008, the list of batsmen to have scored 10,000 Test runs reads this way:

Batsman	Tests	Inns	NO	HS	Runs	Avg	100	50
Brian Lara (WI)	131	232	6	400*	11953	52.89	34	48
Sachin Tendulkar (Ind)	147	238	25	248*	11782	55.31	39	49
Allan Border (Aust)	156	265	44	205	11174	50.56	27	63
Steve Waugh (Aust)	168	260	46	200	10927	51.06	32	50
Sunil Gavaskar (Ind)	125	214	16	236*	10122	51.12	34	45
Rahul Dravid (Ind)	122	210	26	270	10098	54.88	25	51
Ricky Ponting (Aust)	118	197	26	257	10042	58.73	35	40

I am very proud of this record, just as I was proud when I went past 10,000 ODI runs last year (something Lara and Tendulkar have also done), but the achievement at the top of my list is that I have played in so many winning teams. Scoring a hundred for the sake of it will never excite me; getting involved in a one-on-one contest that might decide a big match in our favour always will.

for me to have a decision as to whether or not I enforce the follow-on or not.

On this occasion, we closed at 7–479, and it was that man again, Michael Clarke, who took two wickets before stumps, but the weather was no good on day three and in what play was available and then into day four Shivnarine Chanderpaul kept us at bay. Throughout, Brett Lee performed magnificently, and he produced arguably his best-ever spell of reverse-swing bowling when he took 5–5 in a stunning 19-ball sequence. The West Indies were 4–311 when I brought him back on to bowl, and fourth ball of the second over of his new spell, he had Dwayne Bravo caught down the legside. Next ball, a quick inswinging yorker, Denesh Ramdin was lbw and then first ball of his next

A RELUCTANT SLIPPER

One of the hardest things to do in cricket is field at first slip to a spinner when you're not used to it. On television, things can look as if they're happening slowly, but out in the middle it's a very different story. It's hard for keepers, especially if the ball is turning and fizzing, ball after ball, and it's tough for the guy at slip, too. This was especially true when Warney was bowling, because he could really make the ball spin and bounce; it'd be on you before you knew it! If a leggie pitches the ball on or just outside a leg-stump line, and the batsman goes forward and the keeper moves to try to get a sight of the ball, it can be hopeless for the man at slip, who won't see the ball until it zips past the keeper's gloves or even flies over his shoulder. Some 'easy' slip catches taken off spinners are actually quite brilliant.

In the lead-up to the first Test, with Matt Hayden out and Michael Clarke not here either, we didn't have a first slip for the spinners, so I put myself in there for the warm-up game at Trelawny and did manage to take a catch off Stuart MacGill's bowling. However, everything seemed fast to me. I was never genuinely comfortable or relaxed if the ball looked like coming in my direction.

Afterwards, to compensate, I took one of the 'catching ramps' we now have, a device that has a rounded edge on its near end and rails up each side so that if someone kneeling a couple of metres away throws a ball into it, the rebound will kick off at different angles. It's excellent for short-catching practice, and here I took things a step further, by placing a chair over the top of it, so I couldn't see the man throwing the ball. Consequently, the ball was on to me in a hurry, sometimes at an angle I least expected, and it certainly made me more confident going into the first Test.

Even so, when Pup arrived for the second Test, I was straight out of there!

over, Darren Sammy was also trapped in front. That over cost Bing three runs, and he conceded two from his next over before leaving the field briefly to change his spikes. When he returned, he produced a double wicket maiden — Jerome Taylor, fooled by a slower delivery; Daren Powell, lbw to a fast in-dipper — and then he bowled a dynamic over to Chanderpaul, before Mitchell

Johnson got Fidel Edwards, the last wicket of the innings. Afterwards, Bing described his burst as 'the best spell I have bowled with the old ball … those six overs are the reason why I play Test cricket'. It was superb stuff — he had the ball going both ways, quick and late, almost impossible to counter.

My second declaration of the game left the home team requiring 372 in the final three sessions and though we snared two wickets early and a third before lunch, Sarwan and Chanderpaul batted confidently until well into the final session. In the end, the slow wicket beat us all, and I was left to defend our bowlers at the post-Test media conference and to think about the future.

TUESDAY, JUNE 10

The tour itinerary gave us a welcome nine-day break between the second and third Tests, and we took advantage by putting the bats and ball away for four days while we took a brief holiday. At the same time I had my feet up, I seemed to be spending a fair amount of time getting the latest updates from the casualty ward.

I was worried about Brett Lee, who seemed absolutely spent after his huge effort throughout the second Test, but of chief concern was the news that Brad Haddin is carrying a broken ring finger on his right hand, and while I doubt it will cause him to miss the last game of the series, the selectors decided to bring WA keeper Luke Ronchi into the squad, just in case. Luke arrived here in Bridgetown on Sunday. Hadds actually damaged the digit during the first day of his first Test, and carried the injury into the game in Antigua, not realising it was a fracture. Subsequent X-rays confirmed the break. I would imagine unless the doctors warn he could do long-term damage, he'll keep playing for sure. Most encouragingly, Simon Katich, who suffered a rib injury in Antigua when he ducked into a Daren Powell bouncer early in his first-innings century, had been cleared of any long-term discomfort and looks a certain starter. I know he's been putting plenty of ice on the battered area, and while he was moving gingerly for a few days, he's starting to get his flexibility back now.

Both Hadds and Kato have waited a long while to get the opportunities in Test cricket they are enjoying on this tour. And both are going extremely well — Kato with his hundred in Antigua and Hadds with his nine dismissals so far in the series. They are tough men, not the sort of blokes who'd let some bruised ribs or a busted finger prevent them continuing their Test careers.

Our expectation is that the Kensington Oval deck in Bridgetown will be much faster than the wickets we've seen so far on tour. I quite fancy the idea of letting our pacemen loose on the Windies' top order, not least because their players have, from time to time out in the middle during the first two Tests, mentioned to our batsmen that they 'can't wait' until they get us to Barbados. I don't think there are too many Aussie batsmen losing sleep about this threat, and I'm pretty sure our batsmen will enjoy game on a fast wicket a little bit more than theirs. I have always felt that Gayle (if he plays) and Sarwan are susceptible to extra bounce in a wicket, especially early in their innings, and a couple of their other top-order players might also be worth attacking in this way.

One group who will benefit from a quicker wicket will be the spectators. Over the past few days there has been a lot of talk about different initiatives that could be introduced to help Test cricket, such as a world Test championship. My view is that if there is a problem with the excitement levels in Test cricket these days, it comes back to the flat wickets we're playing on. Fans would rather watch a five-day game played in Brisbane, Perth or Bridgetown than the wickets we've endured in Melbourne and

Antigua this season. There's much more happening, more bouncers, more batsmen ducking and weaving and sometimes falling on their backsides, more catches behind the wicket, more hook shots. That's the sort of Test cricket I grew up watching and loving. That's what I'd love to see in the Test starting Thursday.

TUESDAY, JUNE 17

Third Test, West Indies v Australia at Bridgetown (June 12–16):
Australia 251(A Symonds 52) and 5–439 dec (PA Jaques 108, SM Katich 157) defeated **West Indies** 216 (S Chanderpaul 79*; MG Johnson 4–41) and 387 (XM Marshall 85, S Chanderpaul 50, DJ Bravo 69) by 87 runs

It was the day before the Test, and I called the boys into a circle at training to tell them that Beau Casson was about to become Australia's 401st Test cricketer. Beau's reaction to the news underlined how much the baggy green means to Australian cricketers — he choked right up, overcome that something he's been dreaming about for years was about to come true. I know he was a little embarrassed by his reaction, but he shouldn't have been — I love the fact that playing for Australia means so much to him.

I was also able to confirm that Brad Haddin would play; having just got his first Test cap, I knew there was no way Hadds was going to step aside, not for a broken finger. They breed keepers tough, we all know that.

The next day, all the talk about a bouncy Bridgetown pitch seemed to be on the money, as Chris Gayle won the toss and sent us in, and then their bowlers reduced us to 7–226 before rain washed out the last 40 minutes of the day's play. Only Andrew Symonds was able to put a score together, as the Windies' quicks kept bouncing us and we tried to match them in the aggression

ON THE IMPROVE

I only made 18 and 39 here in Bridgetown, but I'll still look back on the past month as one in which I often batted as well as I have ever done in my life. This is an extremely satisfying result for me because I worked on a few things coming here that I felt would make me a better player, and I feel like they've come off.

As I analysed my form in the Tests and one-day games in Australia, I came to the conclusion that my pre-delivery movements — the 'triggers' I do naturally as the bowler delivers the ball — weren't as assertive as they needed to be. As I struggled at times against India, especially in the Commonwealth Bank series, I told myself to stay still for as long as possible as the ball began its journey towards me, as if that would rectify my problems, but with hindsight all that did was give me a fraction less time to react and play my shots. During our pre-tour camp, I decided to trust my technique more and also be more proactive with these triggers, get them completed a split second before the bowler let go of the ball, and this has given me so much more time during my innings here.

stakes. Four or five times, bumpers sailed over the head of keeper Denesh Ramdin and down to the sightscreen for wides. Three of the first five wickets fell to top edges, hooks or pulls gone wrong, while I was lbw to Jerome Taylor, the third time in a row he's dismissed me during the series. Next day, our fast men squared the ledger by knocking them over for 216, giving us a lead of 35, but after that — just as Ramnaresh Sarwan told us it would before the game — all the life went out of the wicket, and the last three days reverted to the same style of the first two Tests: a war of attrition.

The two men who took the heat out of the contest were our opening bats, Phil Jaques and Simon Katich, who both made gutsy hundreds. Jaquesy's effort was important for him, because — coming so soon after his second innings 76 in Antigua — it put to bed the suggestions that have been made that he needs Matthew Hayden at the other end if he wants to make runs in

Test cricket. Their stand of 223 is the third highest ever made by an Australian opening pair in the Caribbean (behind the 382 scored by Bob Simpson and Bill Lawry in Bridgetown in 1965 and the 242 by Matt Hayden and Justin Langer in Antigua), and in the context of the game, coming as it did after two meagre first-innings team totals, it was a fantastic piece of work. As the No. 3, ready to go in as soon as a wicket fell, I couldn't help but admire their performance. The only negative I could think of is that one of them will probably lose his place in the side for our next Test match, because Haydos is, of course, a certain selection. People have been saying that we are in decline, yet here we have a situation where a bloke who has scored a hundred in

THAT'S MY JOB

Our Test record for 2007–08 is nine games, six wins, two draws, one loss. When I was asked how I'd look back on this West Indies series, I replied this way:

'I think all the guys who have been given an opportunity in the last 12 months have stood up and done a really great job. Simon Katich has been terrific for us at the top of the order, and Phil Jaques bounced back to form in this game. Beau Casson makes his debut and takes wickets for us on the last day, which is what you need from a spinner. So all the guys who have come into the side can hold their head up high and say that they've done a really good job for the team over the last few weeks.

'I actually said when some of the more senior players moved on that I felt it was going to be one of the more exciting periods in my career to have some new, fresh faces around the team. I thought it was going to be exciting, and it has been. It has been great.

'I have enjoyed having guys making their debuts and guys who have played a handful of Tests in the side because I feel I have a lot to offer to those guys by way of experience and know-how in certain situations in games. If I can go and say one thing to them that is going to help them out in situations in games, I feel that's my job.'

each of his most recent two Tests is unsure of his position for our next game. That suggests a depth of talent that few teams in world cricket can match.

By the time we declared, the West Indies needed what would have been a world record 475 to win the game, and we got home comfortably enough despite putting in a sub-standard fielding effort. We missed at least four catches on the fourth day, and also a couple of run out chances, and just about the only highlight of the day was Beau Casson's first Test wicket, which came, ironically, as a result of a brilliant catch by Phil Jaques at short leg. Xavier Marshall, out for 85, was the batsman.

They went into the final day of the series at 3–235, and there was talk of a repeat of their famous victory from 2003, when they scored 7–418 to beat us in Antigua, but I was confident we'd win. It did take us a while to dig Chanderpaul out, but once we got him, lbw Clark for 50, just four balls after Casson dismissed Dwayne Bravo, the game was as good as over. Even so, they kept battling and battling, displaying some real character to make us fight all the way to the winning post. Maybe the days of us demolishing teams are over, and now we're going to have to grind out our victories. The final winning margin was 87 runs. Beau finished with 3–86 from 25 overs, and I thought he got better and better the longer the Test went. What you want from your spinner on day five is to get some crucial breakthroughs, and he did that for us.

I'm pretty satisfied with the way we played in this Test series, even if our effort in winning 2–0 has been described as 'disappointing' in some quarters. I guess that reflects how the two teams have been going in recent years, but I'm old enough to remember back to the 1980s, when the Windies routinely beat Australia time and time again. This has been an engrossing series, with all three Tests going into the fifth day, and it has featured some superb batting and tremendous bowling. That we won without Hayden and Gilchrist, and essentially without Stuart MacGill, too, adds to the achievement. Lee, Clark, Katich, Clarke, Jaques and Symonds all did some terrific things, and I was happy to top the Australian team's batting aggregates, though I was a long way behind Chanderpaul, who averaged an extraordinary 147.33 over the three matches. The West Indian bowlers were much better this time than they were in 2003, especially their quicks, and my suspicion is that their whole team will improve on their recent Test record in upcoming series. When they do that, it will help put the quality of our effort here in perspective.

SUNDAY, JUNE 22

Twenty20 international, at Bridgetown (June 20): **Australia** 3–97 (11 overs: L Ronchi 36) lost to **West Indies** 3–102 (9.1 overs: XM Marshall 36) by seven wickets

Tour game, University of West Indies Vice Chancellor's XI v the Australians, at Three Ws Oval, Bridgetown (June 21): **Australians** 6–337 (50 overs: SR Watson 95, MEK Hussey 50, MJ Clarke 53, DJ Hussey 55) defeated **UWI Vice Chancellor's XI** 126 (33.1 overs: D Ramdin 43; NW Bracken 3–25) by 211 runs

It wasn't that long ago that a Twenty20 game on tour was just an exhibition, a promotional tool for the sport that hardly rated on the same level as a Test match or a one-day international. Things have changed. Losing that semi-final in Cape Town last September hurt us, and we want to improve when the next Twenty20 world championship is held in England in 2009. Between now and then, Australia has only a handful of Twenty20 games scheduled, so every game is precious for us, because it gives us a rare chance to practise our skills, as a team, in match conditions.

That process began with the two Twenty20 internationals we played in Australia in 2007–08, and was supposed to continue here. However, the game was ruined by the weather, reduced to an 11-over slog that, a little crazily, the Windies won by seven wickets with 11 balls to spare. That must be considered a thrashing! It was hardly the ideal international debut for Shaun Marsh and Luke Ronchi, though the two could take some comfort from their opening partnership of 57 from six overs. Our total of 97 didn't seem like enough, and then, first ball of

THE REVERSE SLOG

It's amazing how small the world of cricket can be at times, and we saw an example of this last week when England's Kevin Pietersen played a couple of remarkable shots in a one-dayer against New Zealand at Chester-le-Street, and soon after I was being asked when we were going to start doing the same. I've seen footage of Pietersen reverse-sweeping a six before, but this was different — he was taking guard as a right-hander but then switched to leftie and clubbed Scott Styris for a couple of sixes, one forward of square and the other to wide long-on.

I was quick to say that I am very impressed with Pietersen's innovative skills and his power, but for the moment at least — maybe until we've done some more work in the nets — I would prefer to see my blokes stick to more conventional methods.

'It's probably something historically that we haven't been that good at, improvising that much as a batting group,' I said. 'We've managed with our own skill to be able to hit to different areas. But there's no reason why any of our players can't do that. A few of us muck around with doing it in the nets, and Symmo sort of uses the back of the bat when he plays his. We are probably more deflectors when we reverse sweep rather than six hitters.'

Because Pietersen has the ability to pull off these reverse slogs (as they're being called), he has an extra way of 'getting inside' a bowler's mind as he's coming into bowl. That's one thing a batsman wants to do in one-day cricket, in any form of cricket really, so I have to admire him for that.

their innings, Xavier Marshall top-edged a reasonable 'first-upper' from Brett Lee for six, backward of square, and it was all downhill from there.

Shaun is part of our team for the one-day matches, while Luke is staying on until we get confirmation one way or the other on Brad Haddin's fitness. There is some thought that Hadds will be better off resting his broken finger, rather than putting it through the stress of five more games. Our full squad for the ODI series is: Ricky Ponting (captain), Michael Clarke (vice-captain), Nathan Bracken, Stuart Clark, Mitchell Johnson, Brad Haddin (Luke Ronchi), James Hopes, David Hussey, Michael Hussey, Brett Lee, Shaun Marsh, Andrew Symonds, Shane Watson and Cameron White.

A few of the boys were coming off interesting IPL campaigns, most notably Shane Watson, who was named the player of the tournament after scoring 474 runs and taking 17 wickets for Warney's triumphant Rajasthan Royals. Shaun Marsh was a key man for the Kings XI Punjab as they went all the way to the final, scoring his runs at a rate of almost 140 runs per 100 balls, while David Hussey did some excellent work for my team, Kolkata. The day after our Twenty20 disappointment, we played a 50-over game against a University of West Indies Vice Chancellor's XI at the good-looking 3Ws Oval in Bridgetown, and Watto slammed 95 from 85 balls, giving every indication he's in the peak of form. These next few games could be very important for him — as everyone knows, I'm a big fan and it would be great if he could finish on a high what has been in many ways, because of injury, a wasted season for him. He'll definitely open the batting in the first ODI.

In the game against the Vice Chancellor's XI, Watto shared a 68-run opening stand with Shaun Marsh, who scored 38, and later the younger Hussey crunched five sixes, including four in two overs, to bring up a rapid-fire half century. When we bowled, all our blokes had a decent run, with Cameron White, who during the upcoming series will be out to stake a claim for the spinner's spot left vacant by Brad Hogg, looking pretty good during an eight-over spell. As far as dress rehearsals go, for us this one was excellent.

IN THE DAYS AFTER the third Test, the questions over the future of the Champions Trophy, scheduled for Pakistan in September — a matter that had been bubbling in the background throughout the tour — came to the surface once again, this time because Cricket Australia had announced it was sending a security expert to Pakistan to get the very latest on the situation there.

It was difficult for us cricketers to make comment on the political situation in Pakistan, because we simply don't know precisely what is going on. When I was asked, three days ago, how the team was thinking, I replied, 'You don't have to be Einstein to figure there will be some concern among our team. It's not just because we're Australian cricketers. Anyone travelling to Pakistan would have some sort of concern.'

It is hard for me to be any more decisive than that. We understand that it will be good for the game and great for Pakistan if the tournament goes ahead, so we are comfortable with the final decision being delayed. 'We don't know if we're going, and if we do go, we don't know if individuals are going to pull out,' I said. 'We all know we're expected to go contractually if selected on the tour, but it will come down to the individual and what they feel at the time.'

We are aware that some incidents have occurred in different parts of Pakistan in recent weeks. Every time something happens, we're asked about it almost immediately. All we can do is continue to be guided by the experts.

With Michael Clarke (left) and North Melbourne AFL legend Glenn Archer (in the helmet) at practice during the Test series against India.

Brett Lee has just dismissed VVS Laxman (on ground) with a fast one at the MCG.

Above: Harbhajan Singh (arm upraised) sets off on his victory celebration after dismissing me during our second innings in Sydney.

Above left: Mike Hussey (centre) lays down the law to his batting partner Matt Hayden's runner (me) later in the same innings.

Above right: Are you supposed to acknowledge the applause yourself when the bloke you've been running for has just made a big hundred?

A group of ecstatic Aussies after Stuart Clark dismisses Sachin Tendulkar on the last day at the SCG.

I catch a deflection off the pad of MS Dhoni as things get tense during the final session.

Michael Clarke (far left) has just had Ishant Sharma caught at slip by Mike Hussey, to extend our winning run in Tests to 16 games.

Left: I've rarely been as excited after a Test victory as I was in Sydney.

Below: However, the mood changed in the days that followed. Here I'm in Perth with Brad Hogg on our way to a meeting where we learned that charges concerning Hoggy's alleged abuse of some Indian players had been dropped.

Above: India's outstanding young fast bowler Ishant Sharma (arms upraised) has just had me caught at slip on the final day of the third Test at the WACA.

Below: Andrew Symonds was Anil Kumble's 600th Test wicket.

Right: My hundred in Adelaide was hardly my prettiest, but given the circumstances it was one of my most satisfying.

Above: James Hopes on the fly during the Commonwealth Bank Series.

During the summer, Brett Lee could do almost anything, even balance on Sanath Jayasuriya's bat during the Australia–Sri Lanka one-dayer in Sydney.

Adam Gilchrist reacts to reaching his century against Sri Lanka, as he farewelled the WACA faithful in style during the Commonwealth Bank Series.

Three more 'postcards', all from 2008. Top: Sachin Tendulkar walks off the Adelaide Oval on the final day of the third Test. Middle: An Aussie fan sits by the pool in Antigua while the big screen shows the two captains, Ramnaresh Sarwan and me, with the umpires checking if the conditions have dried out enough for play to recommence. Bottom: The National Stadium in Grenada, venue for the third ODI of our Caribbean tour, my last game before I returned home with a damaged wrist.

On July 26, 2008, Rianna and I welcomed our beautiful baby girl, Emmy Charlotte, into the world. From day one, Emmy was doing great, and we felt blessed that because of the wrist injury I suffered in the West Indies, I'd get to spend longer at home with her than would otherwise have been the case. We couldn't be happier.

'To Cricket Australia and the players' association's credit, I think they've handled the last couple of tours there very well,' I said. 'Obviously, the government's involvement last time probably helped us all out.'

The other thing I needed to stress is that this is not just a problem for us Australians. Sometimes, I wonder if some commentators realise this. 'I'm sure some of the England players will have some concerns, as well as a lot of the New Zealand players who have been confronted with this stuff before, in Sri Lanka and Pakistan.' I said. 'It won't just be Australian players. There will be a few other teams who will be thinking long and hard if the tour does go ahead there.'

WE WERE IN A terrific mood after our demolition job on the Vice Chancellor's team yesterday, but that changed in an instant. I can't remember ever feeling lower on a cricket tour than how I felt late last night when I was told that Jane McGrath had passed away a few hours earlier in Sydney. Jane was an extraordinary person, and the grace, courage and dignity she showed during her 10-year battle with cancer is something I will never forget. Nor will I forget how friendly she was from the first time we were introduced, her constant good humour and her unique ability to keep her husband Glenn in line. She was a tremendous mother to their children, James and Holly, and I keep thinking about them all, and what Glenn and the kids must be going through. We're a tight ship, the Australian cricket family, and we've taken a heavy blow.

The Aussie team flew into St Vincent this morning, and later in the day, at our team meeting, we discussed exactly how we could pay tribute to Jane, her work and her bravery. And so we'll all be wearing pink ribbons during the first game of our one-day series, to be played here on Tuesday. Jane and Glenn, through the McGrath Foundation, have raised an enormous amount of money for cancer research and cancer sufferers, and the colour pink has become something of a trademark. Andrew Symonds and Matthew Hayden have used pink batting grips on their bats during Test matches — they did so famously during a match-winning partnership against England at the MCG last season. We'll all be doing that during the one-dayer … and thinking about her a lot, too.

SATURDAY, JUNE 28

Game One, at St Vincent (June 24): Australia 8–273 (50 overs: SE Marsh 81, MEK Hussey 44, BJ Haddin 50) defeated **West Indies** 189 (39.5 overs: NW Bracken 4–31) by 84 runs

Game Two, at Grenada (June 27): Australia 5–213 (50 overs: MJ Clarke 55, MEK Hussey 62, CL White 40) defeated **West Indies** 8–140 (41 overs: S Chanderpaul 45*; MJ Clarke 3–26) by 63 runs (DL method)

This is an important series for us — one, because we have to start putting right the disappointment of the Commonwealth Bank Series; and two, because of the opportunities it offers to the guys who haven't played a lot of international cricket. And we began well in St Vincent, with Shaun Marsh marking his ODI debut with a man-of-the-match performance as we crushed the home team with 10.1 overs to spare, and then followed up with a professional display here in Grenada, where we didn't get a lot of help from the weather but still prevailed comfortably. And we did so without Andrew Symonds in either encounter, because he is still troubled by the back ailment he picked up in the third Test, and by Brad Haddin in game two, after he finally conceded his finger could do with a rest. Hadds is now heading home, and Luke Ronchi will look after the wicketkeeping duties for the rest of the series.

As much as we'll miss our No. 1 gloveman, I have to say I've

LIKE FATHER, LIKE SON

Shaun Marsh is an absolute dead ringer for his dad, our former coach Geoff 'Swampy' Marsh, not just in his looks, but also his mannerisms, the way he talks, his cheeky grin, his personality. It's unbelievable. Just the other day, I was sitting with David Boon, who is over here at the moment as the travelling Australian selector. He used to open the batting for Australia with Geoff Marsh and was his best mate in the team.

When Shaun walked out to bat, Boonie and I looked at each other and realised we were thinking the same thing: *'That's Swamp!'* It was the same when he walked off a while later, muttering to himself about the mistake that had cost him his wicket. With the bat, I reckon Shaun's got more in his repertoire than his father, and I'm sure he'll match his old man by playing quite a bit of cricket for Australia.

been impressed with Luke from the day he got over here. Whenever a new player comes into the Australian set-up, we try to arrange a meeting — involving the player, captain, vice-captain, manager and coach — to go over what's expected and the little things that we live and die by in the Australian team. Mostly, the young guys sit back and listen, just try to take it all in. Luke was different, more outgoing, and I found that refreshing. This natural inclination to get on the front foot comes out in his batting, which looks pretty dynamic to me.

One thing I always say to the new guys is don't sit in your room expecting that a senior player will call you and ask you down to the bar or out for a beer. Be proactive and do the asking, otherwise — because we've all got so much on — it could be a couple of weeks before we spend any decent time together. More than anyone else among the new guys, Luke has grabbed this invitation.

BEFORE THE FIRST GAME, we observed a minute's silence for Jane McGrath, and throughout the day's play I was touched by the number of people in the crowd, not all of them Australian supporters, who were wearing something pink. It was surprising, but also nice, in the time we were on the island, how many locals stopped us in the street, to express their sympathies, which I took as a great tribute to Jane, and also a reflection on the impact Glenn has had as a cricketer in these parts. I'm not sure fast bowlers are supposed to be that popular outside their own country. The mood within our squad remains sombre: she was a very special woman and I think it'll take me quite a while to fully come to terms with her passing.

The government in St Vincent had declared the day a public holiday, and obviously hoped the locals would have plenty of good cricket to cheer about, but we were firmly in charge from the time Watson and Marsh started the game with an opening stand of 75. The pitch wasn't easy to bat on, but Shaun was in excellent touch, scoring at a run a ball until he was dismissed for 81 in the 31st over. Not even West Indies captain Chris Gayle's unusual tactics, which included the use of five separate bowlers in the first eight overs — including an off-spinner (Gayle himself) bowling the second over of the innings— could unsettle him.

The Windies' reply was never on target, and ended unhappily with the crowd throwing a truckload of plastic bottles onto the field after Darren Sammy was bowled by Nathan Bracken. A couple of the earlier batsmen weren't happy when they were given out lbw, and now Bracks was bowling left-arm round the wicket with Brad Haddin standing up to the stumps. Sammy went for a slog, missed, and the ball clipped the top of the off-stump and then ran away off Hadds' pad for a 'single'. The umpire gave him out immediately, but Sammy didn't know what had happened, and he lingered for a while. Making things worse, the first replay shown on the television in the home team's dressing room was inconclusive, and soon people up there were waving at Sammy, telling him to stay put. I went up to the umpire and said, 'Do you want to check it out, mate?' But he replied, 'No, I saw it hit the stumps, it's definitely out.'

I think there was subsequently some communication with the video umpire, who confirmed it was out. He'd seen a different replay. But by this stage it was too late, the spectators in the 'Double Decker Stand' were hurling bottles onto the field, and this forced James Hopes, who had been fielding at deep point, to quickly leave the boundary for the safety of the fielding circle. I was focused on the game when this happened, and must admit I was surprised when I first saw him standing near me.

'What are you doing here?' I asked.

'I can't go back out there,' he replied.

That was when I realised how bad the problem was. Not all the bottles, James told me, were empty.

Play was stopped for 10 or 15 minutes while the outfield was cleared, and the final few minutes of the game were played with local constabulary lining the boundary rope and the ground announcer begging the fans to stop throwing any more objects onto the arena. It was one of those situations where, because no one was hurt, we're okay to move on, but at the time it wasn't funny.

Our win was really good and I was very pleased after the game. 'It's a pretty formidable squad that we've got here, with a lot of flexibility,' I said, reflecting a mounting confidence. 'The flexibility around our group at the moment is probably as good as I've seen it around the Australian team.'

We saw more of this in game two, my 300th ODI, a match played on a dodgy wicket and interrupted by the weather. At the halfway stage of the match, after we'd made 'only' 5–213 from our 50 overs, many people must have suspected we were in trouble. But we knew that was a very competitive score, which was built on a

THE 300-GAME CLUB

Three hundred games is a big milestone in the AFL, and maybe that's the reason I'm feeling so satisfied at reaching 300 ODIs. Glenn Archer, the great North Melbourne footballer, and a friend of mine, played a club record 311 games for the Kangaroos, and I remember when he reached 300 how I really respected the fact that he could stay in the game for that long. It's a lot of warm-ups! You have to do a lot of things right in a major sport to achieve longevity, and while gaining records or reaching landmarks has never been a motivator for me, I am proud that I've had the durability to hang around for so long, and that I've maintained a certain quality that has meant they've had to keep picking me.

The statistics here are correct as at the end of my 300th game, which was played on June 29, but as is the way of modern cricket, the table is changing rapidly. For example, Sanath Jayasuriya, Muttiah Muralitharan and Chaminda Vaas all played in an Asia Cup ODI for Sri Lanka against Pakistan earlier today and are due to appear in another one-dayer tomorrow. The reason I include this table is to show the class of the cricketers who played 300 ODIs before I managed to reach the landmark. I feel honoured to have joined their 'club'.

Players with 300 or More ODI Appearances

Player	Games	Career	Runs	Avg	Wkts	Avg	Ct	St
Sachin Tendulkar (Ind)	417	1989–2008	16361	44.34	154	44.13	122	–
Sanath Jayasuriya (SL)	412	1989–2008	12390	32.35	310	36.30	117	–
Inzamam-ul-Haq (Pak)	378	1991–2007	11739	39.53	3	21.33	113	–
Wasim Akram (Pak)	356	1984–2003	3717	16.52	502	23.53	88	–
Mohammad Azharuddin (Ind)	334	1985–2000	9378	36.92	12	39.92	156	–
Rahul Dravid (Ind)	333	1996–2007	10585	39.50	4	42.50	193	14
Steve Waugh (Aust)	325	1986–2002	7569	32.91	195	34.67	111	–
Chaminda Vaas (SL)	316	1994–2008	1982	13.76	395	27.42	59	–
Sourav Ganguly (Ind)	311	1992–2007	11363	41.02	100	38.49	100	–
Aravinda de Silva (SL)	308	1984–2003	9284	34.90	106	39.41	95	–
Muttiah Muralitharan (SL)	306	1993–2008	521	5.85	467	23.03	122	–
Shaun Pollock (SA)	303	1996–2008	3519	26.46	393	24.51	108	–
Ricky Ponting (Aust)	300	1995–2008	11044	43.14	3	34.67	135	–

100-run partnership between the two Michaels, Clarke and Hussey, who adapted to the conditions and worked a lot of ones and twos to keep our innings on track. Cameron White's swashbuckling 40, scored from 39 balls, was also very important (it was no mean trick scoring at better than a run a ball on that deck). Brett Lee then came out and dismissed Xavier Marshall with the first ball of the innings — giving Luke Ronchi a catch from his first ball in ODI cricket — and the Windies never recovered.

MY OLD MATE ADAM Gilchrist and I share a common flaw in that we both struggle to accept the bad mistakes and poor decisions that occur on the cricket field. We do tend to wear our hearts on our sleeve in this regard, which is why we've been reported a few too many times over the years. (Not too many people realise that about Gilly, but it's true!) Maybe we're just too competitive; perhaps it's because we've been captain and vice-captain that we feel obliged to speak up when we see an injustice. However, I am aware that sometimes I haven't filed my protests in the right way, and the impression that can leave is never a good one.

Here in Grenada, during my 300th ODI, I was reported by the umpires after I questioned a 'not out' verdict. It wasn't this decision on its own that irritated me; there had been a number of mistakes made during the Tests and the one-dayers, helping and harming both teams, and in the end they drove us all mad. This time, I moved myself into bat-pad on the legside and straightaway there was a big edge, huge appeal, not out. I looked at the umpire and said, with arms outstretched, 'How can that not be out?' And that cost me 30 per cent of my match fee. Soon after, I had separate conversations with James Sutherland and Michael Brown from Cricket Australia, and they both quickly raised the matter. 'How did you get reported again?' asked James. 'Mate, they were four for fifty at the time!' said Brownie.

'I don't care if they are four for 10 or none for 410, if things happen in the game that I think shouldn't happen, I'm going to react to them,' I replied. I'm prepared to concede that I should try to rein my over-reactions in, but I don't think I'm ever going to be able to just stay mute, shrug my shoulders and accept bad mistakes as just being part of the game. That's not me.

MONDAY, JUNE 30

Game Three, at Grenada (June 29): West Indies 223 (48 overs: CH Gayle 53; NW Bracken 3–26) lost to **Australia** 3–227 (40.3 overs: SR Watson 126, RT Ponting 69) by seven wickets

It's amazing these days how guys will come into the Australian set-up for the first time and I will hardly know them. It's not like we've crossed paths that often in domestic cricket, because I play so few games for Tassie. For example, when Chris Rogers came into the Test XI in Perth during the last India series, the only times I'd played against him was in an ING Cup one-dayer in Perth in December 2002 and during the 2005 Ashes tour, when he scored 56 and 209 for Leicestershire against us.

In past seasons, the only other chance I got to share time with guys outside the Australian squad was during a pre-season camp, when as captain I find there's usually quite a bit happening. So it was good for me to be able to spend four weeks with David Hussey as a team-mate with the Knight Riders in the IPL, because it meant, when he came to the West Indies to play in the one-day series, I already knew and liked the bloke. Trouble was, he was quickly seeking me out for some more footy bets. I had to pay up during our time together in the IPL, after I gave the Fremantle Dockers six goals start against

FASTEST TO 300 ODI WICKETS

During the third game of this one-day series, Brett Lee became the 10th bowler to take 300 ODI wickets and the fastest, in terms of games played, to achieve this feat. He did so by a substantial margin, too — 15 games quicker than his closest challenger, Pakistan's Waqar Younis. Bing is the second Australian, after Glenn McGrath, to reach the 300-wickets milestone.

Bowler	Career	ODIs	Total ODIs	Wkts	Avg	Best	4w
Brett Lee (Aust)	2000–2008	171	171	300	22.83	5–22	19
Waqar Younis (Pak)	1989–2003	186	262	416	23.84	7–36	27
Glenn McGrath (Aust)	1993–2007	200	250	381	22.02	7–15	16
Muttiah Muralitharan (SL)	1993–2008	202	307	472	22.86	7–30	22
Wasim Akram (Pak)	1984–2003	208	356	502	23.53	5–15	23
Shaun Pollock (SA)	1996–2008	217	303	393	24.51	6–35	17
Javagal Srinath (Ind)	1991–2003	219	229	315	28.09	5–23	10
Anil Kumble (Ind)	1990–2007	234	271	337	30.90	6–12	10
Chaminda Vaas (SL)	1994–2008	235	317	396	27.40	8–19	13
Sanath Jayasuriya (SL)	1989–2008	396	413	310	36.30	6–29	12

Note: All stats are correct as at June 30, 2008, the date of the third Australia–West Indies ODI; 'ODIs' indicates the number of one-day internationals it took the bowler to reach 300 ODI wickets; 'Total ODIs' indicates the number of one-day internationals the bowler played during his career, or has played to June 30; 'Wkts' indicates career wickets and 'Avg' indicates the bowling average for those career wickets.

Geelong, and now he wanted to back St Kilda against the Kangaroos. I took him on, but lost again when the Saints kicked six goals in the final quarter to win by 15.

In contrast, I can't begin to tell you how much I enjoyed being up the other end as Shane Watson careered towards his first international century. Even the nagging pain I was feeling in my right wrist couldn't detract from the pleasure I felt, watching a bloke who has gone through far more than his fair share of injuries over the past few years power his way to three figures. We came together in the first over, after Shaun Marsh was dismissed, and went on to add 190 at just about a run a ball. My contribution was 69 from 83; Shane finished with 126 from 122, and we were able to cruise home with seven wickets and nine-and-a-half overs to spare. We'd won the series at the earliest opportunity.

The most surprising aspect of all this was the lack of drive shown by our opponents, who seemed to accept their fate very early in the contest. Even though they got that early wicket, their intensity in the field dropped away after just three or four overs. We played well, no doubt about it, but a series was on the line so we expected a bit more from the West Indians. But we can't be worried about their mindset, and I don't want to let it detract too much from our great form. What I want to do now is win the last two games as well, to balance a glitch in our record from 2003, when we won the first four games of a seven-match series but lost the last three.

My big worry is that I might not be in a position to contribute to this assignment. When I got home last night there were a number of text messages on my phone, one of which was from a friend in Australia who congratulated me on the way I pushed the ball around, getting plenty of singles, to give Watto the strike as much as possible. That sounds good, but the truth is that my wrist was aching, and it was impossible for me to put any power into my shots.

I was on 26 when it happened. I played a pull shot off Dwayne Bravo, and as I was running up the pitch for a single I thought, *That feels weird, something's up*. Daren Powell botched up his pick up on the boundary and the ball went for four, and as I walked back past Watto, I said flatly, 'I've done something to my wrist.' I hit seven fours in my innings, but six of them came in the first half of my knock, and at the end I was struggling to even pick my bat up. Unless the injury improves there is little chance I'll be right for game four in St Kitts.

If I am out, Pup will get his first chance to captain his country in a one-day international and my guess is that David Hussey will come into the side to make his ODI debut. Even before my injury, we were keen to given David and Stuart Clark a game, as they are yet to appear in the series, and I'd also like to see Cameron White given another opportunity. But I know it would be tough on the blokes who have been playing to ask them to have a rest when we are so close to the end of the tour. It's not like we can say, 'We're resting you for next week.' As always in these situations caused by having such a strong depth of talent to pick from, deep down you don't feel all that disappointed that you can't give everyone a go. When you are faced with these kinds of selection conundrums, you know the team is not travelling too badly, and that the future is looking all right.

THURSDAY, JULY 10

Game Four, at St Kitts (July 4): Australia 8–282 (50 overs: A Symonds 87, DJ Hussey 50) defeated **West Indies** 6–281 (50 overs: CH Gayle 92, RR Sarwan 63, S Chanderpaul 53; B Lee 3–64) by one run

Game Five, at St Kitts (July 6): Australia 8–341 (50 overs: SE Marsh 49, L Ronchi 64, MEK Hussey 51, A Symonds 66, DJ Hussey 52; FH Edwards 3–86, RR Sarwan 3–57) defeated **West Indies** 172 (39.5 overs: SE Findlay 59; MG Johnson 5–29) by 169 runs

I never expected to be dictating this final diary entry in Australia, but that was the reality after the doctors ruled me out of the final two matches of the tour. The advice was to get home, have the wrist fully checked out, with the expectation being that I'd need surgery. That being the case — in fact, the injury is more severe than anyone realised — it was important that I went under the knife as soon as possible, because there are matches on the horizon: one-dayers against Bangladesh in late August/early September, possibly the Champions Trophy (a final decision is still to be made), a tour of India, then another home season. I had the operation done in Melbourne straight after I absorbed the specialist's opinion, and the initial prognosis is that eventually it'll be good as new. For the moment, however, golf is right out, and it's extremely doubtful I'll be playing in the Bangladesh series.

The doctors explained that I'd torn ligaments and damaged the sheath that keeps the main tendon in my wrist in place. I've watched the replay of that pull shot off Bravo 100 times, and I can't see anything unusual in my body actions that could have caused such a major injury, so maybe it's just one of those things that happen over time, like a rubber band you keep stretching until it finally snaps. On the field, we put a bit of tape around it, which sort of kept things in place, but that was always only going to be a temporary fix. The doc says it's an injury he's seen a few times with tennis players, and when you think about the way we use the bottom hand when playing a pull shot, that's not too dissimilar to hitting a forehand. That might help explain why it happened.

Of course, part of me was very disappointed to be leaving the team in the Caribbean with the job not quite done. But there was also the delight in knowing I'd be getting home to Rianna early; our baby is due in mid-August and I love the idea of being able to spend the next few weeks around the house as the 'expectant' father. We are about to enter a whole new stage of our life together, and I can't wait for the next chapter to begin.

Back in the Caribbean, the boys duly completed a clean sweep of the one-day series, winning a thriller in game four and then destroying the home team in the finale, on the back of the biggest ever one-day innings total made by an Australian team against the West Indies. Luke Ronchi, batting three, made a fifty that took only 22 balls to complete, only for David Hussey to do even better, reaching his half-century from 19 deliveries. Mitchell Johnson then took 5–29, which for me revived memories of his stirring spell in Vadodara last October, when he took 5–26 and shattered the Indian middle-order.

That game, and the controversy the crowd there instigated, now seems so long ago. A season that started with a shock Twenty20 loss to Zimbabwe in Cape Town and featured plenty of controversy and acrimony along the way ended on a real high in St Kitts, and for that I am very grateful. I'm glad I was a part of all of it, I'll never forget it, but I hope I never have to go through another year like it before my career is through.

THE PONTING FOUNDATION

TUESDAY, JULY 22

Two weeks ago, I was in a Melbourne hospital having surgery on my wrist. Last night, I was in Sydney for the launch of the Ponting Foundation — an occasion which, if it works out the way we hope, will turn out to be the most significant event I was involved in during the time covered by this book.

Over the past few years I have done some work and Rianna has done plenty for the Children's Cancer Institute Australia, a fantastic organisation whose ultimate ambition is to save the lives of all children with cancer and to ensure the best possible quality of life for children's cancer sufferers and their families. Now, we feel we have reached the stage where we can do more, to continue to avidly support CCIA but also raise funds for other charities — such as the highly respected Redkite (formerly the Malcolm Sargent Cancer Fund for Children in Australia) — who work so effectively in the same area. This is why we have established the Foundation. We want to be innovative and relentless in the way we go about raising money, and be in a position where if we find a worthy cause — a young boy or girl who might need to fly to the States for some special treatment, for example — we're immediately in a position to help.

We were originally going to launch the Foundation following the Sydney Test last January, but because of the negative mood that game created we decided to wait until after the West Indies tour. Had we gone ahead during the summer, the cynics might have sneered that it was just a gesture to try to boost my image, which some people obviously saw as tarnished. Instead, by waiting, we've been able to focus on the positives. We were surrounded last night by friends and family, and some of Australia's top business people and smartest minds. The mood was fantastic and I came away convinced we will be successful.

From very early in my cricket career, I loved sharing time with children, at things like coaching clinics and promotional events, and — maybe because of my 'working class' roots — I've always been big on everyone, kids and adults alike, getting a reasonable crack at life. My involvement with childhood cancer charities started when I went to lunch one day in Sydney with a number of successful business types and some sporting identities. Also there was Phil Kearns, the former captain of the Wallabies, and as we sat around a boardroom table talking about a wide range of subjects — cricket, rugby, business and then charity work — I was asked what charity most appealed to me.

'Anything with children,' I replied generally. I'd always been willing to help when invited, but I'd never been formally linked to a specific organisation.

The same question was put to Kearnsy, and he revealed he was on the CCIA board. Before we went our separate ways he had arranged for Rianna and me to visit the Sydney Children's Hospital at Randwick, to 'help the kids out' as he put it. All he wanted me to do was turn up, say hello, have a chat and try to brighten up their day. Luckily for me, it turned into much, much more than that.

The experience really touched us. As I explained at the launch last night, 'We didn't walk out with dry eyes.' Rianna and I were deeply affected by how bright and bubbly the kids were, even though they were going through hell, and how their mums and dads, in such a dignified fashion, were so supportive and persistent as they went through their own kind of hell with them. The impact and injustice of the disease was always evident, yet the wards aren't miserable places. We left with our minds numbed by conflicting feelings of hope and sadness. I took a number of phone numbers and promised to keep in touch, which I did. Sometimes the news was great, but not always. I'd receive text messages from parents who'd say that their boy or girl was out of hospital and doing great, but then a month later came another message explaining that the child had passed away. I've always thought I was lucky in life; that one visit convinced me of this many thousands of times over.

The first child we saw was a six-month baby boy who had just been diagnosed with leukaemia. The little bloke didn't know what was happening to him, but his mum and dad sure did. Their lives have been turned totally upside down. All the kids at the Children's Hospital know they are sick, that they have to stay in hospital for a while and that sometimes they feel terrible, but somehow they retain much of their chirpiness. There's a toughness about them, too. Occasional visits by musicians, clowns, TV stars and sporting personalities help a little; their innate courage and optimism help a lot. Ever since that first visit, Rianna and I have tried to do our bit — by using our time and my profile as a cricketer — to make a difference. The Ponting Foundation is the next stage in that process. It's not something I'll throw a few autographed bats at, attend a function or two and think about a couple of times a year. It's much bigger than that. We're committed to doing this as well as we possibly can.

Our first child is due in about three weeks, and I can't wait to be a dad. It's a funny feeling, being the expectant father. I'm slightly anxious, in a way I imagine most first-time parents are, because having a newborn to look after is like nothing I've ever done before, and none of the baby books I've glanced at have convinced me I'm going to be a natural. However, that snippet of worry is overwhelmed by the huge buzz of anticipation that tells me this is going to be the most exciting period of my life. I imagine most debutant dads before me felt this way, too, including the fathers I've met in the children's cancer wards. They would never have known what was ahead of them. Because I've seen those situations, seen how difficult parenthood can sometimes be, I think it will make me hug my new son or daughter that little bit tighter, make me appreciate every day even more. My great hope is that by the time he or she is old enough to play a cover drive, I'll be as well known for the success of our Foundation as I am for any runs I might have scored or Tests we might have won.

SCORES AND AVERAGES

*'Whenever you have a big changeover of players,
as we've had in the last 18 months, it's
very satisfying to continue to win games and
to win series.'*

— Ricky Ponting, July 8, 2008

ICC WORLD TWENTY20

IN SOUTH AFRICA, SEPTEMBER 2007

TOURNAMENT SUMMARY

GROUP MATCHES

Date	Match	Venue	Result
Sept 11	South Africa v West Indies	Johannesburg	South Africa won by eight wickets
Sept 12	Kenya v New Zealand	Durban	New Zealand won by nine wickets
Sept 12	Pakistan v Scotland	Durban	Pakistan won by 51 runs
Sept 12	Australia v Zimbabwe	Cape Town	Zimbabwe won by five wickets
Sept 13	Bangladesh v West Indies	Johannesburg	Bangladesh won by six wickets
Sept 13	England v Zimbabwe	Cape Town	England won by 50 runs
Sept 13	India v Scotland	Durban	No Result
Sept 14	Kenya v Sri Lanka	Johannesburg	Sri Lanka won by 172 runs
Sept 14	Australia v England	Cape Town	Australia won by eight wickets
Sept 14	India v Pakistan	Durban	Match tied
Sept 15	New Zealand v Sri Lanka	Johannesburg	Sri Lanka won by seven wickets
Sept 15	South Africa v Bangladesh	Cape Town	South Africa won by seven wickets
Sept 16	India v New Zealand	Johannesburg	New Zealand won by 10 runs
Sept 16	Australia v Bangladesh	Cape Town	Australia won by nine wickets
Sept 16	South Africa v England	Cape Town	South Africa won by 19 runs
Sept 17	Pakistan v Sri Lanka	Johannesburg	Pakistan won by 33 runs
Sept 18	England v New Zealand	Durban	New Zealand won by five runs
Sept 18	Australia v Pakistan	Johannesburg	Pakistan won by six wickets
Sept 18	Bangladesh v Sri Lanka	Johannesburg	Sri Lanka won by 64 runs
Sept 19	South Africa v New Zealand	Durban	South Africa won by six wickets
Sept 19	England v India	Durban	India won by 18 runs
Sept 20	Australia v Sri Lanka	Cape Town	Australia won by 10 wickets
Sept 20	Bangladesh v Pakistan	Cape Town	Pakistan won by four wickets
Sept 20	South Africa v India	Durban	India won by 37 runs

SEMI-FINALS

Date	Match	Venue	Result
Sept 22	New Zealand v Pakistan	Cape Town	Pakistan won by six wickets
Sept 22	Australia v India	Durban	India won by 15 runs

FINAL

Date	Match	Venue	Result
Sept 24	India v Pakistan	Johannesburg	India won by five runs

GAME FOUR
AUSTRALIA V ZIMBABWE (GROUP B)
Newlands, Cape Town

12 September 2007 (20-over match)

Result: Zimbabwe won by five wickets • Toss: Australia

Umpires: Asad Rauf (Pakistan) and AL Hill (New Zealand)

TV umpire: IL Howell (South Africa) • Match referee: RS Madugalle (Sri Lanka)

Player of the match: BRM Taylor (Zimbabwe)

Australia innings		R	M	B	4	6
AC Gilchrist	c Matsikenyeri b Chigumbura	4	9	6	0	0
ML Hayden	c Taylor b Chigumbura	4	2	2	1	0
RT Ponting	c Chigumbura b Brent	8	14	15	1	0
A Symonds	st Taylor b Masakadza	33	40	25	4	0
MEK Hussey	run out	15	20	23	1	0
BJ Hodge	not out	35	36	22	2	2
BJ Haddin	c Chigumbura b Utseya	6	7	12	0	0
B Lee	b Brent	13	6	7	1	1
MG Johnson	run out	9	5	5	1	0
NW Bracken	c Sibanda b Chigumbura	4	1	3	0	0
Extras	(b 1, w 6)	7				
Total	(9 wickets; 20 overs)	138				

DID NOT BAT: SR Clark

FALL OF WICKETS: 1–7 (Hayden, 0.4 ov), 2–12 (Gilchrist, 2.2 ov), 3–19 (Ponting, 3.6 ov), 4–48 (Hussey, 9.2 ov), 5–86 (Symonds, 13.4 ov), 6–102 (Haddin, 16.2 ov), 7–119 (Lee, 18.1 ov), 8–134 (Johnson, 19.3 ov), 9–138 (Bracken, 19.6 ov)

BOWLING: E Chigumbura 3-0-20-3; GB Brent 4-0-19-2; T Mupariwa 3-0-23-0; CJ Chibhabha 3-0-17-0; P Utseya 4-0-28-1; T Taibu 2-0-21-0; H Masakadza 1-0-9-1

Zimbabwe innings (target: 139 runs from 20 overs)		R	M	B	4	6
V Sibanda	c Gilchrist b Bracken	23	16	15	5	0
BRM Taylor	not out	60	80	45	4	2
CJ Chibhabha	c Gilchrist b Clark	15	13	14	3	0
T Taibu	c Gilchrist b Johnson	0	3	6	0	0
S Matsikenyeri	c Gilchrist b Clark	3	11	8	0	0
H Masakadza	lbw Lee	27	28	2	0	
E Chigumbura	not out	4	6	3	0	0
Extras	(lb 4, w 3)	7				
Total	(5 wickets; 19.5 overs)	139				

DID NOT BAT: KM Dabengwa, P Utseya, GB Brent, T Mupariwa

FALL OF WICKETS: 1–31 (Sibanda, 3.5 ov), 2–54 (Chibhabha, 6.6 ov), 3–55 (Taibu, 7.6 ov), 4–70 (Matsikenyeri, 10.5 ov), 5–123 (Masakadza, 18.3 ov)

BOWLING: B Lee 4-0-31-1; NW Bracken 3.5-0-25-1; SR Clark 4-0-22-2; MG Johnson 4-0-26-1; A Symonds 2-0-11-0; BJ Hodge 2-0-20-0

Twenty20 international debuts: Brad Hodge and Mitchell Johnson

GAME NINE
AUSTRALIA V ENGLAND (GROUP B)
Played at Newlands, Cape Town
14 September 2007 (20-over match)

Result: Australia won by eight wickets • Toss: England
Umpires: Asad Rauf (Pakistan) and IL Howell (South Africa)
TV umpire: AL Hill (New Zealand) • Match referee: RS Madugalle (Sri Lanka)
Player of the match: NW Bracken (Australia)

England innings		R	M	B	4	6
DL Maddy	c Hussey b Clark	20	33	20	3	0
MJ Prior	c Bracken b Johnson	17	19	17	1	1
LJ Wright	c Gilchrist b Johnson	3	7	6	0	0
KP Pietersen	b Bracken	21	30	20	2	0
PD Collingwood	lbw Lee	18	12	11	2	1
A Flintoff	c Clark b Johnson	31	24	19	4	1
OA Shah	c Clarke b Bracken	14	15	13	0	1
AD Mascarenhas	run out	4	8	6	0	0
CP Schofield	c Gilchrist b Clark	1	4	4	0	0
SCJ Broad	b Bracken	1	4	3	0	0
RJ Kirtley	not out	2	3	4	0	0
Extras	(nb 3)	3				
Total	(all out; 20 overs)	135				

FALL OF WICKETS: 1–29 (Prior, 4.5 ov), 2–37 (Wright, 6.4 ov), 3–48 (Maddy, 7.3 ov), 4–73 (Collingwood, 10.3 ov), 5–97 (Pietersen, 13.1 ov), 6–127 (Flintoff, 16.6 ov), 7–128 (Shah, 17.4 ov), 8–132 (Schofield, 18.5 ov), 9–132 (Mascarenhas, 18.6 ov), 10–135 (Broad, 19.6 ov)

BOWLING: B Lee 4–0–31–1; NW Bracken 4–0–16–3; SR Clark 4–0–24–2; MG Johnson 4–0–22–3; A Symonds 2–0–28–0; MJ Clarke 2–0–14–0

Australia innings		R	M	B	4	6
AC Gilchrist	c Flintoff b Schofield	45	36	28	5	1
ML Hayden	not out	67	61	43	11	1
RT Ponting	c & b Flintoff	20	18	16	1	1
A Symonds	not out	2	5	2	0	0
Extras	(lb 2)	2				
Total	(2 wickets; 14.5 overs)	136				

DID NOT BAT: MEK Hussey, BJ Hodge, MJ Clarke, B Lee, MG Johnson, NW Bracken, SR Clark

FALL OF WICKETS: 1–78 (Gilchrist, 8.2 ov), 2–120 (Ponting, 13.3 ov)

BOWLING: SJ Broad 3–0–23–0; A Flintoff 4–0–25–1; PD Collingwood 1–0–16–0; RJ Kirtley 1–0–17–0; AD Mascarenhas 2–0–22–0; CP Schofield 3.5–0–31–1

GAME 14
AUSTRALIA V BANGLADESH (GROUP F)
Newlands, Cape Town
16 September 2007 (20-over match)

Result: Australia won by nine wickets • Toss: Australia
Umpires: Asad Rauf (Pakistan) and IL Howell (South Africa)
TV umpire: AL Hill (New Zealand) • Match referee: RS Madugalle (Sri Lanka)
Player of the match: B Lee (Australia)

Bangladesh innings		R	M	B	4	6
Tamim Iqbal	c Ponting b Clarke	32	44	40	3	0
Nazimuddin	c Ponting b Johnson	11	21	17	2	0
Aftab Ahmed	c Hodge b Bracken	31	51	34	2	0
Mohammad Ashraful	c Symonds b Clark	7	11	6	1	0
Shakib Al Hasan	c Gilchrist b Lee	16	13	11	1	1
Mashrafe Mortaza	b Lee	0	1	1	0	0
Alok Kapali	lbw Lee	0	1	1	0	0
Farhad Reza	c Hussey b Bracken	4	13	13	0	0
Mushfiqur Rahim	not out	3	3	2	0	0
Abdur Razzak	not out	0	2	0	0	0
Extras	(b 1, lb 2, w 11, nb 5)	19				
Total	(8 wickets; 20 overs)	123				

DID NOT BAT: Syed Rasel

FALL OF WICKETS: 1–40 (Nazimuddin, 6.6 ov), 2–65 (Tamim Iqbal, 10.5 ov), 3–82 (Mohammad Ashraful, 13.1 ov), 4–108 (Shakib Al Hasan, 16.3 ov), 5–108 (Mashrafe Mortaza, 16.4 ov), 6–108 (Alok Kapali, 16.5 ov), 7–120 (Aftab Ahmed, 19.3 ov), 8–120 (Farhad Reza, 19.4 ov)

BOWLING: B Lee 4–0–27–3; NW Bracken 3–0–14–2; SR Clark 4–0–13–1; MG Johnson 4–0–28–1; A Symonds 2–0–10–0; MJ Clarke 3–0–28–1

Australia innings		R	M	B	4	6
AC Gilchrist	run out	43	41	28	1	4
ML Hayden	not out	73	51	48	9	3
RT Ponting	not out	6	9	8	0	0
Extras	(w 1, nb 1)	2				
Total	(1 wicket; 13.5 overs)	124				

DID NOT BAT: A Symonds, MEK Hussey, BJ Hodge, MJ Clarke, B Lee, MG Johnson, NW Bracken, SR Clark

Fall of wicket: 1–104 (Gilchrist, 11.3 ov)

BOWLING: Mashrafe Mortaza 3.5–0–27–0; Syed Rasel 2–0–25–0; Abdur Razzak 4–0–34–0; Shakib Al Hasan 2–0–15–0; Alok Kapali 2–0–23–0

GAME 18
AUSTRALIA V PAKISTAN (GROUP F)
New Wanderers Stadium, Johannesburg
18 September 2007 (20-over match)
Result: Pakistan won by six wickets • Toss: Pakistan
Umpires: MR Benson (England) and NJ Llong (England)
TV umpire: DJ Harper (Australia) • Match referee: BC Broad (England)
Player of the match: Misbah-ul-Haq (Pakistan)

Australia innings		R	M	B	4	6
AC Gilchrist	c M Hafeez b Sohail Tanvir	24	18	12	5	0
ML Hayden	c Younis Khan b Sohail Tanvir	1	6	5	0	0
RT Ponting	b Mohammad Hafeez	27	40	26	3	0
A Symonds	b Shahid Afridi	29	18	18	5	0
MEK Hussey	c Imran Nazir b Sohail Tanvir	37	37	25	3	1
BJ Hodge	c Younis Khan b M Asif	36	36	29	3	0
MJ Clarke	run out	0	3	1	0	0
B Lee	not out	2	6	3	0	0
MG Johnson	not out	1	1	1	0	0
Extras	(b 1, lb 3, w 3)	7				
Total	(7 wickets; 20 overs)	164				

DID NOT BAT: NW Bracken, SR Clark

FALL OF WICKETS: 1–8 (Hayden, 1.3 ov), 2–32 (Gilchrist, 3.4 ov), 3–80 (Symonds, 8.5 ov), 4–92 (Ponting, 11.1 ov), 5–155 (Hussey, 17.5 ov), 6–159 (Clarke, 18.4 ov), 7–162 (Hodge, 19.3 ov)

BOWLING: Mohammad Asif 4–0–34–1; Sohail Tanvir 4–0–31–3; Shahid Afridi 4–1–35–1; Mohammad Hafeez 4–0–31; Umar Gul 4–0–29–0

Pakistan innings		R	M	B	4	6
Imran Nazir	c Johnson b Clark	10	12	10	1	1
Mohammad Hafeez	c Clarke b Clark	15	15	11	2	1
Salman Butt	lbw Johnson	11	16	12	2	0
Younis Khan	c Lee b Clark	4	5	3	1	0
Shoaib Malik	not out	52	58	38	4	2
Misbah-ul-Haq	not out	66	51	42	7	1
Extras	(lb 1, w 5, nb 1)	7				
Total	(4 wickets; 19.1 overs)	165				

DID NOT BAT: Shahid Afridi, Kamran Akmal, Mohammad Asif, Umar Gul, Sohail Tanvir

FALL OF WICKETS: 1–25 (Imran Nazir, 3.1 ov), 2–27 (Mohammad Hafeez, 3.4 ov), 3–35 (Younis Khan, 5.1 ov), 4–46 (Salman Butt, 6.4 ov)

BOWLING: B Lee 4–0–30–0; NW Bracken 4–0–35–0; SR Clark 4–0–27–3; MG Johnson 4–0–28–1; A Symonds 2.1–0–27–0; MJ Clarke–1–0–17–0

GAME 22
AUSTRALIA V SRI LANKA (GROUP F)
Newlands, Cape Town
20 September 2007 (20-over match)

Result: Australia won by 10 wickets • Toss: Australia
Umpires: Asad Rauf (Pakistan) and IL Howell (South Africa)
TV umpire: AL Hill (New Zealand) • Match referee: RS Madugalle (Sri Lanka)
Player of the match: SR Clark (Australia)

Sri Lanka innings		R	M	B	4	6
WU Tharanga	c Lee b Bracken	4	10	8	0	0
ST Jayasuriya	lbw Lee	0	2	2	0	0
KC Sangakkara	c Clarke b Clark	22	38	23	3	0
DPMD Jayawardene	c Clark b Lee	1	2	2	0	0
LPC Silva	c Lee b Clark	6	12	11	1	0
TM Dilshan	c Gilchrist b Clark	3	7	5	0	0
J Mubarak	c Symonds b Watson	28	33	26	3	0
MF Maharoof	c Clarke b Clark	0	1	2	0	0
WPUJC Vaas	c Lee b Symonds	21	34	28	1	0
SL Malinga	not out	12	13	10	0	1
CRD Fernando	c & b Bracken	0	2	2	0	0
Extras	(lb 1, w 1, nb 2)	4				
Total	(all out; 19.3 overs)	101				

FALL OF WICKETS: 1–1 (Jayasuriya, 0.3 ov), 2–9 (Tharanga, 1.6 ov), 3–11 (Jayawardene, 2.4 ov), 4–21 (Silva, 5.3 ov), 5–30 (Dilshan, 7.3 ov), 6–43 (Sangakkara, 9.3 ov), 7–43 (Maharoof, 9.5 ov), 8–83 (Mubarak, 16.2 ov), 9–99 (Vaas, 18.5 ov), 10–101 (Fernando, 19.3 ov)

BOWLING: B Lee 4–0–27–2; NW Bracken 3.3–0–14–2; MG Johnson 4–0–18–0; SR Clark 4–0–20–4; SR Watson 3.2–0–19–1; A Symonds 0.4–0–2–1

Australia innings		R	M	B	4	6
AC Gilchrist	not out	31	44	25	4	0
ML Hayden	not out	58	44	38	7	2
Extras	(b 4, lb 2, w 6, nb 1)	13				
Total	(0 wickets; 10.2 overs)	102				

DID NOT BAT: BJ Hodge, A Symonds, MEK Hussey, MJ Clarke, SR Watson, B Lee, MG Johnson, NW Bracken, SR Clark

BOWLING: WPUJC Vaas 2–0–21–0; CRD Fernando 3–1–12–0; MF Maharoof 2–0–34–0; TM Dilshan 2–0–13–0; SL Malinga 1–0–8–0; J Mubarak 0.2–0–8–0

SECOND SEMI-FINAL
AUSTRALIA V INDIA
Kingsmead, Durban
22 September 2007 (20-over match)

Result: India won by 15 runs • Toss: India
Umpires: Asad Rauf (Pakistan) and MR Benson (England)
TV umpire: BR Doctrove (West Indies) • Match referee: BC Broad (England)
Player of the match: Yuvraj Singh (India)

India innings		R	M	B	4	6
G Gambhir	c Hodge b Johnson	24	37	25	4	0
V Sehwag	c Gilchrist b Johnson	9	25	13	1	0
RV Uthappa	run out	34	38	28	1	3
Yuvraj Singh	c Hussey b Clarke	70	38	30	5	5
MS Dhoni	run out	36	21	18	4	1
RG Sharma	not out	8	11	5	0	1
IK Pathan	not out	0	1	1	0	0
Extras	(lb 6, w 1)	7				
Total	(5 wickets; 20 overs)	188				

DID NOT BAT: Harbhajan Singh, Joginder Sharma, S Sreesanth, RP Singh

FALL OF WICKETS: 1–30 (Sehwag, 5.2 ov), 2–41 (Gambhir, 7.6 ov), 3–125 (Uthappa, 14.3 ov), 4–155 (Yuvraj Singh, 17.3 ov), 5–184 (Dhoni, 19.5 ov)

BOWLING: B Lee 4–0–25–0; NW Bracken 4–0–38–0; SR Clark 4–0–38–0; MG Johnson 4–0–31–2; A Symonds 3–0–37–0; MJ Clarke 1–0–13–1

Australia innings		R	M	B	4	6
AC Gilchrist	b Sreesanth	22	21	13	2	2
ML Hayden	b Sreesanth	62	61	47	4	4
BJ Hodge	c Joginder Sharma b Pathan	11	15	10	0	1
A Symonds	b Pathan	43	37	26	3	2
MEK Hussey	c Yuvraj b Joginder Sharma	13	28	12	0	1
MJ Clarke	b Harbhajan	3	2	3	0	0
BJ Haddin	not out	5	14	8	0	0
B Lee	b Joginder Sharma	2	1	2	0	0
MG Johnson	not out	4	2	1	1	0
Extras	(lb 3, w 3, nb 2)	8				
Total	(7 wickets; 20 overs)	173				

DID NOT BAT: NW Bracken, SR Clark

FALL OF WICKETS: 1–36 (Gilchrist, 5.1 ov), 2–68 (Hodge, 8.4 ov), 3–134 (Hayden, 14.4 ov), 4–156 (Symonds, 16.4 ov), 5–159 (Clarke, 17.1 ov), 6–167 (Hussey, 19.3 ov), 7–169 (Lee, 19.5 ov)

BOWLING: RP Singh 4–0–33–0; S Sreesanth 4–1–12–2; IK Pathan 4–0–44–2; Joginder Sharma 3–0–37–2; Harbhajan Singh 4–0–24; V Sehwag 1–0–20–0

ICC WORLD TWENTY20 — AUSTRALIAN AVERAGES

BATTING AND FIELDING

Batsman	T20s	Inns	NO	Runs	HS	Ave	100	50	Ct	St
ML Hayden	6	6	3	265	73*	88.33	0	4	0	0
BJ Hodge	6	3	1	82	36	41.00	0	0	2	0
A Symonds	6	4	1	107	43	35.67	0	0	2	0
AC Gilchrist	6	6	1	169	45	33.80	0	0	9	0
MEK Hussey	6	3	0	65	37	21.67	0	0	3	0
RT Ponting	4	4	1	61	27	20.33	0	0	2	0
MG Johnson	6	3	2	14	9	14.00	0	0	1	0
BJ Haddin	2	2	1	11	6	11.00	0	0	0	0
B Lee	6	3	1	17	13	8.50	0	0	4	0
NW Bracken	6	1	0	4	4	4.00	0	0	2	0
MJ Clarke	5	2	0	3	3	1.50	0	0	4	0
SR Clark	6	–	–	–	–	–	–	–	2	0
SR Watson	1	–	–	–	–	–	–	–	0	0

BOWLING

Bowler	Overs	Mdns	Runs	Wkts	Best	Ave	4w
SR Clark	24.0	0	144	12	4–20	12.00	1
NW Bracken	22.2	0	142	8	3–16	17.75	0
SR Watson	3.2	0	19	1	1–19	19.00	0
MG Johnson	24.0	0	153	8	3–22	19.13	0
B Lee	24.0	0	171	7	3–27	24.43	0
MJ Clarke	7.0	0	72	2	1–13	36.00	0
A Symonds	11.5	0	115	1	1–2	115.00	0
BJ Hodge	2.0	0	20	0	–	–	0

AUSTRALIA'S TWENTY20 INTERNATIONALS BEFORE 2007–08

Date	Opponent	Venue	Result
February 17, 2005	New Zealand	Auckland	Won by 44 runs
June 13, 2005	England	Southampton	Lost by 100 runs
January 9, 2006	South Africa	Brisbane	Won by 95 runs
February 24, 2006	South Africa	Johannesburg	Lost by two runs
January 9, 2007	England	Sydney	Won by 77 runs

Best Australian performances in these matches
Best batting: Ricky Ponting — 98 not out v New Zealand in Auckland, 2004–05.
Best bowling: Michael Kasprowicz — 4–29 v New Zealand in Auckland, 2004–05.

Notes:
1. The only two men to play in all five of these matches were Ricky Ponting and Michael Clarke.
2. The only other half-centuries scored by Australian batsmen in these matches were Damien Martyn's 96 and Andrew Symonds' 54 not out v South Africa at the Gabba in 2005–06.
3. The only other instance of an Australian bowler taking three or more wickets in any of these matches was Glenn McGrath's 3–31 v England in 2005.

AUSTRALIA IN INDIA
SEPTEMBER–OCTOBER 2007

FIRST ONE-DAY INTERNATIONAL

INDIA V AUSTRALIA
M Chinnaswamy Stadium, Bangalore
29 September 2007 (50-over match)
Result: No Result • Toss: Australia
Umpires: SA Bucknor (West Indies) and SL Shastri (India)
TV umpire: AM Saheba (India) • Match referee: BC Broad (England)

Australia innings		R	M	B	4	6
AC Gilchrist	c Yuvraj Singh b Khan	12	11	11	2	0
ML Hayden	b Sreesanth	34	75	39	5	1
BJ Hodge	lbw Sreesanth	0	6	5	0	0
MJ Clarke	run out	130	202	132	10	3
A Symonds	lbw Sreesanth	7	11	7	1	0
BJ Haddin	st Dhoni b Yuvraj Singh	69	99	83	7	1
JR Hopes	c Tendulkar b Khan	37	31	25	4	0
B Lee	not out	0	1	0	0	0
Extras	(b 4, lb 1, w 11, nb 2)	18				
Total	(7 wickets; 50 overs)	307				

DID NOT BAT: GB Hogg, SR Clark, MG Johnson

FALL OF WICKETS: 1–14 (Gilchrist, 2.1 ov), 2–18 (Hodge, 3.1 ov), 3–78 (Hayden, 14.2 ov), 4–90 (Symonds, 16.3 ov), 5–234 (Haddin, 41.5 ov), 6–307 (Hopes, 49.5 ov), 7–307 (Clarke, 49.6 ov)

BOWLING: Z Khan 10–0–64–2; S Sreesanth 10–0–55–3; RP Singh 10–0–67–0; IK Pathan 8–0–38–0; RR Powar 6–1–50–0; Yuvraj Singh 6–0–28–1

India innings		R	M	B	4	6
G Gambhir	not out	4	12	10	1	0
SR Tendulkar	lbw Johnson	0	9	6	0	0
IK Pathan	not out	0	2	0	0	0
Extras	(b 4, w 1)	5				
Total	(1 wicket; 2.4 overs)	9				

DID NOT BAT: SC Ganguly, R Dravid, Yuvraj Singh, MS Dhoni, RR Powar, RP Singh, Z Khan, S Sreesanth

FALL OF WICKETS: 1–1 (Tendulkar, 1.6 ov)

BOWLING: B Lee 1.4–1–4–0; MG Johnson 1–0–1–1

SECOND ONE-DAY INTERNATIONAL

INDIA V AUSTRALIA
Nehru Stadium, Kochi
2 October 2007 (50-over match)

Result: Australia won by 84 runs • Toss: India
Umpires: SA Bucknor (West Indies) and SL Shastri (India)
TV umpire: GA Pratapkumar (India) • Match referee: BC Broad (England)
Player of the match: BJ Haddin (Australia)

Australia innings		R	M	B	4	6
AC Gilchrist	c Tendulkar b Khan	0	4	5	0	0
ML Hayden	b Pathan	75	136	89	5	3
BJ Hodge	c Dhoni b Sreesanth	3	10	10	0	0
MJ Clarke	st Dhoni b Pathan	27	59	38	3	0
A Symonds	c & b Sreesanth	87	131	83	9	2
BJ Haddin	not out	87	89	69	8	3
JR Hopes	c Dravid b Sreesanth	4	11	4	0	0
B Lee	not out	2	4	2	0	0
Extras	(b 4, lb 2, w 15)	21				
Total	(6 wickets; 50 overs)	306				

DID NOT BAT: GB Hogg, SR Clark, MG Johnson

FALL OF WICKETS: 1–3 (Gilchrist, 0.6 ov), 2–8 (Hodge, 3.1 ov), 3–66 (Clarke, 15.3 ov), 4–160 (Hayden, 31.1 ov), 5–268 (Symonds, 46.5 ov), 6–297 (Hopes, 49.2 ov)

BOWLING: Z Khan 10–1–55–1; S Sreesanth 9–0–67–3; IK Pathan 10–0–47–2; Harbhajan Singh 10–0–57–0; RR Powar 5–0–30–0; SR Tendulkar 3–0–22–0; Yuvraj Singh 3–0–22–0

India innings		R	M	B	4	6
G Gambhir	b Johnson	7	13	13	1	0
SR Tendulkar	c Symonds b Clark	16	43	25	1	1
RV Uthappa	lbw Clark	41	59	30	4	2
Yuvraj Singh	c Hayden b Hopes	10	14	10	0	1
R Dravid	c Johnson b Hogg	31	57	48	3	1
MS Dhoni	c Hodge b Hogg	58	134	88	2	2
IK Pathan	run out	1	9	7	0	0
Harbhajan Singh	st Gilchrist b Clarke	4	12	10	0	0
RR Powar	b Clarke	17	17	18	1	1
Z Khan	c Hodge b Hogg	3	16	14	0	0
S Sreesanth	not out	7	34	25	0	0
Extras	(b 4, lb 6, w 10, nb 7)	27				
Total	(all out; 47.3 overs)	222				

FALL OF WICKETS: 1–11 (Gambhir, 3.1 ov), 2–58 (Tendulkar, 8.5 ov), 3–79 (Yuvraj Singh, 11.4 ov), 4–87 (Uthappa, 14.2 ov), 5–136 (Dravid, 25.1 ov), 6–139 (Pathan, 26.6 ov), 7–154 (Harbhajan Singh, 30.3 ov), 8–179 (Powar, 34.6 ov), 9–190 (Khan, 39.2 ov), 10–222 (Dhoni, 47.3 ov)

BOWLING: B Lee 7–0–44–0; MG Johnson 9–1–46–1; SR Clark 6–0–14–2; JR Hopes 7–0–33–1; MJ Clarke 9–1–35–2; GB Hogg 9.3–0–40–3

THIRD ONE-DAY INTERNATIONAL

INDIA V AUSTRALIA
Rajiv Gandhi International Stadium, Hyderabad
5 October 2007 (50-over match)

Result: Australia won by 47 runs • Toss: Australia
Umpires: SA Bucknor (West Indies) and SL Shastri (India)
TV umpire: GA Pratapkumar (India) • Match referee: BC Broad (England)
Player of the match: A Symonds (Australia)

Australia innings		R	M	B	4	6
AC Gilchrist	b Pathan	29	65	31	3	0
ML Hayden	c Dhoni b Pathan	60	109	70	10	0
RT Ponting	c Sreesanth b Yuvraj Singh	25	64	43	3	0
MJ Clarke	c Pathan b Khan	59	89	71	4	0
A Symonds	c Uthappa b Sreesanth	89	83	67	5	5
BJ Hodge	b Khan	3	4	7	0	0
JR Hopes	c Dravid b Sreesanth	11	15	11	0	0
B Lee	not out	0	1	0	0	0
Extras	(b 2, lb 3, w 9)	14				
Total	(7 wickets; 50 overs)	290				

DID NOT BAT: GB Hogg, SR Clark, MG Johnson

FALL OF WICKETS: 1–76 (Gilchrist, 13.2 ov), 2–112 (Hayden, 20.3 ov), 3–135 (Ponting, 28.2 ov), 4–258 (Clarke, 44.6 ov), 5–263 (Hodge, 46.4 ov), 6–290 (Symonds, 49.5 ov), 7–290 (Hopes, 49.6 ov)

BOWLING: Z Khan 10–1–61–2; S Sreesanth 9–0–58–2; IK Pathan 10–0–57–2; Harbhajan Singh 10–1–38–0; Yuvraj Singh 7–0–49–1; SR Tendulkar 4–0–22–0

India innings		R	M	B	4	6
G Gambhir	lbw Lee	6	12	11	0	0
SR Tendulkar	b Hogg	43	119	71	6	0
RV Uthappa	lbw Johnson	0	4	3	0	0
R Dravid	c Hayden b Lee	0	5	4	0	0
Yuvraj Singh	b Johnson	121	177	115	12	3
MS Dhoni	c Gilchrist b Lee	33	49	37	4	0
RG Sharma	c Lee b Hopes	1	3	4	0	0
IK Pathan	lbw Hogg	3	7	4	0	0
Harbhajan Singh	not out	19	38	22	1	1
Z Khan	c & b Hogg	3	13	4	0	0
S Sreesanth	b Clark	1	11	12	0	0
Extras	(b 1, lb 3, w 8, nb 1)	13				
Total	(all out; 47.4 overs)	243				

FALL OF WICKETS: 1–10 (Gambhir, 2.5 ov), 2–11 (Uthappa, 3.5 ov), 3–13 (Dravid, 4.5 ov), 4–108 (Tendulkar, 24.6 ov), 5–173 (Dhoni, 35.6 ov), 6–176 (Sharma, 36.6 ov), 7–183 (Pathan, 38.3 ov), 8–219 (Yuvraj Singh, 43.1 ov), 9–226 (Khan, 44.3 ov), 10–243 (Sreesanth, 47.4 ov)

BOWLING: B Lee 8–1–37–3; MG Johnson 10–0–51–2; SR Clark 8.4–1–44–1; JR Hopes 10–0–43–1; GB Hogg 9–0–46–3; BJ Hodge 2–0–18–0

FOURTH ONE-DAY INTERNATIONAL

INDIA V AUSTRALIA
Played at Sector 16 Stadium, Chandigarh
8 October 2007 (50-over match)

Result: India won by eight runs • Toss: India
Umpires: SA Bucknor (West Indies) and SL Shastri (India)
TV umpire: GA Pratapkumar (India) • Match referee: BC Broad (England)
Player of the match: MS Dhoni (India)

India innings		R	M	B	4	6
SC Ganguly	c Gilchrist b Hopes	41	95	59	6	0
SR Tendulkar	run out	79	184	119	7	0
Yuvraj Singh	c Ponting b Hopes	39	61	55	5	0
MS Dhoni	not out	50	59	35	5	1
R Dravid	b Bracken	13	15	14	2	0
RV Uthappa	not out	30	16	18	6	0
Extras	(b 1, lb 7, w 31)	39				
Total	(4 wickets; 50 overs)	291				

DID NOT BAT: IK Pathan, M Kartik, Harbhajan Singh, Z Khan, RP Singh

FALL OF WICKETS: 1–91 (Ganguly, 19.6 ov), 2–174 (Yuvraj Singh, 35.6 ov), 3–221 (Tendulkar, 41.5 ov), 4–244 (Dravid, 45.5 ov)

BOWLING: B Lee 7–1–26–0; NW Bracken 10–0–78–1; MG Johnson 8–0–51–0; JR Hopes 9–0–43–2; A Symonds 7–0–39–0; GB Hogg 9–0–46–0

Australia innings		R	M	B	4	6
AC Gilchrist	c Khan b Singh	18	25	17	1	1
ML Hayden	c Khan b Kartik	92	156	92	11	2
RT Ponting	st Dhoni b Pathan	29	62	33	5	0
MJ Clarke	c & b Harbhajan	6	13	15	1	0
A Symonds	b Singh	75	103	84	3	1
BJ Hodge	st Dhoni b Harbhajan	17	36	29	1	0
JR Hopes	not out	23	30	20	1	0
GB Hogg	run out	0	1	1	0	0
B Lee	not out	5	14	9	0	0
Extras	(lb 5, w 13)	18				
Total	(7 wickets; 50 overs)	283				

DID NOT BAT: NW Bracken, MG Johnson

FALL OF WICKETS: 1–37 (Gilchrist, 5.1 ov), 2–122 (Ponting, 18.2 ov), 3–132 (Clarke, 21.4 ov), 4–190 (Hayden, 33.5 ov), 5–246 (Hodge, 43.2 ov), 6–268 (Symonds, 46.5 ov), 7–268 (Hogg, 46.6 ov)

BOWLING: Z Khan 9–0–68–0; RP Singh 10–1–66–2; IK Pathan 10–0–46–1; SC Ganguly 1–0–7–0; Harbhajan Singh 10–0–43–2; M Kartik 10–0–48–1

FIFTH ONE-DAY INTERNATIONAL

INDIA V AUSTRALIA
Reliance Stadium, Vadodara
11 October 2007 (50-over match)
Result: Australia won by nine wickets • Toss: India
Umpires: Aleem Dar (Pakistan) and AM Saheba (India)
TV umpire: SL Shastri (India) • Match referee: BC Broad (England)
Player of the match: MG Johnson (Australia)

India innings		R	M	B	4	6
SC Ganguly	run out	0	5	4	0	0
SR Tendulkar	c Gilchrist b Lee	47	128	73	9	0
R Dravid	lbw Lee	0	1	1	0	0
Yuvraj Singh	c Gilchrist b Johnson	1	16	7	0	0
RV Uthappa	lbw Johnson	5	17	6	1	0
MS Dhoni	c Gilchrist b Johnson	4	12	7	1	0
IK Pathan	c Gilchrist b Johnson	26	84	63	2	1
Harbhajan Singh	c Bracken b Hogg	5	6	3	1	0
M Kartik	c Gilchrist b Johnson	0	11	4	0	0
Z Khan	c Gilchrist b Bracken	28	51	44	0	2
RP Singh	not out	12	44	27	1	0
Extras	(b 4, lb 6, w 9, nb 1)	20				
Total	(all out; 39.4 overs)	148				

FALL OF WICKETS: 1–5 (Ganguly, 0.4 ov), 2–5 (Dravid, 0.5 ov), 3–12 (Yuvraj Singh, 3.5 ov), 4–33 (Uthappa, 7.1 ov), 5–43 (Dhoni, 9.2 ov), 6–92 (Tendulkar, 25.3 ov), 7–105 (Harbhajan Singh, 26.6 ov), 8–106 (Pathan, 27.4 ov), 9–107 (Kartik, 29.1 ov), 10–148 (Khan, 39.4 ov)

BOWLING: B Lee 9–0–42–2; MG Johnson 10–0–26–5; GB Hogg 9–1–28–1; JR Hopes 3–0–13–0; NW Bracken 8.4–0–29–1

Australia innings		R	M	B	4	6
AC Gilchrist	not out	79	111	77	7	4
ML Hayden	b Singh	29	52	39	4	0
RT Ponting	not out	39	59	39	5	0
Extras	(lb 1, w 1)	2				
Total	(1 wicket; 25.5 overs)	149				

DID NOT BAT: MJ Clarke, BJ Hodge, A Symonds, GB Hogg, JR Hopes, B Lee, NW Bracken, MG Johnson

Fall of wicket: 1–54 (Hayden, 12.5 ov)

BOWLING: Harbhajan Singh 9–0–36–0; Z Khan 3–0–23–0; M Kartik 7.5–1–52–0; RP Singh 2–0–15–1; IK Pathan 2–0–11–0; SR Tendulkar 2–0–11–0

SIXTH ONE-DAY INTERNATIONAL

INDIA V AUSTRALIA
Vidarbha Cricket Association Ground, Nagpur
14 October 2007 (50-over match)

Result: Australia won by 18 runs • Toss: Australia
Umpires: Aleem Dar (Pakistan) and AM Saheba (India)
TV umpire: SL Shastri (India) • Match referee: BC Broad (England)
Player of the match: A Symonds (Australia)

Australia innings		R	M	B	4	6
AC Gilchrist	c Uthappa b Pathan	51	74	47	8	0
MJ Clarke	c Dhoni b Khan	0	2	1	0	0
RT Ponting	c Dravid b Harbhajan	49	62	44	7	1
BJ Hodge	c Dravid b Kartik	20	29	28	4	0
A Symonds	not out	107	139	88	9	4
BJ Haddin	c Tendulkar b Sreesanth	25	59	53	0	1
JR Hopes	c Dravid b Khan	39	40	30	5	0
B Lee	run out	17	10	9	1	1
MG Johnson	run out	1	2	1	0	0
Extras	(lb 3, w 4, nb 1)	8				
Total	(8 wickets; 50 overs)	317				

DID NOT BAT: GB Hogg, NW Bracken

FALL OF WICKETS: 1–2 (Clarke, 0.3 ov), 2–98 (Ponting, 14.4 ov), 3–102 (Gilchrist, 15.5 ov), 4–129 (Hodge, 21.5 ov), 5–204 (Haddin, 37.6 ov), 6–294 (Hopes, 47.4 ov), 7–315 (Lee, 49.4 ov), 8–317 (Johnson, 49.6 ov)

BOWLING: Z Khan 10–0–62–2; S Sreesanth 8–0–64–1; IK Pathan 9–0–60–1; Harbhajan Singh 8–0–56; M Kartik 9–1–37–1; Yuvraj Singh 1–0–15–0; SR Tendulkar 5–0–20–0

India innings		R	M	B	4	6
SC Ganguly	c Hodge b Hogg	86	161	111	7	2
SR Tendulkar	st Gilchrist b Hopes	72	105	72	9	1
IK Pathan	c Clarke b Hogg	29	41	29	3	2
R Dravid	c Hodge b Hogg	7	32	13	0	0
Yuvraj Singh	lbw Hogg	6	10	11	1	0
MS Dhoni	c Ponting b Johnson	26	44	29	2	1
RV Uthappa	c Hopes b Johnson	44	33	28	5	2
Harbhajan Singh	not out	6	9	5	1	0
Z Khan	not out	3	6	3	0	0
Extras	(b 4, lb 8, w 7, nb 1)	20				
Total	(7 wickets; 50 overs)	299				

DID NOT BAT: M Kartik, S Sreesanth

FALL OF WICKETS: 1–140 (Tendulkar, 24.6 ov), 2–189 (Pathan, 32.6 ov), 3–203 (Ganguly, 36.1 ov), 4–213 (Yuvraj Singh, 38.3 ov), 5–218 (Dravid, 40.3 ov), 6–290 (Uthappa, 48.1 ov), 7–290 (Dhoni, 48.4 ov)

BOWLING: B Lee 7–0–50–0; MG Johnson 9–1–39–2; NW Bracken 8–0–54–0; JR Hopes 4–0–30–1; A Symonds 10–0–39–0; GB Hogg 10–0–49–4; MJ Clarke 2–0–26–0

SEVENTH ONE-DAY INTERNATIONAL

INDIA V AUSTRALIA
Wankhede Stadium, Mumbai
17 October 2007 (50-over match)
Result: India won by two wickets • Toss: Australia
Umpires: Aleem Dar (Pakistan) and AM Saheba (India)
TV umpire: GA Pratapkumar (India) • Match referee: BC Broad (England)
Player of the match: M Kartik (India) • Player of the series: A Symonds (Australia)

Australia innings		R	M	B	4	6
MJ Clarke	lbw Khan	0	1	1	0	0
AC Gilchrist	c Harbhajan b Pathan	19	51	26	4	0
RT Ponting	c Dhoni b Singh	57	129	78	9	0
BJ Hodge	c Karthik b Kartik	16	50	29	2	0
A Symonds	c Tendulkar b Kartik	0	2	1	0	0
BJ Haddin	lbw Kartik	19	48	38	3	0
JR Hopes	b Kartik	22	46	23	3	0
GB Hogg	c Uthappa b Kartik	0	4	3	0	0
B Lee	c Singh b Kartik	0	1	1	0	0
MG Johnson	not out	24	42	31	2	1
NW Bracken	c Harbhajan b Singh	3	25	18	0	0
Extras	(b 4, lb 3, w 26)	33				
Total	(all out; 41.3 overs)	193				

FALL OF WICKETS: 1–0 (Clarke, 0.1 ov), 2–60 (Gilchrist, 9.2 ov), 3–117 (Hodge, 19.5 ov), 4–117 (Symonds, 19.6 ov), 5–129 (Ponting, 26.1 ov), 6–162 (Haddin, 31.1 ov), 7–162 (Hogg, 31.4 ov), 8–162 (Lee, 31.5 ov), 9–177 (Hopes, 35.5 ov), 10–193 (Bracken, 41.3 ov)

BOWLING: Z Khan 9–1–22–1; RP Singh 8.3–1–59–2; IK Pathan 5–0–23–1; SC Ganguly 2–0–24–0; Harbhajan Singh 7–0–31; M Kartik 10–3–27–6

India innings		R	M	B	4	6
SC Ganguly	c Gilchrist b Johnson	0	9	7	0	0
SR Tendulkar	b Lee	21	52	36	4	0
KD Karthik	c Gilchrist b Johnson	0	12	6	0	0
Yuvraj Singh	c Gilchrist b Bracken	15	47	26	2	0
RV Uthappa	lbw Clarke	47	100	59	4	2
MS Dhoni	c Gilchrist b Bracken	5	22	11	1	0
IK Pathan	c Clarke b Hopes	0	4	5	0	0
Harbhajan Singh	c Ponting b Johnson	19	73	49	1	0
Z Khan	not out	31	66	43	3	1
M Kartik	not out	21	48	34	3	0
Extras	(b 4, lb 12, w 20)	36				
Total	(8 wickets; 46 overs)	195				

DID NOT BAT: RP Singh

FALL OF WICKETS: 1–3 (Ganguly, 1.4 ov), 2–8 (Karthik, 3.4 ov), 3–38 (Tendulkar, 10.2 ov), 4–49 (Yuvraj Singh, 13.5 ov), 5–63 (Dhoni, 17.5 ov), 6–64 (Pathan, 18.5 ov), 7–129 (Uthappa, 31.3 ov), 8–143 (Harbhajan Singh, 35.4 ov)

BOWLING: B Lee 10–1–37–1; MG Johnson 10–0–46–3; NW Bracken 10–3–30–2; JR Hopes 5–0–13–1; GB Hogg 8–0–40–0; MJ Clarke 3–0–13–1

TWENTY20 INTERNATIONAL

INDIA V AUSTRALIA
Brabourne Stadium, Mumbai
20 October 2007 (20-over match)

Result: India won by seven wickets • Toss: Australia
Umpires: AM Saheba (India) and SL Shastri (India)
TV umpire: GA Pratapkumar (India) • Match referee: BC Broad (England)
Player of the match: G Gambhir (India)

Australia innings		R	M	B	4	6
AC Gilchrist	b Singh	12	3	5	3	0
ML Hayden	b Harbhajan	17	34	19	1	2
RT Ponting	b Pathan	76	79	53	13	0
A Symonds	run out	20	23	18	1	0
BJ Hodge	b Pathan	2	7	6	0	0
MJ Clarke	not out	25	22	15	2	0
BJ Haddin	not out	5	6	4	0	0
Extras	(lb 2, w 7)	9				
Total	(5 wickets; 20 overs)	166				

DID NOT BAT: B Lee, BW Hilfenhaus, NW Bracken, SR Clark

FALL OF WICKETS: 1–12 (Gilchrist, 0.5 ov), 2–60 (Hayden, 6.6 ov), 3–110 (Symonds, 13.1 ov), 4–116 (Hodge, 14.6 ov), 5–158 (Ponting, 18.6 ov)

BOWLING: RP Singh 4–0–39–1; S Sreesanth 4–0–47–0; IK Pathan 4–0–34–2; Harbhajan Singh 4–0–17–1; M Kartik 4–0–27–0

India innings		R	M	B	4	6
G Gambhir	c Ponting b Hilfenhaus	63	74	52	6	1
V Sehwag	c Gilchrist b Lee	5	12	4	1	0
RV Uthappa	c Gilchrist b Clarke	35	38	26	6	0
Yuvraj Singh	not out	31	34	25	1	3
MS Dhoni	not out	9	11	5	0	1
Extras	(lb 12, w 9, nb 3)	24				
Total	(3 wickets; 18.1 overs)	167				

DID NOT BAT: RG Sharma, IK Pathan, M Kartik, Harbhajan Singh, RP Singh, S Sreesanth

FALL OF WICKETS: 1–20 (Sehwag, 2.2 ov), 2–102 (Uthappa, 10.3 ov), 3–143 (Gambhir, 15.4 ov)

BOWLING:

B Lee 3.1–0–35–1; NW Bracken 2–0–19–0; BW Hilfenhaus 4–0–28–1; SR Clark 4–0–33–0; A Symonds 3–0–26–0; MJ Clarke 2–0–14–1

AUSTRALIA IN INDIA ONE-DAY SERIES — AVERAGES

AUSTRALIAN BATTING AND FIELDING

Batsman	ODIs	Inns	NO	Runs	HS	Ave	100	50	Ct	St
A Symonds	7	6	1	365	107*	73.00	1	3	1	0
BJ Haddin	4	4	1	200	87*	66.67	0	2	0	0
ML Hayden	5	5	0	290	92	58.00	0	3	2	0
RT Ponting	5	5	1	199	57	49.75	0	1	3	0
MJ Clarke	7	6	0	222	130	37.00	1	1	2	0
AC Gilchrist	7	7	1	208	79*	34.67	0	2	12	2
JR Hopes	7	6	1	136	39	27.20	0	0	1	0
MG Johnson	7	2	1	25	24*	25.00	0	0	1	0
B Lee	7	6	4	24	17	12.00	0	0	1	0
BJ Hodge	7	6	0	59	20	9.83	0	0	4	0
NW Bracken	4	1	0	3	3	3.00	0	0	1	0
GB Hogg	7	2	0	0	0	0.00	0	0	1	0
SR Clark	3	–	–	–	–	–	–	–	0	0

AUSTRALIAN BOWLING

Bowler	Overs	Mdns	Runs	Wkts	Best	Ave	4w
MG Johnson	57.0	2	260	14	5–26	18.57	1
SR Clark	14.4	1	58	3	2–14	19.33	0
GB Hogg	54.3	1	249	11	4–49	22.64	1
MJ Clarke	14.0	1	74	3	2–35	24.67	0
JR Hopes	38.0	0	175	6	2–43	29.17	0
B Lee	49.4	4	240	6	3–37	40.00	0
NW Bracken	36.4	3	191	4	2–30	47.75	0
A Symonds	17.0	0	78	0	–	–	0
BJ Hodge	2.0	0	18	0	–	–	0

AUSTRALIAN CENTURIES AND FIVE WICKETS IN AN INNINGS

Michael Clarke's 130 in game one was his third century in one-day international cricket, in his 113th ODI.

Mitchell Johnson's 5–26 in game five was his first five-for in one-day international cricket, in his 23rd ODI.

Andrew Symonds' 107 not out in game six was his sixth century in one-day international cricket, in his 176th ODI.

INDIAN BATTING AND FIELDING

Batsman	ODIs	Inns	NO	Runs	HS	Ave	100	50	Ct	St
SR Tendulkar	7	7	0	278	79	39.71	0	2	4	0
MS Dhoni	7	6	1	176	58	35.20	0	2	4	4
RV Uthappa	6	6	1	167	47	33.40	0	0	3	0
Yuvraj Singh	7	6	0	192	121	32.00	1	0	1	0
SC Ganguly	5	4	0	127	86	31.75	0	1	0	0
Z Khan	7	5	2	68	31*	22.67	0	0	2	0
M Kartik	4	2	1	21	21*	21.00	0	0	0	0
Harbhajan Singh	6	5	2	53	19*	17.67	0	0	3	0
RR Powar	2	1	0	17	17	17.00	0	0	0	0
IK Pathan	7	6	1	59	29	11.80	0	0	1	0
R Dravid	6	5	0	51	31	10.20	0	0	5	0
G Gambhir	3	3	1	17	7	8.50	0	0	0	0
S Sreesanth	4	2	1	8	7*	8.00	0	0	2	0
RG Sharma	1	1	0	1	1	1.00	0	0	0	0
KD Karthik	1	1	0	0	0	0.00	0	0	1	0
RP Singh	4	1	1	12	12*	–	0	0	1	0

INDIAN BOWLING

Bowler	Overs	Mdns	Runs	Wkts	Best	Ave	4w
M Kartik	36.5	5	164	8	6–27	20.50	1
S Sreesanth	36.0	0	244	9	3–55	27.11	0
IK Pathan	54.0	0	282	7	2–47	40.29	0
RP Singh	30.3	2	207	5	2–59	41.40	0
Z Khan	61.0	3	355	8	2–61	44.38	0
Yuvraj Singh	17.0	0	114	2	1–28	57.00	0
Harbhajan Singh	54.0	1	261	3	2–43	87.00	0
SR Tendulkar	14.0	0	75	0	–	–	0
RR Powar	11.0	1	80	0	–	–	0
SC Ganguly	3.0	0	31	0	–	–	0

AUSTRALIA V SRI LANKA TEST SERIES
NOVEMBER 2007

FIRST TEST (WARNE–MURALITHARAN TROPHY)

AUSTRALIA V SRI LANKA
The Gabba, Brisbane
8–12 November 2007
Result: Australia won by an innings and 40 runs • Toss: Sri Lanka
Umpires: AL Hill (New Zealand) and RE Koertzen (South Africa)
TV umpire: PD Parker (Australia) • Match referee: MJ Procter (South Africa)
Player of the match: B Lee (Australia)

Australia first innings		R	M	B	4	6
PA Jaques	st P Jayawardene b Murali	100	283	203	14	0
ML Hayden	c Muralitharan b Vaas	43	97	63	5	0
RT Ponting	st P Jayawardene b Murali	56	128	85	7	0
MEK Hussey	c Atapattu b Fernando	133	354	249	13	2
MJ Clarke	not out	145	367	249	14	1
A Symonds	not out	53	67	61	7	0
Extras	(b 4, lb 12, w 1, nb 4)	21				
Total	(4 wickets dec; 151 overs)	551				

DID NOT BAT: AC Gilchrist, B Lee, MG Johnson, SR Clark, SCG MacGill

FALL OF WICKETS: 1–69 (Hayden, 22.2 ov), 2–183 (Ponting, 51.5 ov), 3–216 (Jaques, 65.5 ov), 4–461 (Hussey, 135.1 ov)

BOWLING: WPUJC Vaas 28–6–102–1; MF Maharoof 34–6–107–0; CRD Fernando 34–3–130–1; M Muralitharan 50–4–170–2; ST Jayasuriya 4–0–18–0; TT Samaraweera 1–0–8–0

Sri Lanka first innings		R	M	B	4	6
MS Atapattu	c Jaques b Johnson	51	273	183	5	0
ST Jayasuriya	c Gilchrist b Lee	7	12	7	1	0
MG Vandort	c Gilchrist b Lee	0	18	12	0	0
DPMD Jayawardene	c Gilchrist b Clark	14	49	35	2	0
TT Samaraweera	c Gilchrist b Johnson	13	55	28	2	0
LPC Silva	c Clarke b Clark	40	60	45	6	0
HAPW Jayawardene	lbw Lee	37	165	104	5	0
MF Maharoof	b Symonds	21	53	54	3	0
WPUJC Vaas	b MacGill	8	15	15	2	0
CRD Fernando	c Johnson b Lee	7	15	10	0	0
M Muralitharan	not out	6	10	4	1	0
Extras	(lb 1, nb 6)	7				
Total	(all out; 81.5 overs)	211				

FALL OF WICKETS: 1–7 (Jayasuriya, 2.5 ov), 2–11 (Vandort, 6.5 ov), 3–45 (DPMD Jayawardene, 18.5 ov), 4–65 (Samaraweera, 29.2 ov), 5–119 (Silva, 41.5 ov), 6–153 (Atapattu, 61.3 ov), 7–181 (Maharoof, 75.1 ov), 8–198 (Vaas, 78.6 ov), 9–198 (HAPW Jayawardene, 79.3 ov), 10–211 (Fernando, 81.5 ov)

BOWLING: B Lee 17.5–9–26–4; MG Johnson 18–2–49–2; SCG MacGill 25–5–79–1; SR Clark 16–4–46–2; A Symonds 5–3–10–1

Sri Lanka second innings (following on)

		R	M	B	4	6
MS Atapattu	c Gilchrist b Symonds	16	63	42	1	1
ST Jayasuriya	c Ponting b Lee	39	87	49	6	1
MG Vandort	b MacGill	82	255	170	10	0
DPMD Jayawardene	c Gilchrist b Johnson	49	144	119	5	0
TT Samaraweera	c Hussey b Johnson	20	65	65	2	0
LPC Silva	c Hussey b Lee	43	96	63	5	0
HAPW Jayawardene	lbw Clark	1	36	21	0	0
MF Maharoof	b Lee	18	34	29	4	0
WPUJC Vaas	not out	11	46	26	2	0
CRD Fernando	b Lee	4	12	6	1	0
M Muralitharan	b Clark	4	9	8	0	0
Extras	(b 4, lb 3, nb 6)	13				
Total	(all out; 99.2 overs)	300				

FALL OF WICKETS: 1–53 (Atapattu, 13.3 ov), 2–65 (Jayasuriya, 18.2 ov), 3–167 (DPMD Jayawardene, 52.6 ov), 4–213 (Vandort, 73.4 ov), 5–215 (Samaraweera, 74.3 ov), 6–226 (HAPW Jayawardene, 83.1 ov), 7–259 (Maharoof, 90.5 ov), 8–281 (Silva, 94.1 ov), 9–290 (Fernando, 96.5 ov), 10–300 (Muralitharan, 99.2 ov)

BOWLING: B Lee 27–7–86–4; MG Johnson 19–5–47–2; SR Clark 22.2–3–75–2; A Symonds 6–1–21–1; SCG MacGill 25–3–64–1

Stumps scores

Day one: Australia first innings 3–242 (MEK Hussey 28, MJ Clarke 5, 76 overs)
Day two: Sri Lanka first innings 2–31 (MS Atapattu 19, DPMD Jayawardene 5, 16 overs)
Day three: Sri Lanka second innings 2–80 (MG Vandort 15, DPMD Jayawardene 8, 22 overs)
Day four: Sri Lanka second innings 5–218 (LPC Silva 5, HAPW Jayawardene 0, 78 overs)

SECOND TEST (WARNE–MURALITHARAN TROPHY)

AUSTRALIA V SRI LANKA
Bellerive Oval, Hobart
16–20 November 2007

Result: Australia won by 96 runs • Toss: Australia
Umpires: Aleem Dar (Pakistan) and RE Koertzen (South Africa)
TV umpire: PD Parker (Australia) • Match referee: MJ Procter (South Africa)
Player of the match: B Lee (Australia) • Player of the series: B Lee (Australia)

Australia first innings		R	M	B	4	6
PA Jaques	c Fernando b Jayasuriya	150	329	237	18	0
ML Hayden	c P Jayawardene b Fernando	17	86	56	0	0
RT Ponting	c M Jayawardene b Murali	31	94	66	2	0
MEK Hussey	lbw Fernando	132	282	220	18	1
MJ Clarke	c P Jayawardene b Malinga	71	174	123	8	0
A Symonds	not out	50	133	71	4	1
AC Gilchrist	not out	67	90	77	7	3
Extras	(b 5, lb 1, w 1, nb 17)	24				
Total	(5 wickets dec; 139 overs)	542				

DID NOT BAT: B Lee, MG Johnson, SR Clark, SCG MacGill

FALL OF WICKETS: 1–48 (Hayden, 19.1 ov), 2–133 (Ponting, 40.5 ov), 3–285 (Jaques, 78.5 ov), 4–410 (Hussey, 110.2 ov), 5–447 (Clarke, 118.2 ov)

BOWLING: SL Malinga 35–6–156–1; MF Maharoof 23–4–82–0; CRD Fernando 26–4–134–2; M Muralitharan 46–4–140–1; ST Jayasuriya 9–1–24–1

Sri Lanka first innings		R	M	B	4	6R
MS Atapattu	c Clarke b Lee	25	102	74	3	0
MG Vandort	b Lee	14	74	45	1	0
KC Sangakkara	c Hussey b Johnson	57	120	76	9	0
DPMD Jayawardene	c Clarke b Lee	104	271	194	13	0
ST Jayasuriya	b MacGill	3	18	15	0	0
LPC Silva	c Gilchrist b MacGill	4	31	17	0	0
HAPW Jayawardene	c Gilchrist b Clark	0	14	5	0	0
MF Maharoof	run out	19	43	35	1	0
CRD Fernando	c Gilchrist b Lee	2	14	8	0	0
SL Malinga	b Clark	1	48	24	0	0
M Muralitharan	not out	1	3	4	0	0
Extras	(lb 7, nb 9)	16				
Total	(all out; 81.2 overs)	246				

FALL OF WICKETS: 1–41 (Vandort, 17.1 ov), 2–54 (Atapattu, 21.4 ov), 3–127 (Sangakkara, 41.3 ov), 4–134 (Jayasuriya, 46.2 ov), 5–152 (Silva, 52.5 ov), 6–163 (HAPW Jayawardene, 55.4 ov), 7–196 (Maharoof, 66.3 ov), 8–207 (Fernando, 69.5 ov), 9–243 (Malinga, 80.1 ov), 10–246 (DPMD Jayawardene, 81.2 ov)

BOWLING: B Lee 23.2–4–82–4; MG Johnson 17–3–44–1; SR Clark 16–6–32–2; SCG MacGill 25–5–81–2

Australia second innings		R	M	B	4	6
PA Jaques	c Vandort b Malinga	68	140	95	6	0
ML Hayden	lbw Muralitharan	33	70	48	4	0
RT Ponting	not out	53	137	102	2	1
MEK Hussey	not out	34	67	48	1	1
Extras	(b 2, lb 1, nb 19)	22				
Total	(2 wickets dec; 46 overs)	210				

DID NOT BAT: MJ Clarke, A Symonds, AC Gilchrist, B Lee, MG Johnson, SR Clark, SCG MacGill

FALL OF WICKETS: 1–83 (Hayden, 14.6 ov), 2–154 (Jaques, 29.3 ov)

BOWLING: SL Malinga 12–0–61–1; CRD Fernando 12–1–50–0; M Muralitharan 20–1–90–1; ST Jayasuriya 2–0–6–0

Sri Lanka second innings		R	M	B	4	6
MS Atapattu	c Jaques b Lee	80	215	164	9	0
MG Vandort	c sub (RJG Lockyear) b Johnson	4	19	9	0	0
KC Sangakkara	c Ponting b Clark	192	431	282	27	1
DPMD Jayawardene	b Lee	0	3	1	0	0
ST Jayasuriya	c Gilchrist b Lee	45	111	77	6	0
LPC Silva	c Ponting b Johnson	0	17	9	0	0
HAPW Jayawardene	lbw Johnson	0	1	1	0	0
MF Maharoof	c Lee b MacGill	4	31	26	0	0
CRD Fernando	run out	2	5	1	0	0
SL Malinga	not out	42	90	58	5	3
M Muralitharan	b Lee	15	25	12	1	1
Extras	(b 1, lb 6, w 6, nb 13)	26				
Total	(all out; 104.3 overs)	410				

FALL OF WICKETS: 1–15 (Vandort, 3.3 ov), 2–158 (Atapattu, 50.5 ov), 3–158 (DPMD Jayawardene, 50.6 ov), 4–265 (Jayasuriya, 74.3 ov), 5–272 (Silva, 77.3 ov), 6–272 (HAPW Jayawardene, 77.4 ov), 7–284 (Maharoof, 83.5 ov), 8–290 (Fernando, 84.1 ov), 9–364 (Sangakkara, 99.4 ov), 10–410 (Muralitharan, 104.3 ov)

BOWLING: B Lee 26.3–3–87–4; MG Johnson 28–4–101–3; SR Clark 24–5–103–1; SCG MacGill 20–1–102–1; MJ Clarke 6–1–10–0

Stumps scores
Day one: Australia first innings 3–329 (MEK Hussey 101, MJ Clarke 8, 90 overs)
Day two: Sri Lanka first innings 0–30 (MS Atapattu 18, MG Vandort 12, 12 overs)
Day three: Australia second innings 1–111 (PA Jaques 53, RT Ponting 7, 20 overs)
Day four: Sri Lanka second innings 3–247 (KC Sangakkara 109, ST Jayasuriya 33, 70 overs)

AUSTRALIA V SRI LANKA TEST SERIES — AVERAGES

AUSTRALIAN BATTING AND FIELDING

Batsman	Tests	Inns	NO	Runs	HS	Ave	100	50	Ct	St
MJ Clarke	2	2	1	216	145*	216.00	1	1	3	0
MEK Hussey	2	3	1	299	133	149.50	2	0	3	0
PA Jaques	2	3	0	318	150	106.00	2	1	2	0
RT Ponting	2	3	1	140	56	70.00	0	2	3	0
ML Hayden	2	3	0	93	43	31.00	0	0	0	0
A Symonds	2	2	2	103	53*	–	0	2	0	0
AC Gilchrist	2	1	1	67	67*	–	0	1	10	0
SR Clark	2	–	–	–	–	–	–	–	0	0
MG Johnson	2	–	–	–	–	–	–	–	1	0
B Lee	2	–	–	–	–	–	–	–	1	0
SCG MacGill	2	–	–	–	–	–	–	–	0	0

AUSTRALIAN BOWLING

Bowler	Overs	Mdns	Runs	Wkts	Best	Ave	5w	10w
A Symonds	11.0	4	31	2	1–10	15.50	0	0
B Lee	94.4	23	281	16	4–26	17.56	0	0
MG Johnson	82.0	14	241	8	3–101	30.13	0	0
SR Clark	78.2	18	256	7	2–32	36.57	0	0
SCG MacGill	95.0	14	326	5	2–81	65.20	0	0
MJ Clarke	6.0	1	10	0	–	–	0	0

DEBUT: Mitchell Johnson made his Test debut in the first Test.

AUSTRALIAN CENTURIES

Phil Jaques' 100 in the first Test was his first century in Test cricket, in his third Test.

Michael Hussey's 133 in the first Test was his sixth century in Test cricket, in his 17th Test.

Michael Clarke's 145 not out in the first Test was his sixth century in Test cricket, in his 28th Test.

Phil Jaques' 150 in the second Test was his second century in Test cricket, in his fourth Test.

Michael Hussey's 132 in the second Test was his seventh century in Test cricket, in his 18th Test.

SRI LANKAN BATTING AND FIELDING

Batsman	Tests	Inns	NO	Runs	HS	Ave	100	50	Ct	St
KC Sangakkara	1	2	0	249	192	124.50	1	1	0	0
MS Atapattu	2	4	0	172	80	43.00	0	2	1	0
SL Malinga	1	2	1	43	42*	43.00	0	0	0	0
DPMD Jayawardene	2	4	0	167	104	41.75	1	0	1	0
MG Vandort	2	4	0	100	82	25.00	0	1	1	0
ST Jayasuriya	2	4	0	94	45	23.50	0	0	0	0
LPC Silva	2	4	0	87	43	21.75	0	0	0	0
WPUJC Vaas	1	2	1	19	11*	19.00	0	0	0	0
TT Samaraweera	1	2	0	33	20	16.50	0	0	0	0
MF Maharoof	2	4	0	62	21	15.50	0	0	0	0
M Muralitharan	2	4	2	26	15	13.00	0	0	1	0
HAPW Jayawardene	2	4	0	38	37	9.50	0	0	2	2
CRD Fernando	2	4	0	15	7	3.75	0	0	1	0

SRI LANKAN BOWLING

Bowler	Overs	Mdns	Runs	Wkts	Best	Ave	5w	10w
ST Jayasuriya	15.0	1	48	1	1–24	48.00	0	0
M Muralitharan	116.0	9	400	4	2–170	100.00	0	0
WPUJC Vaas	28.0	6	102	1	1–102	102.00	0	0
CRD Fernando	72.0	8	314	3	2–134	104.67	0	0
SL Malinga	47.0	6	217	2	1–61	108.50	0	0
TT Samaraweera	1.0	0	8	0	–	–	0	0
MF Maharoof	57.0	10	189	0	–	–	0	0

NEW ZEALAND IN AUSTRALIA
DECEMBER 2007
TWENTY20 INTERNATIONAL

AUSTRALIA V NEW ZEALAND
WACA Ground, Perth
11 December 2007 (20-over match)
Result: Australia won by 54 runs • Toss: Australia
Umpires: SJ Davis (Australia) and PD Parker (Australia)
TV umpire: BNJ Oxenford (Australia) • Match referee: RS Mahanama (Sri Lanka)
Player of the match: A Symonds (Australia)

Australia innings		R	M	B	4	6
AC Gilchrist	c Patel b Gillespie	1	2	5	0	0
MJ Clarke	c Taylor b Vettori	33	43	26	3	1
MEK Hussey	st McCullum b Patel	22	22	16	4	0
A Symonds	not out	85	64	46	7	3
AC Voges	c Taylor b Patel	26	25	20	3	0
LA Pomersbach	c Taylor b Gillespie	15	16	7	1	1
AA Noffke	run out	0	1	0	0	0
B Lee	not out	0	3	1	0	0
Extras	(lb 2, w 1, nb 1)	4				
Total	(6 wickets; 20 overs)	186				

DID NOT BAT: NW Bracken, MG Johnson, SW Tait

FALL OF WICKETS: 1–5 (Gilchrist, 1.2 ov), 2–51 (Hussey, 6.4 ov), 3–71 (Clarke, 9.4 ov), 4–151 (Voges, 16.4 ov), 5–183 (Pomersbach, 19.4 ov), 6–184 (Noffke, 19.5 ov)

BOWLING: KD Mills 4-0-35-0; MR Gillespie 4-1-39-2; JDP Oram 3-0-32-0; JS Patel 4-0-40-2; DL Vettori 4-0-24-1; SB Styris 1-0-14-0

New Zealand innings		R	M	B	4	6
L Vincent	c Gilchrist b Lee	0	2	1	0	0
BB McCullum	c Gilchrist b Lee	13	23	15	0	1
JM How	c Gilchrist b Tait	4	34	18	0	0
SB Styris	c Bracken b Johnson	18	34	15	4	0
LRPL Taylor	b Tait	0	3	2	0	0
MS Sinclair	c Gilchrist b Johnson	0	6	4	0	0
JDP Oram	not out	66	56	31	5	6
DL Vettori	b Noffke	3	9	4	0	0
KD Mills	c Johnson b Noffke	4	8	8	1	0
MR Gillespie	run out	4	14	6	0	0
JS Patel	b Noffke	4	9	8	1	0
Extras	(b 4, lb 5, w 6, nb 1)	16				
Total	(all out; 18.3 overs)	132				

FALL OF WICKETS: 1–0 (Vincent, 0.1 ov), 2–21 (McCullum, 4.3 ov), 3–29 (How, 6.1 ov), 4–30 (Taylor, 6.3 ov), 5–31 (Sinclair, 7.5 ov), 6–49 (Styris, 9.6 ov), 7–59 (Vettori, 11.4 ov), 8–69 (Mills, 13.2 ov), 9–104 (Gillespie, 16.1 ov), 10–132 (Patel, 18.3 ov)

BOWLING: B Lee 4-0-17-2; NW Bracken 2-0-8-0; MG Johnson 3-0-19-2; SW Tait 4-0-22-2; AA Noffke 3.3-1-18-3; A Symonds 2-0-39-0

Twenty20 international debuts: Ashley Noffke, Luke Pomersbach, Shaun Tait, Adam Voges

FIRST ONE-DAY INTERNATIONAL (CHAPPELL–HADLEE TROPHY)

AUSTRALIA V NEW ZEALAND
Adelaide Oval
14 December 2007 (50-over match)

Result: Australia won by seven wickets • Toss: New Zealand
Umpires: MR Benson (England) and SJ Davis (Australia)
TV umpire: BNJ Oxenford (Australia) • Match referee: RS Mahanama (Sri Lanka)
Player of the match: RT Ponting (Australia)

New Zealand innings		R	M	B	4	6
L Vincent	c Hopes b Lee	5	16	11	1	0
BB McCullum	c Bracken b Hogg	96	165	103	12	1
JM How	c Hayden b Tait	20	85	59	1	0
SB Styris	c Gilchrist b Tait	5	8	10	0	0
LRPL Taylor	c Tait b Lee	50	69	52	1	3
JDP Oram	not out	32	67	38	3	0
MS Sinclair	c Hogg b Hopes	2	8	10	0	0
DL Vettori	b Tait	18	26	20	0	0
KD Mills	not out	7	5	2	0	1
Extras	(b 1, lb 5, w 8, nb 5)	19				
Total	(7 wickets; 50 overs)	254				

DID NOT BAT: MR Gillespie, CS Martin

FALL OF WICKETS: 1–16 (Vincent, 2.6 ov), 2–115 (How, 22.4 ov), 3–123 (Styris, 24.5 ov), 4–175 (McCullum, 35.3 ov), 5–197 (Taylor, 40.5 ov), 6–201 (Sinclair, 43.1 ov), 7–241 (Vettori, 48.6 ov)

BOWLING: B Lee 10–0–48–2; NW Bracken 10–3–52–0; SW Tait 10–0–59–3; JR Hopes 10–0–40–1; GB Hogg 10–1–49–1

Australia innings		R	M	B	4	6
AC Gilchrist	c Taylor b Martin	51	43	29	6	2
ML Hayden	c & b Mills	17	35	17	1	0
RT Ponting	not out	107	158	108	13	0
MJ Clarke	c Vincent b Mills	48	117	76	6	0
A Symonds	not out	28	32	28	3	0
Extras	(w 1, nb 3)	4				
Total	(3 wickets; 42.3 overs)	255				

DID NOT BAT: MEK Hussey, JR Hopes, B Lee, GB Hogg, SW Tait, NW Bracken

FALL OF WICKETS: 1–69 (Hayden, 6.5 ov), 2–75 (Gilchrist, 7.6 ov), 3–210 (Clarke, 35.3 ov)

BOWLING: KD Mills 10–1–68–2; MR Gillespie 10–0–72–0; CS Martin 9–1–52–1; JDP Oram 4.3–0–25–0; DL Vettori 8–0–32–0; SB Styris 1–0–6–0

SECOND ONE-DAY INTERNATIONAL (CHAPPELL–HADLEE TROPHY)

AUSTRALIA V NEW ZEALAND
Sydney Cricket Ground
16 December 2007 (50-over match)
Result: No Result • Toss: New Zealand
Umpires: MR Benson (England) and SJ Davis (Australia)
TV umpire: BNJ Oxenford (Australia) • Match referee: RS Mahanama (Sri Lanka)

New Zealand innings		R	M	B	4	6
L Vincent	c Ponting b Lee	0	1	2	0	0
BB McCullum	c Hogg b Lee	5	17	6	1	0
JM How	c Hayden b Bracken	4	8	8	1	0
SB Styris	not out	12	22	13	2	0
LRPL Taylor	not out	5	15	8	0	0
Extras	(w 3, nb 1)	4				
Total	(3 wickets; 6 overs)	30				

DID NOT BAT: JDP Oram, GJ Hopkins, DL Vettori, KD Mills, JS Patel, CS Martin

FALL OF WICKETS: 1–0 (Vincent, 0.2 ov), 2–7 (How, 1.5 ov), 3–12 (McCullum, 2.5 ov)

BOWLING: B Lee 3–0–12–2; NW Bracken 3–0–18–1

Australia: ML Hayden, AC Gilchrist, RT Ponting, MEK Hussey, MJ Clarke, A Symonds, JR Hopes, B Lee, GB Hogg, SW Tait, NW Bracken

THIRD ONE-DAY INTERNATIONAL (CHAPPELL–HADLEE TROPHY)
AUSTRALIA V NEW ZEALAND
Bellerive Oval, Hobart
20 December 2007 (50-over match)

Result: Australia won by 114 runs • Toss: New Zealand
Umpires: MR Benson (England) and PD Parker (Australia)
TV umpire: BNJ Oxenford (Australia) • Match referee: RS Mahanama (Sri Lanka)
Player of the match: RT Ponting (Australia) • Player of the series: RT Ponting (Australia)

Australia innings		R	M	B	4	6
ML Hayden	c Mills b Oram	29	51	32	4	0
MJ Clarke	c & b Gillespie	7	15	13	1	0
RT Ponting	not out	134	198	133	10	2
MEK Hussey	c How b Oram	9	34	17	1	0
A Symonds	lbw Mills	52	71	63	4	0
BJ Haddin	run out	26	28	25	2	1
JR Hopes	run out	20	20	17	2	0
B Lee	not out	0	1	0	0	0
Extras	(lb 3, w 2)	5				
Total	(6 wickets; 50 overs)	282				

DID NOT BAT: GB Hogg, SW Tait, NW Bracken

FALL OF WICKETS: 1–16 (Clarke, 3.2 ov), 2–56 (Hayden, 11.2 ov), 3–87 (Hussey, 19.1 ov), 4–201 (Symonds, 38.4 ov), 5–246 (Haddin, 45.4 ov), 6–280 (Hopes, 49.5 ov)

BOWLING: KD Mills 10-0-59-1; MR Gillespie 8-0-68-1; JDP Oram 10-1-34-2; DL Vettori 10-0-42-0; JS Patel 8-0-58-0; SB Styris 4-0-18-0

New Zealand innings		R	M	B	4	6
JM How	c Haddin b Lee	2	20	15	0	0
BB McCullum	c Haddin b Lee	6	13	8	1	0
MS Sinclair	lbw Hopes	14	38	17	2	0
SB Styris	b Lee	75	130	79	9	2
LRPL Taylor	lbw Tait	13	15	19	1	0
JDP Oram	c Lee b Hopes	2	13	8	0	0
GJ Hopkins	c Clarke b Hogg	9	26	17	1	0
DL Vettori	c Haddin b Hogg	0	2	3	0	0
KD Mills	b Tait	7	17	14	1	0
MR Gillespie	c Symonds b Hogg	24	29	24	3	1
JS Patel	not out	1	5	2	0	0
Extras	(lb 4, w 9, nb 2)	15				
Total	(all out; 34 overs)	168				

FALL OF WICKETS: 1–7 (McCullum, 2.5 ov), 2–8 (How, 4.2 ov), 3–43 (Sinclair, 11.1 ov), 4–60 (Taylor, 14.5 ov), 5–72 (Oram, 17.3 ov), 6–88 (Hopkins, 23.3 ov), 7–88 (Vettori, 23.6 ov), 8–118 (Mills, 28.2 ov), 9–158 (Styris, 32.5 ov), 10–168 (Gillespie, 33.6 ov)

BOWLING: B Lee 9-0-47-3; NW Bracken 5-0-21-0; SW Tait 8-1-30-2; JR Hopes 6-0-17-2; GB Hogg 6-1-49-3

CHAPPELL–HADLEE TROPHY SERIES — AVERAGES

AUSTRALIAN BATTING AND FIELDING

Batsman	ODIs	Inns	NO	Runs	HS	Ave	100	50	Ct	St
A Symonds	3	2	1	80	52	80.00	0	1	1	0
AC Gilchrist	2	1	0	51	51	51.00	0	1	1	0
MJ Clarke	3	2	0	55	48	27.50	0	0	1	0
BJ Haddin	1	1	0	26	26	26.00	0	0	3	0
ML Hayden	3	2	0	46	29	23.00	0	0	2	0
JR Hopes	3	1	0	20	20	20.00	0	0	1	0
MEK Hussey	3	1	0	9	9	9.00	0	0	0	0
RT Ponting	3	2	2	241	134*	–	2	0	1	0
B Lee	3	1	1	0	0*	–	0	0	1	0
NW Bracken	3	–	–	–	–	–	–	–	1	0
GB Hogg	3	–	–	–	–	–	–	–	2	0
SW Tait	3	–	–	–	–	–	–	–	1	0

AUSTRALIAN BOWLING

Bowler	Overs	Mdns	Runs	Wkts	Best	Ave	4w
B Lee	22.0	0	107	7	3–47	15.29	0
SW Tait	18.0	1	89	5	3–59	17.80	0
JR Hopes	16.0	0	57	3	2–17	19.00	0
GB Hogg	16.0	2	98	4	3–49	24.50	0
NW Bracken	18.0	3	91	1	1–18	91.00	0

AUSTRALIAN CENTURIES

Ricky Ponting's 107 not out in game one was his 24th century in one-day international cricket, in his 286th ODI.

Ricky Ponting's 134 not out in game three was his 25th century in one-day international cricket, in his 288th ODI.

NEW ZEALAND BATTING AND FIELDING

Batsman	ODIs	Inns	NO	Runs	HS	Ave	100	50	Ct	St
SB Styris	3	3	1	92	75	46.00	0	1	0	0
BB McCullum	3	3	0	107	96	35.67	0	1	0	0
LRPL Taylor	3	3	1	68	50	34.00	0	1	1	0
JDP Oram	3	2	1	34	32*	34.00	0	0	0	0
MR Gillespie	2	1	0	24	24	24.00	0	0	1	0
KD Mills	3	2	1	14	7*	14.00	0	0	2	0
DL Vettori	3	2	0	18	18	9.00	0	0	0	0
GJ Hopkins	2	1	0	9	9	9.00	0	0	0	0
JM How	3	3	0	26	20	8.67	0	0	1	0
MS Sinclair	2	2	0	16	14	8.00	0	0	0	0
L Vincent	2	2	0	5	5	2.50	0	0	1	0
JS Patel	2	1	1	1	1*	–	0	0	0	0
CS Martin	2	–	–	–	–	–	–	–	0	0

NEW ZEALAND BOWLING

Bowler	Overs	Mdns	Runs	Wkts	Best	Ave	4w
JDP Oram	14.3	1	59	2	2–34	29.50	0
KD Mills	20.0	1	127	3	2–68	42.33	0
CS Martin	9.0	1	52	1	1–52	52.00	0
MR Gillespie	18.0	0	140	1	1–68	140.00	0
DL Vettori	18.0	0	74	0	–	–	0
JS Patel	8.0	0	58	0	–	–	0
SB Styris	5.0	0	24	0	–	–	0

AUSTRALIA V INDIA TEST SERIES
DECEMBER 2007–JANUARY 2008

FIRST TEST (BORDER–GAVASKAR TROPHY)

AUSTRALIA V INDIA
Melbourne Cricket Ground
26–29 December 2007

Result: Australia won by 337 runs • Toss: Australia
Umpires: MR Benson (England) and BF Bowden (New Zealand) • TV umpire: SJ Davis (Australia)
Match referee: MJ Procter (South Africa) • Player of the match: ML Hayden (Australia)

Australia first innings		R	M	B	4	6
PA Jaques	st Dhoni b Kumble	66	142	108	8	0
ML Hayden	c Dravid b Khan	124	268	183	9	0
RT Ponting	b Khan	4	21	13	0	0
MEK Hussey	lbw Kumble	2	4	3	0	0
MJ Clarke	c Laxman b Singh	20	82	60	0	0
A Symonds	c sub (KD Karthik) b Kumble	35	59	42	5	0
AC Gilchrist	c Tendulkar b Kumble	23	58	42	1	0
GB Hogg	c Dravid b Khan	17	54	44	0	0
B Lee	lbw Kumble	0	11	12	0	0
MG Johnson	not out	15	58	35	1	1
SR Clark	c Harbhajan b Khan	21	30	23	3	0
Extras	(lb 5, w 2, nb 9)	16				
Total	(all out; 92.4 overs)	343				

FALL OF WICKETS: 1–135 (Jaques, 33.4 ov), 2–162 (Ponting, 38.5 ov), 3–165 (Hussey, 39.3 ov), 4–225 (Clarke, 59.1 ov), 5–241 (Hayden, 62.3 ov), 6–281 (Symonds, 71.4 ov), 7–288 (Gilchrist, 75.3 ov), 8–294 (Lee, 79.2 ov), 9–312 (Hogg, 86.1 ov), 10–343 (Clark, 92.4 ov)

BOWLING: Z Khan 23.4–1–94–4; RP Singh 20–3–82–1; Harbhajan Singh 20–3–61–0; SC Ganguly 3–1–15–0; A Kumble 25–4–84–5; SR Tendulkar 1–0–2–0.

India first innings		R	M	B	4	6
W Jaffer	c Gilchrist b Lee	4	38	27	0	0
R Dravid	lbw Clark	5	103	66	0	0
VVS Laxman	c Ponting b Lee	26	98	56	1	0
SR Tendulkar	b Clark	62	113	77	7	1
SC Ganguly	b Hogg	43	134	79	1	1
Yuvraj Singh	c Gilchrist b Clark	0	10	11	0	0
MS Dhoni	lbw Clark	0	2	2	0	0
A Kumble	c Gilchrist b Lee	27	93	76	4	0
Harbhajan Singh	c Clarke b Hogg	2	29	24	0	0
Z Khan	c Gilchrist b Lee	11	24	14	2	0
RP Singh	not out	2	8	6	0	0
Extras	(b 4, lb 3, nb 7)	14				
Total	(all out; 71.5 overs)	196				

FALL OF WICKETS: 1–4 (Jaffer, 8.3 ov), 2–31 (Dravid, 21.4 ov), 3–55 (Laxman, 30.1 ov), 4–120 (Tendulkar, 45.1 ov), 5–122 (Yuvraj Singh, 47.4 ov), 6–122 (Dhoni, 47.6 ov), 7–166 (Ganguly, 60.1 ov), 8–173 (Harbhajan, 66.6 ov), 9–193 (Kumble, 69.6 ov), 10–196 (Khan, 71.5 ov)

BOWLING: B Lee 19.5–6–46–4; MG Johnson 13–5–25–0; A Symonds 3–1–8–0; SR Clark 15–4–28–4; GB Hogg 21–3–82–2.

Australia second innings		R	M	B	4	6
PA Jaques	c & b Kumble	51	162	103	5	0
ML Hayden	c Ganguly b Harbhajan	47	84	54	6	0
RT Ponting	c Dravid b Harbhajan	3	9	7	0	0
MEK Hussey	c Tendulkar b Singh	36	95	84	0	0
MJ Clarke	st Dhoni b Kumble	73	154	113	5	0
A Symonds	lbw Khan	44	75	52	4	2
AC Gilchrist	c Singh b Harbhajan	35	83	59	4	0
GB Hogg	not out	35	59	50	1	2
B Lee	not out	11	26	19	1	0
Extras	(lb 3, nb 13)	16				
Total	(7 wickets dec; 88 overs)	351				

FALL OF WICKETS: 1–83 (Hayden, 18.5 ov), 2–89 (Ponting, 20.2 ov), 3–139 (Jaques, 38.2 ov), 4–161 (Hussey, 45.1 ov), 5–243 (Symonds, 61.5 ov), 6–288 (Clarke, 73.1 ov), 7–316 (Gilchrist, 80.5 ov)

BOWLING: ; Z Khan 20–2–93–1; RP Singh 16–1–50–1; A Kumble 25–2–102–2; Harbhajan Singh 26–0–101–3; SR Tendulkar 1–0–2–0

India second innings		R	M	B	4	6
R Dravid	lbw Symonds	16	154	114	2	0
W Jaffer	c Gilchrist b Lee	15	67	40	2	0
VVS Laxman	c Clarke b Clark	42	171	112	6	0
SR Tendulkar	c Gilchrist b Lee	15	31	21	1	0
SC Ganguly	c Ponting b Hogg	40	142	78	5	0
Yuvraj Singh	lbw Hogg	5	16	10	1	0
MS Dhoni	c Gilchrist b Johnson	11	32	32	2	0
A Kumble	c Gilchrist b Johnson	8	26	21	1	0
Harbhajan Singh	run out	0	3	0	0	0
Z Khan	not out	0	16	2	0	0
RP Singh	b Johnson	2	14	20	0	0
Extras	(b 1, nb 6)	7				
Total	(all out; 74 overs)	161				

FALL OF WICKETS: 1–26 (Jaffer, 15.3 ov), 2–54 (Dravid, 34.3 ov), 3–77 (Tendulkar, 41.3 ov), 4–118 (Laxman, 53.4 ov), 5–125 (Yuvraj Singh, 56.2 ov), 6–144 (Dhoni, 63.6 ov), 7–157 (Kumble, 69.6 ov), 8–157 (Harbhajan Singh, 70.1 ov), 9–157 (Ganguly, 70.3 ov), 10–161 (Singh, 73.6 ov)

BOWLING: B Lee 14–3–43–2; MG Johnson 15–6–21–3; SR Clark 15–9–20–1; GB Hogg 17–3–51–2; A Symonds 13–5–25–1

Stumps scores
Day one: Australia first innings 9–337 (MG Johnson 10, SR Clark 21, 90 overs)
Day two: Australia second innings 0–32 (PA Jaques 10, ML Hayden 22, 8 overs)
Day three: India second innings 0–6 (R Dravid 3, W Jaffer 2, 8 overs)

SECOND TEST (BORDER–GAVASKAR TROPHY)

AUSTRALIA V INDIA
Sydney Cricket Ground
2–6 January 2008
Result: Australia won by 122 runs • Toss: Australia
Umpires: MR Benson (England) and SA Bucknor (West Indies)
TV umpire: BNJ Oxenford (Australia) • Match referee: MJ Procter (South Africa)
Player of the match: A Symonds (Australia)

Australia first innings		R	M	B	4	6
PA Jaques	c Dhoni b Singh	0	11	9	0	0
ML Hayden	c Tendulkar b Singh	13	43	26	2	0
RT Ponting	lbw Harbhajan	55	128	69	9	0
MEK Hussey	c Tendulkar b Singh	41	100	79	3	0
MJ Clarke	lbw Harbhajan	1	11	4	0	0
A Symonds	not out	162	344	226	18	2
AC Gilchrist	c Tendulkar b Singh	7	14	8	1	0
GB Hogg	c Dravid b Kumble	79	149	102	10	0
B Lee	lbw Kumble	59	132	121	10	0
MG Johnson	c Ganguly b Kumble	28	29	30	5	0
SR Clark	lbw Kumble	0	5	4	0	0
Extras	(b 2, lb 9, w 4, nb 3)	18				
Total	(all out; 112.3 overs)	463				

FALL OF WICKETS: 1–0 (Jaques, 2.3 ov), 2–27 (Hayden, 8.4 ov), 3–119 (Ponting, 29.5 ov), 4–119 (Hussey, 30.1 ov), 5–121 (Clarke, 31.4 ov), 6–134 (Gilchrist, 34.5 ov), 7–307 (Hogg, 71.1 ov), 8–421 (Lee, 102.5 ov), 9–461 (Johnson, 110.6 ov), 10–463 (Clark, 112.3 ov)

BOWLING: RP Singh 26–3–124–4; I Sharma 23–3–87–0; SC Ganguly 6–1–13–0; Harbhajan Singh 27–3–108–2; A Kumble 25.3–0–106–4; SR Tendulkar 5–0–14–0

India first innings		R	M	B	4	6
W Jaffer	b Lee	3	27	25	0	0
R Dravid	c Hayden b Johnson	53	240	160	9	0
VVS Laxman	c Hussey b Hogg	109	218	142	18	0
SR Tendulkar	not out	154	429	243	14	1
SC Ganguly	c Hussey b Hogg	67	116	78	7	1
Yuvraj Singh	lbw Lee	12	36	24	2	0
MS Dhoni	c Gilchrist b Lee	2	19	13	0	0
A Kumble	c Gilchrist b Lee	2	11	5	0	0
Harbhajan Singh	c Hussey b Johnson	63	152	92	8	0
RP Singh	c Gilchrist b Clark	13	33	22	2	0
I Sharma	c & b Lee	23	44	34	5	0
Extras	(b 4, lb 13, w 6, nb 8)	31				
Total	(all out; 138.2 overs)	532				

FALL OF WICKETS: 1–8 (Jaffer, 6.4 ov), 2–183 (Dravid, 52.6 ov), 3–185 (Laxman, 53.6 ov), 4–293 (Ganguly, 77.6 ov), 5–321 (Yuvraj Singh, 86.5 ov), 6–330 (Dhoni, 90.6 ov), 7–345 (Kumble, 92.5 ov), 8–474 (Harbhajan Singh, 122.1 ov), 9–501 (Singh, 129.3 ov), 10–532 (Sharma, 138.2 ov)

BOWLING: B Lee 32.2–5–119–5; MG Johnson 37–2–148–2; SR Clark 25–3–80–1; A Symonds 7–1–19–0; GB Hogg 30–2–121–2; MJ Clarke 7–1–28–0

Australia second innings		R	M	B	4	6
PA Jaques	c Yuvraj Singh b Kumble	42	110	82	5	0
ML Hayden	c Jaffer b Kumble	123	304	196	12	0
RT Ponting	c Laxman b Harbhajan	1	7	4	0	0
MEK Hussey	not out	145	340	259	16	0
MJ Clarke	c Dravid b Kumble	0	1	1	0	0
A Symonds	c Dhoni b Singh	61	159	100	7	0
AC Gilchrist	c Yuvraj Singh b Kumble	1	8	4	0	0
GB Hogg	c Dravid b Harbhajan	1	5	2	0	0
B Lee	not out	4	5	3	0	0
Extras	(b 3, lb 8, w 3, nb 9)	23				
Total	(7 wickets dec; 107 overs)	401				

FALL OF WICKETS: 1–85 (Jaques, 25.1 ov), 2–90 (Ponting, 26.4 ov), 3–250 (Hayden, 70.4 ov), 4–250 (Clarke, 70.5 ov), 5–378 (Symonds, 104.1 ov), 6–393 (Gilchrist, 105.4 ov), 7–395 (Hogg, 106.1 ov)

BOWLING: RP Singh 16–2–74–1; I Sharma 14–2–59–0; Harbhajan Singh 33–6–92; A Kumble 40–3–148–4; SR Tendulkar 2–0–6–0; Yuvraj Singh 2–0–11–0

India second innings		R	M	B	4	6
R Dravid	c Gilchrist b Symonds	38	152	103	6	0
W Jaffer	c Clarke b Lee	0	4	4	0	0
VVS Laxman	lbw Clark	20	52	34	3	0
SR Tendulkar	b Clark	12	33	16	3	0
SC Ganguly	c Clarke b Lee	51	90	56	9	0
Yuvraj Singh	c Gilchrist b Symonds	0	2	3	0	0
MS Dhoni	lbw Symonds	35	117	82	6	0
A Kumble	not out	45	130	111	7	0
Harbhajan Singh	c Hussey b Clarke	7	29	14	1	0
RP Singh	lbw Clarke	0	1	1	0	0
I Sharma	c Hussey b Clarke	0	2	3	0	0
Extras	(nb 2)	2				
Total	(all out; 70.5 overs)	210				

FALL OF WICKETS: 1–3 (Jaffer, 0.5 ov), 2–34 (Laxman, 11.5 ov), 3–54 (Tendulkar, 17.4 ov), 4–115 (Dravid, 33.1 ov), 5–115 (Yuvraj Singh, 33.4 ov), 6–137 (Ganguly, 40.2 ov), 7–185 (Dhoni, 61.2 ov), 8–210 (Harbhajan Singh, 70.1 ov), 9–210 (Singh, 70.2 ov), 10–210 (Sharma, 70.5 ov)

BOWLING: B Lee 13–3–34–2; MG Johnson 11–4–33–0; SR Clark 12–4–32–2; GB Hogg 14–2–55–0; A Symonds 19–5–51–3; MJ Clarke 1.5–0–5–3

Stumps scores
Day one: Australia first innings 7–376 (A Symonds 137, B Lee 31, 89 overs)
Day two: India first innings 3–216 (SR Tendulkar 9, SC Ganguly 21, 62 overs)
Day three: Australia second innings 0–13 (PA Jaques 8, ML Hayden 5, 5 overs)
Day four: Australia second innings 4–282 (MEK Hussey 87, A Symonds 14, 83 overs)

THIRD TEST (BORDER–GAVASKAR TROPHY)

AUSTRALIA V INDIA
WACA Ground, Perth
16–19 January 2008
Result: India won by 72 runs • Toss: India
Umpires: Asad Rauf (Pakistan) and BF Bowden (New Zealand)
TV umpire: BNJ Oxenford (Australia) • Match referee: MJ Procter (South Africa)
Player of the match: IK Pathan (India)

India first innings		R	M	B	4	6
W Jaffer	c Gilchrist b Lee	16	94	53	2	0
V Sehwag	c Gilchrist b Johnson	29	80	58	6	0
R Dravid	c Ponting b Symonds	93	278	183	14	0
SR Tendulkar	lbw Lee	71	175	128	9	0
SC Ganguly	c Hussey b Johnson	9	17	12	2	0
VVS Laxman	c Tait b Lee	27	89	56	3	0
MS Dhoni	lbw Clark	19	84	52	2	0
IK Pathan	lbw Johnson	28	73	44	4	0
A Kumble	c Rogers b Clark	1	10	6	0	0
RP Singh	c Hussey b Johnson	0	7	2	0	0
I Sharma	not out	0	5	5	0	0
Extras	(lb 19, w 9, nb 9)	37				
Total	(all out; 98.2 overs)	330				

FALL OF WICKETS: 1–57 (Sehwag, 16.4 ov), 2–59 (Jaffer, 19.2 ov), 3–198 (Tendulkar, 57.4 ov), 4–214 (Ganguly, 60.5 ov), 5–278 (Dravid, 77.6 ov), 6–284 (Laxman, 81.4 ov), 7–328 (Dhoni, 95.4 ov), 8–330 (Pathan, 96.6 ov), 9–330 (Kumble, 97.1 ov), 10–330 (Singh, 98.2 ov)

BOWLING: B Lee 24–5–71–3; MG Johnson 28.2–7–86–4; SR Clark 17–4–45–2; SW Tait 13–1–59–0; A Symonds 10–1–36–1; MJ Clarke 6–1–14–0

Australia first innings		R	M	B	4	6
PA Jaques	c Laxman b Pathan	8	17	13	1	0
CJL Rogers	lbw Pathan	4	14	9	1	0
RT Ponting	c Dravid b Sharma	20	50	35	2	0
MEK Hussey	c Dhoni b Singh	0	10	8	0	0
MJ Clarke	c Dhoni b Sharma	23	58	34	3	0
A Symonds	c Dravid b Kumble	66	103	70	7	1
AC Gilchrist	c Dhoni b Singh	55	116	61	9	0
B Lee	c Dhoni b Singh	11	48	43	0	0
MG Johnson	not out	6	31	14	1	0
SR Clark	c Dhoni b Singh	0	2	3	0	0
SW Tait	c & b Kumble	8	10	11	2	0
Extras	(b 4, lb 1, w 4, nb 2)	11				
Total	(all out; 50 overs)	212				

FALL OF WICKETS: 1–12 (Rogers, 3.3 ov), 2–13 (Jaques, 3.5 ov), 3–14 (Hussey, 6.2 ov), 4–43 (Ponting, 14.3 ov), 5–61 (Clarke, 18.2 ov), 6–163 (Symonds, 35.4 ov), 7–192 (Gilchrist, 42.4 ov), 8–195 (Lee, 46.3 ov), 9–195 (Clark, 46.6 ov), 10–212 (Tait, 49.6 ov)

BOWLING: RP Singh 14–2–68–4; IK Pathan 17–2–63–2; I Sharma 7–0–34–2; A Kumble 12–1–42–2

India second innings		R	M	B	4	6
W Jaffer	c Hussey b Clark	11	45	27	1	0
V Sehwag	b Clark	43	86	61	7	0
IK Pathan	c Ponting b Clark	46	133	64	6	0
R Dravid	c Gilchrist b Lee	3	5	5	0	0
SR Tendulkar	lbw Lee	13	33	25	2	0
SC Ganguly	c Clarke b Johnson	0	7	3	0	0
VVS Laxman	c Gilchrist b Lee	79	228	156	8	0
MS Dhoni	c Gilchrist b Symonds	38	100	87	2	2
A Kumble	c Clarke b Symonds	0	2	4	0	0
RP Singh	c Gilchrist b Clark	30	73	59	3	1
I Sharma	not out	4	5	1	1	0
Extras	(lb 14, w 5, nb 8)	27				
Total	(all out; 80.4 overs)	294				

FALL OF WICKETS: 1–45 (Jaffer, 9.3 ov), 2–79 (Sehwag, 17.3 ov), 3–82 (Dravid, 18.2 ov), 4–116 (Tendulkar, 24.4 ov), 5–125 (Ganguly, 25.5 ov), 6–160 (Pathan, 34.3 ov), 7–235 (Dhoni, 62.1 ov), 8–235 (Kumble, 62.5 ov), 9–286 (Singh, 79.5 ov), 10–294 (Laxman, 80.4 ov)

BOWLING: B Lee 20.4–4–54–3; MG Johnson 10–0–58–1; SR Clark 19–4–61–4; SW Tait 8–0–33–0; MJ Clarke 13–2–38–0; A Symonds 10–2–36–2

Australia second innings		R	M	B	4	6
CJL Rogers	c Dhoni b Pathan	15	22	18	3	0
PA Jaques	c Jaffer b Pathan	16	46	30	3	0
RT Ponting	c Dravid b Sharma	45	139	71	6	0
MEK Hussey	lbw Singh	46	165	113	5	0
MJ Clarke	st Dhoni b Kumble	81	160	134	10	0
A Symonds	lbw Kumble	12	18	14	1	1
AC Gilchrist	b Sehwag	15	51	22	2	0
B Lee	c Laxman b Sehwag	0	8	6	0	0
MG Johnson	not out	50	101	80	5	2
SR Clark	c Dhoni b Pathan	32	55	35	3	1
SW Tait	b Singh	4	15	8	1	0
Extras	(lb 6, w 8, nb 10)	24				
Total	(all out; 86.5 overs)	340				

FALL OF WICKETS: 1–21 (Rogers, 5.1 ov), 2–43 (Jaques, 9.4 ov), 3–117 (Ponting, 33.1 ov), 4–159 (Hussey, 44.6 ov), 5–177 (Symonds, 49.4 ov), 6–227 (Gilchrist, 60.3 ov), 7–229 (Lee, 62.2 ov), 8–253 (Clarke, 71.1 ov), 9–326 (Clark, 83.6 ov), 10–340 (Tait, 86.5 ov)

BOWLING: RP Singh 21.5–4–95–2; IK Pathan 16–2–54–3; I Sharma 17–0–63–1; A Kumble 24–2–98–2; V Sehwag 8–1–24–2

Stumps scores
Day one: India first innings 6–297 (MS Dhoni 8, IK Pathan 8, 84 overs)
Day two: India second innings 1–52 (V Sehwag 29, IK Pathan 2, 11 overs)
Day three: Australia second innings 2–65 (RT Ponting 24, MEK Hussey 5, 15 overs)

FOURTH TEST (BORDER–GAVASKAR TROPHY)

AUSTRALIA V INDIA
Adelaide Oval
24–28 January 2008

Result: Match drawn • Toss: India
Umpires: Asad Rauf (Pakistan) and BF Bowden (New Zealand)
TV umpire: SJ Davis • Match referee: MJ Procter (South Africa)
Player of the match: SR Tendulkar (India) • Player of the series: B Lee (Australia)

India first innings		R	M	B	4	6
V Sehwag	c Hayden b Lee	63	152	90	6	0
IK Pathan	c Gilchrist b Johnson	9	34	21	2	0
R Dravid	c Ponting b Johnson	18	73	55	0	0
SR Tendulkar	c Hogg b Lee	153	342	205	13	3
SC Ganguly	lbw Hogg	7	42	29	1	0
VVS Laxman	c Gilchrist b Lee	51	134	102	5	0
MS Dhoni	c Symonds b Johnson	16	75	64	1	0
A Kumble	c Gilchrist b Johnson	87	249	205	9	0
Harbhajan Singh	c Gilchrist b Symonds	63	135	103	7	0
RP Singh	c Johnson b Clarke	0	3	4	0	0
I Sharma	not out	14	80	48	1	0
Extras	(b 8, lb 21, w 3, nb 13)	45				
Total	(all out; 152.5 overs)	526				

FALL OF WICKETS: 1–34 (Pathan, 7.3 ov), 2–82 (Dravid, 23.2 ov), 3–122 (Sehwag, 32.5 ov), 4–156 (Ganguly, 41.6 ov), 5–282 (Laxman, 73.3 ov), 6–336 (Dhoni, 89.4 ov), 7–359 (Tendulkar, 96.3 ov), 8–466 (Harbhajan Singh, 131.3 ov), 9–468 (Singh, 132.3 ov), 10–526 (Kumble, 152.5 ov)

BOWLING: B Lee 36–4–101–3; MG Johnson 37.5–6–126–4; SR Clark 1–6–92–0; GB Hogg 31–2–119–1; MJ Clarke 10–0–39–1; A Symonds 7–0–20–1

Australia first innings		R	M	B	4	6
PA Jaques	b Kumble	60	219	159	3	0
ML Hayden	b Sharma	103	271	200	10	1
RT Ponting	b Sehwag	140	396	266	10	0
MEK Hussey	b Pathan	22	81	66	1	0
MJ Clarke	c Laxman b Sharma	118	315	243	8	0
A Symonds	b Sharma	30	110	63	5	0
AC Gilchrist	c Sehwag b Pathan	14	19	18	1	0
GB Hogg	not out	16	86	42	1	0
B Lee	c Dhoni b Pathan	1	5	4	0	0
MG Johnson	c Sharma b Harbhajan	13	32	28	2	0
SR Clark	b Sehwag	3	8	8	0	0
Extras	(b 10, lb 12, w 10, nb 11)	43				
Total	(all out; 181 overs)	563				

FALL OF WICKETS: 1–159 (Jaques, 52.4 ov), 2–186 (Hayden, 63.4 ov), 3–241 (Hussey, 83.4 ov), 4–451 (Ponting, 148.6 ov), 5–490 (Clarke, 160.1 ov), 6–506 (Gilchrist, 163.6 ov), 7–527 (Symonds, 170.3 ov), 8–528 (Lee, 171.2 ov), 9–557 (Johnson, 177.6 ov), 10–563 (Clark, 180.6 ov)

BOWLING: RP Singh 4–0–14–0; IK Pathan 36–2–112–3; I Sharma 40–6–115–3; Harbhajan Singh 48–5–128–1; A Kumble 30–4–109–1; V Sehwag 19–2–51–2; SR Tendulkar 1–0–6–0; SC Ganguly 3–1–6–0

India second innings		R	M	B	4	6
V Sehwag	c Gilchrist b Symonds	151	354	236	11	2
IK Pathan	lbw Johnson	0	7	6	0	0
R Dravid	retired hurt	11	98	64	2	0
SR Tendulkar	run out	13	67	36	1	0
SC Ganguly	c Hussey b Johnson	18	51	38	1	0
VVS Laxman	c Gilchrist b Lee	12	39	30	0	0
MS Dhoni	c Hayden b Lee	20	58	44	3	0
A Kumble	not out	9	63	52	0	0
Harbhajan Singh	c Ponting b Hogg	7	22	20	0	0
I Sharma	not out	2	15	20	0	0
Extras	(b 9, lb 9, w 3, nb 5)	26				
Total	(7 wickets dec; 90 overs)	269				

FALL OF WICKETS: 1–2 (Pathan, 1.5 ov), 2–128 (Tendulkar, 37.6 ov), 3–162 (Ganguly, 49.2 ov), 4–186 (Laxman, 56.6 ov), 5–237 (Dhoni, 70.6 ov), 6–253 (Sehwag, 77.4 ov), 7–264 (Harbhajan Singh, 84.2 ov)

BOWLING: B Lee 27–3–74–2; MG Johnson 16–1–33–2; A Symonds 22–4–52–1; SR Clark 12–3–37–0; GB Hogg 12–3–53–1; MJ Clarke 1–0–2–0

Stumps scores

Day one: India first innings 5–309 (SR Tendulkar 124, MS Dhoni 6, 86 overs)
Day two: Australia first innings 0–62 (PA Jaques 21, ML Hayden 36, 21 overs)
Day three: Australia first innings 3–322 (RT Ponting 79, MJ Clarke 37, 111 overs)
Day four: India second innings 1–45 (V Sehwag 31, R Dravid 11, 17 overs)

AUSTRALIA V INDIA TEST SERIES — AVERAGES

AUSTRALIAN BATTING AND FIELDING

Batsman	Tests	Inns	NO	Runs	HS	Ave	100	50	Ct	St
ML Hayden	3	5	0	410	124	82.00	3	0	3	0
A Symonds	4	7	1	410	162*	68.33	1	2	1	0
MG Johnson	4	5	3	112	50*	56.00	0	1	1	0
GB Hogg	3	5	2	148	79	49.33	0	1	1	0
MEK Hussey	4	7	1	292	145*	48.67	1	0	9	0
MJ Clarke	4	7	0	316	118	45.14	1	2	6	0
RT Ponting	4	7	0	268	140	38.29	1	1	6	0
PA Jaques	4	7	0	243	66	34.71	0	3	0	0
AC Gilchrist	4	7	0	150	55	21.43	0	1	25	0
B Lee	4	7	2	86	59	17.20	0	1	1	0
SR Clark	4	5	0	56	32	11.20	0	0	0	0
CJL Rogers	1	2	0	19	15	9.50	0	0	1	0
SW Tait	1	2	0	12	8	6.00	0	0	1	0

AUSTRALIAN BOWLING

Bowler	Overs	Mdns	Runs	Wkts	Best	Ave	5w	10w
B Lee	186.5	33	542	24	5–119	22.58	1	0
A Symonds	91.0	19	247	9	3–51	27.44	0	0
SR Clark	146.0	37	395	14	4–28	28.21	0	0
MJ Clarke	38.5	4	126	4	3–5	31.50	0	0
MG Johnson	168.1	31	530	16	4–86	33.13	0	0
GB Hogg	125.0	15	481	8	2–51	60.13	0	0
SW Tait	21.0	1	92	0	–	–	0	0

DEBUT: Chris Rogers made his Test debut in the third Test.

AUSTRALIAN CENTURIES AND FIVE WICKETS IN AN INNINGS

Matthew Hayden's 124 in the first Test was his 28th century in Test cricket, in his 92nd Test.

Andrew Symonds' 162 not out in the second Test was his second Test century, in his 17th Test.

Brett's Lee's 5–119 in the second Test was his eighth five-for in Test cricket, in his 63rd Test.

Matthew Hayden's 123 in the second Test was his 29th century in Test cricket, in his 93rd Test.

Michael Hussey's 145 not out in the second Test was his eighth century in Test cricket, in his 20th Test.

Matthew Hayden's 103 in the fourth Test was his 30th century in Test cricket, in his 92nd Test.

Ricky Ponting's 140 in the fourth Test was his 34th century in Test cricket, in his 116th Test.

Michael Clarke's 118 in the fourth Test was his sixth century in Test cricket, in his 33rd Test.

INDIAN BATTING AND FIELDING

Batsman	Tests	Inns	NO	Runs	HS	Ave	100	50	Ct	St
V Sehwag	2	4	0	286	151	71.50	1	1	1	0
SR Tendulkar	4	8	1	493	154*	70.43	2	2	5	0
VVS Laxman	4	8	0	366	109	45.75	1	2	5	0
R Dravid	4	8	1	237	93	33.86	0	2	9	0
A Kumble	4	8	2	179	87	29.83	0	1	2	0
SC Ganguly	4	8	0	235	67	29.38	0	2	2	0
Harbhajan Singh	3	6	0	142	63	23.67	0	2	1	0
I Sharma	3	6	4	43	23	21.50	0	0	1	0
IK Pathan	2	4	0	83	46	20.75	0	0	0	0
MS Dhoni	4	8	0	141	38	17.63	0	0	10	3
Z Khan	1	2	1	11	11	11.00	0	0	0	0
W Jaffer	3	6	0	49	16	8.17	0	0	2	0
RP Singh	4	7	1	47	30	7.83	0	0	1	0
Yuvraj Singh	2	4	0	17	12	4.25	0	0	2	0

INDIAN BOWLING

Bowler	Overs	Mdns	Runs	Wkts	Best	Ave	5w	10w
V Sehwag	27.0	3	75	4	2–24	18.75	0	0
IK Pathan	69.0	6	229	8	3–54	28.63	0	0
A Kumble	181.3	16	689	20	5–84	34.45	1	0
Z Khan	43.4	3	187	5	4–94	37.40	0	0
RP Singh	117.5	15	507	13	4–68	39.00	0	0
I Sharma	101.0	11	358	6	3–115	59.67	0	0
Harbhajan Singh	154.0	17	490	8	3–101	61.25	0	0
SC Ganguly	12.0	3	34	0	–	–	0	0
SR Tendulkar	10.0	0	30	0	–	–	0	0
Yuvraj Singh	2.0	0	11	0	–	–	0	0

TWENTY20 INTERNATIONAL

AUSTRALIA V INDIA
Melbourne Cricket Ground
1 February 2008 (20-over match)
Result: Australia won by nine wickets • Toss: India
Umpires: BNJ Oxenford (Australia) and SJA Taufel (Australia)
TV umpire: RL Parry (Australia) • Match referee: JJ Crowe (New Zealand)
Player of the match: MJ Clarke (Australia)

India innings		R	M	B	4	6
G Gambhir	c Hopes b Bracken	9	9	6	1	0
V Sehwag	run out	0	5	3	0	0
KD Karthik	b Lee	8	9	8	1	0
RV Uthappa	c DJ Hussey b Bracken	1	7	3	0	0
RG Sharma	b Hopes	8	15	8	1	0
MS Dhoni	c Lee b DJ Hussey	9	30	27	0	0
IK Pathan	c Gilchrist b Bracken	26	41	30	0	0
P Kumar	c Voges b Noffke	6	8	10	0	0
Harbhajan Singh	c Clarke b Voges	1	5	3	0	0
S Sreesanth	c Hodge b Voges	0	1	1	0	0
I Sharma	not out	3	8	6	0	0
Extras	(w 3)	3				
Total	(all out; 17.3 overs)	74				

FALL OF WICKETS: 1–5 (Sehwag, 0.5 ov), 2–12 (Gambhir, 1.4 ov), 3–20 (Karthik, 2.6 ov), 4–20 (Uthappa, 3.2 ov), 5–32 (RG Sharma, 6.4 ov), 6–49 (Dhoni, 11.4 ov), 7–60 (Kumar, 14.1 ov), 8–63 (Harbhajan Singh, 15.2 ov), 9–63 (Sreesanth, 15.3 ov), 10–74 (Pathan, 17.3 ov)

BOWLING: B Lee 3–0–13–1; NW Bracken 2.3–1–11–3; AA Noffke 4–0–23–1; JR Hopes 3–0–10–1; DJ Hussey 3–0–12–1; AC Voges 2–0–5–2

Australia innings		R	M	B	4	6
AC Gilchrist	c Gambhir b Kumar	25	34	22	2	1
MJ Clarke	not out	37	50	36	1	1
BJ Hodge	not out	10	15	10	0	0
Extras	(b 1, lb 1, w 1)	3				
Total	(1 wicket; 11.2 overs)	75				

DID NOT BAT: MEK Hussey, A Symonds, DJ Hussey, B Lee, JR Hopes, NW Bracken, AA Noffke, AC Voges

FALL OF WICKETS: 1–57 (Gilchrist, 7.3 ov)

BOWLING: IK Pathan 3–0–18–0; S Sreesanth 3–0–25–0; P Kumar 2–0–15–1; I Sharma 1.2–0–8–0; Harbhajan Singh 2–0–7–0

Twenty20 international debut: David Hussey

COMMONWEALTH BANK SERIES

AUSTRALIA, INDIA, SRI LANKA
FEBRUARY–MARCH 2008

GAME ONE

AUSTRALIA V INDIA
The Gabba, Brisbane
3 February 2008 (50-over match)
Result: No Result • Toss: India

Umpires: SJ Davis (Australia) and RE Koertzen (South Africa)

TV umpire: BNJ Oxenford (Australia) • Match referee: JJ Crowe (New Zealand)

India innings		R	M	B	4	6
V Sehwag	b Bracken	6	15	8	1	0
SR Tendulkar	hit wicket b Lee	10	30	17	1	0
G Gambhir	lbw Johnson	39	74	51	4	0
RG Sharma	c Gilchrist b Lee	29	68	43	5	0
MK Tiwary	b Lee	2	15	16	0	0
MS Dhoni	c Ponting b Lee	37	102	61	1	0
RV Uthappa	c Clarke b Noffke	5	17	13	0	0
IK Pathan	run out	21	51	40	0	1
Harbhajan Singh	c Clarke b Lee	27	27	19	3	0
S Sreesanth	run out	4	4	3	0	0
I Sharma	not out	1	2	1	0	0
Extras	(lb 7, w 4, nb 2)	13				
Total	(all out; 45 overs)	194				

FALL OF WICKETS: 1–12 (Sehwag, 3.2 ov), 2–26 (Tendulkar, 6.3 ov), 3–91 (Gambhir, 19.2 ov), 4–93 (RG Sharma, 20.6 ov), 5–94 (Tiwary, 22.2 ov), 6–102 (Uthappa, 26.1 ov), 7–147 (Pathan, 38.6 ov), 8–189 (Dhoni, 44.1 ov), 9–190 (Harbhajan Singh, 44.3 ov), 10–194 (Sreesanth, 44.6 ov)

BOWLING: B Lee 9–2–27–5; NW Bracken 9–0–55–1; AA Noffke 9–0–46–1; MG Johnson 9–2–33–1; JR Hopes 6–0–17–0; MJ Clarke 2–0–5–0; A Symonds 1–0–4–0

Australia innings		R	M	B	4	6
AC Gilchrist	c Dhoni b Sreesanth	14	21	17	2	0
JR Hopes	b I Sharma	17	28	12	4	0
RT Ponting	c Sehwag b Sreesanth	0	12	2	0	0
MJ Clarke	not out	2	17	8	0	0
A Symonds	not out	5	11	6	1	0
Extras	(b 4, w 4, nb 5)	13				
Total	(3 wickets; 7.2 overs)	51				

DID NOT BAT: MEK Hussey, BJ Haddin, B Lee, NW Bracken, AA Noffke, MG Johnson

FALL OF WICKETS: 1–33 (Gilchrist, 3.6 ov), 2–38 (Hopes, 4.4 ov), 3–39 (Ponting, 5.2 ov)

BOWLING: IK Pathan 2–0–23–0; S Sreesanth 3.2–0–17–2; I Sharma 2–0–7–1

GAME TWO

INDIA V SRI LANKA
The Gabba, Brisbane
5 February 2008 (50-over match)

Result: No result • Toss: India
Umpires: SJ Davis (Australia) and RE Koertzen (South Africa)
TV umpire: BNJ Oxenford (Australia) • Match referee: JJ Crowe (New Zealand)

India innings		R	M	B	4	6
V Sehwag	c Sangakkara b Amerasinghe	33	87	39	2	1
SR Tendulkar	b Malinga	35	70	52	2	0
G Gambhir	not out	102	159	101	10	1
Yuvraj Singh	c Jayawardene b Muralitharan	2	14	11	0	0
RG Sharma	c Sangakkara b Muralitharan	0	1	2	0	0
MS Dhoni	not out	88	124	95	5	1
Extras	(lb 3, w 4)	7				
Total	(4 wickets; 50 overs)	267				

DID NOT BAT: RV Uthappa, IK Pathan, Harbhajan Singh, S Sreesanth, I Sharma

FALL OF WICKETS: 1–68 (Tendulkar, 14.3 ov), 2–80 (Sehwag, 17.1 ov), 3–83 (Yuvraj Singh, 20.3 ov), 4–83 (RG Sharma, 20.5 ov)

BOWLING: WPUJC Vaas 10–0–72–0; SL Malinga 10–1–56–1; MKDI Amerasinghe 10–2–30–1; M Muralitharan 10–0–51–2; CK Kapugedera 6–0–23–0; TM Dilshan 1–0–8–0; ST Jayasuriya 3–0–24–0

Sri Lanka: WU Tharanga, ST Jayasuriya, KC Sangakkara, DPMD Jayawardene, TM Dilshan, LPC Silva, CK Kapugedera, WPUJC Vaas, SL Malinga, MKDI Amerasinghe, M Muralitharan

---

DEBUT: Ashley Noffke made his ODI debut in the opening game of the Commonwealth Bank Series.

AUSTRALIAN CENTURIES AND FIVE WICKETS IN AN INNINGS DURING THE COMMONWEALTH BANK SERIES

Brett's Lee's 5–27 in game one was his seventh five-for in one-day international cricket, in his 161st ODI.

Nathan Bracken's 5–47 in game three was his second five-for in one-day international cricket, in his 76th ODI.

Adam Gilchrist's 118 in game six was his 16th century in one-day international cricket, in his 281st ODI.

Ricky Ponting's 124 in game 10 was his 26th century in one-day international cricket, in his 295th ODI.

Brett's Lee's 5–58 in game 10 was his eighth five-for in one-day international cricket, in his 165th ODI.

GAME THREE

AUSTRALIA V SRI LANKA
Sydney Cricket Ground
8 February 2008 (50-over match)

Result: Australia won by 128 runs • Toss: Australia
Umpires: AL Hill (New Zealand) and SJA Taufel (Australia)
TV umpire: PD Parker (Australia) • Match referee: JJ Crowe (New Zealand)
Player of the match: NW Bracken (Australia)

Australia innings		R	M	B	4	6
AC Gilchrist	lbw Kapugedera	61	136	81	3	1
ML Hayden	c Jayawardene b Amerasinghe	42	57	50	5	0
RT Ponting	c Jayawardene b Vaas	9	34	22	1	0
MJ Clarke	not out	77	126	86	2	1
A Symonds	c Kapugedera b Vaas	12	19	17	0	0
MEK Hussey	c Dilshan b Amerasinghe	10	23	13	1	0
JR Hopes	c Dilshan b Malinga	34	36	29	2	0
B Lee	not out	0	1	2	0	0
Extras	(lb 2, w 6)	8				
Total	(6 wickets; 50 overs)	253				

DID NOT BAT: NW Bracken, GB Hogg, MG Johnson

FALL OF WICKETS: 1–65 (Hayden, 12.5 ov), 2–88 (Ponting, 19.5 ov), 3–139 (Gilchrist, 31.4 ov), 4–160 (Symonds, 36.4 ov), 5–190 (Hussey, 41.4 ov), 6–253 (Hopes, 49.4 ov)

BOWLING: WPUJC Vaas 10–1–34–2; SL Malinga 10–0–55–1; MKDI Amerasinghe 10–0–66–2; M Muralitharan 10–0–42–0; CK Kapugedera 10–0–54–1

Sri Lanka innings		R	M	B	4	6
WU Tharanga	c Gilchrist b Bracken	10	23	18	1	0
ST Jayasuriya	b Lee	7	21	13	1	0
KC Sangakkara	lbw Bracken	42	65	41	7	0
DPMD Jayawardene	c Gilchrist b Johnson	6	29	16	0	0
LPC Silva	c Gilchrist b Hogg	7	39	32	0	0
TM Dilshan	c Lee b Bracken	14	17	10	0	1
CK Kapugedera	c Hayden b Bracken	0	2	2	0	0
WPUJC Vaas	run out	18	34	30	3	0
SL Malinga	run out	2	17	10	0	0
M Muralitharan	c Symonds b Bracken	11	17	14	0	1
MKDI Amerasinghe	not out	0	10	4	0	0
Extras	(lb 3, w 4, nb 1)	8				
Total	(all out; 31.3 overs)	125				

FALL OF WICKETS: 1–18 (Jayasuriya, 4.6 ov), 2–18 (Tharanga, 5.1 ov), 3–57 (Jayawardene, 11.3 ov), 4–74 (Sangakkara, 19.3 ov), 5–81 (Silva, 20.6 ov), 6–84 (Kapugedera, 21.3 ov), 7–93 (Dilshan, 23.5 ov), 8–105 (Malinga, 27.3 ov), 9–114 (Vaas, 29.1 ov), 10–125 (Muralitharan, 31.3 ov)

BOWLING: B Lee 7–1–34–1; NW Bracken 8.3–0–47–5; MG Johnson 5–3–9–1; JR Hopes 5–0–15–0; GB Hogg 6–1–17–1

GAME FOUR

AUSTRALIA V INDIA
Melbourne Cricket Ground
10 February 2008 (50-over match)
Result: India won by five wickets • Toss: Australia
Umpires: RE Koertzen (South Africa) and SJA Taufel (Australia)
TV umpire: RL Parry (Australia) • Match referee: JJ Crowe (New Zealand)
Player of the match: I Sharma (India)

Australia innings		R	M	B	4	6
AC Gilchrist	lbw Sreesanth	0	2	3	0	0
ML Hayden	c Dhoni b I Sharma	25	30	21	5	0
RT Ponting	c Tendulkar b I Sharma	9	39	15	0	0
MJ Clarke	c RG Sharma b Pathan	11	36	27	1	0
A Symonds	c Dhoni b I Sharma	14	47	24	1	0
MEK Hussey	not out	65	122	88	4	0
BJ Haddin	st Dhoni b Harbhajan	5	29	31	0	0
B Lee	c Dhoni b Pathan	10	44	35	0	0
MG Johnson	c Uthappa b Sreesanth	3	10	8	0	0
NW Bracken	c Tendulkar b Sreesanth	1	10	9	0	0
SR Clark	c Dhoni b I Sharma	0	2	1	0	0
Extras	(b 1, lb 3, w 9, nb 3)	16				
Total	(all out; 43.1 overs)	159				

FALL OF WICKETS: 1–1 (Gilchrist, 0.3 ov), 2–37 (Hayden, 5.2 ov), 3–47 (Ponting, 7.2 ov), 4–64 (Clarke, 12.5 ov), 5–75 (Symonds, 17.5 ov), 6–92 (Haddin, 25.2 ov), 7–145 (Lee, 38.2 ov), 8–151 (Johnson, 40.4 ov), 9–155 (Bracken, 42.5 ov), 10–159 (Clark, 43.1 ov)

BOWLING: S Sreesanth 9–0–31–3; I Sharma 9.1–1–38–4; IK Pathan 8–0–26–2; Harbhajan Singh 8–2–19–1; V Sehwag 5–0–24–0; Yuvraj Singh 2–0–11–0; SR Tendulkar 2–0–6–0

India innings		R	M	B	4	6
V Sehwag	lbw Bracken	11	18	19	2	0
SR Tendulkar	c Lee b Johnson	44	123	54	3	0
IK Pathan	lbw Johnson	18	35	30	1	0
G Gambhir	c Clarke b Lee	21	50	43	2	0
Yuvraj Singh	c Hussey b Clark	3	31	14	0	0
RG Sharma	not out	39	86	61	2	0
MS Dhoni	not out	17	72	54	0	0
Extras	(lb 2, w 5)	7				
Total	(5 wickets; 45.5 overs)	160				

DID NOT BAT: RV Uthappa, Harbhajan Singh, S Sreesanth, I Sharma

FALL OF WICKETS: 1–18 (Sehwag, 3.6 ov), 2–54 (Pathan, 11.2 ov), 3–89 (Gambhir, 21.6 ov), 4–96 (Tendulkar, 25.4 ov), 5–102 (Yuvraj Singh, 28.3 ov)

BOWLING: B Lee 9–0–42–1; NW Bracken 10–0–35–1; SR Clark 10–1–26–1; MG Johnson 10–1–24–2; MJ Clarke 4–0–12–0; A Symonds 2.5–0–19–0

GAME FIVE

INDIA V SRI LANKA
Manuka Oval, Canberra
12 February 2008 (50-over match)

Result: Sri Lanka won by eight wickets (D/L method) • Toss: Sri Lanka
Umpires: AL Hill (New Zealand) and BNJ Oxenford (Australia)
TV umpire: PD Parker (Australia) • Match referee: JJ Crowe (New Zealand)
Player of the match: TM Dilshan (Sri Lanka)

India innings (29 overs maximum)		R	M	B	4s	6s
V Sehwag	c Muralitharan b Kulasekara	14	34	18	2	0
SR Tendulkar	c Kulasekara b Maharoof	32	41	30	4	0
G Gambhir	run out	35	58	33	3	0
RG Sharma	not out	70	93	64	6	1
MS Dhoni	run out	31	33	26	3	0
Yuvraj Singh	c Muralitharan b Malinga	6	3	3	1	0
RV Uthappa	not out	0	3	0	0	0
Extras	(lb 1, w 6)	7				
Total	(5 wickets; 29 overs)	195				

DID NOT BAT: IK Pathan, Harbhajan Singh, S Sreesanth, I Sharma

FALL OF WICKETS: 1–45 (Sehwag, 7.3 ov), 2–49 (Tendulkar, 8.2 ov), 3–113 (Gambhir, 19.6 ov), 4–181 (Dhoni, 27.4 ov), 5–192 (Yuvraj Singh, 28.3 ov)

BOWLING: WPUJC Vaas 6–1–39–0; SL Malinga 6–0–45–1; MF Maharoof 6–0–33–1; KMDN Kulasekara 6–0–41–1; M Muralitharan 5–0–36–0

Sri Lanka innings		R	M	B	4s	6s
TM Dilshan	not out	62	90	59	6	1
ST Jayasuriya	c Dhoni b I Sharma	27	20	13	2	2
KC Sangakkara	c I Sharma b Harbhajan	10	19	10	1	0
DPMD Jayawardene	not out	36	49	35	1	0
Extras	(lb 6, w 10, nb 3)	19				
Total	(2 wickets; 19 overs)	154				

DID NOT BAT: MF Maharoof, LPC Silva, CK Kapugedera, WPUJC Vaas, SL Malinga, KMDN Kulasekara, M Muralitharan

FALL OF WICKETS: 1–45 (Jayasuriya, 3.5 ov), 2–69 (Sangakkara, 7.1 ov)

BOWLING: S Sreesanth 3–0–48–0; I Sharma 4–0–26–1; IK Pathan 4–0–30–0; Harbhajan Singh 4–0–15; SR Tendulkar 2–0–15–0; V Sehwag 2–0–14–0

GAME SIX

AUSTRALIA V SRI LANKA
WACA Ground, Perth
15 February 2008 (50-over match)

Result: Australia won by 63 runs • Toss: Australia
Umpires: DJ Harper and RE Koertzen (South Africa)
TV umpire: PD Parker • Match referee: JJ Crowe (New Zealand)
Player of the match: AC Gilchrist (Australia)

Australia innings		R	M	B	4	6
AC Gilchrist	c Kapugedera b Malinga	118	194	132	9	3
ML Hayden	c Maharoof b Malinga	4	17	11	0	0
RT Ponting	c Jayawardene b Vaas	25	35	25	4	0
MJ Clarke	st Sangakkara b Muralitharan	43	105	69	4	0
A Symonds	c Sangakkara b Maharoof	4	5	8	0	0
MEK Hussey	c Jayawardene b Kulasekara	25	53	28	0	1
JR Hopes	c Jayasuriya b Kulasekara	2	10	5	0	0
GB Hogg	b Malinga	5	11	10	0	0
B Lee	b Malinga	2	12	6	0	0
MG Johnson	run out	0	2	1	0	0
NW Bracken	not out	1	5	4	0	0
Extras	(b 1, lb 1, w 4, nb 1)	7				
Total	(all out; 49.4 overs)	236				

FALL OF WICKETS: 1–16 (Hayden, 3.6 ov), 2–66 (Ponting, 12.1 ov), 3–171 (Clarke, 36.2 ov), 4–177 (Symonds, 37.4 ov), 5–206 (Gilchrist, 43.2 ov), 6–217 (Hopes, 45.1 ov), 7–232 (Hogg, 47.4 ov), 8–232 (Hussey, 48.1 ov), 9–233 (Johnson, 48.4 ov), 10–236 (Lee, 49.4 ov)

BOWLING: WPUJC Vaas 10–0–35–1; SL Malinga 9.4–1–47–4; MF Maharoof 10–0–53–1; KMDN Kulasekara 10–0–52–2; M Muralitharan 10–0–47–1

Sri Lanka innings		R	M	B	4	6
TM Dilshan	b Johnson	11	23	13	2	0
ST Jayasuriya	c Hopes b Bracken	12	14	10	2	0
KC Sangakkara	b Lee	80	180	114	4	0
DPMD Jayawardene	c Ponting b Johnson	21	27	25	4	0
LPC Silva	c Symonds b Bracken	0	11	10	0	0
CK Kapugedera	c Hussey b Hopes	26	71	60	2	0
MF Maharoof	c sub (BJ Haddin) b Hogg	7	25	16	1	0
WPUJC Vaas	c Gilchrist b Hogg	0	1	1	0	0
KMDN Kulasekara	c Symonds b Bracken	0	5	7	0	0
SL Malinga	b Johnson	5	15	18	1	0
M Muralitharan	not out	0	2	0	0	0
Extras	(lb 7, w 3, nb 1)	11				
Total	(all out; 45.3 overs)	173				

FALL OF WICKETS: 1–29 (Jayasuriya, 3.1 ov), 2–35 (Dilshan, 4.2 ov), 3–71 (Jayawardene, 10.5 ov), 4–76 (Silva, 13.6 ov), 5–129 (Kapugedera, 32.5 ov), 6–159 (Maharoof, 39.1 ov), 7–159 (Vaas, 39.2 ov), 8–160 (Kulasekara, 40.5 ov), 9–173 (Malinga, 44.6 ov), 10–173 (Sangakkara, 45.3 ov)

BOWLING: B Lee 8.3–0–49–1; NW Bracken 8–2–21–3; MG Johnson 10–2–29–3; JR Hopes 9–1–26–1; GB Hogg 10–1–41–2

GAME SEVEN

AUSTRALIA V INDIA
Adelaide Oval
17 February 2008 (50-over match)
Result: Australia won by 50 runs • Toss: Australia
Umpires: AL Hill (New Zealand) and PD Parker (Australia)
TV umpire: RL Parry (Australia) • Match referee: JJ Crowe (New Zealand)
Player of the match: MJ Clarke (Australia)

Australia innings		R	M	B	4	6
AC Gilchrist	b I Sharma	15	30	17	3	0
ML Hayden	c Dhoni b Pathan	13	63	34	0	1
RT Ponting	c RG Sharma b Patel	10	24	14	1	0
MJ Clarke	c I Sharma b Pathan	79	175	108	6	0
A Symonds	c Uthappa b I Sharma	3	22	12	0	0
MEK Hussey	c Dhoni b Pathan	5	38	21	0	0
JR Hopes	st Dhoni b Harbhajan	19	36	18	2	0
GB Hogg	run out	32	62	52	2	0
MG Johnson	not out	9	22	13	0	0
NW Bracken	c Dhoni b Pathan	0	3	4	0	0
SR Clark	not out	8	12	9	0	0
Extras	(lb 2, w 6, nb 2)	10				
Total	(9 wickets; 50 overs)	203				

FALL OF WICKETS: 1–25 (Gilchrist, 5.3 ov), 2–41 (Ponting, 10.1 ov), 3–43 (Hayden, 11.3 ov), 4–50 (Symonds, 15.4 ov), 5–73 (Hussey, 23.4 ov), 6–112 (Hopes, 30.2 ov), 7–184 (Hogg, 45.1 ov), 8–187 (Clarke, 46.1 ov), 9–187 (Bracken, 46.5 ov)

BOWLING: S Sreesanth 8–0–35–0; I Sharma 9–1–32–2; MM Patel 9–1–31–1; IK Pathan 10–1–41–4; Harbhajan Singh 10–0–40–1; Yuvraj Singh 4–0–22–0

India innings		R	M	B	4	6
G Gambhir	c Ponting b Johnson	34	77	42	3	0
SR Tendulkar	lbw Bracken	5	23	15	1	0
IK Pathan	c Hayden b Hopes	14	46	30	2	0
RG Sharma	c Gilchrist b Hopes	1	12	3	0	0
Yuvraj Singh	c Clark b Hogg	26	65	44	3	1
MS Dhoni	run out	37	97	50	1	0
RV Uthappa	c Gilchrist b Johnson	18	57	36	1	0
Harbhajan Singh	c Gilchrist b Johnson	4	8	6	0	0
S Sreesanth	st Gilchrist b Hogg	1	15	4	0	0
I Sharma	not out	2	21	10	0	0
MM Patel	c Gilchrist b Bracken	0	11	9	0	0
Extras	(lb 2, w 8, nb 1)	11				
Total	(all out; 41.2 overs)	153				

FALL OF WICKETS: 1–20 (Tendulkar, 4.4 ov), 2–55 (Pathan, 13.5 ov), 3–59 (Gambhir, 14.5 ov), 4–59 (RG Sharma, 15.1 ov), 5–115 (Yuvraj Singh, 27.6 ov), 6–134 (Dhoni, 34.3 ov), 7–141 (Harbhajan Singh, 35.6 ov), 8–150 (Uthappa, 37.5 ov), 9–152 (Sreesanth, 38.4 ov), 10–153 (Patel, 41.2 ov)

BOWLING: NW Bracken 7.2–1–21–2; SR Clark 8–1–33–0; MG Johnson 10–1–42–3; JR Hopes 6–3–16–2; GB Hogg 8–1–30–2; A Symonds 2–0–9–0

GAME EIGHT

INDIA V SRI LANKA
Adelaide Oval
19 February 2008 (50-over match)
Result: India won by two wickets • Toss: Sri Lanka
Umpires: AL Hill (New Zealand) and PD Parker (Australia)
TV umpire: RL Parry (Australia) • Match referee: JJ Crowe (New Zealand)
Player of the match: KC Sangakkara (Sri Lanka)

Sri Lanka innings		R	M	B	4s	6s
TM Dilshan	c Dhoni b Patel	4	2	4	1	0
ST Jayasuriya	run out	0	14	3	0	0
KC Sangakkara	c Kumar b Pathan	128	241	155	12	0
DPMD Jayawardene	run out	71	171	99	4	1
CK Kapugedera	run out	1	5	5	0	0
LPC Silva	c Uthappa b Harbhajan	21	54	30	0	0
MF Maharoof	not out	3	5	4	0	0
WPUJC Vaas	not out	1	2	1	0	0
Extras	(lb 4, w 4, nb 1)	9				
Total	(6 wickets; 50 overs)	238				

DID NOT BAT: SL Malinga, MKDI Amerasinghe, M Muralitharan

FALL OF WICKETS: 1–4 (Dilshan, 0.4 ov), 2–6 (Jayasuriya, 2.3 ov), 3–159 (Jayawardene, 37.4 ov), 4–161 (Kapugedera, 38.4 ov), 5–234 (Sangakkara, 48.6 ov), 6–235 (Silva, 49.3 ov)

BOWLING: MM Patel 9–2–38–1; I Sharma 10–0–44–0; IK Pathan 10–0–44–1; P Kumar 10–0–49–0; Harbhajan Singh 10–0–54–1; Yuvraj Singh 1–0–5–0

India innings		R	M	B	4s	6s
G Gambhir	c Sangakkara b Amerasinghe	15	58	34	2	0
SR Tendulkar	b Malinga	0	6	2	0	0
RV Uthappa	run out	10	42	28	0	0
RG Sharma	c Silva b Muralitharan	24	74	36	1	0
Yuvraj Singh	b Vaas	76	115	70	10	1
MS Dhoni	not out	50	140	68	0	0
IK Pathan	b Amerasinghe	31	62	41	4	0
P Kumar	c Jayawardene b Amerasinghe	6	13	8	0	0
Harbhajan Singh	lbw b Malinga	3	8	6	0	0
I Sharma	not out	0	6	2	0	0
Extras	(lb 14, w 10)	24				
Total	(8 wickets; 49.1 overs)	239				

DID NOT BAT: MM Patel

FALL OF WICKETS: 1–2 (Tendulkar, 1.1 ov), 2–33 (Uthappa, 9.6 ov), 3–35 (Gambhir, 11.4 ov), 4–99 (RG Sharma, 23.2 ov), 5–158 (Yuvraj Singh, 32.6 ov), 6–216 (Pathan, 45.3 ov), 7–229 (Kumar, 47.4 ov), 8–236 (Harbhajan Singh, 48.4 ov)

BOWLING: WPUJC Vaas 10–0–27–1; SL Malinga 10–1–37–2; MKDI Amerasinghe 10–0–49–3; MF Maharoof 6.1–0–43–0; M Muralitharan 10–0–44–1; ST Jayasuriya 2–0–14–0; TM Dilshan 1–0–11–0

GAME NINE

AUSTRALIA V SRI LANKA
Melbourne Cricket Ground
22 February 2008 (50-over match)
Result: Australia won by 24 runs (D/L method) • Toss: Sri Lanka
Umpires: RE Koertzen (South Africa) and SJA Taufel (Australia)
TV umpire: RL Parry (Australia) • Match referee: JJ Crowe (New Zealand)
Player of the match: MEK Hussey (Australia)

Australia innings		R	M	B	4	6
AC Gilchrist	b Vaas	6	18	11	0	0
ML Hayden	c Silva b Maharoof	23	64	53	3	0
RT Ponting	run out	11	58	34	0	0
MJ Clarke	c & b Muralitharan	50	118	69	4	0
A Symonds	c Sangakkara b Maharoof	4	15	6	0	0
MEK Hussey	not out	64	129	98	1	0
JR Hopes	st Sangakkara b Muralitharan	11	20	16	0	0
GB Hogg	c Dilshan b Malinga	4	6	4	0	0
MG Johnson	not out	6	11	9	0	0
Extras	(b 2, w 3)	5				
Total	(7 wickets; 50 overs)	184				

DID NOT BAT: NW Bracken, SR Clark

FALL OF WICKETS: 1–12 (Gilchrist, 4.3 ov), 2–39 (Hayden, 15.1 ov), 3–44 (Ponting, 17.6 ov), 4–54 (Symonds, 21.1 ov), 5–144 (Clarke, 42.1 ov), 6–166 (Hopes, 46.3 ov), 7–173 (Hogg, 47.5 ov)

BOWLING: WPUJC Vaas 10–1–34–1; SL Malinga 10–1–44–1; MF Maharoof 10–1–20–2; M Muralitharan 10–0–37–2; MKDI Amerasinghe 10–0–47–0

Sri Lanka innings		R	M	B	4	6
MDK Perera	lbw Clark	1	15	11	0	0
ST Jayasuriya	c Ponting b Clark	0	5	1	0	0
KC Sangakkara	c Symonds b Hopes	22	103	59	0	0
DPMD Jayawardene	c Gilchrist b Bracken	27	57	45	3	0
LPC Silva	not out	16	54	47	0	0
TM Dilshan	not out	9	18	14	0	0
Extras	(lb 1, w 1)	2				
Total	(4 wickets; 29.3 overs)	77				

DID NOT BAT: MF Maharoof, WPUJC Vaas, SL Malinga, MKDI Amerasinghe, M Muralitharan

FALL OF WICKETS: 1–0 (Jayasuriya, 1.1 ov), 2–3 (Perera, 3.1 ov), 3–42 (Jayawardene, 16.2 ov), 4–64 (Sangakkara, 24.5 ov)

BOWLING: NW Bracken 6–1–13–1; SR Clark 5–1–8–2; MG Johnson 7–1–17–0; JR Hopes 7–2–23–1; GB Hogg 4.3–1–15–0

GAME 10

AUSTRALIA V INDIA
Sydney Cricket Ground
24 February 2008 (50-over match)

Result: Australia won by 18 runs • Toss: Australia
Umpires: DJ Harper (Australia) and AL Hill (New Zealand)
TV umpire: BNJ Oxenford (Australia) • Match referee: JJ Crowe (New Zealand)
Player of the match: RT Ponting (Australia)

Australia innings		R	M	B	4	6
AC Gilchrist	c Dhoni b Sreesanth	16	12	7	3	0
ML Hayden	run out	54	98	62	5	1
RT Ponting	c Pathan b Sreesanth	124	190	133	7	1
MJ Clarke	c RG Sharma b Sehwag	31	41	38	0	0
A Symonds	b I Sharma	59	54	49	6	2
MEK Hussey	not out	15	14	10	0	0
JR Hopes	run out	4	8	3	0	0
B Lee	run out	0	1	0	0	0
Extras	(lb 5, w 8, nb 1)	14				
Total	(7 wickets; 50 overs)	317				

DID NOT BAT: GB Hogg, NW Bracken, SR Clark

FALL OF WICKETS: 1–21 (Gilchrist, 2.3 ov), 2–131 (Hayden, 20.3 ov), 3–194 (Clarke, 31.5 ov), 4–296 (Symonds, 47.2 ov), 5–304 (Ponting, 48.1 ov), 6–317 (Hopes, 49.5 ov), 7–317 (Lee, 49.6 ov)

BOWLING: S Sreesanth 8–0–58–2; I Sharma 10–0–65–1; IK Pathan 9–0–73–0; Harbhajan Singh 9–0–50–0; V Sehwag 6–0–28–1; Yuvraj Singh 8–0–38–0

India innings		R	M	B	4	6
V Sehwag	c Gilchrist b Clark	17	39	19	3	0
SR Tendulkar	lbw Lee	2	3	3	0	0
G Gambhir	st Gilchrist b Hogg	113	177	119	9	1
RG Sharma	c Gilchrist b Bracken	1	3	3	0	0
Yuvraj Singh	c Gilchrist b Clark	5	6	3	1	0
MS Dhoni	c Gilchrist b Lee	36	84	66	4	0
RV Uthappa	c Hussey b Lee	51	95	46	4	1
IK Pathan	c Bracken b Hopes	22	25	21	2	0
Harbhajan Singh	c Gilchrist b Lee	20	16	11	3	0
S Sreesanth	not out	3	2	4	0	0
I Sharma	b Lee	2	4	0	0	0
Extras	(b 6, lb 5, w 12, nb 4)	27				
Total	(all out; 49.1 overs)	299				

FALL OF WICKETS: 1–3 (Tendulkar, 0.5 ov), 2–45 (Sehwag, 8.4 ov), 3–46 (RG Sharma, 9.1 ov), 4–51 (Yuvraj Singh, 10.2 ov), 5–149 (Dhoni, 30.3 ov), 6–216 (Gambhir, 39.1 ov), 7–257 (Pathan, 44.5 ov), 8–290 (Harbhajan Singh, 47.4 ov), 9–290 (Uthappa, 47.5 ov), 10–299 (I Sharma, 49.1 ov)

BOWLING: B Lee 9.1–1–58–5; NW Bracken 10–0–53–1; SR Clark 10–0–55–2; JR Hopes 6–0–27–1; GB Hogg 9–0–62–1; MJ Clarke 5–0–33–0

GAME 11

INDIA V SRI LANKA
Bellerive Oval, Hobart
26 February 2008 (50-over match)
Result: India won by seven wickets • Toss: India
Umpires: RE Koertzen (South Africa) and SJA Taufel (Australia)
TV umpire: BNJ Oxenford (Australia) • Match referee: JJ Crowe (New Zealand)
Player of the match: P Kumar (India)

Sri Lanka innings		R	M	B	4s	6s
MDK Perera	b I Sharma	8	15	13	1	0
ST Jayasuriya	c Dhoni b Pathan	34	88	44	2	1
KC Sangakkara	c Dhoni b Kumar	33	47	42	4	0
DPMD Jayawardene	c RG Sharma b Kumar	3	12	11	0	0
LPC Silva	c Dhoni b Kumar	0	7	4	0	0
TM Dilshan	lbw b I Sharma	8	20	12	1	0
CK Kapugedera	c & b Harbhajan	57	119	86	4	0
WPUJC Vaas	c Gambhir b I Sharma	0	10	7	0	0
SL Malinga	c Uthappa b I Sharma	12	56	36	0	0
M Muralitharan	b Kumar	13	31	27	1	0
MKDI Amerasinghe	not out	0	2	1	0	0
Extras	(lb 5, w 6)	11				
Total	(all out; 47.1 overs)	179				

FALL OF WICKETS: 1–15 (Perera, 3.2 ov), 2–72 (Sangakkara, 14.1 ov), 3–77 (Jayawardene, 16.5 ov), 4–81 (Silva, 18.3 ov), 5–81 (Jayasuriya, 19.3 ov), 6–93 (Dilshan, 23.3 ov), 7–93 (Vaas, 25.4 ov), 8–139 (Malinga, 38.4 ov), 9–179 (Muralitharan, 46.5 ov), 10–179 (Kapugedera, 47.1 ov)

BOWLING: MM Patel 9–0–51–0; I Sharma 10–0–41–4; IK Pathan 10–2–23–1; P Kumar 0–2–31–4; Harbhajan Singh 4.1–0–17–1; Yuvraj Singh 4–0–11–0

India innings		R	M	B	4s	6s
RV Uthappa	c Amerasinghe b Malinga	11	7	9	2	0
SR Tendulkar	c Silva b Muralitharan	63	92	54	10	0
G Gambhir	not out	63	125	89	5	0
Yuvraj Singh	c Dilshan b Perera	36	31	35	4	1
RG Sharma	not out	3	8	7	0	0
Extras	(w 4)	4				
Total	(3 wickets; 32.2 overs)	180				

DID NOT BAT: P Kumar, IK Pathan, MS Dhoni, Harbhajan Singh, I Sharma, MM Patel

FALL OF WICKETS: 1–18 (Uthappa, 1.5 ov), 2–120 (Tendulkar, 20.1 ov), 3–171 (Yuvraj Singh, 29.4 ov)

BOWLING: WPUJC Vaas 6–0–29–0; SL Malinga 6–0–36–1; MKDI Amerasinghe 7–0–40–0; M Muralitharan 8.2–0–54–1; ST Jayasuriya 1–0–4–0; MDK Perera 4–0–17–1

POINTS TABLE AFTER GAME 12

Team	Played	Won	Lost	NR	Tied	BP	Points	Run Rate
Australia	8	5	2	1	–	4	26	+0.769
India	8	3	3	2	–	1	17	+0.121
Sri Lanka	8	2	5	1	–	0	10	-0.949

GAME 12

AUSTRALIA V SRI LANKA
Melbourne Cricket Ground
29 February 2008 (50-over match)
Result: Sri Lanka won by 13 runs • Toss: Sri Lanka
Umpires: DJ Harper (Australia) and AL Hill (New Zealand) • TV umpire: BNJ Oxenford (Australia)
Match referee: JJ Crowe (New Zealand) • Player of the match: AC Gilchrist (Australia)

Sri Lanka innings		R	M	B	4	6
MDK Perera	lbw Lee	5	20	12	0	0
ST Jayasuriya	c Hussey b Bracken	23	42	32	2	1
KC Sangakkara	c Hussey b Johnson	11	35	26	2	0
DPMD Jayawardene	lbw Hogg	50	95	66	5	0
CK Kapugedera	c Gilchrist b Hopes	2	33	23	0	0
TM Dilshan	run out	62	96	70	3	0
LPC Silva	c Johnson b Bracken	35	66	48	4	0
KMDN Kulasekara	b Bracken	14	29	22	1	0
SL Malinga	c Hopes b Lee	0	4	1	0	0
M Muralitharan	b Bracken	1	4	2	0	0
MKDI Amerasinghe	not out	5	5	2	1	0
Extras	(lb 1, w 8, nb 4)	13				
Total	(all out; 50 overs)	221				

FALL OF WICKETS: 1–12 (Perera, 4.4 ov), 2–32 (Jayasuriya, 9.2 ov), 3–42 (Sangakkara, 12.3 ov), 4–61 (Kapugedera, 19.5 ov), 5–125 (Jayawardene, 31.6 ov), 6–185 (Dilshan, 44.2 ov), 7–206 (Silva, 47.4 ov), 8–208 (Malinga, 48.2 ov), 9–212 (Muralitharan, 49.2 ov), 10–221 (Kulasekara, 49.6 ov)

BOWLING: B Lee 10–1–55–2; NW Bracken 10–3–29–4; MG Johnson 10–1–54–1; JR Hopes 8–0–32–1; GB Hogg 10–1–33–1; MJ Clarke 2–0–17–0

Australia innings		R	M	B	4	6
AC Gilchrist	c Malinga b Kulasekara	83	78	50	11	2
JR Hopes	b Muralitharan	28	70	42	3	0
RT Ponting	lbw Kulasekara	1	25	11	0	0
MJ Clarke	b Amerasinghe	0	11	11	0	0
A Symonds	c Sangakkara b Amerasinghe	0	9	4	0	0
MEK Hussey	b Kapugedera	5	48	25	0	0
BJ Haddin	lbw Malinga	7	14	13	0	0
GB Hogg	lbw Muralitharan	21	49	35	0	0
B Lee	b Jayasuriya	37	80	59	2	1
MG Johnson	c Jayawardene b Amerasinghe	3	17	13	0	0
NW Bracken	not out	14	42	26	1	0
Extras	(lb 3, w 6)	9				
Total	(all out; 48.1 overs)	208				

FALL OF WICKETS: 1–107 (Hopes, 14.4 ov), 2–113 (Gilchrist, 15.4 ov), 3–115 (Clarke, 18.3 ov), 4–115 (Ponting, 19.3 ov), 5–115 (Symonds, 20.1 ov), 6–123 (Haddin, 23.2 ov), 7–142 (Hussey, 29.3 ov), 8–158 (Hogg, 34.5 ov), 9–173 (Johnson, 39.1 ov), 10–208 (Lee, 48.1 ov)

BOWLING: SL Malinga 9–1–48–1; KMDN Kulasekara 10–3–36–2; MKDI Amerasinghe 10–2–44–3; M Muralitharan 10–0–42–2; CK Kapugedera 6–0–24–1; MDK Perera 3–0–11–0; ST Jayasuriya 0.1–0–0–1

FIRST FINAL

AUSTRALIA V INDIA
Sydney Cricket Ground
2 March 2008 (50-over match)
Result: India won by six wickets • Toss: Australia
Player of the match: SR Tendulkar (India)
Umpires: DJ Harper (Australia) and RE Koertzen (South Africa)
TV umpire: BNJ Oxenford (Australia) • Match referee: JJ Crowe (New Zealand)

Australia innings		R	M	B	4	6
AC Gilchrist	c Yuvraj Singh b Kumar	7	13	7	1	0
ML Hayden	c Chawla b Harbhajan	82	115	88	10	0
RT Ponting	b Kumar	1	7	5	0	0
MJ Clarke	c Dhoni b I Sharma	4	7	8	1	0
A Symonds	c Kumar b Harbhajan	31	71	44	4	0
MEK Hussey	run out	45	87	67	2	0
JR Hopes	c Dhoni b Yuvraj Singh	15	40	37	1	0
GB Hogg	not out	23	47	31	0	0
B Lee	c RG Sharma b Pathan	17	9	10	3	0
MG Johnson	not out	6	12	3	0	0
Extras	(b 1, w 7)	8				
Total	(8 wickets; 50 overs)	239				

DID NOT BAT: NW Bracken

FALL OF WICKETS: 1–16 (Gilchrist, 2.4 ov), 2–19 (Ponting, 4.2 ov), 3–24 (Clarke, 5.5 ov), 4–124 (Symonds, 23.1 ov), 5–135 (Hayden, 27.3 ov), 6–173 (Hopes, 38.5 ov), 7–212 (Hussey, 46.6 ov), 8–231 (Lee, 48.6 ov)

BOWLING: P Kumar 10–1–49–2; I Sharma 8–0–32–1; IK Pathan 7–0–63–1; Harbhajan Singh 10–0–38–2; PP Chawla 10–0–33–0; Yuvraj Singh 4–0–18–1; RG Sharma 1–0–5–0

India innings		R	M	B	4	6
RV Uthappa	c Hussey b Hopes	17	74	33	2	0
SR Tendulkar	not out	117	235	120	10	0
G Gambhir	run out	3	9	4	0	0
Yuvraj Singh	b Hogg	10	33	21	1	0
RG Sharma	b Hopes	66	108	87	6	0
MS Dhoni	not out	15	21	12	3	0
Extras	(b 4, lb 2, w 6, nb 2)	14				
Total	(4 wickets; 45.5 overs)	242				

DID NOT BAT: P Kumar, IK Pathan, Harbhajan Singh, I Sharma, PP Chawla

FALL OF WICKETS: 1–50 (Uthappa, 10.6 ov), 2–56 (Gambhir, 12.4 ov), 3–87 (Yuvraj Singh, 18.5 ov), 4–210 (RG Sharma, 41.3 ov)

BOWLING: B Lee 9–0–33–0; NW Bracken 8–0–42–0; MG Johnson 10–0–70–0; JR Hopes 8.5–0–42–2; GB Hogg 7–0–38–1; MJ Clarke 3–0–11–0

SECOND FINAL

AUSTRALIA V INDIA
The Gabba, Brisbane
4 March 2008 (50-over match)

Result: India won by nine runs • Toss: India
Umpires: AL Hill (New Zealand) and SJA Taufel (Australia)
TV umpire: BNJ Oxenford (Australia) • Match referee: JJ Crowe (New Zealand)
Player of the match: P Kumar (India) • Player of the series: NW Bracken (Australia)

India innings		R	M	B	4	6
RV Uthappa	c Hopes b Clark	30	99	49	1	0
SR Tendulkar	c Ponting b Clarke	91	176	121	7	0
G Gambhir	c Johnson b Clarke	15	21	16	1	0
Yuvraj Singh	c Hayden b Symonds	38	27	38	2	2
MS Dhoni	c Clarke b Bracken	36	52	37	2	1
RG Sharma	c Symonds b Clarke	2	6	5	0	0
IK Pathan	b Bracken	12	24	20	1	0
Harbhajan Singh	lbw Lee	3	7	3	0	0
P Kumar	c Ponting b Bracken	7	7	7	1	0
PP Chawla	not out	6	8	2	1	0
S Sreesanth	not out	1	4	2	0	0
Extras	(lb 5, w 12)	17				
Total	(9 wickets; 50 overs)	258				

FALL OF WICKETS: 1–94 (Uthappa, 20.5 ov), 2–121 (Gambhir, 25.2 ov), 3–175 (Yuvraj Singh, 34.6 ov), 4–205 (Tendulkar, 39.2 ov), 5–209 (Sharma, 41.1 ov), 6–237 (Pathan, 47.2 ov), 7–240 (Dhoni, 47.6 ov), 8–249 (Harbhajan Singh, 48.5 ov), 9–255 (Kumar, 49.3 ov)

BOWLING: B Lee 10-0-58-1; NW Bracken 9-1-31-3; SR Clark 6-0-32-1; MG Johnson 6-0-33-0; JR Hopes 6-0-20-0; MJ Clarke 10-0-52-3; A Symonds 3-0-27-1

Australia innings		R	M	B	4	6
AC Gilchrist	c Dhoni b Kumar	2	3	3	0	0
ML Hayden	run out	55	122	68	7	0
RT Ponting	c Yuvraj Singh b Kumar	1	9	7	0	0
MJ Clarke	b Kumar	17	29	22	1	0
A Symonds	lbw Harbhajan	42	81	56	2	1
MEK Hussey	c Dhoni b Sreesanth	44	66	42	3	0
JR Hopes	c Chawla b Pathan	63	105	80	4	1
B Lee	b Kumar	7	20	12	0	0
MG Johnson	c Dhoni b Sreesanth	8	9	6	1	0
NW Bracken	c Chawla b Pathan	1	7	2	0	0
SR Clark	not out	0	2	0	0	0
Extras	(lb 2, w 7)	9				
Total	(all out; 49.4 overs)	249				

FALL OF WICKETS: 1–2 (Gilchrist, 0.3 ov), 2–8 (Ponting, 2.3 ov), 3–32 (Clarke, 8.6 ov), 4–121 (Hayden, 25.4 ov), 5–123 (Symonds, 25.6 ov), 6–199 (Hussey, 41.6 ov), 7–228 (Lee, 46.4 ov), 8–238 (Johnson, 48.2 ov), 9–247 (Bracken, 49.2 ov), 10–249 (Hopes, 49.4 ov)

BOWLING: P Kumar 10-2-46-4; S Sreesanth 9-0-43-2; IK Pathan 8.4-0-54-2; Harbhajan Singh 10-0-44-1; PP Chawla 9-0-45-0; Yuvraj Singh 3-0-15-0

COMMONWEALTH BANK SERIES — AVERAGES

AUSTRALIAN BATTING AND FIELDING

Batsman	ODIs	Inns	NO	Runs	HS	Ave	100	50	Ct	St
MEK Hussey	10	9	3	278	65*	46.33	0	2	6	0
MJ Clarke	10	10	2	314	79	39.25	0	3	4	0
ML Hayden	8	8	0	298	82	37.25	0	3	3	0
AC Gilchrist	10	10	0	322	118	32.20	1	2	16	2
JR Hopes	9	9	0	193	63	21.44	0	1	3	0
GB Hogg	7	5	1	85	32	21.25	0	0	0	0
A Symonds	10	10	1	174	59	19.33	0	1	5	0
RT Ponting	10	10	0	191	124	19.10	1	0	6	0
B Lee	8	7	1	73	37	12.17	0	0	2	0
MG Johnson	9	7	3	35	9*	8.75	0	0	2	0
SR Clark	5	3	2	8	8*	8.00	0	0	1	0
BJ Haddin	3	2	0	12	7	6.00	0	0	0	0
NW Bracken	10	5	2	17	14*	5.67	0	0	1	0
AA Noffke	1	–	–	–	–	–	–	–	0	0

AUSTRALIAN BOWLING

Bowler	Overs	Mdns	Runs	Wkts	Best	Ave	4w
NW Bracken	85.5	8	347	21	5–47	16.52	1
B Lee	71.4	5	356	16	5–27	22.25	2
SR Clark	39.0	3	154	6	2–8	25.67	0
JR Hopes	61.5	6	218	8	2–16	27.25	0
MG Johnson	77.0	11	311	11	3–29	28.27	0
GB Hogg	54.3	5	236	8	2–30	29.50	0
MJ Clarke	26.0	0	130	3	3–52	43.33	0
AA Noffke	9.0	0	46	1	1–46	46.00	0
A Symonds	8.5	0	59	1	1–27	59.00	0

INDIAN BATTING AND FIELDING

Batsman	ODIs	Inns	NO	Runs	HS	Ave	100	50	Ct	St
MS Dhoni	10	9	4	347	88*	69.40	0	2	19	2
G Gambhir	10	10	2	440	113	55.00	2	1	1	0
SR Tendulkar	10	10	1	399	117*	44.33	1	2	2	0
RG Sharma	10	10	3	235	70*	33.57	0	2	5	0
Yuvraj Singh	9	9	0	202	76	22.44	0	1	2	0
RV Uthappa	10	8	1	142	51	20.29	0	1	4	0
IK Pathan	10	6	0	118	31	19.67	0	0	1	0
V Sehwag	5	5	0	81	33	16.20	0	0	1	0
Harbhajan Singh	10	5	0	57	27	11.40	0	0	1	0
P Kumar	4	2	0	13	7	6.50	0	0	2	0
I Sharma	9	4	3	5	2*	5.00	0	0	2	0
S Sreesanth	7	4	2	9	4	4.50	0	0	0	0
MK Tiwary	1	1	0	2	2	2.00	0	0	0	0
MM Patel	3	1	0	0	0	0.00	0	0	0	0
PP Chawla	2	1	1	6	6*	–	0	0	3	0

INDIAN BOWLING

Bowler	Overs	Mdns	Runs	Wkts	Best	Ave	4w
P Kumar	40.0	5	175	10	4–31	17.50	2
I Sharma	62.1	2	285	14	4–38	20.36	2
S Sreesanth	40.2	0	232	9	3–31	25.77	0
IK Pathan	68.4	3	377	11	4–41	34.27	1
Harbhajan Singh	65.1	2	277	8	2–38	34.63	0
MM Patel	27.0	3	120	2	1–31	60.00	0
V Sehwag	13.0	0	66	1	1–28	66.00	0
Yuvraj Singh	26.0	0	120	1	1–18	120.00	0
PP Chawla	19.0	0	78	0	–	–	0
SR Tendulkar	4.0	0	21	0	–	–	0
RG Sharma	1.0	0	5	0	–	–	0

SRI LANKAN BATTING AND FIELDING

Batsman	ODIs	Inns	NO	Runs	HS	Ave	100	50	Ct	St
KC Sangakkara	8	7	0	326	128	46.57	1	1	6	2
DPMD Jayawardene	8	7	1	214	71	35.67	0	2	7	0
TM Dilshan	8	7	2	170	62*	34.00	0	2	4	0
CK Kapugedera	7	5	0	86	57	17.20	0	1	2	0
LPC Silva	8	6	1	79	35	15.80	0	0	3	0
ST Jayasuriya	8	7	0	103	34	14.71	0	0	1	0
MF Maharoof	4	2	1	10	7	10.00	0	0	1	0
WU Tharanga	2	1	0	10	10	10.00	0	0	0	0
M Muralitharan	8	4	1	25	13	8.33	0	0	3	0
KMDN Kulasekara	3	2	0	14	14	7.00	0	0	1	0
WPUJC Vaas	7	4	1	19	18	6.33	0	0	0	0
SL Malinga	8	4	0	19	12	4.75	0	0	1	0
MDK Perera	3	3	0	14	8	4.67	0	0	0	0
MKDI Amerasinghe	6	3	3	5	5*	–	0	0	1	0

SRI LANKAN BOWLING

Bowler	Overs	Mdns	Runs	Wkts	Best	Ave	4w
KMDN Kulasekara	26.0	3	129	5	2–36	25.80	0
MDK Perera	7.0	0	28	1	1–17	28.00	0
SL Malinga	70.4	5	368	12	4–47	30.67	1
MKDI Amerasinghe	57.0	4	276	9	3–44	30.67	0
MF Maharoof	32.1	1	149	4	2–20	37.25	0
M Muralitharan	73.2	0	353	9	2–37	39.22	0
ST Jayasuriya	6.1	0	42	1	1–0	42.00	0
CK Kapugedera	22.0	0	101	2	1–24	50.50	0
WPUJC Vaas	62.0	3	270	5	2–34	54.00	0
TM Dilshan	2.0	0	19	0	–	–	0

AUSTRALIA IN THE WEST INDIES

MAY–JULY 2008

FIRST TEST (THE FRANK WORRELL TROPHY)

WEST INDIES V AUSTRALIA

Sabina Park, Kingston, Jamaica

22–26 May 2008

Result: Australia won by 95 runs • Toss: Australia

Umpires: Aleem Dar (Pakistan) and RB Tiffin (Zimbabwe)

TV umpire: N Malcolm (West Indies) • Match referee: RS Mahanama (Sri Lanka)

Player of the match: SR Clark (Australia)

Australia first innings		R	M	B	4	6
PA Jaques	lbw Edwards	9	37	23	1	0
SM Katich	c Sammy b Edwards	12	18	11	3	0
RT Ponting	c Parchment b Bravo	158	354	224	16	1
MEK Hussey	c Bravo b Jaggernauth	56	186	146	6	0
BJ Hodge	c Ramdin b Edwards	67	212	122	9	1
MG Johnson	c Powell b Sammy	22	113	53	3	0
A Symonds	not out	70	158	115	8	2
BJ Haddin	c Ramdin b Sammy	11	41	35	1	0
B Lee	lbw Edwards	4	8	6	1	0
SR Clark	c Bravo b Powell	3	28	16	0	0
SCG MacGill	b Edwards	2	30	12	0	0
Extras	(b 2, lb 13, nb 2)	17				
Total	(all out; 126.5 overs)	431				

FALL OF WICKETS: 1–18 (Katich, 3.4 ov), 2–37 (Jaques, 7.3 ov), 3–174 (Hussey, 49.6 ov), 4–293 (Ponting, 84.1 ov), 5–326 (Hodge, 92.1 ov), 6–350 (Johnson, 101.2 ov), 7–368 (Haddin, 111.3 ov), 8–383 (Lee, 114.4 ov), 9–399 (Clark, 120.5 ov), 10–431 (MacGill, 126.5 ov)

BOWLING: DBL Powell 29–4–99–1; FH Edwards 26.5–4–104–5; DJG Sammy 29–7–78–2; DJ Bravo 22–6–61–1; AS Jaggernauth 20–0–74–1

West Indies first innings		R	M	B	4	6
DS Smith	b Clark	32	69	53	3	0
BA Parchment	c Haddin b Clark	9	105	60	1	0
RR Sarwan	c Haddin b Clark	7	21	9	1	0
RS Morton	c Clark b MacGill	67	193	135	10	2
S Chanderpaul	c Hussey b MacGill	118	381	276	13	1
DJ Bravo	c Katich b Lee	46	81	60	4	3
D Ramdin	c Haddin b Lee	0	9	9	0	0
DJG Sammy	c Jaques b Johnson	0	3	3	0	0
DBL Powell	b Lee	3	15	17	0	0
FH Edwards	c Haddin b Johnson	1	63	19	0	0
AS Jaggernauth	not out	0	13	7	0	0
Extras	(b 2, lb 10, w 3, nb 14)	29				
Total	(all out; 106 overs)	312				

FALL OF WICKETS: 1–47 (Smith, 14.6 ov), 2–62 (Sarwan, 18.2 ov), 3–68 (Parchment, 20.3 ov), 4–196 (Morton, 62.3 ov), 5–260 (Bravo, 84.3 ov), 6–262 (Ramdin, 86.4 ov), 7–263 (Sammy, 87.3 ov), 8–268 (Powell, 90.5 ov), 9–298 (Edwards, 102.5 ov), 10–312 (Chanderpaul, 105.6 ov)

BOWLING: B Lee 28–7–63–3; MG Johnson 26–6–63–2; SR Clark 19–2–59–3; SCG MacGill 22–2–100–2; A Symonds 11–4–15–0

Australia second innings		R	M	B	4	6
PA Jaques	c Ramdin b Edwards	4	5	5	1	0
SM Katich	lbw Edwards	1	35	22	0	0
RT Ponting	c Bravo b Powell	5	6	7	0	0
MEK Hussey	b Powell	1	25	15	0	0
MG Johnson	c Ramdin b Powell	4	14	13	1	0
BJ Hodge	c Ramdin b Bravo	27	105	53	4	0
A Symonds	c Sammy b Bravo	79	225	118	9	3
BJ Haddin	c Morton b Bravo	23	90	76	2	0
B Lee	c Ramdin b Edwards	9	41	31	1	0
SR Clark	not out	1	4	1	0	0
SCG MacGill	c Morton b Bravo	0	2	1	0	0
Extras	(b 2, lb 10, nb 1)	13				
Total	(all out; 56.5 overs)	167				

FALL OF WICKETS: 1–5 (Jaques, 1.4 ov), 2–10 (Ponting, 2.6 ov), 3–12 (Katich, 7.4 ov), 4–12 (Hussey, 8.3 ov), 5–18 (Johnson, 10.5 ov), 6–70 (Hodge, 27.1 ov), 7–144 (Haddin, 47.5 ov), 8–162 (Lee, 55.6 ov), 9–166 (Symonds, 56.3 ov), 10–167 (MacGill, 56.5 ov)

BOWLING: DBL Powell 15–5–36–3; FH Edwards 16–3–40–3; DJ Bravo 18.5–3–47–4; AS Jaggernauth 3–0–22–0; DJG Sammy 4–0–10–0

West Indies second innings		R	M	B	4	6
DS Smith	lbw Clark	28	133	77	3	0
BA Parchment	c Haddin b Clark	15	32	30	1	0
RR Sarwan	c Symonds b Clark	12	86	31	1	0
RS Morton	lbw Lee	9	52	30	2	0
S Chanderpaul	c & b Lee	11	59	35	2	0
DJ Bravo	c Johnson b Clark	0	16	11	0	0
D Ramdin	run out	36	91	61	5	0
DJG Sammy	lbw Clark	35	115	80	6	0
DBL Powell	c Haddin b MacGill	27	51	35	6	0
FH Edwards	not out	9	23	14	2	0
AS Jaggernauth	c Jaques b MacGill	0	1	1	0	0
Extras	(b 4, lb 2, nb 3)	9				
Total	(all out; 67 overs)	191				

FALL OF WICKETS: 1–22 (Parchment, 7.3 ov), 2–55 (Sarwan, 20.6 ov), 3–60 (Smith, 24.1 ov), 4–74 (Morton, 31.5 ov), 5–80 (Bravo, 34.6 ov), 6–82 (Chanderpaul, 35.3 ov), 7–149 (Ramdin, 55.5 ov), 8–172 (Sammy, 62.1 ov), 9–191 (Powell, 66.5 ov), 10–191 (Jaggernauth, 66.6 ov)

BOWLING: B Lee 22–6–81–2; SR Clark 20–8–32–5; MG Johnson 11–3–29–0; SCG MacGill 14–2–43–2

Stumps scores
Day one: Australia first innings 4–301 (BJ Hodge 53, MG Johnson 1, 87 overs)
Day two: West Indies first innings 3–115 (RS Morton 23, S Chanderpaul 25, 37 overs)
Day three: Australia second innings 4–17 (MG Johnson 4, BJ Hodge 0, 10 overs)
Day four: West Indies second innings 1–46 (DS Smith 19, RR Sarwan 8, 18 overs)

SECOND TEST (THE FRANK WORRELL TROPHY)

WEST INDIES V AUSTRALIA
Sir Vivian Richards Stadium, North Sound, Antigua
30 May–3 June 2008
Result: Match drawn • Toss: Australia
Umpires: MR Benson (England) and RB Tiffin (Zimbabwe)
TV umpire: N Malcolm (West Indies) • Match referee: RS Mahanama (Sri Lanka)
Player of the match: S Chanderpaul (West Indies)

Australia first innings		R	M	B	4	6
PA Jaques	lbw Bravo	17	71	47	2	0
SM Katich	c Ramdin b Taylor	113	416	248	9	0
RT Ponting	c Marshall b Taylor	65	184	123	5	0
MEK Hussey	c Chanderpaul b Sammy	10	56	38	2	0
MJ Clarke	c Marshall b Powell	110	310	187	12	0
A Symonds	c Ramdin b Edwards	18	31	19	3	0
BJ Haddin	c Morton b Taylor	33	86	55	6	0
B Lee	not out	63	114	82	8	1
MG Johnson	not out	29	26	26	3	0
Extras	(lb 7, w 5, nb 9)	21				
Total	(7 wickets dec; 136 overs)	479)				

DID NOT BAT: SR Clark, SCG MacGill

FALL OF WICKETS: 1–36 (Jaques, 14.3 ov), 2–172 (Ponting, 52.6 ov), 3–199 (Hussey, 65.2 ov), 4–271 (Katich, 84.5 ov), 5–296 (Symonds, 91.3 ov), 6–360 (Haddin, 109.3 ov), 7–414 (Clarke, 126.5 ov)

BOWLING: DBL Powell 29–3–101–1; FH Edwards 28–6–98–1; JE Taylor 27–5–95–3; DJ Bravo 24–4–80–1; DJG Sammy 21–2–71–1; RR Sarwan 7–0–27–0

West Indies first innings		R	M	B	4	6
DS Smith	c Symonds b Johnson	16	46	30	3	0
XM Marshall	lbw Clarke	53	110	69	8	0
RR Sarwan	c Clarke b MacGill	65	173	146	4	1
RS Morton	c Katich b Clarke	2	2	5	0	0
S Chanderpaul	not out	107	352	236	12	0
DJ Bravo	c Haddin b Lee	45	191	127	2	3
D Ramdin	lbw Lee	0	1	1	0	0
DJG Sammy	lbw Lee	0	4	2	0	0
JE Taylor	b Lee	20	23	26	2	1
DBL Powell	lbw Lee	0	2	2	0	0
FH Edwards	c Haddin b Johnson	0	17	10	0	0
Extras	(b 17, lb 13, w 2, nb 12)	44				
Total	(all out; 107 overs)	352				

FALL OF WICKETS: 1–55 (Smith, 9.2 ov), 2–103 (Marshall, 26.1 ov), 3–105 (Morton, 26.6 ov), 4–182 (Sarwan, 53.6 ov), 5–314 (Bravo, 95.4 ov), 6–314 (Ramdin, 95.5 ov), 7–318 (Sammy, 97.1 ov), 8–341 (Taylor, 103.2 ov), 9–341 (Powell, 103.4 ov), 10–352 (Edwards, 106.6 ov)

BOWLING: B Lee 21–7–59–5; MG Johnson 24–5–72–2; SR Clark 14–0–39–0; SCG MacGill 21–1–107–1; MJ Clarke 15–7–20–2; A Symonds 12–3–25–0

Australia second innings		R	M	B	4	6
PA Jaques	c Ramdin b Taylor	76	187	136	8	1
MEK Hussey	c Ramdin b Bravo	40	110	94	3	0
RT Ponting	lbw Taylor	38	88	48	4	0
MJ Clarke	run out	10	28	24	0	0
A Symonds	not out	43	83	53	4	0
BJ Haddin	lbw Edwards	7	32	12	1	0
B Lee	c Ramdin b Edwards	4	32	13	0	0
Extras	(b 8, lb 6, w 3, nb 9)	26				
Total	(6 wickets dec; 61.5 overs)	244				

FALL OF WICKETS: 1–74 (Hussey, 27.6 ov), 2–163 (Jaques, 45.2 ov), 3–178 (Ponting, 47.3 ov), 4–186 (Clarke, 50.6 ov), 5–222 (Haddin, 57.1 ov), 6–244 (Lee, 61.5 ov)

BOWLING: DBL Powell 13–3–47–0; FH Edwards 7.5–1–28–2; JE Taylor 12–0–33–2; DJG Sammy 12–1–45–0; DJ Bravo 14–1–59–1; RR Sarwan 3–0–18–0

West Indies second innings		R	M	B	4	6
DS Smith	c Hussey b Lee	0	21	16	0	0
XM Marshall	c Haddin b Clark	5	53	32	1	0
RR Sarwan	c Hussey b Johnson	128	381	241	18	1
RS Morton	lbw Lee	14	74	42	2	0
S Chanderpaul	not out	77	336	180	8	0
DJ Bravo	c sub (BJ Hodge) b Lee	1	14	14	0	0
D Ramdin	not out	21	47	45	3	0
Extras	(lb 8, nb 12)	20				
Total	(5 wickets; 93 overs)	266				

FALL OF WICKETS: 1–4 (Smith, 4.4 ov), 2–19 (Marshall, 11.3 ov), 3–84 (Morton, 28.1 ov), 4–227 (Sarwan, 81.1 ov), 5–236 (Bravo, 84.1 ov)

BOWLING: B Lee 21–5–51–3; SR Clark 18–8–22–1; MJ Clarke 6–3–16–0; MG Johnson 20–3–70–1; SCG MacGill 19–2–75–0; MEK Hussey 6–2–14–0; A Symonds 3–0–10–0

Stumps scores
Day one: Australia first innings 3–259 (SM Katich 113, MJ Clarke 38, 82 overs)
Day two: West Indies first innings 3–125 (RR Sarwan 32, S Chanderpaul 5, 35 overs)
Day three: West Indies first innings 4–255 (S Chanderpaul 55, DJ Bravo 29, 71 overs)
Day four: Australia second innings 6–244 (A Symonds 43, 61.5 overs)

THIRD TEST (THE FRANK WORRELL TROPHY)

WEST INDIES V AUSTRALIA
Kensington Oval, Bridgetown, Barbados
12–16 June 2008
Result: Australia won by 87 runs • Toss: West Indies
Umpires: Aleem Dar (Pakistan) and MR Benson (England)
TV umpire: GE Greaves (West Indies) • Match referee: RS Mahanama (Sri Lanka)
Player of the match: SM Katich (Australia) • Player of the series: S Chanderpaul (West Indies)

Australia first innings		R	M	B	4	6
PA Jaques	c Ramdin b Taylor	31	45	35	4	1
SM Katich	c Gayle b Edwards	36	129	72	5	0
RT Ponting	lbw Taylor	18	31	21	0	2
MEK Hussey	c Powell b Bravo	12	22	25	0	1
MJ Clarke	c Ramdin b Bravo	0	3	3	0	0
A Symonds	c Chattergoon b Bravo	52	141	84	5	1
BJ Haddin	lbw Benn	32	91	66	6	0
B Casson	lbw Edwards	10	78	44	1	0
B Lee	not out	23	72	46	3	1
MG Johnson	c Benn b Taylor	0	8	8	0	0
SR Clark	b Edwards	1	9	7	0	0
Extras	(lb 7, w 21, nb 8)	36				
Total	(all out; 67.1 overs)	251				

FALL OF WICKETS: 1–46 (Jaques, 10.2 ov), 2–75 (Ponting, 16.1 ov), 3–96 (Hussey, 22.3 ov), 4–96 (Clarke, 22.6 ov), 5–111 (Katich, 29.1 ov), 6–198 (Haddin, 48.4 ov), 7–213 (Symonds, 52.3 ov), 8–244 (Casson, 63.1 ov), 9–245 (Johnson, 64.6 ov), 10–251 (Clark, 67.1 ov)

BOWLING: DBL Powell 11–5–43–0; FH Edwards 16.1–4–55–3; JE Taylor 12–2–46–3; CH Gayle 7–2–6–0; DJ Bravo 15–5–61–3; SJ Benn 6–0–33–1

West Indies first innings		R	M	B	4	6
CH Gayle	c Casson b Lee	14	23	14	3	0
S Chattergoon	c Haddin b Lee	6	13	10	1	0
RR Sarwan	c Hussey b Clark	20	46	25	2	1
XM Marshall	c Casson b Symonds	39	102	61	6	0
S Chanderpaul	not out	79	226	142	12	1
DJ Bravo	c Haddin b Johnson	29	86	57	4	1
D Ramdin	c Clarke b Johnson	1	16	12	0	0
JE Taylor	c Katich b Clarke	0	7	9	0	0
SJ Benn	c Haddin b Johnson	3	14	14	0	0
DBL Powell	c Haddin b Lee	9	6	6	2	0
FH Edwards	c Ponting b Johnson	1	26	11	0	0
Extras	(lb 7, nb 8)	15				
Total	(all out; 58.5 overs)	216				

FALL OF WICKETS: 1–11 (Chattergoon, 2.5 ov), 2–26 (Gayle, 4.2 ov), 3–64 (Sarwan, 11.1 ov), 4–108 (Marshall, 25.1 ov), 5–168 (Bravo, 44.3 ov), 6–188 (Ramdin, 48.1 ov), 7–189 (Taylor, 49.6 ov), 8–195 (Benn, 52.5 ov), 9–204 (Powell, 53.5 ov), 10–216 (Edwards, 58.5 ov)

BOWLING: B Lee 15–2–64–3; SR Clark 15–4–41–1; MG Johnson 11.5–3–41–4; A Symonds 8–4–17–1; B Casson 7–1–43–0; MJ Clarke 2–0–3–1

Australia second innings		R	M	B	4	6
PA Jaques	c Ramdin b Edwards	108	303	224	9	0
SM Katich	c sub (DJG Sammy) b Benn	157	488	332	14	0
RT Ponting	c sub (RS Morton) b Powell	39	94	72	2	1
MEK Hussey	c Bravo b Benn	18	59	48	2	0
MJ Clarke	not out	48	145	107	6	0
A Symonds	c Chanderpaul b Benn	2	8	9	0	0
BJ Haddin	not out	45	107	83	5	1
Extras	(b 5, lb 2, w 5, nb 5, pen 5)	22				
Total	(5 wickets dec; 145 overs)	439				

FALL OF WICKETS: 1–223 (Jaques, 72.3 ov), 2–299 (Ponting, 94.3 ov), 3–330 (Hussey, 109.3 ov), 4–358 (Katich, 117.1 ov), 5–360 (Symonds, 119.2 ov)

BOWLING: DBL Powell 16–6–40–1; FH Edwards 14–3–52–1; JE Taylor 22–3–64–0; CH Gayle 16–3–45–0; SJ Benn 47–7–154–3; DJ Bravo 23–4–63–0; XM Marshall 2–2–0–0; RR Sarwan 5–0–9–0

West Indies second innings		R	M	B	4	6
CH Gayle	c Lee b Clark	26	74	45	4	0
XM Marshall	c Jaques b Casson	85	198	146	12	1
RR Sarwan	lbw Clarke	43	87	56	6	0
S Chanderpaul	lbw Clark	50	201	131	5	0
DJ Bravo	c Jaques b Casson	69	163	133	5	4
D Ramdin	lbw Clark	8	51	27	1	0
JE Taylor	c Haddin b Johnson	31	53	36	6	0
S Chattergoon	c Haddin b Lee	13	34	14	1	0
SJ Benn	c Hussey b Casson	13	34	25	2	0
DBL Powell	c Haddin b Lee	6	27	18	1	0
FH Edwards	not out	5	21	15	1	0
Extras	(b 10, lb 8, w 8, nb 12)	38				
Total	(all out; 105.4 overs)	387				

FALL OF WICKETS: 1–64 (Gayle, 15.3 ov), 2–159 (Sarwan, 35.5 ov), 3–181 (Marshall, 44.1 ov), 4–303 (Bravo, 82.6 ov), 5–303 (Chanderpaul, 83.3 ov), 6–345 (Ramdin, 93.3 ov), 7–351 (Taylor, 94.2 ov), 8–375 (Chattergoon, 99.3 ov), 9–375 (Benn, 100.5 ov), 10–387 (Powell, 105.4 ov)

BOWLING: B Lee 25.4–3–109–2; SR Clark 24–8–58–3; MG Johnson 12–0–72–1; B Casson 25–3–86–3; MJ Clarke 17–1–38–1; A Symonds 2–0–6–0

Stumps scores

Day one: Australia first innings 7–226 (B Casson 6, B Lee 7, 56.4 overs)
Day two: Australia second innings 0–35 (PA Jaques 13, SM Katich 17, 14 overs)
Day three: Australia second innings 3–330 (SM Katich 148, MJ Clarke 0, 112 overs)
Day four: West Indies second innings 3–235 (S Chanderpaul 27, DJ Bravo 30, 59 overs)

WEST INDIES V AUSTRALIA TEST SERIES — AVERAGES

AUSTRALIAN BATTING AND FIELDING

Batsman	Tests	Inns	NO	Runs	HS	Ave	100	50	Ct	St
A Symonds	3	6	2	264	79	66.00	0	3	2	0
SM Katich	3	5	0	319	157	63.80	2	0	3	0
MJ Clarke	2	4	1	168	110	56.00	1	0	2	0
RT Ponting	3	6	0	323	158	53.83	1	1	1	0
BJ Hodge	1	2	0	94	67	47.00	0	1	0	0
PA Jaques	3	6	0	245	108	40.83	1	1	4	0
B Lee	3	5	2	103	63*	34.33	0	1	2	0
BJ Haddin	3	6	1	151	45*	30.20	0	0	16	0
MEK Hussey	3	6	0	137	56	22.83	0	1	5	0
MG Johnson	3	4	1	55	29*	18.33	0	0	1	0
B Casson	1	1	0	10	10	10.00	0	0	2	0
SR Clark	3	3	1	5	3	2.50	0	0	1	0
SCG MacGill	2	2	0	2	2	1.00	0	0	0	0

AUSTRALIAN BOWLING

Bowler	Overs	Mdns	Runs	Wkts	Best	Ave	5w	10w
MJ Clarke	40.0	11	77	4	2–20	19.25	0	0
SR Clark	110.0	30	251	13	5–32	19.30	1	0
B Lee	132.4	30	427	18	5–59	23.72	1	0
MG Johnson	104.5	20	347	10	4–41	34.70	0	0
B Casson	32.0	4	129	3	3–86	43.00	0	0
SCG MacGill	76.0	7	325	5	2–43	65.00	0	0
A Symonds	36.0	11	73	1	1–17	73.00	0	0
MEK Hussey	6.0	2	14	0	–	–	0	0

DEBUTS: Brad Haddin and Beau Casson made their Test debuts during the series — Haddin in the first Test, Casson in the third.

AUSTRALIAN CENTURIES AND FIVE WICKETS IN AN INNINGS

Ricky Ponting's 158 in the first Test was his 35th century in Test cricket, in his 117th Test.

Stuart Clark's 5–32 in the first Test was his second five-for in Test cricket, in his 16th Test.

Simon Katich's 113 in the second Test was his third century in Test cricket, in his 25th Test.

Michael Clarke's 110 in the second Test was his seventh century in Test cricket, in his 34th Test.

Brett's Lee's 5–59 in the second Test was his ninth five-for in Test cricket, in his 67th Test.

Phil Jaques' 108 in the third Test was his third century in Test international cricket, in his 11th Test.

Simon Katich's 157 in the third Test was his fourth century in Test cricket, in his 26th Test.

WEST INDIAN BATTING AND FIELDING

Batsman	Tests	Inns	NO	Runs	HS	Ave	100	50	Ct	St
S Chanderpaul	3	6	3	442	118	147.33	2	3	2	0
RR Sarwan	3	6	0	275	128	45.83	1	1	0	0
XM Marshall	2	4	0	182	85	45.50	0	2	2	0
DJ Bravo	3	6	0	190	69	31.67	0	1	4	0
RS Morton	2	4	0	92	67	23.00	0	1	3	0
CH Gayle	1	2	0	40	26	20.00	0	0	1	0
DS Smith	2	4	0	76	32	19.00	0	0	0	0
JE Taylor	2	3	0	51	31	17.00	0	0	0	0
D Ramdin	3	6	1	66	36	13.20	0	0	14	0
BA Parchment	1	2	0	24	15	12.00	0	0	1	0
DJG Sammy	2	3	0	35	35	11.67	0	0	2	0
S Chattergoon	1	2	0	19	13	9.50	0	0	1	0
DBL Powell	3	5	0	45	27	9.00	0	0	2	0
SJ Benn	1	2	0	16	13	8.00	0	0	1	0
FH Edwards	3	5	2	16	9*	5.33	0	0	0	0
AS Jaggernauth	1	2	1	0	0*	0.00	0	0	0	0

WEST INDIAN BOWLING

Bowler	Overs	Mdns	Runs	Wkts	Best	Ave	5w	10w
FH Edwards	108.5	21	377	15	5–104	25.13	1	0
JE Taylor	73.0	10	238	8	3–46	29.75	0	0
DJ Bravo	116.5	23	371	10	4–47	37.10	0	0
SJ Benn	53.0	7	187	4	3–154	46.75	0	0
DBL Powell	113.0	26	366	6	3–36	61.00	0	0
DJG Sammy	66.0	10	204	3	2–78	68.00	0	0
AS Jaggernauth	23.0	0	96	1	1–74	96.00	0	0
CH Gayle	23.0	5	51	0	–	–	0	0
RR Sarwan	15.0	0	54	0	–	–	0	0
XM Marshall	2.0	2	0	0	–	–	0	0

TWENTY20 INTERNATIONAL

WEST INDIES V AUSTRALIA
Kensington Oval, Bridgetown, Barbados
20 June 2008 (20-over match)

Result: West Indies won by seven wickets • Toss: West Indies
Umpires: BR Doctrove (West Indies) and CR Duncan (West Indies)
TV umpire: GE Greaves (West Indies) • Match referee: RS Mahanama (Sri Lanka)
Player of the match: XM Marshall (West Indies)

Australia innings (11 overs maximum)		R	M	B	4	6
SE Marsh	c Marshall b Roach	29	44	22	1	2
L Ronchi	c Taylor b Roach	36	33	22	6	1
SR Watson	not out	17	27	15	1	1
DJ Hussey	c Perkins b Bravo	0	3	2	0	0
CL White	not out	10	12	6	1	0
Extras	(lb 2, w 2, nb 1)	5				
Total	(3 wickets; 11 overs)	97				

DID NOT BAT: RT Ponting, MJ Clarke, MEK Hussey, B Lee, MG Johnson, JR Hopes

FALL OF WICKETS: 1–57 (Ronchi, 5.6 ov), 2–72 (Marsh, 7.5 ov), 3–72 (DJ Hussey, 8.2 ov)

BOWLING: JE Taylor 2–0–23–0; SJ Benn 2–0–19–0; FH Edwards 2–0–12–0; KAJ Roach 3–0–29–2; DJ Bravo 2–0–12–1

West Indies innings		R	M	B	4	6
XM Marshall	run out	36	24	15	3	3
WKD Perkins	run out	9	32	11	1	0
D Ramdin	c Johnson b Watson	8	11	6	1	0
DJ Bravo	not out	28	23	15	1	3
ADS Fletcher	not out	7	19	8	1	0
Extras	(b 6, lb 1, w 7)	14				
Total	(3 wickets; 9.1 overs)	102				

DID NOT BAT: KA Pollard, DJG Sammy, SJ Benn, KAJ Roach, FH Edwards, JE Taylor

FALL OF WICKETS: 1–53 (Marshall, 3.3 ov), 2–59 (Perkins, 4.6 ov), 3–64 (Ramdin, 5.3 ov)

BOWLING: B Lee 2–0–26–0; MG Johnson 2–0–30–0; SR Watson 2.1–0–17–1; JR Hopes 2–0–14–0; CL White 1–0–8–0

Twenty20 international debuts: Shaun Marsh and Luke Ronchi

FIRST ONE-DAY INTERNATIONAL

WEST INDIES V AUSTRALIA
Arnos Vale Ground, Kingstown, St Vincent
24 June 2008 (50-over match)
Result: Australia won by 84 runs • Toss: West Indies
Umpires: Asad Rauf (Pakistan) and BR Doctrove (West Indies)
TV umpire: CR Duncan (West Indies) • Match referee: RS Mahanama (Sri Lanka)
Player of the match: SE Marsh (Australia)

Australia innings		R	M	B	4	6
SE Marsh	c Gayle b Sammy	81	129	97	7	1
SR Watson	lbw Bravo	31	59	27	4	0
RT Ponting	b Taylor	5	24	20	0	0
MJ Clarke	c Ramdin b Sammy	9	24	23	0	0
MEK Hussey	c Pollard b Gayle	44	89	58	1	0
BJ Haddin	c Pollard b Benn	50	56	52	4	1
CL White	lbw Sarwan	8	17	8	1	0
JR Hopes	b Bravo	9	11	9	1	0
B Lee	not out	12	8	5	0	1
MG Johnson	not out	3	1	1	0	0
Extras	(b 3, lb 5, w 13)	21				
Total	(8 wickets; 50 overs)	273				

DID NOT BAT: NW Bracken

FALL OF WICKETS: 1–75 (Watson, 12.5 ov), 2–96 (Ponting, 18.3 ov), 3–117 (Clarke, 24.3 ov), 4–140 (Marsh, 30.4 ov), 5–231 (Haddin, 44.4 ov), 6–248 (Hussey, 47.1 ov), 7–251 (White, 48.1 ov), 8–269 (Hopes, 49.4 ov)

BOWLING: JE Taylor 7-0-30-1; CH Gayle 10-0-55-1; FH Edwards 3-0-22-0; DJ Bravo 8-0-54-2; SJ Benn 10-0-39-1; RR Sarwan 5-0-34-1; DJG Sammy 7-1-31-2

West Indies innings		R	M	B	4	6
XM Marshall	c Haddin b Lee	6	13	11	1	0
CH Gayle	lbw Bracken	20	37	26	3	0
RR Sarwan	c Hussey b Lee	2	25	11	0	0
ADS Fletcher	run out	26	70	43	2	0
DJ Bravo	lbw Clarke	33	51	37	4	0
KA Pollard	c Haddin b Johnson	11	30	20	0	1
D Ramdin	b Watson	31	55	38	1	0
DJG Sammy	b Bracken	33	59	35	2	0
JE Taylor	c Haddin b Bracken	11	11	10	0	1
SJ Benn	c Clarke b Bracken	7	9	6	1	0
FH Edwards	not out	1	2	2	0	0
Extras	(w 8)	8				
Total	(all out; 39.5 overs)	189				

FALL OF WICKETS: 1–11 (Marshall, 2.6 ov), 2–29 (Gayle, 7.5 ov), 3–29 (Sarwan, 8.1 ov), 4–80 (Bravo, 19.1 ov), 5–92 (Fletcher, 22.5 ov), 6–111 (Pollard, 27.1 ov), 7–163 (Ramdin, 35.4 ov), 8–178 (Taylor, 37.5 ov), 9–186 (Sammy, 39.1 ov), 10–189 (Benn, 39.5 ov)

BOWLING: B Lee 9-1-37-2; NW Bracken 5.5-0-31-4; MG Johnson 7-0-42-1; JR Hopes 5-0-14-0; MJ Clarke 4-1-15-1; CL White 6-0-32-0; SR Watson 3-0-18-1

SECOND ONE-DAY INTERNATIONAL

WEST INDIES V AUSTRALIA
National Cricket Stadium, St George's, Grenada
27 June 2008 (50-over match)

Result: Australia won by 63 runs (D/L method) • Toss: Australia
Umpires: Asad Rauf (Pakistan) and N Malcolm (West Indies)
TV umpire: BR Doctrove (West Indies) • Match referee: RS Mahanama (Sri Lanka)
Player of the match: MJ Clarke (Australia)

Australia innings		R	M	B	4	6
SE Marsh	c Browne b Powell	12	23	22	1	0
SR Watson	lbw Taylor	0	5	3	0	0
RT Ponting	c Gayle b Taylor	13	37	17	2	0
MJ Clarke	lbw Benn	56	142	98	6	0
MEK Hussey	c Marshall b Bravo	62	151	105	2	1
CL White	not out	40	55	39	3	0
JR Hopes	not out	17	24	17	1	0
Extras	(b 3, w 9, nb 1)	13				
Total	(5 wickets; 50 overs)	213				

DID NOT BAT: L Ronchi, B Lee, MG Johnson, NW Bracken

FALL OF WICKETS: 1–3 (Watson, 0.6 ov), 2–19 (Marsh, 5.1 ov), 3–35 (Ponting, 8.6 ov), 4–135 (Clarke, 37.6 ov), 5–175 (Hussey, 44.6 ov)

BOWLING: JE Taylor 10–2–47–2; DBL Powell 10–2–29–1; DJ Bravo 10–2–35–1; DJG Sammy 5–0–18–0; KA Pollard 2–0–11–0; SJ Benn 10–0–54–1; CH Gayle 3–0–16–0

West Indies innings		R	M	B	4	6
XM Marshall	c Ronchi b Lee	0	1	1	0	0
CH Gayle	c Ponting b Johnson	10	39	24	2	0
ADS Fletcher	b Hopes	19	68	44	3	0
S Chanderpaul	not out	45	147	77	1	0
DJ Bravo	c Hussey b Watson	3	21	21	0	0
PA Browne	c White b Clarke	1	16	18	0	0
KA Pollard	c Watson b Clarke	0	2	2	0	0
DJG Sammy	c Johnson b Clarke	9	30	23	1	0
DBL Powell	b Watson	21	10	12	1	2
SJ Benn	not out	23	23	26	2	0
Extras	(lb 2, w 5, nb 2)	9				
Total	(8 wickets; 41 overs)	140				

DID NOT BAT: JE Taylor

FALL OF WICKETS: 1–0 (Marshall, 0.1 ov), 2–23 (Gayle, 7.5 ov), 3–41 (Fletcher, 15.2 ov), 4–49 (Bravo, 20.5 ov), 5–53 (Browne, 24.4 ov), 6–53 (Pollard, 24.6 ov), 7–74 (Sammy, 30.6 ov), 8–105 (Powell, 34.4 ov)

BOWLING: B Lee 7–1–25–1; NW Bracken 9–0–32–0; MG Johnson 4–0–14–1; SR Watson 7–1–22–2; JR Hopes 8–3–19–1; MJ Clarke 6–0–26–3

THIRD ONE-DAY INTERNATIONAL

WEST INDIES V AUSTRALIA
National Cricket Stadium, St George's, Grenada
29 June 2008 (50-over match)

Result: Australia won by seven wickets • Toss: Australia
Umpires: Asad Rauf (Pakistan) and N Malcolm (West Indies)
TV umpire: BR Doctrove (West Indies) • Match referee: RS Mahanama (Sri Lanka)
Player of the match: SR Watson (Australia)

West Indies innings		R	M	B	4	6
CH Gayle	run out	53	85	54	5	3
XM Marshall	c Ronchi b Watson	35	101	65	4	0
RR Sarwan	c Symonds b Johnson	31	73	43	2	0
S Chanderpaul	c Ronchi b Symonds	32	46	49	2	0
DJ Bravo	lbw Symonds	7	14	10	0	0
ADS Fletcher	st Ronchi b Bracken	12	26	16	2	0
D Ramdin	b Bracken	21	42	30	1	0
DJG Sammy	c & b Lee	3	12	6	0	0
DBL Powell	run out	2	11	4	0	0
FH Edwards	not out	7	11	9	1	0
SJ Benn	b Bracken	1	5	0	0	0
Extras	(lb 6, w 10, nb 3)	19				
Total	(all out; 48 overs)	223				

FALL OF WICKETS: 1–86 (Gayle, 17.4 ov), 2–99 (Marshall, 20.2 ov), 3–160 (Chanderpaul, 32.6 ov), 4–168 (Sarwan, 35.5 ov), 5–172 (Bravo, 36.6 ov), 6–195 (Fletcher, 41.3 ov), 7–211 (Sammy, 44.3 ov), 8–214 (Ramdin, 45.3 ov), 9–220 (Powell, 46.4 ov), 10–223 (Benn, 47.6 ov)

BOWLING: B Lee 9–1–36–1; NW Bracken 9–0–26–3; MG Johnson 8–1–41–1; JR Hopes 3–0–23–0; A Symonds 7–0–42–2; SR Watson 5–0–23–1; MJ Clarke 7–0–26–0

Australia innings		R	M	B	4	6
SE Marsh	b Edwards	0	5	5	0	0
SR Watson	c Sarwan b Sammy	126	161	122	15	2
RT Ponting	c Marshall b Gayle	69	142	83	7	0
MJ Clarke	not out	11	30	23	0	0
A Symonds	not out	8	16	12	1	0
Extras	(lb 2, w 9, nb 2)	13				
Total	(3 wickets; 40.3 overs)	227				

DID NOT BAT: MEK Hussey, L Ronchi, JR Hopes, B Lee, MG Johnson, NW Bracken

FALL OF WICKETS: 1–1 (Marsh, 0.5 ov), 2–191 (Ponting, 33.2 ov), 3–207 (Watson, 36.3 ov)

BOWLING: FH Edwards 6–0–35–1; DBL Powell 6–0–33–0; SJ Benn 10–1–59–0; DJ Bravo 9–0–47–0; DJG Sammy 4–0–20–1; CH Gayle 5–0–26–1; XM Marshall 0.3–0–5–0

FOURTH ONE-DAY INTERNATIONAL

WEST INDIES V AUSTRALIA
Warner Park, Basseterre, St Kitts
4 July 2008 (50-over match)

Result: Australia won by one run • Toss: West Indies
Umpires: Asad Rauf (Pakistan) and SA Bucknor (West Indies)
TV umpire: N Malcolm (West Indies) • Match referee: RS Mahanama (Sri Lanka)
Player of the match: A Symonds (Australia)

Australia innings		R	M	B	4	6
SE Marsh	c Ramdin b Powell	16	60	34	2	0
SR Watson	c Ramdin b Powell	20	38	22	4	0
MEK Hussey	c Bravo b Sammy	37	84	46	4	0
MJ Clarke	lbw Miller	36	77	51	3	0
A Symonds	c Bravo b Edwards	87	94	78	10	2
DJ Hussey	c sub (KAJ Roach) b Gayle	50	89	51	1	2
JR Hopes	c Sarwan b Edwards	0	2	1	0	0
L Ronchi	c Marshall b Bravo	12	19	9	1	0
B Lee	not out	7	15	9	0	0
MG Johnson	not out	0	3	1	0	0
Extras	(lb 7, w 7, nb 3)	17				
Total	(8 wickets; 50 overs)	282				

DID NOT BAT: NW Bracken

FALL OF WICKETS: 1–41 (Watson, 7.5 ov), 2–56 (Marsh, 11.4 ov), 3–116 (MEK Hussey, 23.6 ov), 4–129 (Clarke, 28.5 ov), 5–256 (Symonds, 46.1 ov), 6–256 (Hopes, 46.2 ov), 7–266 (DJ Hussey, 47.4 ov), 8–279 (Ronchi, 49.3 ov)

BOWLING: FH Edwards 10–0–53–2; DBL Powell 10–1–66–2; DJ Bravo 10–0–57–1; DJG Sammy 4–0–18–1; NO Miller 10–1–56–1; CH Gayle 6–1–25–1

West Indies innings		R	M	B	4	6
CH Gayle	c Hopes b Watson	92	173	92	6	4
XM Marshall	lbw Lee	0	2	2	0	0
RR Sarwan	c Ronchi b Lee	63	117	79	6	1
S Chanderpaul	b Bracken	53	132	71	4	0
DJ Bravo	b Hopes	31	47	32	2	1
SE Findlay	c M Hussey b Lee	9	22	14	0	1
D Ramdin	not out	5	16	9	0	0
DJG Sammy	not out	3	6	3	0	0
Extras	(lb 6, w 17, nb 2)	25				
Total	(6 wickets; 50 overs)	281				

DID NOT BAT: DBL Powell, FH Edwards, NO Miller

FALL OF WICKETS: 1–1 (Marshall, 0.3 ov), 2–138 (Sarwan, 23.4 ov), 3–188 (Gayle, 33.4 ov), 4–247 (Bravo, 42.6 ov), 5–271 (Findlay, 47.2 ov), 6–275 (Chanderpaul, 48.6 ov)

BOWLING: B Lee 10–0–64–3; NW Bracken 10–0–50–1; MG Johnson 10–0–40–0; JR Hopes 10–0–63–1; DJ Hussey 2–0–20–0; SR Watson 7–0–33–1; MJ Clarke 1–0–5–0

FIFTH ONE-DAY INTERNATIONAL

WEST INDIES V AUSTRALIA
Warner Park, Basseterre, St Kitts
6 July 2008 (50-over match)
Result: Australia won by 169 runs • Toss: Australia
Umpires: Asad Rauf (Pakistan) and SA Bucknor (West Indies)
TV umpire: N Malcolm (West Indies) • Match referee: RS Mahanama (Sri Lanka)
Player of the match: L Ronchi (Australia) • Player of the series: SR Watson (Australia)

Australia innings		R	M	B	4	6
SE Marsh	c Ramdin b Edwards	49	99	57	7	0
SR Watson	c Powell b Bravo	29	59	40	4	0
L Ronchi	c Ramdin b Miller	64	53	28	5	6
MJ Clarke	c Ramdin b Sarwan	5	20	10	0	0
MEK Hussey	c Findlay b Edwards	51	106	56	3	0
A Symonds	c Ramdin b Edwards	66	86	80	6	1
DJ Hussey	c Powell b Sarwan	52	35	21	4	4
JR Hopes	c Fletcher b Sarwan	18	24	11	3	0
B Lee	not out	0	1	0	0	0
Extras	(lb 3, w 1, nb 3)	7				
Total	(8 wickets; 50 overs)	341				

DID NOT BAT: MG Johnson, NW Bracken

FALL OF WICKETS: 1–70 (Watson, 12.5 ov), 2–129 (Marsh, 19.2 ov), 3–150 (Ronchi, 21.1 ov), 4–152 (Clarke, 22.1 ov), 5–265 (Symonds, 43.5 ov), 6–280 (MEK Hussey, 45.6 ov), 7–341 (DJ Hussey, 49.5 ov), 8–341 (Hopes, 49.6 ov)

BOWLING: FH Edwards 9–0–86–3; DBL Powell 10–0–50–0; DJ Bravo 10–0–74–1; CH Gayle 2–0–33–0; NO Miller 10–0–38–1; RR Sarwan 9–1–57–3

West Indies innings		R	M	B	4	6
CH Gayle	c Ronchi b Johnson	5	6	8	1	0
XM Marshall	lbw Watson	17	58	30	3	0
RR Sarwan	c Hopes b Johnson	7	17	11	1	0
S Chanderpaul	c Lee b Clarke	38	67	49	4	0
SE Findlay	not out	59	111	74	5	1
DJ Bravo	c D Hussey b Symonds	13	18	20	1	0
ADS Fletcher	st Ronchi b Clarke	1	2	4	0	0
D Ramdin	c M Hussey b Symonds	3	4	6	0	0
DBL Powell	b Johnson	10	22	25	1	0
NO Miller	c Watson b Johnson	8	15	11	1	0
FH Edwards	c Hopes b Johnson	0	2	1	0	0
Extras	(lb 2, w 9)	11				
Total	(all out; 39.5 overs)	172				

FALL OF WICKETS: 1–6 (Gayle, 1.3 ov), 2–21 (Sarwan, 5.4 ov), 3–56 (Marshall, 11.6 ov), 4–92 (Chanderpaul, 20.3 ov), 5–129 (Bravo, 27.2 ov), 6–131 (Fletcher, 28.0 ov), 7–138 (Ramdin, 29.4 ov), 8–158 (Powell, 35.6 ov), 9–172 (Miller, 39.4 ov), 10–172 (Edwards, 39.5 ov)

BOWLING: B Lee 9–0–42–0; MG Johnson 7.5–1–29–5; NW Bracken 5–0–19–0; SR Watson 5–0–23–1; MJ Clarke 6–0–34–2; A Symonds 7–0–23–2

WEST INDIES V AUSTRALIA ONE-DAY SERIES — AVERAGES

AUSTRALIAN BATTING AND FIELDING

Batsman	ODIs	Inns	NO	Runs	HS	Ave	100	50	Ct	St
A Symonds	3	3	1	161	87	80.50	0	2	1	0
DJ Hussey	2	2	0	102	52	51.00	0	2	1	0
BJ Haddin	1	1	0	50	50	50.00	0	1	3	0
MEK Hussey	5	4	0	194	62	48.50	0	2	4	0
CL White	2	2	1	48	40*	48.00	0	0	1	0
SR Watson	5	5	0	206	126	41.20	1	0	2	0
L Ronchi	4	2	0	76	64	38.00	0	1	5	2
SE Marsh	5	5	0	158	81	31.60	0	1	0	0
MJ Clarke	5	5	1	117	56	29.25	0	1	1	0
RT Ponting	3	3	0	87	69	29.00	0	1	1	0
JR Hopes	5	4	1	44	18	14.67	0	0	3	0
B Lee	5	3	3	19	12*	–	0	0	2	0
MG Johnson	5	2	2	3	3*	–	0	0	1	0
NW Bracken	5	–	–	–	–	–	–	–	0	0

AUSTRALIAN BOWLING

Bowler	Overs	Mdns	Runs	Wkts	Best	Ave	4w
A Symonds	14.0	0	65	4	2–23	16.25	0
MJ Clarke	24.0	1	106	6	3–26	17.67	0
NW Bracken	38.5	0	158	8	4–31	19.75	1
SR Watson	27.0	1	119	6	2–22	19.83	0
MG Johnson	36.5	2	166	8	5–29	20.75	1
B Lee	44.0	3	204	7	3–64	29.14	0
JR Hopes	26.0	3	119	2	1–19	59.50	0
CL White	6.0	0	32	0	–	–	0
DJ Hussey	2.0	0	20	0	–	–	0

DEBUTS: Shaun Marsh, Luke Ronchi and David Hussey made their ODI debuts during the series — Marsh in game one, Ronchi in game two and Hussey in game four.

AUSTRALIAN CENTURIES AND FIVE WICKETS IN AN INNINGS

Shane Watson's 126 in game three was his first century in one-day international cricket, in his 68th ODI.

Mitchell Johnson's 5–29 in game five was his second five-for in one-day international cricket, in his 39th ODI.

WEST INDIAN BATTING AND FIELDING

Batsman	ODIs	Inns	NO	Runs	HS	Ave	100	50	Ct	St
SE Findlay	2	2	1	68	59*	68.00	0	1	1	0
S Chanderpaul	4	4	1	168	53	56.00	0	1	0	0
CH Gayle	5	5	0	180	92	36.00	0	2	2	0
RR Sarwan	4	4	0	103	63	25.75	0	1	2	0
D Ramdin	4	4	1	60	31	20.00	0	0	7	0
DJ Bravo	5	5	0	87	33	17.40	0	0	2	0
DJG Sammy	4	4	1	48	33	16.00	0	0	0	0
SJ Benn	3	3	1	31	23*	15.50	0	0	0	0
ADS Fletcher	4	4	0	58	26	14.50	0	0	1	0
XM Marshall	5	5	0	58	35	11.60	0	0	3	0
DBL Powell	4	3	0	33	21	11.00	0	0	2	0
JE Taylor	2	1	0	11	11	11.00	0	0	0	0
FH Edwards	4	3	2	8	7*	8.00	0	0	0	0
NO Miller	2	1	0	8	8	8.00	0	0	0	0
KA Pollard	2	2	0	11	11	5.50	0	0	2	0
PA Browne	1	1	0	1	1	1.00	0	0	1	0

WEST INDIAN BOWLING

Bowler	Overs	Mdns	Runs	Wkts	Best	Ave	4w
DJG Sammy	20.0	1	87	4	2–31	21.75	0
RR Sarwan	14.0	1	91	4	3–57	22.75	0
JE Taylor	17.0	2	77	3	2–47	25.67	0
FH Edwards	28.0	0	196	6	3–86	32.67	0
NO Miller	20.0	1	94	2	1–38	47.00	0
CH Gayle	26.0	1	155	3	1–25	51.67	0
DJ Bravo	47.0	2	267	5	2–54	53.40	0
DBL Powell	36.0	3	178	3	2–66	59.33	0
SJ Benn	30.0	1	152	2	1–39	76.00	0
KA Pollard	2.0	0	11	0	–	–	0
XM Marshall	0.3	0	5	0	–	–	0

AUSTRALIAN TEST TEAM AVERAGES 2007–08

BATTING AND FIELDING

Batsman	Tests	Inns	NO	Runs	HS	Ave	100	50	Ct	St
A Symonds	9	15	5	777	162*	77.00	1	7	3	0
SM Katich	3	5	0	319	157	63.80	2	0	3	0
MJ Clarke	8	13	2	700	145*	63.64	3	3	11	0
ML Hayden	5	8	0	503	124	62.88	3	0	3	0
MEK Hussey	9	16	2	728	145*	52.00	3	1	17	0
PA Jaques	9	16	0	806	150	50.38	3	5	6	0
GB Hogg	3	5	2	148	79	49.33	0	1	1	0
RT Ponting	9	16	1	731	158	48.73	2	4	10	0
BJ Hodge	1	2	0	94	67	47.00	0	1	0	0
MG Johnson	9	9	4	167	50*	33.40	0	1	3	0
AC Gilchrist	6	8	1	217	67*	31.00	0	2	35	0
BJ Haddin	3	6	1	151	45*	30.20	0	0	16	0
B Lee	9	12	4	189	63*	23.63	0	2	4	0
B Casson	1	1	0	10	10	10.00	0	0	2	0
CJL Rogers	1	2	0	19	15	9.50	0	0	1	0
SR Clark	9	8	1	61	35	8.71	0	0	1	0
SW Tait	1	2	0	12	8	6.00	0	0	1	0
SCG MacGill	4	2	0	2	2	1.00	0	0	0	0

AUSTRALIAN BOWLING

Bowler	Overs	Mdns	Runs	Wkts	Best	Ave	5w	10w
A Symonds	138.0	34	251	12	3–51	20.92	0	0
B Lee	414.1	86	1250	58	5–59	21.55	2	0
SR Clark	334.2	85	902	34	5–32	26.53	1	0
MJ Clarke	84.5	16	213	8	3–5	26.63	0	0
MG Johnson	355.0	65	1118	34	4–41	32.88	0	0
B Casson	32.0	4	129	3	3–86	43.00	0	0
GB Hogg	125.0	15	481	8	2–51	60.13	0	0
SCG MacGill	171.0	21	651	10	2–43	65.10	0	0
SW Tait	21.0	1	92	0	–	–	0	0
MEK Hussey	6.0	2	14	0	–	–	0	0

NOTE: AUSTRALIA PLAYED NINE TEST MATCHES IN 2007–08, AS FOLLOWS:

Opponent	Tests	Won	Lost	Drawn	Tied
India	4	2	1	1	–
Sri Lanka	2	2	–	–	–
West Indies	3	2	–	1	–
Total	9	6	1	2	–

AUSTRALIAN ODI TEAM AVERAGES 2007–08

BATTING AND FIELDING

Batsman	ODIs	Inns	NO	Runs	HS	Ave	100	50	Ct	St
DJ Hussey	2	2	0	102	52	51.00	0	2	1	0
CL White	2	2	1	48	40*	48.00	0	0	1	0
A Symonds	23	21	4	780	107*	45.88	1	7	8	0
ML Hayden	16	15	0	634	92	42.27	0	6	7	0
RT Ponting	21	20	3	718	134*	42.24	3	2	11	0
SR Watson	5	5	0	206	126	41.20	1	0	2	0
BJ Haddin	9	8	1	288	87*	41.14	0	3	6	0
L Ronchi	4	2	0	76	64	38.00	0	1	5	2
MJ Clarke	25	23	3	708	130	35.40	1	5	8	0
MEK Hussey	18	14	3	381	65*	34.64	0	4	10	0
AC Gilchrist	19	18	1	581	118	34.18	1	5	29	4
SE Marsh	5	5	0	158	81	31.60	0	1	0	0
JR Hopes	24	20	2	393	63	21.83	0	1	8	0
B Lee	23	17	9	116	37	14.50	0	0	6	0
GB Hogg	17	7	1	85	0	14.17	0	0	3	0
MG Johnson	21	11	6	63	24*	12.60	0	0	4	0
BJ Hodge	7	6	0	59	20	9.83	0	0	4	0
SR Clark	5	3	2	8	8*	8.00	0	0	1	0
NW Bracken	22	6	2	20	14*	5.00	0	0	3	0
SR Clark	3	–	–	–	–	–	–	–	0	0
SW Tait	3	–	–	–	–	–	–	–	1	0
AA Noffke	1	–	–	–	–	–	–	–	0	0

BOWLING

Bowler	Overs	Mdns	Runs	Wkts	Best	Ave	4w
SW Tait	18.0	1	89	5	3–59	17.80	0
SR Clark	14.4	1	58	3	2–14	19.33	0
SR Watson	27.0	1	119	6	2–22	19.83	0
MG Johnson	170.5	15	737	33	5–26	22.33	2
NW Bracken	179.2	14	787	34	5–47	23.15	2
B Lee	187.2	12	907	36	5–27	25.19	2
GB Hogg	125.0	8	583	23	4–49	25.35	1
SR Clark	39.0	3	154	6	2–8	25.67	0
MJ Clarke	64.0	2	310	12	3–26	25.83	0
JR Hopes	141.5	9	569	19	2–16	29.95	0
A Symonds	39.5	0	202	5	2–23	40.40	0
AA Noffke	9.0	0	46	1	1–46	46.00	0
CL White	6.0	0	32	0	–	–	0
BJ Hodge	2.0	0	18	0	–	–	0
DJ Hussey	2.0	0	20	0	–	–	0

Note: Australia played 25 one-day internationals in 2007–08: 13 against India (six wins, five losses, two no-results); three against New Zealand (two wins, one no-result); four against Sri Lanka (three wins, one loss); five against the West Indies (five wins).

AUSTRALIAN TWENTY20 TEAM AVERAGES 2007–08

BATTING AND FIELDING

Batsman	T20s	Inns	NO	Runs	HS	Ave	100	50	Ct	St
ML Hayden	7	7	3	282	73*	70.50	0	4	0	0
MJ Clarke	9	5	3	98	37*	49.00	0	0	5	0
L Ronchi	1	1	0	36	36	36.00	0	0	0	0
A Symonds	9	8	2	212	85*	35.33	0	1	2	0
RT Ponting	6	5	1	137	76	34.25	0	1	3	0
BJ Hodge	8	5	2	94	36	31.33	0	0	3	0
SE Marsh	1	1	0	29	29	29.00	0	0	0	0
AC Voges	2	1	0	26	26	26.00	0	0	1	0
AC Gilchrist	9	9	1	207	45	25.88	0	0	16	0
MEK Hussey	9	4	0	87	37	17.40	0	0	3	0
BJ Haddin	3	3	2	16	6	16.00	0	0	0	0
LA Pomersbach	1	1	0	15	15	15.00	0	0	0	0
MG Johnson	8	3	2	14	9	14.00	0	0	2	0
B Lee	10	4	2	17	13	8.50	0	0	5	0
NW Bracken	9	1	0	4	4	4.00	0	0	3	0
AA Noffke	2	1	0	0	0	0.00	0	0	0	0
DJ Hussey	2	1	0	0	0	0.00	0	0	1	0
SR Watson	2	1	1	17	17*	–	0	0	0	0
CL White	1	1	1	10	10*	–	0	0	0	0
SR Clark	7	–	–	–	–	–	–	–	2	0
BW Hilfenhaus	1	–	–	–	–	–	–	–	0	0
JR Hopes	2	–	–	–	–	–	–	–	1	0
SW Tait	1	–	–	–	–	–	–	–	0	0

BOWLING

Bowler	Overs	Mdns	Runs	Wkts	Best	Ave	4w
AC Voges	2.0	0	5	2	2–5	2.50	0
AA Noffke	7.3	1	41	4	3–18	10.25	0
SW Tait	4.0	0	22	2	2–22	11.00	0
DJ Hussey	3.0	0	12	1	1–12	12.00	0
SR Clark	28.0	0	177	12	4–20	14.75	1
NW Bracken	28.5	1	180	11	3–11	16.36	0
SR Watson	5.3	0	36	2	1–17	18.00	0
MG Johnson	29.0	0	202	10	3–22	20.20	0
B Lee	36.1	0	262	11	3–27	23.82	0
JR Hopes	5.0	0	24	1	1–10	24.00	0
BW Hilfenhaus	4.0	0	28	1	1–28	28.00	0
MJ Clarke	9.0	0	86	3	1–13	28.67	0
A Symonds	16.5	0	180	1	1–2	180.00	0
BJ Hodge	2.0	0	20	0	–	–	0
CL White	1.0	0	8	0	–	–	0

Note: Australia played 10 Twenty20 internationals in 2007–08, for five wins (over England, Bangladesh, Sri Lanka, India and New Zealand) and five losses (to Zimbabwe, Pakistan, India twice and the West Indies).

PHOTOGRAPHS

All the photographs that appear in *Captain's Diary 2008* — except for the shot of Ricky, Rianna and Emmy Ponting that appears on the final page of the third colour section — come from Getty Images. The photographers responsible for the images in the colour sections are:

SECTION ONE

Page 1 — Tom Shaw.

Page 2 — All: Hamish Blair.

Page 3 — All: Hamish Blair.

Page 4 — Both: Hamish Blair.

Page 5 — Both: Hamish Blair.

Page 6 — Top: Tom Shaw. Middle: Hamish Blair. Bottom: Cameron Spencer.

Page 7 — Top: Cameron Spencer. Bottom: Quinn Rooney.

Page 8 — Top: Quinn Rooney. Bottom left and right: Cameron Spencer.

SECTION TWO

Page 1 — Top left and right: Tom Shaw. Bottom left: Julian Herbert. Bottom right: Hamish Blair.

Page 2 — Top left and right: Hamish Blair. Bottom left: Quinn Rooney. Bottom right: Cameron Spencer.

Page 3 — Top left and right: Paul Kane. Bottom left: Quinn Rooney. Bottom right: Mark Dadswell.

Page 4 — Top left and right: Mark Nolan. Bottom left: Robert Cianflone. Bottom right: Paul Kane.

Page 5 — Top and middle: Quinn Rooney. Bottom: Cameron Spencer.

Page 6 — Top: Ezra Shaw. Middle: Chris McGrath. Bottom: Doug Benc.

Page 7 — Top left: Mark Nolan. Top right and bottom: Harry How.

Page 8 — Top left, bottom left and right: Chris McGrath. Top right: Doug Benc.

SECTION THREE

Page 1 — Top left: Robert Gray. Top right: Mark Dadswell. Bottom: Quinn Rooney

Page 2 — Top: Ezra Shaw. Bottom left and right: Cameron Spencer.

Page 3 — Top and middle: Mark Nolan. Bottom: Cameron Spencer.

Page 4 — Top: Mark Nolan. Bottom: Paul Kane

Page 5 — Top and bottom left: Robert Cianflone. Bottom right: Simon Cross.

Page 6 — Top: Lucas Dawson. Bottom left: Cameron Spencer. Bottom right: Paul Kane.

Page 7 — Top: Robert Cianflone. Middle and bottom: Doug Benc.

Page 8 — Newspix/James Elsby.